TOM BROKAW

The
GREATEST
GENERATION

The
GREATEST
GENERATION
SPEAKS

RANDOM
HOUSE

Published in the United States by Random House, an imprint of The Random Hous Publishing Group, a division of Random House, Inc., New York, and simultaneousl in Canada by Random House of Canada Limited, Toronto.

RANDOM HOUSE and colophon are registered trademarks of Random House, Inc.

The Greatest Generation was originally published in the United States in 1998 anc subsequently in 2004 with a new preface by the author by Random House, an imprint of The Random House Publishing Group, a division of Random House, Inc New York.

The Greatest Generation Speaks was originally published in the United States in 19' by Random House, an imprint of The Random House Publishing Group, a division (Random House, Inc., New York.

Cover design by Amy King
Front endpapers: Library of Congress
Rear endpapers: National Archives
Title-page photos: UPI/Corbis-Bettmann

ISBN 978-0-385-36426-3

A Cataloging-in-Publication record has been established for *The Greatest Generatic* with the Library of Congress under the ISBN 0-375-50202-5 and for *The Greatest Generation Speaks* under the ISBN 0-375-50394-3.

www.atrandom.com

Printed in China

Book design by Carole Lowenstein

1 2 3 4 5 6 7 8 9 10

2013 Random House Leatherbound Edition

THE GREATEST GENERATION

TOM
BROKAW

·

THE
GREATEST
GENERATION

RANDOM HOUSE

NEW YORK

For Meredith, of course,
and her parents,
Vivian and Merritt Auld,
and my parents,
Jean and Anthony "Red" Brokaw

Preface to the
New Edition

When *The Greatest Generation* was first published, I hoped that it would be a success, but, frankly, I was unprepared for the magnitude of the book's popularity and for the emotional reaction it triggered across generational lines, especially within families of World War II veterans. I returned to some of the original research in an effort to determine the source of the response, which came in waves that washed across the normal fault lines of America— rich and poor, conservative and liberal, rural and metropolitan, believer and nonbeliever.

One of the seminal sources of military information about World War II is the brilliant work of John Keegan, the estimable British historian. In the preface to his book titled simply *The Second World War* he writes, "The Second World War is the largest single event in human history, fought across six of the world's seven continents and all its oceans. It killed fifty million human beings, left hundreds of millions of others wounded in mind or body and materially devastated much of the heartland of civilization."

The physical scope of the war, the political consequences, and the cost to humanity were, of course, unprecedented. World War II was total immersion for the countries and the people involved. Moreover, for the people I write about in this book, it was the first formative experience of their young adult years. Every day for four years they knew, intensely, great danger, separation, death, heroism, uncertainty, accomplishment, and cruelty.

They finished the war determined to have more peaceful and prosperous lives, these children of first a global economic depression and then a war that engulfed the world. Postwar political and economic developments pushed them swiftly into a new era; shortly after first Germany and then Japan surrendered, the Cold War began. Americans at home rushed to start families and build communities and careers, all of which had been deferred by the demands of war and deprivation.

However, they did not abandon their sense of duty and service to their community and nation. Indeed, it was encoded in them as a result of their personal experiences first in the Great Depression and then in World War II. In these times, individual and collective survival depended on a selfless sense of commitment to a common cause.

I have especially enjoyed telling the story of three wounded young veterans from different outfits who by chance were in the same hospital ward when the war was over, recovering from their grievous wounds. One was from a prominent Michigan family, another from a poor Kansas family, and the third was a Japanese American from Hawaii. As they struggled to heal their bodies, they quickly became friends and talked into the night about their postwar plans.

They decided that public service—politics—was an appealing future. They had already given so much for their country, but they were prepared to give more. They left the hospital and returned to their communities to pursue their dreams. They were reunited several years later when all three were in the U.S. Senate. They were Senator Robert Dole of Kansas, the Republican presidential nominee in 1996; the late Senator Phil Hart of Michigan, who was often called "the conscience of the Senate" and for whom the Hart Senate Office Building is named; and Daniel Inouye of Hawaii, the first Japanese American elected to the Senate and a recipient of the Medal of Honor in 2000, a delayed recognition of his heroics in the Italian campaign in World War II.

Now members of the greatest generation are in their late seventies and eighties. We are losing them at an ever-faster pace, and their obituaries again remind us of their commitment to public service and community. The death notices mention their service during World War II and then typically recite a long list of service-club memberships, school-board activities, special projects related to their professions or talents, church or synagogue memberships. Several retired members of the greatest generation I've come to know volunteer at inner city schools or homeless shelters and hospitals.

In ways that I could not have anticipated, these and other accounts of the remarkable lives of members of the greatest generation are providing a valuable context for us during these tumultuous early years of a new century. That was clear to me a week or so after the horrific attacks of 9/11. I encountered a grieving young New York City fireman in a restaurant not far from St. Patrick's Cathedral. He was dressed in his formal blues, having just attended another funeral of another fallen comrade. We talked for a while about the great sadness in the city, and then, as I turned to leave, he took my hand and shook it firmly, his expression matching his grip, and he said, "Mr. Brokaw, watch my generation now, just watch us."

On assignment in Iraq, I was startled to see how many well-worn copies of *The Greatest Generation* turned up when I visited infantry outfits. Many young American military men and women of today seem to identify with their predecessors, who at the same age faced a dangerous and uncertain world.

That is especially comforting to me when word comes that one of the featured subjects in *The Greatest Generation* has died. I miss them, their nobility and courage, then and now and over the length of good, useful lives. Many of them told me that having their membership in this distinctive generation written about in the book gave them some unanticipated recognition at a time when they thought they would likely just slip quietly away. Chesterfield Smith, the powerhouse Florida lawyer who as president of the American Bar Association stood up to President Richard M. Nixon following the Saturday Night Massacre in 1973, spent his final days in a hospital, handing out copies of *The Greatest Generation* to his doctors and nurses.

My longtime friend Joe Foss, the Marine fighter pilot ace who earned the Congressional Medal of Honor for shooting down a record number of Japanese planes, died in 2003, and his long life of distinction was appropriately celebrated in all the major newspapers. After all, he had been governor of South Dakota, the first commissioner of the American Football League, and the president of the National Rifle Association. Still, the accounts almost always mentioned, in addition to all that, that he was a charter member of the greatest generation.

When I walked behind the flag-draped caisson bearing Joe Foss's remains, it was a snowy day in Arlington National Cemetery. I thought about the great arc of his life, from boy on a Depression-era South Dakota farm to war hero to national political and sports figure. But most of all, I thought of him as the essence of the common man, who roared to life early every morning, well into his eighties, a born-again Christian who saw his faith as a source of strength, not as a sign of superiority, and a patriot who spent his last days sharing with school children the rewards of civic duty.

One of his political adversaries in South Dakota was George McGovern, a World War II bomber pilot who earned the Distinguished Flying Cross for his heroics. McGovern and Foss represented opposite ends of the political spectrum, yet throughout their lives they maintained a healthy, friendly respect for each other. McGovern shares an even closer relationship with Bob Dole, another conservative Republican, and together they've worked to start an international school lunch program as a means of building bridges to the Third World and of addressing the global shame of hungry children.

The group photo from a gathering in Vancouver, Washington, of many of the individuals featured in the three books I wrote about the greatest generation is a symbol of their long journey and of their achievements. Men and women, white, African American, Hispanic American, Japanese American, state legislators and a U.S. Senator, school teachers and entrepreneurs, a minister and a sports writer, working class and white collar: The photo was a portrait of the America that they had built together.

For me, that common determination to make the world better, to find common ground at home and abroad, is the legacy of this generation as much as the sacrifices made and victories gained during

World War II. In a new century, facing new challenges, members of the greatest generation, in life and death, continue to instruct and inspire me, and us.

TOM BROKAW
February 2004

OVERLEAF: *"Salute to the Greatest Generation" event on June 3, 2000, in Vancouver, Washington, at the Vancouver National Historic Reserve, on the occasion of Tom Brokaw's Marshall Lecture.*
PHOTOGRAPH: JIM GIZZI, HI-CAMR PHOTOGRAPHY

ACKNOWLEDGMENTS

When I first came to fully understand what effect members of the World War II generation had on my life and the world we occupy today, I quickly resolved to tell their stories as a small gesture of personal appreciation. As I did that on television, at dinner parties, and in commencement speeches, it had the effect of a chain letter that no one wanted to disrupt. Everyone seemed to want to share their own stories of parents, other family members, or acquaintances who were charter members of this remarkable generation.

It rapidly became a kind of extended family, and with the encouragement of a number of friends I began to understand that this was a mother lode of material that deserved the permanence a book would represent. It was a daunting undertaking: because there are so many stories to tell and because the lives of these people are so special I didn't want to do anything in a book that would not live up to their deeds, heroic and otherwise.

If I have failed them, it is entirely my fault.

In the course of gathering this material, interviewing the subjects, and collecting the photographs, I had invaluable assistance from the best and brightest of a new generation, young women and young men in their twenties and thirties who came to care about these subjects as passionately as I did.

Elizabeth Bowyer, now a law student at the University of Virginia, and Phil Napoli, a newly minted Ph.D. in history from Columbia, teamed up with Julie Huang, my research assistant at NBC News, to work tirelessly and brilliantly to provide me with an unending supply of stories, facts, insights, and ideas. I am more grateful to them than they'll ever know. I'd also like to thank Tammy Fine, who helped get the project started before moving to Washington and a new assignment on the *Today* show.

Through it all, Erin O'Connor, who runs my NBC life with the organizational and mission-oriented skills of a battlefield commander, was simply peerless in her ability to juggle all of the needs of this book, my NBC News duties, and the considerable logistical demands of both. Metaphorically, if I go into any battle, I want Erin at my side.

Other friends who initially encouraged me to expand my thoughts on the World War II generation into a book include Stephen Ambrose, Ellen Levine of *Good Housekeeping*, and William Styron. I was further encouraged in the effort by reading the works of William Manchester, Paul Fussell, Ben Bradlee, Andy Rooney, and Art Buchwald.

So many ideas came from so many places, but I would be remiss not to single out my pal Mike Barnicle, the best newspaper columnist Boston has ever had; Bob Karolevitz, a fine writer in my hometown who wrote of his generation for the local newspaper, *The Yankton Press and Dakotan*; the astute observations of my friends Kurt Andersen and Frank Gannon; and my NBC colleagues, who offered to share notes and enthusiasm and tolerated my fits of frustration, distraction, and emotion.

Special thanks go to Craig Leake and Andrea Malin, my colleagues on the NBC documentary also called *The Greatest Generation.* They were simultaneously able to get some of these stories on screen while also helping me get them on the pages of this book. I could not be more proud to be associated with both of them on both projects.

Also, since a book is about more than writing it and publishing it, I am deeply grateful for the counsel and expertise of my business manager, Kenneth Starr. (No, not *that* Ken Starr. This is a New Yorker with an altogether different line of work.)

And what can I say of the keen eye, the great heart, and the indomitable spirit of the woman who has been commander in chief on this project, Kate Medina, my editor at Random House? Her enthusiasm for the subject, coolness under fire when the schedule was shattered by events in Washington and elsewhere, and, most of all, her friendship through it all will live in my heart forever. For all that she managed during the last twelve months, Kate deserves her own chapter in this book. And special thanks to the team at Random House who helped produce this book: Meaghan Rady, Benjamin Dreyer, Richard Elman, and Carole Lowenstein.

As always, I'm grateful for the love, encouragement, and tolerance of the women who have made all the difference in my life: Meredith, my wife; Jean, my mother; Jennifer, Andrea, and Sarah, our daughters.

Finally, to the men and women whose stories I did not get to, I am genuinely sorry, for I have loved them all. I hope you will tell them in your own way. To those families and friends of other members of the greatest generation, may I suggest you now begin to ask the questions and hear the stories that have been locked in memory for too long.

TOM BROKAW, *1998*

CONTENTS

THE ARENA

Tom Brokaw, Igloo, South Dakota, U.S. Army Ordnance Depot, 1944

———————•———————

GENERATIONS

In the spring of 1984, I went to the northwest of France, to Normandy, to prepare an NBC documentary on the fortieth anniversary of D-Day, the massive and daring Allied invasion of Europe that marked the beginning of the end of Adolf Hitler's Third Reich. I was well prepared with research on the planning for the invasion—the numbers of men, ships, airplanes, and other weapons involved; the tactical and strategic errors of the Germans; and the names of the Normandy villages that in the midst of battle provided critical support to the invaders. What I was not prepared for was how this experience would affect me emotionally.

The D-Day fortieth-anniversary project awakened my earliest memories. Between the ages of three and five I lived on an Army base in western South Dakota and spent a good deal of my time outdoors in a tiny helmet, shooting stick guns at imaginary German and Japanese soldiers. My father, Red Brokaw, then in his early thirties, was an all-purpose Mr. Fix-It and operator of snowplows and construction machinery, part of a crew that kept the base functioning. When he was drafted, the base commander called him back, reasoning he was more valuable in the job he had. When Dad returned home, it was the first time I saw my mother cry. These were powerful images for an impressionable youngster.

The war effort was all around us. Ammunition was tested on the South Dakota sagebrush prairie before being shipped out to battlefront positions. I seem to remember that one Fourth of July the base commander staged a particularly large firing exercise as a wartime substitute for fireworks. Neighbors always seemed to be going to or coming home from the war. My grandfather Jim Conley followed the war's progress in *Time* magazine and on his maps. There was even a stockade of Italian prisoners of war on the edge of the base. They were often free to wander around the base in their distinctive, baggy POW uniforms, chattering happily in Italian, a curious Mediterranean presence in that barren corner of the Great Plains.

At the same time, my future wife, Meredith Auld, was starting life in Yankton, South Dakota, the Missouri River community that later became the Brokaw family home as well. She saw her father only once during her first five years. He was a front-line doctor with the Army's 34th Regiment and was in the thick of battle from North Africa all the way through Italy. When he returned home, he established a thriving medical practice and was a fixture at our high school sports games. He never spoke to any of us of the horrors he had seen. When one of his sons wore as a casual jacket one of Doc Auld's Army coats with the major's insignia still attached, I remember thinking, "God, Doc Auld was a big deal in the war."

Yet when I arrived in Normandy, those memories had receded, replaced by days of innocence in the fifties, my life as a journalist covering the political turmoil brought on by Vietnam, the social upheaval of the sixties, and Watergate in the seventies. I was much more concerned about the prospects of the Cold War than the lessons of the war of my early years.

I was simply looking forward to what I thought would be an interesting assignment in a part of France celebrated for its hospitality, its seafood, and its Calvados, the local brandy made from apples.

Instead, I underwent a life-changing experience. As I walked the beaches with the American veterans who had landed there and now returned for this anniversary, men in their sixties and seventies, and listened to their stories in the cafés and inns, I was deeply moved and profoundly grateful for all they had done. I realized that they had been all around me as I was growing up and that I had failed to appreciate what they had been through and what they had accomplished. These men and women came of age in the Great Depression, when economic despair hovered over the land like a plague. They had watched their parents lose their businesses, their farms, their jobs, their hopes. They had learned to accept a future that played out one day at a time. Then, just as there was a glimmer of economic recovery, war exploded across Europe and Asia. When Pearl Harbor made it irrefutably clear that America was not a fortress, this generation was summoned to the parade ground and told to train for war. They left their ranches in Sully County, South Dakota, their jobs on the main street of Americus, Georgia, they gave up their place on the assembly lines in Detroit and in the ranks of Wall Street, they quit school or went from cap and gown directly into uniform.

They answered the call to help save the world from the two most powerful and ruthless military machines ever assembled, instruments of conquest in the hands of fascist maniacs.

They faced great odds and a late start, but they did not protest. At a time in their lives when their days and nights should have been filled with innocent adventure, love, and the lessons of the workaday world, they were fighting, often hand to hand, in the most primitive conditions possible, across the bloodied landscape of France, Belgium, Italy, Austria. They fought their way up a necklace of South Pacific islands few had ever heard of before and made them a fixed part of American history—islands with names like Iwo Jima, Guadalcanal, Okinawa. They were in the air every day, in skies filled with terror, and they went to sea on hostile waters far removed from the shores of their homeland.

New branches of the services were formed to get women into uniform, working at tasks that would free more men for combat. Other women went to work in the laboratories and in the factories, developing new medicines, building ships, planes, and tanks, and raising the families that had been left behind.

America's preeminent physicists were engaged in a secret race to build a new bomb before Germany figured out how to harness the atom as a weapon. Without their efforts and sacrifices our world would be a far different place today.

When the war was over, the men and women who had been involved, in uniform and in civilian capacities, joined in joyous and short-lived celebrations, then immediately began the task of rebuilding their lives and the world they wanted. They were mature beyond their years, tempered by what they had been through, disciplined by their military training and sacrifices. They married in record numbers and gave birth to another distinctive generation, the Baby Boomers. They stayed true to their values of personal responsibility, duty, honor, and faith.

They became part of the greatest investment in higher education that any society ever made, a generous tribute from a grateful nation. The GI Bill, providing veterans tuition and spending money for education, was a brilliant and enduring commitment to the nation's future. Campus classrooms and housing were overflowing with young men in their mid-twenties, many of whom had never expected to get a college education. They left those campuses with degrees and a determination to make up for lost time. They were a new kind of army now, moving onto the landscapes of industry, science, art, public policy, all the fields of American life, bringing to them the same passions and discipline that had served them so well during the war.

They helped convert a wartime economy into the most powerful peacetime economy in history. They made breakthroughs in medicine and other sciences. They gave the world new art and literature. They came to understand the need for federal civil rights legislation. They gave America Medicare.

They helped rebuild the economies and political institutions of their former enemies, and they stood fast against the totalitarianism of their former allies, the Russians. They were rocked by the social and political upheaval of the sixties. Many of them hated the long hair, the free love, and, especially, what they saw as the desecration of the flag. But they didn't give up on the new generation.

They weren't perfect. They made mistakes. They allowed McCarthyism and racism to go unchallenged for too long. Women of the World War II generation, who had demonstrated so convincingly that they had so much more to offer beyond their traditional work, were the underpinning for the liberation of their gender, even as many of their husbands resisted the idea. When a new war broke out, many of the veterans initially failed to recognize the differences between their war and the one in Vietnam.

There on the beaches of Normandy, I began to reflect on the

wonders of these ordinary people whose lives are laced with the markings of greatness. At every stage of their lives they were part of historic challenges and achievements of a magnitude the world had never before witnessed.

Although they were transformed by their experiences and quietly proud of what they had done, their stories did not come easily. They didn't volunteer them. I had to keep asking questions or learn to stay back a step or two as they walked the beaches themselves, quietly exchanging memories. NBC News had brought to Normandy several of those ordinary Americans, including Gino Merli, of Wilkes-Barre, Pennsylvania, who landed on D-Day and later won the Congressional Medal of Honor for holding off an attacking wave of German soldiers. This quiet man had stayed at his machine gun, blazing away at the Germans, covering the withdrawal of his fellow Americans, until his position was overrun. He faked his own death twice as the Germans swept past, and then he went back to his machine gun to cut them down from behind. His cunning and courage saved his fellow soldiers, and in a night of battle he killed more than fifty attacking Germans.

We also brought Harry Garton of Bucks County, Pennsylvania, who lost both legs to a land mine later in the war. Merli and Garton had both been in the Army's "Big Red One," the 1st Division. This trip to Normandy was their first time meeting each other and their first journey back to those beaches since they'd landed under greatly different circumstances forty years earlier. Quite coincidentally, they realized they'd been in the same landing craft, so they had matching memories of the chaos and death all around them. Garton said, "I remember all the bodies and all the screaming." Were they scared?, I asked them. Both men had the same answer: they felt alternating fear, rage, calm, and, most of all, an overpowering determination to survive.

As they made their way along Omaha Beach in 1984, they stopped and pointed to a low-lying bluff leading to higher ground. Merli said, "Remember that?" They both stared at a steep, sandy slope, an ordinary beach approach to my eye. "Remember what?" I asked. "Oh," Merli said, "that hillside was loaded with mines, and a unit of sappers had gone first, to find where the mines were. A number of those guys were lying on the hillside, their legs shattered by the explosions. They'd shot themselves up with morphine

*Sam Gibbons and Snow Ball
at Grandparents Gibbonses' house,
Haven Beach, Florida, 1926*

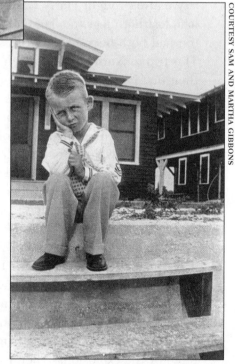

Sam Gibbons, 1927

and they were telling where it was now safe to step. They were about twenty-five yards apart, our guys, calmly telling us how to get up the hill. They were human markers." Garton said, "When I got to the top of that hill, I thought I'd live at least until the next day."

They described the scene as calmly as if they were remembering an egg-toss at a Sunday social back home. It was an instructive moment for me, one of many, and so characteristic. The war stories come reluctantly, and they almost never reflect directly on the bravery of the storyteller. Almost always he or she is singling out someone else for praise.

On that trip to Normandy, I ducked into a small café for lunch on a rainy Sunday. A tall, familiar-looking American approached with a big grin and introduced himself: "Tom, Congressman Sam Gibbons of Florida."

I knew of Gibbons, a veteran Democrat from central Florida, a member of the Ways and Means Committee, but I didn't know much about him.

"Congressman," I said, "what are you doing here?" "Oh, I was here forty years ago," he said with a laugh, "but it was a little different then." With that he clicked a small brass-and-steel cricket he was holding and laughed again.

I knew of the cricket. The paratroopers of the 101st and 82nd Airborne divisions were given the crickets to click if they were separated from their units. As it turned out, most of them were. When I asked Gibbons what had happened to him that day, he sat down and, staring at a far wall, told a harrowing tale that went on for half an hour. In the café, all of us listening were hypnotized by this gangly, jug-eared man in his sixties and the story he was sharing.

Gibbons, a captain in the 101st, was all alone when he landed in a French farm field in the predawn darkness. Using his cricket, he clicked until he got an answer, and then formed a squad of American paratroopers out of other units. They had no idea where they were, and for a time Gibbons thought the invasion had failed because there was no sign of American troops besides his small patched-up patrol.

Gibbons and the other paratroopers with him moved along the country roads between the hedgerows, getting ambushed and fighting back, moving on again, trying to figure out just where they

were. Gibbons even tried to converse with the terrified French villagers, using his high school Spanish. It didn't help. It was eighteen hours before they hooked up with other units.

His original objective, holding the bridges over the Douve River
at a village called St. Côme-du-Mont, turned out to have been a far
tougher assignment than the D-Day planners had realized. It took
a whole division, fire support from U.S. cruisers offshore, and
tanks to take control of the river crossings. By the third day, Gibbons was exhausted, he said, and he was one of only six hundred
or so of the two thousand men in his battalion still on his feet. The
others were all dead or wounded.

As he sat there on that rainy afternoon, describing these scenes
from passing images of his memory, Gibbons's tough-guy demeanor began to change. He softened and then began to weep. His
wife touched his arm and said he didn't have to go on. But he did,
and those of us in his tiny audience were enthralled.

Later, Gibbons told me that he fought his way all across Europe
and into Germany without a scratch. His brother, also in the Army,
was badly wounded, and when the war was over they both enrolled
at the University of Florida law school. They didn't talk much
about the war until one Saturday in the fall term when they decided to try to count up the young Floridians they had known who
hadn't made it back. Gibbons says, "When we got to a hundred we
stopped counting and said, 'To hell with this.' "

Gibbons went on to his career in politics, first in the Florida legislature and then seventeen terms in the U.S. House of Representatives, where he became a champion of free trade as a means of
keeping international tensions under control, a lesson he learned
from the politics of World War II. He was also a solid member of
the ruling Democratic majorities. He initially supported the Vietnam War but says now, "The sorriest vote I ever cast was for the
Tonkin Gulf resolution," the congressional mandate engineered by
President Johnson so he could step up the American efforts in
Vietnam.

Gibbons's personal war experience rarely came up publicly
again, but it did one day in the fall of 1995, after the Republican
Revolution of the year before, when a well-organized class of GOP
Baby Boomers took control of the House, determined to decon-

Martha and Sam Gibbons, 1962

Sam Gibbons, U.S. Army

struct many of the policies put in place by Democrats during their long congressional rule.

Gibbons, now in the minority on the Ways and Means Committee, was furious. The new Republican leadership had cut off debate on Medicare reforms without a hearing. Gibbons stormed from the room, shouting, "You're a bunch of dictators, that's all you are. . . . I had to fight you guys fifty years ago." Gibbons then grabbed the tie of the startled Republican chairman, demanding, "Tell them what you did in there, tell them what you did."

Watching this scene play out on CNN, many of my colleagues were puzzled by the eruption in the normally calm demeanor of Congressman Gibbons. I smiled to myself, thinking of that day in Normandy in 1944 when Gibbons, who was then just twenty-four, learned something about fighting for what you believe in.

When I returned to Normandy for the fiftieth anniversary of D-Day, my wife, Meredith, joined me. By 1994, I felt a kind of missionary zeal for the men and women of World War II, spreading the word of their remarkable lives. I was inspired by them but also by the work of my friend Stephen Ambrose, the plain-talking historian who had written an account of the invasion called *D-Day June 6, 1944: The Climactic Battle of World War II.*

From him I learned that the men told the stories best themselves. So I told Meredith, "Whenever one of these guys comes over to say hello, just ask, 'Where were you that day?' You'll hear some unbelievable stories." And so we did, wherever we went. What we did not know at the time was that an old family friend back in our hometown of Yankton, South Dakota, had played a critical role in D-Day planning.

In fact, we were only vaguely aware that Hod Nielsen had anything to do with World War II. To us, he was the keeper of the flame of high school athletics as a sportswriter and radio sportscaster. In his columns and on the air, he chronicled the individual and team achievements of our local high school, writing generously of the smallest victories, celebrating the stars but always finding some admirable trait to highlight in his descriptions of those of us who were known mostly for just showing up.

What I did not know—nor did any of my high school contemporaries—was that Hod Nielsen, who spent so many of the postwar

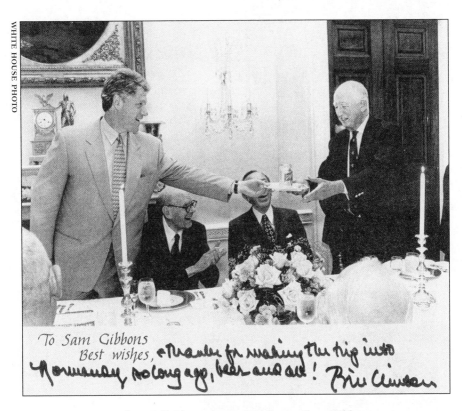

To Sam Gibbons
Best wishes, + Thanks for making the trip into
Normandy so long ago, beer and all! Bill Clinton

President Bill Clinton's presentation to Sam Gibbons,
recalling Gibbons's participation in D-Day—
White House Family Dining Room, May 14, 1994

Hod Nielsen, England, 1942

Hod Nielsen, England, 1943,
returning from a mission

Hod Nielsen, 1995

years making sure our little triumphs received notice, had been a daring photo reconnaissance pilot during World War II. He was in the unit that flew lightly armored P-38s over Normandy just before the invasion, photographing the beaches and fields for the military planners. As soon as they returned from that mission, they were hustled back to Washington to report directly to the legendary commander of the Army Air Corps, General Henry "Hap" Arnold. It's also likely they were spirited out of England quickly to diminish the chances that the identity of their reconnaissance targets would somehow leak.

Hod was one of many in our midst who kept his war years to himself, preferring to concentrate on the generations that followed. He is so characteristic of that time and place in American life. One of four sons of hardworking Scandinavian immigrants, whom he remembers for their loving and frugal ways, Hod doesn't recall a missed meal or a complaint about hard times during the height of the Great Depression.

All four boys in his family were in the service. One brother was killed in action when his bomber was shot down over Europe. The war had been a family trial but also an adventure. Hod had a lot of fun as a freewheeling young officer during pilot training. He managed to avoid getting shot down during numerous reconnaissance missions. He saw a lot of the United States and the world, but when the war was over Hod wanted to return to the familiar life he had known in South Dakota. He says now, "I thought then, If this is the fast track, I don't want any part of it."

Instead, he returned to a career in broadcasting and sportswriting. He's been at it for more than half a century, and he can still get excited about the local high school team's coming football season. He can tell you the whereabouts and the personal and professional fortunes of the athletes long gone from that small city along the Missouri River.

To get a favorable mention in a Hod Nielsen column requires more than a winning touchdown or all-state recognition. He is as likely to write about an athlete's musical ability or scholastic standing or family. As a result, it's always been a little special to read your name beneath his byline. Now that my contemporaries and those who followed us onto the playing fields of Yankton know more about his early life, I am confident they'll feel even greater pride in recognition from this modest and decent man.

During NBC's coverage of the fiftieth anniversary of D-Day, I was asked by Tim Russert on *Meet the Press* my thoughts on what we were witnessing. As I looked over the assembled crowd of veterans, which included everyone from Cabinet officers and captains of industry to retired schoolteachers and machinists, I said, "I think this is the greatest generation any society has ever produced." I know that this was a bold statement and a sweeping judgment, but since then I have restated it on many occasions. While I am periodically challenged on this premise, I believe I have the facts on my side.

This book, I hope, will in some small way pay tribute to those men and women who have given us the lives we have today. It is not the defining history of their generation. Instead, I think of this as like a family portrait. Some of the names and faces you'll recognize immediately. Others are more like your neighbors, the older couple who always fly the flag on the Fourth of July and Veterans Day and spend their vacation with friends they've had for fifty years at a reunion of his military outfit. They seem to have everything they need, but they still count their pennies as if the bottom may drop out tomorrow. Most of all, they love each other, love life and love their country, and they are not ashamed to say just that.

The sad reality is that they are dying at an ever faster pace. They're in the mortality years now, in their seventies and eighties, and the Department of Veterans' Affairs estimates that about thirty-two thousand World War II vets die every month. Not all of them were on the front lines, of course, or even in a critical rear-echelon position, but they were fused by a common mission and a common ethos.

I am in awe of them, and I feel privileged to have been a witness to their lives and their sacrifices. There were so many other people whose stories could have been in this book, who embodied the standards of greatness in the everyday that the people in this book represent, and that give this generation its special quality and distinction. As I came to know many of them, and their stories, I became more convinced of my judgment on that day marking the fiftieth anniversary of D-Day. This is the greatest generation any society has produced.

THE GREATEST GENERATION

THE TIME
OF THEIR LIVES

"This generation of Americans has a rendezvous with destiny."
—Franklin Delano Roosevelt

The year of my birth, 1940, was the fulcrum of America in the twentieth century, when the nation was balanced precariously between the darkness of the Great Depression on one side and the storms of war in Europe and the Pacific on the other. It was a critical time in the shaping of this nation and the world, equal to the revolution of 1776 and the perils of the Civil War. Once again the American people understood the magnitude of the challenge, the importance of an unparalleled national commitment, and, most of all, the certainty that only one resolution was acceptable. The nation turned to its young to carry the heaviest burden, to fight in enemy territory and to keep the home front secure and productive. These young men and women were eager for the assignment. They understood what was required of them, and they willingly volunteered for their duty.

Many of them had been born just twenty years earlier than I, in a time of national promise, optimism, and prosperity, when all things seemed possible as the United States was swiftly taking its place as the most powerful nation in the world. World War I was over, America's industrial might was coming of age with the rise of the auto industry and the nascent communications industry, Wall Street was booming, and the popular culture was rich with the likes of Babe Ruth, Eugene O'Neill, D. W. Griffith, and a new author on the scene, F. Scott Fitzgerald. What those unsuspecting infants could not have realized, of course, was that these were temporary conditions, a false spring to a life that would be buffeted by winds of change dangerous and unpredictable, so fierce that they threatened not just America but the very future of the planet.

Nonetheless, 1920 was an auspicious year for a young person to enter the world as an American citizen. The U.S. population had topped 106 million people, and the landscape was changing rapidly from agrarian to urban, even though one in three Americans still lived on a farm. Women were gaining the right to vote with the ratification of the Nineteenth Amendment, and KDKA in Pittsburgh was broadcasting the first radio signals across the middle of America. Prohibition was beginning, but so was the roaring lifestyle that came with the flouting of Prohibition and the culture that produced it. In far-off Russia the Bolshevik revolution was a bloody affair, but its American admirers were unable to stir comparable passions here.

Five years later this American child born in 1920 still seemed to be poised for a life of ever greater prosperity, opportunity, and excitement. President Calvin "Silent Cal" Coolidge was a benign presence in the White House, content to let the bankers, industrialists, and speculators run the country as they saw fit.

As the twenties roared along, the Four Horsemen of Notre Dame were giving Saturdays new meaning with their college football heroics. Jack Dempsey and Gene Tunney were raising the spectacle of heavyweight boxing matches to new heights of frenzy. Baseball was a daytime game and a true national pastime, from the fabled Yankee Stadium to the sandlots in rural America.

The New Yorker was launched, and the place of magazines occupied a higher order. Flappers were dancing the Charleston; Fitzgerald was publishing The Great Gatsby; the Scopes trial was under way in Tennessee, with Clarence Darrow and William Jennings Bryan in a passionate and theatrical debate on evolution versus the Scriptures. A. Philip Randolph organized the Brotherhood of Sleeping Car Porters, the beginning of a long struggle to force America to face its shameful policies and practices on race.

By the time this young American who had such a promising start reached the age of ten, his earlier prospects were shattered; the fault lines were active everywhere: the stock market was struggling to recover from the crash of 1929, but the damage was too great. U.S. income was falling fast. Thirteen hundred banks closed. Businesses were failing everywhere, sending four and a half million people onto the streets with no safety net. The average American farm family had an annual cash income of four hundred dollars.

Herbert Hoover, as president, seemed to be paralyzed in the face of spreading economic calamity; he was a distant figure of stern bearing whose reputation as an engineering genius and management wizard was quickly replaced by cruel caricatures of his aloofness from the plight of the ever larger population of poor.

Congress passed the disastrous Smoot-Hawley Tariff Act, establishing barriers to world trade and exacerbating an already raging global recession.

Yet Henry Luce managed to launch *Fortune,* a magazine specializing in business affairs. United Airlines and American Airlines, still in their infancy, managed to stay airborne. Lowell Thomas began a nightly national radio newscast on NBC and CBS. *The Lone Ranger* series was heard on radio.

Overseas, three men were plotting to change the world: Adolf Hitler in Germany, Joseph Stalin in Russia, and Mao Zedong in China. In American politics, the New York governor, Franklin Delano Roosevelt, was planning his campaign for the 1932 presidential election.

By 1933, when the baby born in 1920 was entering teenage years, the promise of that early childhood was shattered by crashing world economies. American farmers were able to produce only about sixteen bushels of corn per acre, and the prices were so low that it was more efficient to feed the corn to the hogs than take it to market. It was the year my mother moved with her parents and sister off their South Dakota farm and into a nearby small town, busted by the markets and the merciless drought. They took one milk cow, their pride, and their determination to just keep going somehow.

My mother, who graduated from high school at sixteen, had no hope of affording college, so she went to work in the local post office for a dollar a day. She was doing better than her father, who earned ten cents an hour working at a nearby grain elevator.

My father, an ambitious and skilled construction equipment operator, raced around the Midwest in his small Ford coupe, working hellishly long hours on road crews, hoping he could save enough in the warm weather months to get through another long winter back home in the small wood-frame hotel his sisters ran for railroad men, traveling salesmen, and local itinerants in the Great Plains village founded by his grandfather Richard Brokaw, a Civil War veteran who came to the Great Plains as a cook for railroad crews.

A mass of homeless and unemployed men drifted across the American landscape, looking for work or a handout wherever they could find it. More than thirty million Americans had no income of any kind. The American military had more horses than tanks, and its only action had been breaking up a demonstration of World War I veterans demanding their pension bonuses a year earlier.

Franklin Roosevelt took the oath of office as president of the United States, promising a New Deal for the beleaguered American people, declaring to a nation with more than fifteen million people out of work, "The only thing we have to fear is fear itself."

He pushed through an Emergency Banking Act, a Federal Emergency Relief Act, a National Industrial Recovery Act, and by 1935 set in motion the legislation that would become the Social Security system.

Not everyone was happy. Rich Americans led by the Du Ponts, the founders of General Motors, and big oil millionaires founded the Liberty League to oppose the New Deal. Privately, in the salons of the privileged, Roosevelt was branded a traitor to his class.

In Germany, a former painter with a spellbinding oratorical style took office as chancellor and immediately set out to seize control of the political machinery of Germany with his National Socialist German Workers party, known informally as the Nazis. Adolf Hitler began his long march to infamy. He turned on the Jews, passing laws that denied them German citizenship, codifying the anti-Semitism that eventually led to the concentration camps and the gas chambers, an act of hatred so deeply immoral it will mark the twentieth century forever.

By the late thirties in America, anti-Semitism was the blatant message of Father Charles Coughlin, a messianic Roman Catholic priest with a vast radio audience. Huey Long, the brilliant Louisiana populist, came to power, first as governor and then as a U.S.

senator, preaching in his own spellbinding fashion the power of the little guy against the evils of Wall Street and corporate avarice.

When our young American was reaching eighteen, in 1938, the flames of war were everywhere in the world: Hitler had seized Austria; the campaign against Jews had intensified with Kristallnacht, a vicious and calculated campaign to destroy all Jewish businesses within the Nazi realm. Japan continued its brutal and genocidal war against the Chinese; and in Russia, Stalin was presiding over show trials, deporting thousands to Siberia, and summarily executing his rivals in the Communist party. The Spanish Civil War was a losing cause for the loyalists, and a diminutive fascist general, Francisco Franco, began a reign that would last forty years.

In this riotous year the British prime minister, Neville Chamberlain, believed he had saved his country with a pact negotiated with Hitler at Munich. He returned to England to declare, "I believe it is peace for our time . . . peace with honor."

It was neither.

At home, Roosevelt was in his second term, trying to balance the continuing need for extraordinary efforts to revive the economy with what he knew was the great peril abroad. Congress passed the Fair Labor Standards Act, setting a limit on hours worked and a minimum wage. The federal government began a system of parity payments to farmers and subsidized foreign wheat sales.

In the fall of 1938, Dwight David Eisenhower, a career soldier who had grown up on a small farm outside of Abilene, Kansas, was a forty-eight-year-old colonel in the U.S. Army. He had an infectious grin and a fine reputation as a military planner, but he had no major combat command experience. The winds of war were about to carry him to the highest peaks of military glory and political reward. Ike, as he was called, would become a folksy avatar of his time.

America was entertained by Benny Goodman, Glenn Miller, Woody Guthrie, the music of Hoagy Carmichael, the big-screen film magic of Clark Gable, Cary Grant, Katharine Hepburn, Errol Flynn, Ginger Rogers, Fred Astaire, Bette Davis, Henry Fonda.

At the beginning of a new decade, 1940, just twenty years after our young American entered a world of such great promise and prosperity, it was clear to all but a few delusional isolationists that war would define this generation's coming of age.

France, Belgium, the Netherlands, Luxembourg, Denmark, Norway, and Romania had all fallen to Nazi aggression. German troops controlled Paris. In the east, Stalin was rapidly building up one of the greatest ground armies ever to defend Russia and communism.

Japan signed a ten-year military pact with Germany and Italy, forming an Axis they expected would rule the world before the decade was finished.

Roosevelt, elected to his third term, again by a landslide, was preparing the United States, pushing through the Export Control Act to stop the shipment of war materials overseas. Contracts were arranged for a new military vehicle called the jeep. A fighter plane was developed. It would be designated the P-51 Mustang. Almost 20 percent of the budget FDR submitted to Congress was for defense needs. The first peacetime military draft in U.S. history was activated.

Roosevelt stayed in close touch with his friend, the new prime minister of England, Winston Churchill, who told the English: "I have nothing to offer but blood, toil, tears and sweat." And "We shall not flag or fail . . . we shall fight on the seas and oceans . . . we shall fight on the landing grounds, we shall fight in the fields and on the streets, we shall fight in the hills, we shall never surrender."

Our twenty-year-old American learned something of war by reading *For Whom the Bell Tolls,* by Ernest Hemingway, and something else about the human spirit by watching *The Grapes of Wrath,* the film based on John Steinbeck's novel, directed by John Ford and starring Henry Fonda.

The majority of black Americans were still living in the states of the former Confederacy, and they remained second-class citizens, or worse, in practice and law. Negro men were drafted and placed in segregated military units even as America prepared to fight a fascist regime that had as a core belief the inherent superiority of the Aryan people.

It had been a turbulent twenty years for our young American, and the worst and the best were yet to come. On December 7, 1941, the Japanese attacked Pearl Harbor. Across America on that Sunday afternoon, the stunning news from the radio electrified the nation and changed the lives of all who heard it. Marriages were postponed or accelerated. College was deferred. Plans of any kind for the future were calibrated against the quickening pace of the march to war.

Shortly after the attack, Winston Churchill called FDR from the prime minister's country estate, Chequers. In his book *The Grand Alliance,* Churchill recounted the conversation. "Mr. President, what's this about Japan?" Roosevelt replied, "It's quite true. They have attacked us at Pearl Harbor. We're all in the same boat now."

Churchill couldn't have been happier. He would now have the manpower, the resources, and the political will of the United States actively engaged in this fight for survival. He wrote, "So we had won after all." A few days later, after Germany and Italy had declared war against the United States, Churchill wrote to Anthony Eden, his foreign secretary, who was traveling to Russia, "The accession of the United States makes amends for all, and with time and patience will give us certain victory."

In America, young men were enlisting in the military by the hundreds of thousands. Farm kids from the Great Plains who never expected to see the ocean in their lifetimes signed up for the Navy; brothers followed brothers into the Marines; young daredevils who were fascinated by the new frontiers of flight volunteered for pilot training. Single young women poured into Washington to fill the exploding needs for clerical help as the political capital mobilized for war. Other women, their husbands or boyfriends off to basic training, learned to drive trucks or handle welding torches. The old rules of gender and expectation changed radically with what was now expected of this generation.

My mother and father, with my newborn brother and me in the backseat of the 1938 Ford sedan that would be our family car for the next decade, moved to that hastily constructed Army ammunition depot called Igloo, on the alkaline and sagebrush landscape of far southwestern South Dakota. I was three years old.

It was a monochromatic world, the bleak brown prairie, Army-green cars and trucks, khaki uniforms everywhere. My first impressions of women were not confined to those of my mother caring for my brothers and me at home. I can still see in my mind's eye a woman in overalls carrying a lunch bucket, her hair covered in a red bandanna, swinging out of the big Army truck she had just parked, headed for home at the end of a long day. Women in what

Jean and Anthony "Red" Brokaw at the time of their wedding, 1938

had been men's jobs were part of the new workaday world of a nation at war.

Looking back, I can recall that the grown-ups all seemed to have a sense of purpose that was evident even to someone as young as four, five, or six. Whatever else was happening in our family or neighborhood, there was something greater connecting all of us, in large ways and small.

Indeed there was, and the scope of the national involvement was reflected in the numbers: by 1944, twelve million Americans were in uniform; war production represented 44 percent of the Gross National Product; there were almost nineteen million more workers than there had been five years earlier, and 35 percent of them were women. The nation was immersed in the war effort at every level.

The young Americans of this time constituted a generation birthmarked for greatness, a generation of Americans that would take its place in American history with the generations that had converted the North American wilderness into the United States and infused the new nation with self-determination embodied first in the Declaration of Independence and then in the Constitution and the Bill of Rights.

At the end of the twentieth century the contributions of this generation would be in bold print in any review of this turbulent and earth-altering time. It may be historically premature to judge the greatness of a whole generation, but indisputably, there are common traits that cannot be denied. It is a generation that, by and large, made no demands of homage from those who followed and prospered economically, politically, and culturally because of its sacrifices. It is a generation of towering achievement and modest demeanor, a legacy of their formative years when they were participants in and witness to sacrifices of the highest order. They know how many of the best of their generation didn't make it to their early twenties, how many brilliant scientists, teachers, spiritual and business leaders, politicians and artists were lost in the ravages of the greatest war the world has seen.

The enduring contributions of this generation transcend gender. The world we know today was shaped not just on the front lines of combat. From the Great Depression forward, through the war and into the years of rebuilding and unparalleled progress on almost every front, women were essential to and leaders in the greatest national mobilization of resources and spirit the country had ever known. They were also distinctive in that they raised the place of their gender to new heights; they changed forever the perception and the reality of women in all the disciplines of American life.

Millions of men and women were involved in this tumultuous journey through adversity and achievement, despair and triumph. Certainly there were those who failed to measure up, but taken as a whole this generation did have a "rendezvous with destiny" that went well beyond the outsized expectations of President Roosevelt when he first issued that call to duty in 1936.

The stories that follow represent the lives of some of them. Each is distinctive and yet reflective of the common experiences of that trying time and this generation of greatness.

---•---

ORDINARY
PEOPLE

—————————— • ——————————

When the United States entered World War II, the U.S. government turned to ordinary Americans and asked of them extraordinary service, sacrifice, and heroics. Many Americans met those high expectations, and then returned home to lead ordinary lives.

When the war ended, more than twelve million men and women put their uniforms aside and returned to civilian life. They went back to work at their old jobs or started small businesses; they became big-city cops and firemen; they finished their degrees or enrolled in college for the first time; they became schoolteachers, insurance salesmen, craftsmen, and local politicians. They weren't widely known outside their families or their communities. For many, the war years were enough adventure to last a lifetime. They were proud of what they accomplished but they rarely discussed their experiences, even with each other. They became once again ordinary people, the kind of men and women who always have been the foundation of the American way of life.

Tom Broderick in paratrooper training,
Fort Benning, Georgia, 1944

THOMAS
AND EILEEN
BRODERICK

"What's a handicap? I don't have a handicap."

O**N THE FIFTIETH ANNIVERSARY OF** D-Day, I was broadcasting from the American cemetery overlooking Omaha Beach at Colleville-sur-Mer in Normandy, one of the bloodiest battlefields in American history. The cemetery is at once haunting and beautiful, with 9,386 white marble headstones in long, even lines across the manicured fields of dark green, each headstone marking the death of a brave young American. The anniversary was a somber and celebratory moment, as veterans of that daring and dangerous invasion, unparalleled in the long history of warfare, gathered to pay tribute to those whose sacrifices were marked by the simple headstones and to share with the world their own remarkable stories of survival.

In the course of the extended *Today* show coverage on NBC, we concentrated more on the heroics of those who survived, but then the noted historian Stephen Ambrose interrupted to say, "I think we should talk about what was happening to so many men down there on those beaches. They were terribly wounded. Their stomachs opened. Their faces shot away. Their limbs blown off. That was the reality of that day and we shouldn't forget that."

Ambrose brought us back to the savage nature of war that we often overlook on those occasions when wars are celebrated for what they achieved. For the warriors who live, the consequences of war become a lifelong condition. In its savagery, war strikes at the very idea of a sound and healthy body. In World War II, more than 292,000 Americans were killed in battle, and more than 1.7 million returned home physically affected in some way, from minor afflictions to blindness or missing limbs or paralysis, battle-scarred and exhausted, but oh so happy and relieved to be home. They had survived an extraordinary ordeal, but now they were eager to reclaim their ordinary lives of work, family, church, and community. The war had taught them what mattered most in the lives they wanted now to settle down and live.

Thomas Broderick was a nineteen-year-old premed student at Xavier College in Cincinnati in 1942, trying to decide which branch of the service fit his sense of adventure. This son of a south Chicago working-class family was bright and ambitious, so he enlisted in the Merchant Marine. "They gave us the best deal," he said. "If you didn't like it, you could quit." After ten weeks of training he went on a mission to North Africa on a supply ship. The pay was excellent. The food was abundant. He had a private room on the officers' deck of his ship, the *John W. Brown,* but the trip was long and boring. He wanted out of the Merchant Marine. He wanted to join the Airborne so he could be like those cocky paratroopers he saw stationed in Algiers. "I'd never even been in a plane before," he says, "but it was the challenge I wanted."

His superiors in the Merchant Marine were astonished. Here he was, ready to go back to the security of the Merchant Marine Academy for another eighteen months of accelerated training, and he wanted to quit to join one of the most dangerous outfits in the service. His officer offered him a thirty-day furlough to think it over. Broderick said, "No, my mind's made up." When he returned home, his parents were equally appalled. When he told his draft board what he wanted, the clerk said, "You're nuts. I'll give you another month before we draft you, so you can change your mind." Broderick declined, saying he wanted in now.

Tom Broderick spent seventeen weeks in basic training for the infantry in Mineral Wells, Texas, before heading to Fort Benning, Georgia, to become a member of the 82nd Airborne. When he finished his training, a captain offered him an instructor's job and the rank of sergeant. Again Broderick refused the safer alternative, saying he wanted to stay with his outfit and go overseas.

Broderick's unit shipped out to England as replacements for the 82nd Airborne men lost in the Normandy invasion. In September, Broderick made his first jump into combat, in Holland. He was in the thick of it immediately, the Battle of Arnhem. It was a joint mission of American and British paratroopers, and their objective was to take the Nijmegen bridge to help pave the Allies' way into Germany and to discourage any German counterattack. "We jumped at about five hundred feet because we wanted to be a low target. It was one-thirty in the afternoon.

"The first German I saw I couldn't shoot, because he was riding a bicycle away from me. I couldn't shoot at him because he wasn't shooting at me. Things were different ten minutes later. There were Germans all over the place—they outnumbered us about forty thousand to twenty-eight thousand. It was combat morning, noon, and night."

On the fifth day Broderick made a mistake that would alter his life forever. "I remember being in the foxhole and . . . I was lining up my aim on a German. I got a little high in the foxhole and I got shot clean through the head—through the left temple."

A Catholic chaplain arrived to administer the last rites, but after slipping into unconsciousness, Broderick somehow managed to stay alive until he awoke a few days later in a British hospital. He was relieved to be out of combat but he had a problem: he couldn't see. Why not? he asked. His doctors told him, "When that hemorrhage clears up, you'll be all right." Broderick continued to believe them until he was sent to Dibble General Hospital in Menlo Park, California, one of the two facilities in the nation treating blind veterans.

Finally a doctor told him the truth. He would be blind forever. "I was stunned. I cried, 'Aren't you going to do anything?' " He rushed to a fellow veteran who had been hospitalized with him in England, a man recovering from shrapnel in one of his eyes. "I just cried and cried, and he said to me, 'We knew the whole time, Tom; we just didn't want to tell you.' "

Broderick was angry and disoriented. When the Army made him take a rehabilitation course in Connecticut, he said, "I rebelled—I just didn't want to learn braille. I told them I was going to work in my dad's trucking business just so I could get out of there."

It didn't get much better when he returned to Chicago. He enrolled at Loyola University and the Veterans Administration hired a reader for him, but after only seven weeks Broderick dropped out and went to work for his father. His downslide continued. "They didn't know what to do with me. Dad had me taking orders on the phone because I could still write. But then I heard of people having to call back to get the orders straightened out. I thought, 'Hell, I'm screwing up.'" He quit after a month.

Broderick realized he'd have to learn braille. His Veterans Administration counselor also recommended he enroll in a class in insurance sales, a fast-growing field in postwar America. He learned the insurance business by day and braille by night. Before long the VA found him a job with an elderly insurance broker in his neighborhood. Not too long after that, Broderick had established his own insurance business. He was no longer the young man angry at his fate. He was now prepared to accept his blindness and get on with his life.

Broderick worked six days a week. When he wasn't taking orders by phone with his braille machine and dictating them to his secretary later, he was making house calls at night. He quickly developed a very keen audio sense; many customers he dealt with on the phone were astonished when they finally met him. He'd quickly call out their name when he heard their voice. Until that point they had no idea he was blind.

Later, when he and his wife were having children—seven in all—Broderick would tell each of them the same story as they reached the age when they could understand the real meaning of blindness. His daughter, Katy Broderick Duffy: "He'd tell us how he was hurt in the war and that when he came home he went with his mother to Lourdes, the famous shrine in France, to pray for a miracle. He said that before they put the water on his eyes, he asked the Lord for a favor: 'If I can't have my eyesight back, could you find a girl for me to marry?' And that's how he met my mother. When you're little and you hear that story, you really think it *was* a miracle."

Broderick's wife, Eileen, is a little skeptical of the story, but Tom insists it's true, although his version is a bit breezier. "I said, 'I know we don't always get what we want, but what's right for us. I'm

HE 'LOOKS' TO THE FUTURE

Former Pfc. Thomas Broderick Jr., 20, who has been blind as a result of a German sniper's bullet, shows his two sisters, Patricia (left) and Jacqueline, that he is adept at operating a typewriter, an accomplishment he plans to use in his future work.
(Daily News photo.)

Tom Broderick, feature in the Chicago Tribune, *1944*

really hoping to meet the woman for me—and if you want to throw in the eyes, too, that's okay.' "

Not long after that, Tom and Eileen met on a blind date, no irony intended. Eileen was a twenty-three-year-old nurse and Tom was twenty-seven. She fell in love instantly. "That night, after the date, I went home, woke my cousin up, and said, 'I've met the man I'm going to marry.' She told me I'd been drinking too much and I should go to bed, but I knew.

"You didn't think about his blindness. It just didn't seem to matter. He was so unique. He ran a business by himself and didn't need help from anyone, although it was a little tricky when we went out alone. I'd have to take him to the men's room and ask someone to take him in. I'd stand outside. I think, being a nurse, I was a little more flexible. I understood that it was all just mechanics.

"My father was worried when I said I was marrying Tom. He just didn't understand how Tom could take care of me and a family. But after three or four years of marriage they became very close. Tom's mother started him off right. When he came back from the war she would not allow anyone to use the word *blind* in the house. Tom had to be treated with dignity and respect, and anything he wanted to try, he could do it. When he left his father's business to set out on his own, she was happy."

Tom and Eileen had common roots as strongly faithful Roman Catholic Irish Americans. They settled into a life of the prosperous middle class on the south side of Chicago, where Tom's business continued to flourish and their family grew quickly. During one five-year stretch Eileen had five children, and then another two later. Eileen says, "He was very involved in their upbringing. There were things he could do and those he couldn't. It was kind of trial and error. He couldn't change diapers but he could give them a bottle. We never talked about how to make things work. It wasn't easy, but we did what we had to do."

The Broderick children were part of the equation of making things work. Daughter Katy says, "The blindness was just incidental. I'd see other people who were blind and not well adjusted and think, 'What's wrong with them?' Later I realized not everyone had the strength and determination of my father. When I was little, my friends would say, 'Your father's not blind!' He could just do so many things it didn't seem like he was blind."

Dan Broderick, one of Tom's sons, says his father worked out a system to take care of most of the household chores, including assembling an elaborate stereo system, washing and waxing the car, and changing the storm windows. He refused to succumb to his blindness. He even refused to let Eileen get disability license plates for the family car when they became available. "What's a handicap?" he'd say. "I don't have a handicap."

But then Tom isn't much for cars. Since he can't drive himself, he likes to walk, and his family was expected to do the same. Katy remembers, "We walked everywhere. He hated getting rides. He thought it was a waste."

During his introduction to the world of the blind at the rehabilitation center in Connecticut, Broderick and his friends formed an informal organization to help each other adjust to their new realities. It became the Blinded Veterans Association, and Broderick decided that he should share the lessons of his new life with other veterans who were struggling with their blindness. He began making trips to Chicago-area rehabilitation programs, counseling sightless veterans on the career possibilities in insurance, mortgage sales, and car financing—the hot financial service fields as America exploded out of the cities and into the suburbs.

"I'd tell them about my own struggle—how I was young when I became blind and I knew how they felt. I brought some of them down to my office so they could see the braille machine and what was possible. I don't feel any special bond with other blind organizations or blind people, but I wanted to help veterans. You have to do it. It was no big deal, really."

Tom's son Dan remembers that, during Vietnam, the nearby Veterans Administration office would send over young men who'd lost their sight in that war. "When you first saw them you thought you were at a wake—some of them were suicidal, with their eyes blown out. Mom would go out and get a case of beer, and they'd sit on the porch with my dad and listen to the White Sox game. Then he'd navigate 'em around our house to show them what we had—five bedrooms, a big house. By the end of the night they'd be back on the porch, drinking beer but laughing now."

Another son, Scott: "You know how everyone says their dad is the best. Well, do you know how many people I've heard that from about *my* dad? Friends, neighbors, clients. Every kid thinks it, but to hear it from other people is so gratifying. He never let his disability get in the way of anything."

Tom Broderick in so many ways embodies the best qualities of his generation. He was so eager to get involved in the war he enlisted in two branches of the service. He was gravely wounded, but once he got over the initial understandable anger, he set out to be the best husband, father, businessman, and citizen he could be—sight or no sight. He didn't grow bitter and dependent on others. He didn't blame the world for his condition.

A common lament of the World War II generation is the absence today of personal responsibility. Broderick remembers listening to an NPR broadcast and hearing an account of how two boys found a loaded gun in one of their homes. The visiting boy accidentally shot his friend. The victim's father was on the radio, talking about suing the gun manufacturer. That got to Tom Broderick. "So," he said, "here's this man talking about suing and he's not accepting responsibility for having a loaded gun in the house."

Tom knows something about personal responsibility. He's been forced to live as a blind man for more than fifty years, and when asked about the moment when the lights were literally shot out of his eyes, he says only, "It was my fault for getting too high in the foxhole. That happens sometimes."

CHARLES O.
VAN GORDER, MD

*"If I had my life to do all over again, I'd do it the same way—
go somewhere small where people have a need."*

I T IS NOT SURPRISING, I suppose, that the horrors of war give
birth to a new generation of good Samaritans. Young men and
women who have been so intensely exposed to such inhumanity
often make a silent pledge that if they ever escape this dark world
of death and injuries, this universe of cruelty, they will devote their
lives to good works. Sometimes the pledge is a conscious thought.
Sometimes it is a subconscious reaction to their experiences. This
is the story of a good Samaritan who set out in life to heal, found
his greatest personal and professional tests under fire, and returned
home to his original calling with a renewed sense of mission.

There had never been a military operation remotely approaching
the scale and the complexity of D-Day. It involved 176,000 troops,
more than 12,000 airplanes, almost 10,000 ships, boats, landing
craft, frigates, sloops, and other special combat vessels—all involved in a surprise attack on the heavily fortified north coast of
France, to secure a beachhead in the heart of enemy-held territory
so that the march to Germany and victory could begin. It was daring, risky, confusing, bloody, and ultimately glorious.

It will live forever as a stroke of enduring genius, a military maneuver that, even though it went awry and spilled ashore in chaos,

Dr. Charles Van Gorder, wartime portrait

succeeded. It was so risky that before he launched the invasion, gambling that the small break in the weather would hold, General Dwight Eisenhower personally wrote out a statement taking full responsibility for the failure if it occurred. He was grateful he never had to release it.

A new generation of Americans has a greater appreciation of what was involved on D-Day as a result of Steven Spielberg's stunning film *Saving Private Ryan.* For most younger Americans, D-Day has been a page or two in their history books, or some anniversary ceremony on television with a lot of white-haired men leaning into the winds coming off the English Channel as President Reagan or President Clinton praised their contributions. *Saving Private Ryan,* although a work of fiction, is true to the sound, the fury, the death, the terrible wounds of that day.

Charles O. Van Gorder was a special part of D-Day. He was a thirty-one-year-old captain in the U.S. Army Medical Corps in June 1944, a graduate of the University of Tennessee Medical School. He'd already served in North Africa when he volunteered to be part of a two-team surgical unit that would try something new for D-Day: it would be part of the 101st Airborne assault force, setting up medical facilities in the middle of the fighting instead of safely behind the Allied lines. They knew that casualties would be high and that saving lives would require immediate attention.

So Captain Van Gorder and his colleagues were loaded onto gliders for the flight across the English Channel and into Normandy. These were primitive aircraft, made of tubing, canvas, and plywood, with no engines, of course. They were silent—the element of surprise—and they could land in rough terrain.

Van Gorder remembers, "We landed in the field where we were supposed to, but they forgot one thing: when they put the brakes on, it made that glider just like an ice sled and it went zooming across the field. We hit a tree—which ended up right between the pilot and the copilot. Nobody in my glider was killed, but nearly all the other gliders had someone killed or injured."

That was at four A.M. By nine that same day, June 6, 1944, Van Gorder and his fellow doctors had set up an operating facility, a precursor to the MASH units, the Mobile Army Surgical Hospitals that saved so many lives and, later on television, gave us so much intelligent entertainment.

They were located in a French château; they converted the milk storage room to an operating room, and by late that afternoon the château grounds were covered with hundreds of wounded young Americans. Van Gorder and the other surgeons operated around the clock for thirty-six hours, always wearing their helmets because the château was often in the line of fire. The Army had issued the medical team several cases of Scotch whiskey and Van Gorder later remembered, "The only thing that kept us going was sipping that Scotch. Finally, I got so tired my head fell down into an open abdomen." He was ordered to go back to his tent for some rest. En route, a soldier offered him hot chocolate. When he decided to go back for the hot chocolate, a German bomb hit his tent, demolishing it. It was the first of many narrow escapes for Dr. Van, as he was called.

Altogether, it was a frantic and grisly scene that even now, more than fifty years later, Dr. Van Gorder cannot remove from his memory. "I have flashbacks every day," he says. "All those boys being slaughtered, sometimes two hundred boys and only ten surgeons. The war made me a better doctor because I had to do all kinds of surgery. There were no trauma surgery books before the war to learn from."

Van Gorder's D-Day initiation wasn't the end of his frontline experience; it was only the beginning. His unit stayed with the 101st over the next six months as it fought its way across Europe, headed for the heart of Germany. They were in the thick of the fighting during the long siege in Belgium, and during the Battle of the Bulge.

In December 1944, Dr. Van Gorder and his colleague and friend, Dr. John Rodda, were in the middle of surgery when their makeshift operating room came under heavy fire from German forces. "I was practically lying on my stomach operating on patients," Van Gorder remembers, "because of the shooting coming right into the tent.

"I was the only one who spoke German, so I went to the end of the tent and waved a towel through the flap. I told the German commander we had more than fifty wounded, including German

ABOVE: *Dr. Charles Van Gorder in the Rodda–Van Gorder Hospital and Clinic, Andrews, North Carolina (left to right): Dr. Charles Van Gorder, Dr. John S. Rodda, nurse*

LEFT: *"Captain Charles Van Gorder demonstrates what the well-dressed airborne surgeon wears on an invasion," June 13, 1944*

BELOW: *Charles Van Gorder, MD, 1994*

POWs. He told me to load them up. I had to leave one patient behind with his stomach open." They were taken prisoner on December 19, 1944, Dr. Van Gorder's thirty-second birthday.

Van Gorder had suffered shrapnel wounds in his knees while the operating tent was under fire, so his friend Dr. Rodda supported him as they trekked through the snow under the watchful German guns. Van Gorder is convinced that without Rodda's help the Germans would have shot him as a straggler.

He returned the favor when Rodda became ill. Two young American doctors, who had seen more death and suffering than most graduating classes of doctors were likely to see in a lifetime, were now trying just to keep each other alive. Nothing in medical school had prepared them for this primal struggle of being prisoners of war in a bleak winter landscape in the heart of enemy territory. Back home, their families had no idea of what they were going through, and it was just as well.

Van Gorder, Rodda, and the other prisoners were packed into boxcars, and the train moved them to the north of Germany, where they stayed on a siding for three days, locked inside. "Half of us would stand and half of us would sit in rotation because it was so crowded," Van Gorder remembers.

Van Gorder got out of his confinement when the Germans needed a doctor to operate on a soldier needing an appendectomy. It was almost a fatal mission, however. American planes attacked the German train, not knowing there were Americans aboard. Van Gorder ducked beneath a car to avoid the heavy fire and then told the Germans, "I'm going to let the others out." He risked his life to race into the line of fire and open the boxcar doors. The Americans poured out and immediately ran to a small hill and formed a human sign: USA POWs. The attacking American planes waggled their wings to indicate they understood, and broke off the attack.

The German army was fighting a losing battle, retreating deeper and deeper to the east, taking their prisoners with them. Van Gorder and Rodda were taken first to Poland and then to the Russian border. In the confusion, they escaped and started making their way back west, through Poland. Whenever they came upon a Polish hospital they'd stop to do what they could for the patients there, as most of the Polish doctors had been conscripted by the

Germans. Finally they made their way back to American lines in the spring of 1945. Their war was over.

"When I was finally discharged, I had served five years in the war; I was overseas for thirty months straight," Dr. Van Gorder says without a trace of bitterness. During that time his wife, Helen, a nurse from Nova Scotia he'd met in New Jersey during his residency before the war, gave birth to their first son, Rod. The infant died shortly after birth, a victim of sudden infant death syndrome. Dr. Van Gorder was in North Africa at the time, a long way from his wife's side.

When the war was over, Dr. Van Gorder was headed for New York and a fellowship in reconstructive surgery. No doubt it would have been a high-income, prestigious practice. Before going to New York, however, Van Gorder visited his parents, who had relocated to the North Carolina mountain hamlet of Andrews. It's tucked into the Smoky Mountains in that corner where North Carolina, Tennessee, and Georgia come together. It was a logging community, the very essence of backwoods.

After the turmoil of the war, however, it looked like a little piece of heaven to Dr. Van Gorder. The people were plain and friendly, the village was scenic and tranquil—and there were no doctors. It was the perfect match for a young physician who had experienced enough trauma, turmoil, and uncertainty in five years to last a lifetime. He decided to stay in Andrews and open a practice.

He called his wartime buddy and fellow surgeon John Rodda and invited him to become a partner. Dr. Rodda made one visit to Andrews and saw immediately what had attracted his friend. He agreed to sign on.

They opened a small clinic and mini-hospital above a department store. It consisted of an operating room, X-ray facilities, a blood lab, three examining rooms, and twenty-one beds. For the next ten years they were the only physicians in town. They really didn't intend to stay forever but they quickly came to love their practices, their patients, and their adopted home.

Dr. Van Gorder's son, Chuck, remembers his dad being very busy, and some evenings so exhausted he'd fall asleep at the dinner table. "When the clinic closed at five-thirty in the evening," Chuck recalls, "my mother—who was the nurse—took the names of all the people who were too sick to come to town. We'd all get in the station wagon with our parents and they'd make their nightly rounds of house calls. They did this every night.

"I don't think my dad ever left town the same time as Dr. Rodda. Andrews had a tough element and someone was always getting hurt in a fight or getting shot. Even so, some of the people in town at first didn't trust Dad and Dr. Rodda because they were so young, and folks around here were used to older doctors. So Dad and Dr. Rodda brought in an older doctor from a nearby town to just be in the operating room when they did surgery. In return, they'd operate on that doctor's patients without charging him."

Chuck Van Gorder remains in awe of his father and what he meant to his neighbors. "Even after he retired," he remembers, "people kept asking for him. A friend of mine was working for the power company when he blew his hands off in an accident. He was delirious. He kept screaming, 'I want Dr. Van. Dr. Van will make this all right.' "

Other physicians returning from similar combat experiences made their contributions to postwar America in other ways. Dr. William McDermott—another combat surgeon who went ashore in Normandy and operated in frontline tents across France, at the Battle of the Bulge, and into Germany—was a product of Exeter, Harvard, and a one-year residency at Massachusetts General Hospital before the war. He says of his war experiences, "It was horrible, but the salvation was that you were doing something—you weren't just sitting there and watching the horror. We were always so damn busy and so tired, but I got an enormous amount of experience. It was like running a full-time emergency room twenty-four hours a day."

McDermott was involved in the liberation of one of the most notorious concentration camps, Ebensee. "You never in your life could imagine what it was like," he says. "When I was treating kids in combat I didn't have time to think, but the concentration camp was different. I went into a barracks and there were two men to every cot. They could barely move, but they got themselves up somehow and saluted me. I just about burst into tears. I stayed there for two weeks treating them, but two hundred died every day."

It was an experience that stayed with Dr. McDermott when he returned to the Boston area and began a long, distinguished medical career at Massachusetts General Hospital, Yale, Harvard, and New England Deaconess Hospital. In his eighties, he remains the chairman of the department of surgery at Deaconess and he's the Cheever Professor of Surgery Emeritus at Harvard Medical School, where he was on the faculty for many years.

Dr. McDermott has written several books, including a war memoir called *A Surgeon in Combat*, which recounts his experiences at Ebensee. That, in turn, led to a Boston meeting with a survivor of the camp, Morris Hollander, a Czech Jew. They may have met in the camp, although they couldn't be sure. They did share the same lessons, however. One a Jewish inmate, the other a Roman Catholic doctor, they had both come to understand something about God and man in the barbarity of Ebensee.

In a *Boston Globe* account of their meeting, Dr. McDermott said, "God is a God of necessity. He sets the morals. If people break them, that's their issue, not God's." Hollander responded, "Exactly. . . . Every nation has the ability to do as Germany did."

Dr. McDermott says he remembers the horror of Ebensee to this day, but it remains for him primarily an intensely personal experience. "No," he says, "I didn't share this much with my medical students; I was a little restrained, but if the war came up during discussions, I would remind them of the levels to which humans can sink. It's important for medical students to know those imperfections of the human race."

He also isn't interested in returning to Germany. On one occasion after the war, he had to change planes in the Frankfurt airport, and he got involved in a typical reservations foul-up. In exasperation he said, "Listen, fifteen years ago we had a helluva lot easier time taking Frankfurt than I'm having getting out of Frankfurt now." Dr. McDermott remembers with a short laugh that he got a first-class ticket back to Boston almost immediately.

IN NORTH CAROLINA Dr. Van Gorder applied the lessons of his war experiences to his family of patients, and his philosophy was shared by his wife, Helen. After the death of their firstborn, Helen continued working as a nurse even as the family was wracked by the war. Her two brothers, Canadians, volunteered for the American forces and both were killed. Her husband was always in the thick of battle until he became a prisoner of war. Later the Van Gorders' son, Chuck, would be wounded in Vietnam while serving with his father's old outfit, the 101st Airborne. When Chuck asked his mother how she managed all of that emotional turmoil she answered, "Since I was a little girl I've had trust in the Lord. I had faith it would all work out."

It did work out for the Van Gorders because they did keep their faith in their God, in each other, and in the belief that life is about helping others. They passed that along to their two daughters and their surviving son. That's another legacy of the World War II generation, the strong commitment to family values and community. They were mature beyond their years in their twenties, and when they married and began families it was not a matter of thinking "Well, let's see how this works out . . ."

They applied the same values to their professional lives; they never stopped thinking about how they could improve health care for their community. While they were building their practice, Van Gorder and Rodda realized Andrews deserved more than their modest clinic, so they set out to build a hospital. Dr. Van Gorder became a regular visitor to the state capital in Raleigh, lobbying the governor to apply for federal Hill-Burton funds to build a hospital in Andrews. He succeeded. When the hospital was completed in 1956 it was a community triumph. Local residents working in the mills contributed through a payroll deduction program, sometimes as little as a nickel a week, or through bank contribution programs.

Today the hospital has sixty beds and a full range of medical services, from X rays to surgery. It is being expanded to accommodate sixteen more doctors, in a community that had none when the war ended.

As they steadily expanded the health care services available to the rural logging community, they kept up with the advances in medical technology and they were impressed with the progress in patient care. But Dr. Van Gorder laments the bureaucratic and commercial nature of modern medicine.

"The war taught me the importance of integrity in dealing with people," he says. "I worked with some fine surgeons and we helped each other. Medicine was more altruistic. I just wanted to help people. Kids start out now thinking 'How much money can I make?' not 'What can I do, how much can I help?' "

In the early days of his Andrews practice, his patients often paid with produce from their gardens or with freshly killed game. When that gave way to distant bureaucrats rejecting claims because a code was entered improperly or dictating care instructions, Dr. Van Gorder's enthusiasm for what he loved began to fade. A man who began his medical career operating behind the lines and in the line of fire, a physician who learned more in a week of combat than an insurance clerk could know in a lifetime of paper shuffling, had little patience for the system that was overrunning his love of medicine.

In a small town, physicians are often more than the healers. They are the first citizens in every sense of the phrase. Dr. Van Gorder was a member of the Andrews board of education for twenty years; he was president of the Andrews Lions Club, and he was the grand potentate of the Shrine Temple in Charlotte, North Carolina. It was a life of service that hundreds of thousands of other World War II veterans were living in their hometowns across America.

In Dr. Van Gorder's family, one daughter, Katherine, is a librarian in South Carolina; Suzanne is a nurse and a commander in the Naval Reserve in Florida; son Chuck, who when he returned from Vietnam worked for a time as a nurse, is in the real estate business near Andrews.

Van Gorder's friend and partner, Dr. Rodda, died six years ago, and Van Gorder has been struggling with his own health problems—he suffered a small stroke in 1997—but he's still cheerful and grateful for a full life.

His war experiences, however, now more than fifty years in his past, live on in his memory. "I have flashbacks of the war every day. You can't get it out of your mind. D-Day, all those boys being slaughtered. When I was working in our hospital I thought about it a lot. I thought about how the war taught us to handle things. We learned a lot.

"The thing I am most proud of is that hospital," he says. "If I had my life to do all over again, I'd do it the same way—go somewhere small where people have a need, contribute something to people who need it; help people."

WESLEY KO

"In the war I learned to be self-sufficient. . . . I learned to be a leader. When my business failed I was able to move on, whereas my wife was devastated by the loss."

A SENSE OF personal responsibility and a commitment to honesty is characteristic of this generation. Those were values bred into the young men and women coming of age at the time the war broke out. It's how they were raised. There are always exceptions to the common bonds of any generation, but in talking to the men and women whose stories make up this book I was struck by the connective cords of their lives, wherever they lived or in whatever circumstances.

One after another they volunteered how in their families and in their communities they were expected to be responsible for their behavior, how honesty was assumed to be the rule, not the exception. They also talked matter-of-factly about a sense of duty to their country, a sentiment not much in fashion anymore.

Moreover, in their communities there were always monitors outside their own families to remind them of the ethos of their family and community. I've often said I was raised by the strict standards of my mother and father, and also of the parents of my friends, my teachers, my coaches, my ministers, and by the local businessmen who didn't hesitate to remind me "that's not how you were raised."

Those qualities didn't show up in a statistical survey of America's strengths as the country steeled itself for what seemed an unavoidable war, but they were critical to the nation's preparations,

Wesley Ko, June 1944

for success depended as much on personal resolve as it did on tanks and planes and ships and guns.

The idea of personal responsibility is such a defining characteristic of the World War II generation that when the rules changed later, these men and women were appalled.

Wesley Ko is one of them. In 1988, at the age of seventy, his printing business failed, in part because of government regulations and in part because a relocation deal was seriously flawed. Ko was left with a debt of $1.3 million, a loan he'd personally guaranteed. It never occurred to him to declare personal bankruptcy. Ko had learned early in life the meaning of responsibility and self-sufficiency.

Ko grew up in the Philadelphia area, the son of a Chinese man brought to this country by an American missionary. His father was educated at Princeton and at Temple University and became pastor of a Methodist church for Chinese immigrants in Philadelphia. His mother was the daughter of a Chinese coolie brought to America to work on the railroads, one of the laborers who in the late nineteenth and early twentieth centuries were subjected to the same vicious racial discrimination that African Americans suffered. They were treated like an alien and subhuman population, restricted to the backbreaking work on the railroad, or to hand laundries in their own well-defined ghettos.

Ko's father hoped to escape that with his education, but the Great Depression was especially hard on preachers, who were dependent on their congregations for financial support. Wesley's father was just able to hold on to the family residence by opening a small laundry. Wesley, a bright young man, had hoped to go to college, but it was out of the question in those difficult times.

He went to work in a printing company, and when the war broke out his boss offered to get him a deferment, but Wesley's buddies were all signing up and he wanted to volunteer as well. He was assigned to the officers' training school at Fort Benning, Georgia, and after ninety days he was a second lieutenant in the 82nd Airborne.

"I was apprehensive," he says, "being the only Oriental in the 82nd. I think the 82nd was apprehensive too; I wasn't assigned right away. I guess they thought Orientals couldn't be leaders. I didn't make an issue of it. I was born and raised in this country and I didn't think I was any different." Asian complexions were real burdens for American citizens when their country was at war with Japan; too many of their fellow citizens made no distinction between the enemy and the Asian Americans in their midst. In the end, the Army did recognize Wesley Ko's qualities and installed him as a platoon leader in a new outfit: the 325th Glider Infantry Regiment.

It was the daredevil and dangerous new way to transport troops, including Dr. Van Gorder and his medical unit, when D-Day was launched. A pilot and a copilot steered the glider to what was a controlled crash landing in difficult terrain, ferrying thirteen troops and their equipment at a time.

In the spring of 1942 Ko and his outfit sailed for North Africa, for more training sessions in the demanding conditions of Morocco, Algeria, and Tunisia. "It was very, very hot," he recalls, "a hundred twenty degrees. We had to run for twenty minutes with our packs, then walk twenty minutes. At one point the whole regiment had dysentery. We lost more men training in Africa than in our first combat."

It was the beginning of a three-year ordeal for Wesley Ko. After training in Africa he was almost constantly in combat—first in Sicily on Mount Saint Angelo de Cava, then during the occupation of Naples with steady shelling from Germany's big guns. After Italy, it was more hard-core training, this time in Ireland and England, for the Normandy invasion. Ko was promoted to first lieutenant and given command of a mortar platoon.

On June 7, D-Day plus one, he was in a flight of 250 gliders headed for the north coast of France, where the fighting was very heavy. "When we arrived over Normandy," he says, "we started receiving machine-gun fire. We sat on our flak jackets to give us a little more protection, we were flying so low."

Ko was well trained. "I just didn't think of the danger," he says now. "I guess I was too young, too naive. But it turns out we lost twenty percent of our gliders—they never got into battle. They were either shot down or made a bad landing."

As soon as Ko scrambled from his glider, he was in the thick of the fighting. His regiment began fighting its way from village to vil-

Wesley Ko

Wesley Ko and grandchild

lage, losing many men along the way. Ko had some very close calls in the hellish ten days following D-Day. "I was standing next to one of the operations officers when he was shot and killed. I remember another time taking my binoculars from their case and shrapnel had blown out a lens." Another time, "for the river crossing, the engineers had set up a bridge and we just ran across. We received tremendous fire but you had to keep pushing forward. Different fellows were hit and you had to keep jumping over their bodies."

After thirty-three days straight of combat without replacements, Ko's battalion of 600 men had lost more than half, 323. And it was just the beginning of the drive for Berlin. Holland and the Battle of the Bulge lay ahead.

In the beginning of the Battle of the Bulge, that desperate but ultimately doomed attempt by Hitler to counterattack against the advancing Allied forces, Ko and his men were deployed in defensive positions, in heavy snow, to keep the enemy from overrunning Allied gains. "It was terrible weather, with snow up to your knees," he remembers, ". . . we had our olive-drab uniforms, so we stuck out like sore thumbs."

During one withdrawal Ko and his sergeant were the last to leave. They looked to their left and saw a company of men in snowsuits. Ko relates: "The Germans! We were startled. There were only two of us, so we had to get out of there. We ran through a creek to keep out of sight. To this day I can't remember how I ever got dry."

Ko went on to more fierce fighting at close range, in the attack on the Siegfried line. "The concrete pillboxes were so thick that not even heavy artillery was effective, so the only option was for the men to get close enough to drop grenades. But in order to get close you had to suffer a lot of casualties. In my regiment alone, which had a couple of thousand men, we had close to two hundred killed, more than seven hundred fifty wounded, and forty-nine missing in action."

Ko was promoted to captain and given command of a company as his outfit pushed east, participating in the battle for Cologne, Germany, and assisting in the capture of the 21st German army, which was trying to avoid the Russian troops advancing from the other direction. Ko and his men helped liberate the Wobbelin concentration camp at Ludwigslust. "We dug a mass grave and made every

German citizen in the area who was aware of the situation help us and also attend the burial of the hundreds of dead inmates."

The war was at an end. Captain Wesley Ko had participated in six campaigns in two and a half years, under fire in some of the most important and ferocious battles of the war. He had accumulated enough points for a swift return home. As he put it, "Not many of us made it all the way."

On September 23, 1945, he arrived back in the United States aboard the USS *Constitution*.

When he returned from the war Ko decided to go back to his old printing-plant job, but after a year or so he teamed up with his brother and a friend to open their own business, Komak Printing. They specialized in silk-screening for advertising companies and then began doing custom work for electronics firms. It was hard work but Ko was thriving.

He married his wife, Ruth, in 1950 and they bought a home in the leafy Philadelphia suburb of Chalfont ("James Michener lived there," Ko is proud to point out). They raised a son and two daughters. It was anyone's American dream come true, but especially for the grandson of a Chinese coolie.

It didn't last.

By 1985, when he'd been in business for almost forty years, Ko faced some difficult decisions. The printing business involves a good many chemicals and waste, and the government was cracking down on disposal. His plant was outmoded. Philadelphia was losing business to other metropolitan areas.

He accepted an offer to relocate to upstate New York, in Glens Falls, near Albany. It would be an expensive move—he'd have to personally guarantee the $1.3 million loan—but the Glens Falls chamber of commerce was offering lots of incentives and his son was interested in continuing the business there.

It all looked good on paper. The reality was a nightmare. Ko says the Glens Falls incentives took longer to get in place than promised. He was forced to shut down the Philadelphia plant before starting the other, so there was loss of income and, worse, a break in the continuity with his best customers. By the time he did get the new plant open it was too late. He went out of business after only a year.

"It was a big decision-making time. I couldn't retire. I hadn't taken out Social Security. So at the age of seventy I had to go get a job and start paying back that million-dollar loan." He adds, "I just didn't feel comfortable with declaring bankruptcy. I just didn't think it was the honorable thing to do, even though it would have been easier."

Lessons learned in training and during the war more than four decades earlier were critical during this trying time.

"In the war I learned to be self-sufficient. I matured. I learned to be a leader. When my business failed I was able to move on, whereas my wife was devastated by the loss."

Ko managed to preserve the plant's assets for his principal creditors, and his lawyers negotiated the settlement of other debts at reduced levels. Continuing to live in the small-town environment with local suppliers still carrying Komak debts on their books wasn't easy, but Wesley and Ruth persevered. He managed to get a job as a quality-control manager at a local electronics company and applied the stock options he earned toward the debts he owed. Finally, at the age of seventy-six, Wesley retired, saying, "I have no regrets."

He and Ruth now live near their daughters, in Massachusetts. He's editor of *The Glider Towline,* the newsletter of the surviving members of the 325th Glider Infantry Association. It's filled with chatty reminders of coming reunions and pictures of grandfatherly men in baseball caps bearing the regiment's insignia. One caption reads, "The youth of World War II are the senior citizens of today." A column called "Taps" gets longer with every issue, as it marks the passing of the glider veterans or their wives.

Ko's only regret is that the lessons of his generation are lost on his grandchildren. He was disappointed when his grandson quit the private school he was attending. Now, however, the young man seems to have found a calling as a carpenter, and Wesley is feeling better about his direction.

However, Wesley Ko reflects the common lament of his generation when he says, "Everything comes too easy. Nowadays you just don't make the effort like you did in our day."

JAMES
AND DOROTHY
DOWLING

"I ran that department like a business and in military style."

I N A WAY no one could have anticipated at the time, the military training and discipline required to win World War II became an accelerated course in how to prepare a young generation to run a large, modern, and complex industrial society. Nearly every veteran, however painful the military experience may have been, seems to be grateful for the discipline and leadership training they were exposed to at such a formative age.

James Dowling of Smithtown, New York, is the personification of the difficult times of his generation, the heroics of ordinary men in extraordinary situations in time of war, and the priceless contributions of veterans to the development of postwar America.

He's now seventy-five years old, a grandfather, a founder of the Little League in his hometown, a retired highway superintendent, and a vintage car enthusiast. He's proud of his family, his personal independence, and his contribution to his community. If that sounds like a predictable and bland résumé for a man in his mid-seventies, it is also deceptive, for it masks a life of deprivation, struggle, adventure, heroics, and achievement.

James Dowling was orphaned soon after he was born. His mother died when he was only six months old and his father was unable to

James and Dorothy—home on twenty-four-hour leave

care for this baby and his four brothers and sisters. In those simpler times, when much of social welfare was a matter of good-hearted people, the plight of James and his siblings was made known in church. The minister announced that someone had to take in these children.

James and two of his brothers were taken home by the Conklins, Clarence and Anna. It was not a formal adoption but the Conklins raised these Dowling children as their own. Conklin was a prosperous builder in Smithtown until the Depression hit. At home the electricity was often shut off. So was the telephone. But what James remembers is that no one gave up. His father took odd jobs and always gave a portion of what he earned to creditors until he paid most of them off. Mrs. Conklin took in sewing. They avoided bankruptcy. It wasn't easy, but at that time in small towns bankruptcy was a disgrace to be avoided at all costs.

Besides, James and the others in the family didn't feel deprived. Everyone they knew was going through similar experiences. The family stayed together and made the best of it. The boys spent their days fishing and clamming, getting what jobs they could.

James was fascinated by the relatively new field of aviation. The Conklins lived not too far from where Charles Lindbergh had lifted off for Paris in *The Spirit of St. Louis*. The skies over Long Island were beginning to fill with the new airplanes coming off the production lines at the nearby Grumman plant.

So when war broke out and James was drafted in 1943, at age nineteen, he immediately volunteered for the U.S. Army Air Corps and qualified for bombardier-navigator training. He promised his hometown sweetheart, Dorothy Owen, that when he returned they'd be married. She had no doubt he'd be back, recalling more than a half century later, "He was a cheerful Irishman with blazing red hair. I knew he'd be okay."

Dowling was assigned to the 445th Air Wing of the 8th Air Force and shipped to England, where in 1944 he began bombing runs over Germany, striking at the heart of the German military-industrial complex. By his eighth mission he was lead bombardier-navigator, and on his eleventh mission he was in a world of trouble—a long, long way from the innocence of those summer days back on Long Island.

His squadron was involved in a massive bombing attack on an industrial center near the German town of Kassel in September 1944. There were thirty-seven B-24s on the raid when they came under attack from above and below: antiaircraft fire and Luftwaffe fighter planes. Thirty of the B-24s were lost, including Dowling's. He managed to bail out before it crashed, but as soon as he hit the ground he was captured by German troops and loaded onto one of many boxcars for a three-hundred-mile ride. Their journey, like Dr. Van Gorder's, was often interrupted by strafing attacks from American planes unaware that those German trains were loaded with Americans.

Back in New York, Dowling's family and his sweetheart, Dorothy, were notified he was missing in action.

Dowling spent the next eight months in a German POW camp, Stalag Luft One, near Barth, Germany. Shortly before Christmas 1944, English-speaking German broadcasters read over shortwave radio holiday greetings from American prisoners of war. It was a compassionate act on the part of the Third Reich, wholly at odds with what it was doing on the battlefield and in places such as Dachau and Buchenwald.

Two housewives who heard Dowling's name and message to Dorothy didn't get all the details, so they each sent a postcard on December 22 to Dorothy at her home in Ballston Lake, New York. One postcard was addressed, simply, "Dorothy?" Dorothy's sister had heard the broadcast as well. It was the first message from Dowling since his capture. "Dearest Dorothy, I am all right, sweetheart. I didn't get a scratch or anything. Please tell Mom and Dad. Don't worry about me. We'll get married as soon as I get home again. I love you and miss you terribly, sweetheart, and wish that I could be with you soon. I have lots to tell you when I get back."

A military telegram with the same message arrived five days later, after Christmas. The military message added: "Pending further confirmation, this report does not establish his status as a prisoner of war." A cautionary note to go with the first word that James was still alive.

As the New Year began, the end was near for the Third Reich. James was liberated by advancing Russian troops in May 1945. He

James Dowling and company

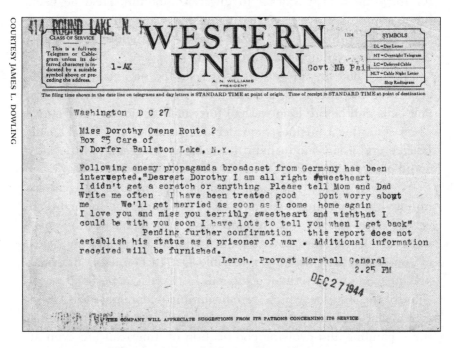

Telegram to Dorothy Owens, December 27, 1944

was headed home shortly thereafter. Before he left he wrote to Dorothy, not knowing that the Christmas message had gotten through. The sentiments were the same from this determined young man: ". . . I am alive and well, can't wait to get home and get married."

Dowling wrote it on a scrap of paper, folded the paper over, addressed it, and mailed it off with no envelope, no return address. Fifty-three years later James and Dorothy still have the note.

HE STAYED in the service for another two years, hoping to become a jet pilot, but when Dorothy became pregnant he decided it was time to go home to Smithtown. But now what? Well, like a lot of returning veterans James was willing to take chances, so he went into business for himself with his father-in-law. They started a seafood trucking business.

James would buy from the returning fishing trawlers late in the afternoon, load his truck, and very early the next morning set off for the Fulton Fish Market in lower Manhattan. He'd be back home at nine A.M. It was a thriving business, but James wondered what to do with all of the spare time he had before the fishing trawlers returned in the late afternoon.

"Since I had my afternoons free I started organizing baseball games for the little kids, including my five sons. I'd buy the bats and balls and before long we had forty or fifty kids in the league. Then some local businessmen decided to start an official Little League and asked me to help. I agreed, as long as the little kids could play.

"We started with four teams and by the seventies we had six hundred boys playing. I was president of the League for eighteen years." Little League was, in many ways, a metaphor for the postwar years. There were now so many children on the playing fields of America it was no longer feasible just to count on informal pickup games to keep them occupied. Little League baseball was a game of the suburbs, which were beginning to dominate the American social landscape. It was extremely well organized, reflecting the expanding and evolving codification of American life even at leisure.

James didn't confine his community service to the Little League, however. In the early 1960s another veteran, the town clerk, asked him to run for superintendent of highways in Smithtown. He had three hours to decide. After talking it over with Dorothy, he decided he could do a good job, so he ran as the candidate of the Democrats, even though he'd never been registered in either party. He defeated a man who'd been in the job for twelve years.

This was no cushy, eight-to-five assignment. From the development of the interstate highway system down to the gridwork of curb, gutter, and asphalt in new developments, the construction of roads was a vital element in the social and economic expansion of postwar America.

As James remembers, "I came into office at a time when all of the young ex-GIs were moving out of Queens and Brooklyn and into new suburban homes. I met with them. They wanted good services, and that meant good roads."

Smithtown was no longer a sleepy little Long Island fishing village backed up to potato fields. Although James had never built a road in his life, his military training had taught him how to organize and move men. He had 175 people reporting to him, and a big task ahead. He had to modernize the Smithtown road system so that it would fit seamlessly with the developments now surrounding it and feed easily into the shopping malls that were beginning to take hold at the edge of town.

He was ahead of his time in many of his techniques. When he ripped up an old road, he'd reprocess the old material and use it as a base for the new road, introducing the concept of recycling to highway construction at a time when most old asphalt was simply carted off to a landfill.

Dowling is especially proud of his snow-removal techniques. He saw a major snowstorm as the highway superintendent's equivalent of battle. He had some experience with clearing airfields during winter storms in the war, so he simply adapted what he had learned: he put more trucks on the road, switched to the new, modern snow tires, introduced new hydraulic systems. Smithtown became so well known for its snow-removal efficiency that the state of New York contracted Dowling to teach other municipalities and counties what he had learned. As he said when I spoke with him, "I ran that department like a business and in military style."

That was not enough for him, however. "I didn't take life for granted," he says. "The most memorable lesson I learned in the war is that life is precious. I really came to appreciate that when we languished in that prison camp. So I am always looking for things to do."

In addition to his duties as highway superintendent and in the seafood trucking business, Dowling also ran a bulldozer business and a small restaurant, for a time. "I was always looking for challenges in life. I think the war years gave me that. And anyone who went through the Depression understood what a dollar was and what it meant to find work. I think I passed these values on to my kids and the people who worked for me. One of the young people who worked for me came by later and said, 'You had a purpose. We came to work every day knowing you had a project for us. You were always looking ahead. You treated us with respect.' "

Dowling didn't discuss the war much until he was in his late fifties, and then he went to a reunion of the 8th Air Force. He came home from that with renewed pride in what he had been through, and began to share his stories with his family. "Now," he says with a chuckle, "my sons and grandsons ask me more about the war. They'll see something on the History Channel and say, 'My grandfather flew through that!' and they're in awe."

That's a change from the earlier years, when he first returned from the war. "After we got back, people didn't talk about it and you didn't ask, even if they were in the same age group and likely served in the war. I didn't know until a few years ago that one of my Little League coaches had been in an air raid that I knew of; it was just like that.

"It didn't really become important to talk about until we were in our sixties. When I went back to the site of our prison camp, I started opening up with my wife and family a little more. I felt I could, because other guys were there. But my pilot would never talk to his wife about it. And two members of our crew, when we tried to get them to reunions, they just didn't want to relive it, I guess."

Three of his sons went to Vietnam and James is proud of that. He's also confident the country and this generation are in good shape. He and Dorothy, his wife since 1945, went into Manhattan a few years ago to march in a veterans' parade, and they were stunned by the number of people "who just came up to us and shook our hands, saying, 'Thanks.' I think the spirit of America is back."

As for his future, James has a few more Model A's to restore and then, as he says, "I will look for some civic project to get involved with, some service to perform."

Dorothy offers the most fitting testimonial. Fifty-three years after she married the young man with the blazing red hair, she laughs when asked the secret to their long love affair. "Simple," she says. "He's a really great guy."

Harry R. Hammond, identification card

REV. HARRY REGINALD "REG" HAMMOND

"I think we were on God's side. The United States has done some foolish things, but in that war I knew we had God with us."

FAITH IN GOD was not a casual part of the lives of the World War II generation. The men and women who went off to war, or stayed home, volunteer that their spiritual beliefs helped them cope with the constant presence of possible death, serious injury, or the other anxieties attendant to the disruptions brought on by war. Helen Van Gorder's faith helped her through the great strains of having a husband, and later a son, in the line of fire. Faith was the twin to love in the marriage of the Brodericks. On the front lines, chaplains were not incidental to the war effort. Some jumped with the Airborne troops on D-Day and others risked their own lives to administer last rites or other comforting words to dying and grievously wounded young men wherever the battle took them. The very nature of war prompted many who participated in it to think more deeply about God and their relationship to a higher being once they returned home.

"God does not bring war upon us. We bring it upon ourselves. Man's inhumanity to man is not God-driven." Harry Reginald

Hammond—Reg to his friends—came to understand the place of God early in his life through the work of his father, a popular Episcopal priest in Ventura, California. He came face-to-face with man's inhumanity to man as a first lieutenant during World War II.

Those lessons remained fresh in Hammond's mind when, more than fifty years later, he was ordained as a priest in the Anglican Orthodox Church at the age of seventy-nine, the oldest person ever ordained in that faith. It was the spiritual outgrowth of a lifetime of service to others and an abiding faith in God. In his family, Reg had always been expected to wear the vestments of a priest, but no one would have guessed it would take so long or that when he finally answered the call it would be in another church.

After all, his father, Stephen, and his four brothers had all been priests in the Episcopal Church. In his early years, Reg seemed destined for a career in the grocery business. After he married Margery MacPherson in 1941, he happily went to work in her father's grocery business until he enlisted in the Army and shipped out for boot camp and then officer's training in North Carolina.

He landed in Normandy a few days after D-Day, and that's when he began to see the horrors of war. He ran a platoon of antiaircraft guns to protect the field artillery of the 90th Infantry Division, an outfit in the thick of some of the worst fighting; at one point the 90th had a casualty rate of 100 percent among its enlisted men; 150 percent among the officers. He was awarded five battle stars and a Bronze Star for meritorious service. "I saw more bodies in a short time than most undertakers will see in a lifetime. Young men dead alongside the road. Every night I would pray for those guys and myself. I think it deepened my faith."

When he returned to California after the war, his father-in-law had sold the grocery business, but Reg still was not ready to follow the path of his father and brothers into the seminary. Instead, like 2.3 million other returning vets, Hammond made use of the GI Bill. He enrolled at the University of California at Santa Barbara.

He started as an economics major. "I thought I'd catch on with one of the big businesses in California, but then I also thought I might like teaching, so I added education to my major. By the time I started student-teaching I knew what I wanted to do. I liked working with kids. I guess I was drawn to service of some kind—

ARMY EXCHANGE
RATION CARD – ETO

No. 4   Date issued 22 Oct '45

Name H.R. Hammond   ASN 01047999

Signature *Harry R Hammond*

Organization RE 3228   APO 562

Signature Unit C.O. *FR Parmentier*
Capt Inf

D7

Harry R. Hammond, ration card

OFFICER'S PAY DATA CARD
Harry R. Hammond, 01047999, 1 Lt, CAC
(Name)   (Serial number)   (Grade and arm or service)

Over 1 years' service 2nd pay period 1 years completed

27 Mar, 19 43

Monthly base pay and longevity	$ 166.67
Additional pay for For Serv	16.67
Rental allowances	75.00
Subsistence 30 day month	42.00
Date 6 January 44 Total, $	283.67
	300.34

Dependents (state names and addresses):
Mrs. Margery B. Hammond (Wife)
2191 El Jardin, Ventura, California

Evidence of dependency (mother) filed with voucher No. _____
_____, 19_____

Accounts of _____
Allotments, class E, $ 230.00 $_____ $_____
Insurance, class D, $_____   Class N, $ 6.70
Pay reservations, class A, $_____
Other deductions, $_____
Subsequent changes in above data with dates thereof:
_____
_____
_____
_____

Changes affecting pay will be entered here and maintained up to date.
W. D., A. G. O. Form No. 77
March 26, 1942   45·57   16—27079-1

Harry R. Hammond, pay data card

the idea of having some effect on the future. A way of paying back, in a sense."

It was the beginning of a pilgrimage through the California public education system, from the San Joaquin Valley to Marin County, north of San Francisco. Hammond began as an elementary school teacher but moved over to administration after a few years, commuting to Los Angeles in the summer months to earn a PhD in education along the way. By the time he retired in 1980 he had served as teacher, principal, assistant superintendent, and superintendent, but he had never completely given up the idea of also serving the church in some formal way.

By then he had started and dropped ordination studies twice. He decided he'd have to be content as a perpetual deacon, a sort of priest's assistant. But then he was unable to finish that training, either. It appeared he would live out his life, as he put it, "as the black sheep" of a family that had sent four other sons to the priesthood.

Besides, he was growing disillusioned with the Episcopal Church in the 1960s, which, like so many institutions at the time, was altering its traditions. "Instead of looking to the Bible for direction," he says, "they were looking to society for direction in terms of sexual behavior, adultery, these kinds of questions."

Eventually Dr. Hammond became so fed up he left the Episcopal Church and helped found a branch of its much more conservative cousin, the Anglican Orthodox Church. It uses the original Book of Common Prayer, which stresses the authority of the church. Anglican Orthodox worshipers place more emphasis on the confession of sins and adhere to a stricter definition of what sin is.

When Dr. Hammond and a few like-minded faithful established their church, there was an immediate problem: the denomination was relatively small, so there were few priests. His friends encouraged him to step up his involvement and follow in the footsteps of his brothers and father into the ministry. Since Hammond had spent so much of his life preparing for this role, the bishop of the Anglican Orthodox Church agreed to let him skip seminary and qualify by taking a lengthy and rigorous test.

When he completed the bishop's test and was ordained, thus fulfilling a calling that had been so much a part of his life for so long, Hammond had "a deep sense of satisfaction . . . a sort of wonderment and pleasure." He was grateful that his brothers, all priests in the Episcopal Church he had left, were supportive of his decision. "My youngest brother had hoped I would stay in the Episcopal Church, but he came to my ordination and participated; you can't ask for more than that." One of his parishioners, Dr. William Henry, says, "Reg embodies the Episcopal priest of the thirties, forties, fifties . . . he has the Book of Common Prayer memorized. When he was ordained it seemed as if he was correcting a mistake."

The Reverend Hammond is using the years he has left to continue the call to service he's heard most of his life. He has an older congregation, so that often means house calls for this seventy-nine-year-old clergyman. He takes communion to the shut-ins, aware that if he was not willing to make the extra effort, the people he serves would be left with no opportunity to observe their faith.

As he goes about his ministerial duties, the Reverend Hammond also remembers his experiences during World War II, when he was praying for the young boys who had been killed or were about to face death in battle. "You needed something to keep you going," he remembers. "It made me realize that there was something much larger than just me. I realized it had to be God. And I think we were on God's side. The United States has done some foolish things, but in that war I knew we had God with us."

*Lloyd Kilmer (with his wife-to-be, Marie Beckwith) with his new wings,
Pampa, Texas*

LLOYD KILMER

"My dad's a piece of work. He's the quintessential GI. What you see is what you get."

NOTHING CAME TOO EASY for Lloyd Kilmer, the son of a Minnesota dairy farmer. When Lloyd was eight years old his father lost the farm to the bank and the family moved onto county assistance in the nearby small town of Stewartville. It was a common migration for farm families across the Midwest and it was a traumatic time in the lives of these proud, independent people.

Typically, everyone in the family went to work wherever they could. Young Lloyd sold newspapers, sacked groceries in the local market, and ran the projector at the movie theater. When he wanted to join the Boy Scouts, a county official lent him the fifty cents for the admission fee. He didn't wear shoes in the summer so that he could have a decent pair in the winter.

He never had a bicycle as a kid, but it's not a bitter memory. "That's the way it was. There wasn't much we could do about it." What Kilmer remembers most about those years is that his father was humiliated when he had to apply to the WPA, the government relief program, for work so that he could feed his family. Kilmer says it left such a deep impression on him he made a pledge. "I never wanted to experience that sort of thing for my wife and family. I was driven toward never letting that happen."

Goals in those difficult times were modest by modern standards. Again and again I have heard from this generation, "We really didn't have any expectations." For too many of them, the idea of any real prosperity was simply too remote. Lloyd Kilmer was the first member of his family to graduate from high school, an achievement of considerable pride. He was working as a bellhop at a hotel in Rochester, Minnesota, home of the Mayo Clinic, when the war broke out.

Kilmer, who had never been in an airplane in his life, knew immediately what he wanted to do. He wanted to become a combat pilot. He enlisted in the Army Air Corps on July 22, 1942, and was accepted for officer's candidate school. Suddenly he went from being a bellhop in a comfortable hotel in a small, prosperous midwestern city to the rigors of pilot training in a succession of bases in Kansas, Oklahoma, and Texas.

Understandably, Kilmer is still very proud that he passed every test along the way and that within one year of the day that he first set foot in an airplane, he was a qualified pilot of a four-engine bomber, the B-24. His girlfriend pinned on him the silver wings and gold bar of a second lieutenant. In return, he gave her an engagement ring paid for by assigning to the jewelry store his ten-thousand-dollar military insurance policy. As he says, "My dreams had come true."

He was assigned to the 448th Bomb Group, 712th Squadron, 2nd Air Division, 8th Air Force, based in England. He was flying combat missions on a regular basis, including D-Day, June 6, 1944. From the cockpit of his plane he could see the first wave of GIs going ashore on those murderous beaches. Kilmer says it is a day that "will live in my mind and heart forever."

Twenty-three days later was another date fixed even more firmly in his memory. On June 29, 1944, his sixteenth mission, Kilmer was on a bombing run over a Nazi tank factory in Germany. He was taking heavy fire from antiaircraft guns on the ground.

"One shell went through the wing, rupturing the gas tanks, disabling an engine, and starting a fire. Another burst knocked the propeller off an engine. Other planes were exploding all around us. We could see parachutes coming out of some—and others with no parachutes. We were in big trouble."

Still, Kilmer, who was just twenty-four years old, was confident they could make it back home or at least to the North Sea, where, if they ditched, they'd be picked up by an Allied sub or ship. "I

Liberation Day—Stalag 7A,
April 29, 1945

Lloyd Kilmer,
aviation cadet, 1943

Lloyd Kilmer's plane,
June 29, 1944, Beemster, Holland

didn't have any real question," he says. "I had a wonderful crew. They were superbly trained. There's no doubt we could make it back. But it didn't work out for us."

They managed to put out the fires on the plane by going into a steep dive, but they were losing too much fuel to make it to safe territory. Kilmer was forced to crash-land in a potato field near Beemster, Holland. They all managed to survive the crash without serious injuries but the Germans had total control of the area, and within a short time Kilmer and his crew were all prisoners of war.

For the next ten months Kilmer was an inmate at two German POW camps. One interrogation was especially memorable for him. After days in solitary confinement, he was repeating only his name, rank, and serial number while being pressed at gunpoint for information about the 8th Air Force. Kilmer was taken to see a German officer.

Kilmer recalls, "The officer said to me, 'Mr. Kilmer, you've been very stubborn. You haven't told us what we want to know, so we're going to tell you what we know about you.' " With that, Kilmer says, the officer pulled out a book describing the activities of Kilmer's bomber squadron, its bombing reports, and biographies of the crews. Kilmer was stunned. Then the German officer said, "You think we're pretty smart, don't you? We know ninety-five percent of what's going on in the American armed forces. However, your government knows *ninety-seven* percent of what's going on in the German armed forces."

That was the end of Kilmer's solitary confinement and interrogation and it was the beginning of the long, cruel fight to survive, days of watching other inmates getting shot as they tried to escape, the same meals of watery cabbage or turnip soup, the cold nights with only a thin blanket for cover. When asked if he ever came close to just giving up the fight to live, Kilmer says, "Nope. I had a bride that I was going to marry. My mother and father, family, and great friends. No, I was going to go home." Those same thoughts were in the minds of so many veterans I interviewed. In the worst of combat or other dangerous situations they were sure they were going to survive to return to the girl back home or to their families.

Kilmer was living in squalid conditions with 125,000 other prisoners at a German camp called Moosburg Stalag 7A in the spring of 1945. He had lost sixty pounds; his weight had dropped below one hundred. He was attending a POW church service on April 29 when the chaplain, a fellow American POW, paused to listen to the small-arms fire that had suddenly erupted around the camp and looked up to see low-flying aircraft. Kilmer chuckles as he remembers the chaplain saying, "Men, we'd better hit the deck."

Not long after that, an American tank rolled through the German barbed wire. Lloyd Kilmer's ordeal was over. To mark the liberation, the American rescuers went to a nearby church steeple where the Nazi swastika was prominently displayed on a flag. Kilmer says the men of Stalag 7A fell quiet as the swastika was lowered and an American flag was raised in its place. In a way he could not have fully appreciated at the time, that became a defining moment in Lloyd Kilmer's life.

When Kilmer got back home he married Marie immediately and the Army arranged for medical and psychiatric treatment at a prisoner-of-war rehabilitation center in Miami Beach. He was eased back into a normal life in time to use the GI Bill and attend the fall term at Creighton University in Omaha in 1946. For a young man who was proud of his high school diploma just four years earlier, this was an unexpected opportunity.

He made the most of it, getting a degree in just three years while selling real estate part-time so successfully that, when he graduated, Omaha's largest firm offered him a full-time job. Kilmer and Marie started a family. Their first son, Lloyd Jr., was born in 1950, and Frank followed four years later. Baby Boomers.

The boys remember Kilmer as a "God-and-country patriot," a stern disciplinarian, and a driven businessman. Kilmer worked long hours in real estate and in a savings and loan company, where he became an officer. He was deeply involved with ex-POW organizations and the VFW. He was a scoutmaster for the local Boy Scout troop and active in his church. He organized a law-enforcement appreciation dinner during the sixties, when "law and order" were fighting words for a new generation.

For his sons, however, Kilmer was a distant figure. Lloyd Jr. and especially Frank had a difficult time relating to him. Lloyd Jr. says his father "always had a rigid set of ethics. He would say, 'This is the way it's going to be.' Other parents threatened to send their kids to military school. My dad followed through." Both boys went to Culver Military Academy in Indiana for a time, a point of pride for their father but far less so for them.

Frank and his father had some monumental arguments during the Vietnam War, when Frank dropped out of college. "It was a very difficult time in my family. And my father felt betrayed by his sons for not agreeing with his values and views about the war in Vietnam and about that era in general."

Kilmer became such a well-known public figure in Omaha that he ran for county clerk and controller in Douglas County, and he won as a Republican at a time when the courthouse was a Democratic stronghold. But at home he was an intensely private man when it came to his past. He never talked to his sons about his war experiences. As Frank says, "His work habits and his devotion to work were typical of men of that generation who went through traumatic experience, and his relative emotional distance was also quite typical."

The boys took their own paths in life. Lloyd Jr. recently received his PhD in education after a quarter century as a school principal. Lloyd Sr. was in the audience when his elder son received the degree. Frank left college and went into a Buddhist monastery for two years before becoming a plumber in California. Both have been married and divorced.

Their often strained relationship with their father was not unique for Baby Boomers, especially when their two worlds diverged so sharply during the sixties. The fathers were wholly unaccustomed to a permissive society. They were happy simply to be alive and, given all they had been through, they had this nagging fear it could all happen again. Their children came of age at a time when excess, not deprivation, was the rule, when their government lied about a new war, when the concepts of duty and honor were mocked.

Those were the two conflicting views of life and of the world in the Kilmer household. Now that both generations have aged and mellowed some, they're slowly finding more common ground.

For Frank it began when his parents moved to Sun City West, a popular retirement community outside of Phoenix. His father noticed that the main boulevard had no flags displayed on the

Fourth of July. Ever since that day, April 29, 1945, when the swastika went down and the American flag went up near his prisoner-of-war camp, Lloyd Kilmer has looked for the Stars and Stripes. He started a campaign to do something about R. H. Johnson Boulevard. "I devised a plan to attach an American flag to each of the hundred power poles along the boulevard," Lloyd says. It's now known as the Boulevard of Flags. Red, white, and blue American flags flutter every twenty yards or so along the thoroughfare that leads to the spacious retirement homes of so many World War II veterans.

They dedicated the Boulevard of Flags on Presidents Day 1989. Lloyd was honored for his role with the Patrick Henry Award for Patriotism, one of the highest awards of the American Legion.

Frank says of his dad, "He will brag about his involvement with the POWs and the VFW and the flag thing. But what I really appreciate about him is how he took care of my mother for ten years when she was really ill."

Shortly after they retired in Arizona, Marie had a series of health problems—a broken hip, then a stroke followed by Alzheimer's disease. The American dream for the Kilmers turned into a nightmare of emotional and physical pain. Lloyd never complained. He simply took care of the love of his life, hiring a nurse a few afternoons a week so he could go shopping. It went on for almost ten years before Marie died. Frank, who had continued following the Buddhist faith after his earlier feuds with his father, was deeply impressed and, for the first time, felt a real bond with him.

They grew even closer when Lloyd met a widow after Marie died. His new love, Ruth, had been married for half a century to another ex-POW. She was a former schoolteacher and the daughter of a small-town Iowa banker. It was a perfect match, but Frank remembers how his father was worried. "He needed affirmation it was okay," Frank says. "What better person to get validation for something he perceived as unconventional than from his nonconformist son?"

Lloyd and Ruth are married and they think of their life in Sun City as paradise. Since her first husband was also a POW, Ruth knows never to serve *anything* containing turnips or cabbage. She also knows to say Lloyd's name softly if she wants to awaken him from a nap; an unexpected touch or a loud "Wake up!" startles him still.

Lloyd remains active in the campaign to get a constitutional amendment to make it illegal to desecrate the flag, and he often attends reunions of his old bomber squadron held by the Ex-POW Association.

As his son Frank says, in a mixture of affection and admiration, "My dad's a piece of work. He's the quintessential GI. What you see is what you get."

———————•———————

GORDON LARSEN

"I didn't talk about the war much. I spent most of my time trying to forget it."

FOR LLOYD KILMER, the war and his experience as a POW was a central theme throughout his life, even if he didn't share that with his family. Other veterans shoved their war experiences to the far corners of their lives and sealed them off as best they could. They could never completely erase the memories or the residual effects of their training, but they were determined to start an entirely new life once the war ended.

In 1953, when I was living in a small town constructed by the Army Corps of Engineers along the Missouri River in South Dakota, I was surrounded by the young veterans of World War II who were busy making up for lost time: raising families, earning a living by building the large hydroelectric dam across the Missouri on this isolated stretch of the Great Plains, trying to forget what they had been through just a few years earlier.

As a talkative kid, friendly to grown-ups, I heard lots of stories about their days during the Depression or their long-ago sports achievements or hunting and fishing lore, but I cannot recall any of the veterans sitting around telling war stories. It just wasn't done.

I do remember one startling comment, however. It came from Gordon Larsen, a popular member of the community. He was a stocky, cheerful young man who worked on a crew that kept the electrical, heating, and plumbing systems going in the town. He had such a lively sense of humor that it was almost worth it to have your furnace break down. Gordon always kept up a lively chatter while he worked on it.

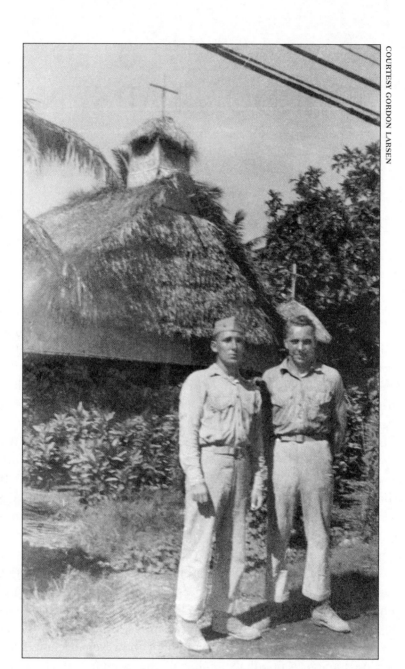

Gordon Larsen (right) at Guadalcanal, 1942

So it was surprising that the morning after Halloween he came into the post office, where my mother worked, and complained about the rowdiness of the high school teenagers the night before. My mother, trying to play to his good humor, said, "Oh, Gordon, what were *you* doing when you were seventeen?"

He looked at her for a moment and said, "I was landing on Guadalcanal." Then he turned and left the post office.

It was a moment that made a deep impression on Mother. She shared it with me when she came home that evening, and we have talked about it often. It was so representative of how quickly times had changed for young people.

Gordon is now seventy-three. He's retired from the Army Corps of Engineers after thirty-five years, having moved on from fixing furnaces to operating the sophisticated control systems in the powerhouses of dams in South Dakota, North Dakota, and Washington. He was surprised when I told him my mother and I remembered that moment in the post office. "I didn't talk about the war much," he said. "I spent most of my time trying to forget it."

Gordon quit high school in Omaha to join the Marines in 1941, following the path of his older brother, Jim. He trained in San Diego with the 3rd Marine Division, 9th Regiment, and immediately shipped out for the Pacific, where he carried the heavy Browning automatic rifle ashore at Guadalcanal, Bougainville, Guam, and Okinawa, participating in some of the heaviest fighting of the war.

He hooked up with Jim, then nineteen, in the 3rd Marines, and they went ashore together at Bougainville. It was a bloody, unforgettable day for Gordon. His brother was hit almost instantly, severely wounded, on the beach. Gordon remembered it vividly. "He bounced around," he said. "He was really hit."

Jim was down in an exposed position, and every time a rescue effort was launched, the Japanese opened up. Gordon's commander told him they couldn't do anything until dark. Jim lay there all day, his life draining from him. Finally, once it was nighttime, they were able to get him back to their lines and transported to a waiting ship.

But too much damage had been done. Gordon's brother died two weeks later in a Denver hospital.

As he told me this story, unprompted, on a telephone call across forty-five years, Gordon's voice grew husky and more distant. "I haven't"—he hesitated and then went on—"I haven't talked about this hardly ever."

He said he still has nightmares about his days in combat, and when I knew him, in the early fifties, when the memories were especially fresh, he said he thought about it all of the time, even when he was entertaining us while fixing our furnace.

There were no psychiatrists in our small community for him to see, even if he had been inclined, which he wasn't. "I just wanted to forget," he said, "I just wanted to get on with my life." Gordon said that when he went into a bar in those days and heard guys talking about combat, it made him sick, so sick he'd just walk out rather than stick around and share the painful memories. Besides, he always figured those who were willing to talk about combat had never really experienced it.

After all the bloody fighting across the island chains leading to Japan, Gordon's outfit was on Guam, preparing to board ships that would take them to the invasion of the mainland. Then word came of the surrender of the Japanese. Gordon's shooting war was over.

He came home with his unit. There had been 240 men in it when he left San Diego three years earlier. Only eight returned alive and uninjured. Gordon says he's never been in touch with any of them. He doesn't want to revisit those days.

He does credit the Marines, however, and that awful experience during his formative years with giving direction to his life. He said he was a wild kid, and he didn't know what would have happened without the discipline of the Marines and the sobering experiences of war.

He came home a man, went to school nights to get his high school diploma, and worked days learning the trade of a furnace-and-heating-system technician. "I was never out of work," he proudly recalled. "I never had to take the 52–20 program"—a government subsidy for returning veterans who couldn't get work—twenty dollars a week for fifty-two weeks.

Most returning veterans went to work or back to school as swiftly as possible. They were acutely aware of what they had lost in their training years. In fact many of them to this day just subtract three, four, or five years from their chronological age in good humor,

Gordon Larsen

laughingly explaining that those were the years they lost during the war.

Gordon's choice of furnace-and-heating work proved to be a good fit. It was a skill in demand, for America was in a building boom and home heating was changing over from coal to oil. After fixing furnaces on Army Corps of Engineers projects, he stepped up to powerhouse operator on the Corps' big hydroelectric dams in the Midwest and West.

He met his wife, Emelia, on the job in Omaha and they raised six children, four boys and two girls. Gordon reveres his Marine Corps connection but he's also grateful his sons never had to serve. As he said of his Marine days, "It was a million-dollar experience, but I wouldn't give you a plugged nickel to go through it again."

Part of that experience was learning the lessons of loyalty and family. As his Marine buddies had been his family in training and in combat, he carried that attitude into his civilian life. He said, "It's hard to explain, but my friends are like my family. I found out in the Marines what that can mean in life, and I'm still that way today."

Life didn't always work out the way Gordon had hoped. When he already had six children of his own and was working two jobs to make ends meet, he took in a young Sioux Indian as a foster child. He just felt sorry for the tot, whose parents were both in jail. The boy lived with the Larsens for several years but grew increasingly difficult to control, at one point attempting to burn down their house. They were forced to send him back to the reservation and they've never heard from him since. This is not an unusual occurrence when white families try to raise young Indians. The cultural differences often become too great to be successfully managed, but Gordon still feels disappointed that it came to a bad end. It was not what he had learned in the Marine Corps, to lose a family member because there was no common ground.

When I talked to this ordinary man with such extraordinary experiences during his teenage years, I was sorry that he hadn't shared them with the young people in our community during the fifties. I understood, of course, why he didn't want to revisit those nightmare years, but I am confident we could have learned something from him.

World War II left another mark on Gordon Larsen—he's an unabashed patriot. That's a part of American life lost on younger generations, he believes. It's a common refrain among World War II veterans, forged as they were on the anvil of military discipline and the call to duty to defend their country against real peril. "Whenever I hear Taps or see a flag go by, I get tears in my eyes. Even now," he said, "and I'm seventy-three."

John Caulfield (far right) with buddies, Panama, 1945

The ROMEO Club—
Retired Old Men Eating Out

JOHN "LEFTY" CAULFIELD

"I have only one regret. My kid never had a Corner."

ALTHOUGH THE WINDS OF WAR had been blowing steadily across the Atlantic and Pacific for some time, it wasn't until the Japanese attacked Pearl Harbor that everyone in the United States finally realized we could not stand idly by while the Axis rolled across Europe and Asia. That stunning surprise attack galvanized the nation as no speech or distant development could. While Pearl Harbor was the explosion that triggered five long years of death, injury, and separation, it also gave Americans everywhere common cause. They talk longingly now about the loss of that bond, that cohesion of national purpose and the personal ties that went with it.

It's a regular topic at the monthly meetings of the ROMEO Club, held in various diners at the edges of Harvard Square, in Cambridge, Massachusetts. John Caulfield, a burly former high school principal, started ROMEO. "Retired old men eating out," he explains. Not just any old men. The guys from Kerry Corner, the Irish working-class neighborhood not far from the leafy sanctuary of Harvard Yard.

In the thirties, Kerry Corner made up about ten square blocks of Cambridge. Caulfield and the others are forever attached to those roots. "I tell ya, where we're from, every three-decker house had four, five kids to every floor, and every morning they were out the door and headed for St. Paul's School." Wood frame homes were divided into three parts for the families that had emigrated from County Kerry, Ireland. These were large families whose lives revolved around work, the Roman Catholic Church, the Democratic party, and whatever sport was in season.

Every guy had a nickname. Hutch, Lefty, Nibby, Mac, Dude, Jabber, Spud, Bugs, Tea Pot—whatever it was, it stuck for life. They were a gang, but not in the modern sense of guns and dope and senseless violence. They were a gang of pals, and when they got into a fight it was with each other, and then, as one of them says, "We shook hands and forgot."

As teenagers they led lives of innocent deprivation. They used the showers at the playground fieldhouse because no one had showers at home. There were no swimming pools so they took their dips in the Charles River. They organized their own baseball and basketball games without the current worries about uniforms and liability insurance. They got whacked by the nuns at St. Paul's, the neighborhood parochial school, when they stepped out of line; and if they went home and complained to their parents, they were likely to be whacked again. Their mothers stayed home and their fathers went off to jobs as laborers, policemen, firemen, plumbers, printers, railroad men.

When Pearl Harbor was attacked, they signed up for the Navy, the Army, the Marines, the Merchant Marine. Someone put up a big banner in the neighborhood—KERRY CORNER'S CONTRIBUTION TO THE UNITED STATES—with a star for every young man who enlisted or who was drafted. Mothers and fathers would gather on the square to organize Christmas packages for the boys who were fighting their way across Europe or the Pacific as infantrymen, radar operators, aircraft controllers, helmsmen, and quartermasters. None became a highly decorated hero or senior officer, but the boys of Kerry Corner, and millions more like them from neighborhoods across the country, were the muscles and bones of the U.S. armed forces.

It was the biggest adventure of their lives. Before Pearl Harbor their world was defined by the ten square blocks of their neighborhood. As Eddie O'Callaghan remembers, "I was glad to get out and get back, but it really was an education because when we were kids a trip to Cape Cod was really a big thing—sixty miles away."

John Caulfield (middle row, second from right), August 1942,
St. Paul's CYO baseball team

Not even the war could separate them. One of their favorite stories was told by the late Angie Backus, a Marine in the Pacific in 1942. His unit had been in heavy fighting on Tulagi for six weeks, with no reinforcements and no fresh supplies. Finally some more Marines landed, so Angie decided to take his mortar crew for a midnight raid on the supply depot. "We sneak down," Angie said, "and we get stopped by a sentry. He looks at me and says, 'Angie, is that you? It's me, Sonny Foster.' Way out in the Pacific, in the middle of the war, I bump into a kid I grew up next door to. Small world, huh?"

Remarkably, only a few from the Kerry gang didn't return. They can count only a half dozen. The others came home to the old neighborhood at the end of the war. But before long it began to change, under pressure from the expansion of Harvard and the rising prosperity in Cambridge. The lads from Kerry Corner were doing well too, and they were able to move to nearby working-class suburbs. In their hearts, however, they'll live on Kerry Corner, as friends, forever.

Some went on to college while others went directly to jobs as machinists, graphic artists, telephone company foremen, state highway patrolmen, or city cops. In the war they were the foot soldiers and common seamen, the men who made the war machinery work. They returned to perform the same invaluable service to greater Boston, just as other members of their generation were doing for other urban areas and small towns across the country.

John "Lefty" Caulfield, the organizer of the ROMEO Club, returned and went to Harvard, which he had attended briefly on a baseball scholarship before enlisting in the Navy. When he re-enrolled in 1946, he had the GI Bill to pay the way—and many classmates who would later make their marks on the world, including Henry Kissinger; James Schlesinger, the former director of the CIA who was also secretary of defense and secretary of energy; Robert Coles, the distinguished psychiatrist who has devoted his life to the study of troubled children; and Amory Houghton of the Corning Glass family.

Caulfield, now a member of the Harvard Athletic Hall of Fame, played four years of varsity baseball, captained the team, and led the Ivy League in hitting. His favorite memory is beating Yale in

1948, when a young Navy veteran was captain of that Harvard rival—George Bush, Yale's first baseman.

That was an unexpected dividend from the war: the mixing of the likes of Lefty Caulfield with a future president of the United States from a country-club upbringing in Connecticut, a long way from Kerry Corner. Caulfield's father died when he was young, and the family was so poor he can remember blankets over the windows to keep the cold out and long waits at the local food bank for free grapefruits, cornmeal, and baked beans.

When Caulfield graduated in 1950, he began a career in education in the Cambridge schools, first teaching math and French while coaching the baseball teams. Later, he was appointed principal at Martin Luther King High School just 150 yards from his old home on the corner of Flagg and Banks streets. He had mixed feelings about the promotion. "I could do more for them as a principal," he explained, "but I missed the family of kids I had as a teacher."

We met upstairs at a ROMEO Club gathering at Charlie's Kitchen, a folksy bar and grill in Cambridge. A few of the members wore hearing aids and, on the whole, they were a pound or two over their ideal weight, but they're a healthy bunch for men in their seventies and eighties. They were wearing caps signifying their old military units or craft unions, a few sports shirts with the name of a club in Florida or down at the Cape. They present visitors with a tiny beaded pin of the American and Irish flags.

It was a big turnout the day I was there, eighteen guys from the old neighborhood and the one woman who's a member, Helen Sheehan, widow of Joe, a legendary figure who starred for the Boston College basketball team after the war. He was killed in an industrial accident later and Helen got his place at the table. When she lost her husband, their boyhood friend, they immediately organized a raffle and raised several thousand dollars so she would have ready cash. They also love to tease her in the most politically incorrect fashion. "Helen's one of the boys; we think she was a man before her sex-change operation." Helen laughs as heartily as any of them.

Father Joe Collins, eighty-four, of the neighborhood parish, St. Paul's, was also there. He's married many of these men and represents the faith that's been such an important part of their lives. Only one has been married to more than one woman and that was because his first wife died. Father Joe always begins and ends the meeting with grace and benediction. When he finishes someone asks, "Is he gone now? Can we swear again?"

They've told and listened to the same stories so many times that when I asked James Maher how long he was in the service, the whole table answered with him in a singsong harmony: "Three years, seven months, and twenty-one days." They all laughed. Mostly, however, they talk about the old days and the differences in life between then and now.

Caulfield believes these monthly gatherings typify the big difference. "I would say camaraderie and the affection everyone has to this day. It's fifty years of this." And something else, according to Caulfield. "I believe we're being victimized by our affluence. We don't appreciate things because you don't work for them." It's a common observation of this generation and all the men around the table nod in agreement.

That leads to a discussion of other lamentable changes, in their eyes. O'Callaghan, who was in one of the units that liberated Dachau, came home from the war and signed on with the Cambridge police department. "I was a detective in the juvenile squad and I took some neglected babies to my home until we could get them into a hospital." Now, he says, hospitals that see evidence of child abuse won't even call the police.

John Caulfield picks up on the theme. "We're afraid to breathe. When I was a principal I hugged all the kids all of the time. The girls *and* the boys. I hugged them to praise them or to get their attention. But you can't do that anymore. Sexual harassment."

John McGowan, a machinist for all the years after the war, says, "Too many people want others to take care of their kids. They're sending them to school at three years old just to get them out of the house." Leo Doyle adds his observations about modern kids: "They don't know how to play, even. They're bored with each other." An impossible concept for the ROMEO crowd. "They sit in front of computer screens. It may be educational but they don't know how to play tag, baseball, whatever the hell else. Part of growing up is learning to fight with each other."

It goes on. Someone says, "You no longer know your next-door neighbor. If someone is sick or dies, no one knows it." Work, which has been so central to their lives, has changed so much. "We went to work for a company and stayed there until we retired. Now they downsize; they're getting rid of you and they don't care."

Someone else says, "Road rage! What's that all about? Why's everyone in such a hurry?"

Leo Doyle on Memorial Day: "When we were kids in grammar school the veterans from World War I would come into our classroom or we'd go down to the auditorium and they'd tell us about some of the things they went through. . . . I gave a talk in a school, and the kids kept strolling in like there was no tomorrow. Hell, when we were there you sat down and kept your mouth shut. I just got back from Wisconsin and I was talking to my great-grandchildren about Memorial Day, and they almost didn't know what I was talking about."

The tone, however, was not bitter. The men of ROMEO and Kerry Corner are too proud and, in a way, so pleasantly surprised by how their lives turned out they have no time for bitterness. Besides, push them a little, and they'll tell you about the success of their kids, the schoolteachers and cops and lawyers. Joe Connally, who returned from the war to work in food services at schools throughout the Boston area, says, "You know, you forget there are so many good kids out there yet. I have a great feeling for the country and the kids coming along." All along the table on the second floor at Charlie's Kitchen, the boys of Kerry Corner pause over their thick hot dogs and French fries, the hamburgers, chicken sandwiches, and beers, and silently nod in agreement.

After all, their own kids are doing well in their jobs and with their families. The promise of America has not dimmed for them, the sons and daughters of Kerry Corner's contribution to the United States in war and peace.

They don't have everything, however. Lefty Caulfield speaks for the table when he says, "I heard a guy say one time, 'I have only one regret. My kid never had a Corner.' "

HOME FRONT

Any war always has at least two fronts: the front line, where the fighting is done, and the home front, which provides the weapons, the supplies, the transportation, the intelligence, the political and moral support. The home front rarely gets equal credit, but World War II required such a massive buildup in such a short time, the home-front effort was as impressive as the fighting in Europe or the Pacific. On factory assembly lines or in shipbuilding yards, in government offices and top secret laboratories, on farms and ranches, the men and women who stayed behind were fully immersed in the war effort. They worked long shifts, rationed gasoline, and ate less meat. They rolled surgical dressings for the Red Cross and collected cigarettes for the boys "over there." They waited for the mail and dreaded the unexpected telegram or visit from the local pastor. Some of them, pressed into duties they had never considered, found new callings in life. It was a radical transformation of America, an evolution still in progress, especially for women.

Charles Briscoe, high school, 1936

CHARLES BRISCOE

*"If you've got a job, there's a way to do it. As a farm kid I
didn't have anyone to ask; I just had to figure it out. So when
I went to Boeing, that's just what I did."*

AMERICA WAS a modern industrial power when it entered the
war, and so the machinery was already in place for converting
production from domestic needs to the tools of war—tanks, jeeps,
ships large and small, submarines, small-bore rifles, and artillery
pieces large enough to launch a shell the size of a full-grown hog.
No industry was as busy or as inventive as the airplane business.
Aircraft designers were drafting new fighter planes and long-range
bombers almost daily.

All this production required another kind of army—one of workers. There was no shortage of men and women ready to earn a
steady wage after the long, lean years of the Great Depression.
Moreover, most of them were used to hard work and long hours.
Many had grown up on farms where the days ran from daybreak to
past sundown, where work meant just that—work—the backbreaking, callus-making kind of work in hayfields and cattle barns,
in primitive kitchens and rudimentary laundry rooms.

Charles Briscoe grew up as the son of an itinerant farmer who
moved restlessly across the Great Plains, looking for work. Briscoe
came of age in the Dust Bowl. "On the fourth of March, 1935," he
says, "I was in a car being pulled by my uncle's car. It was a beautiful day. The sun was shining. Then it turned dark as quickly as
you can clap your hands. I could see nothing. I got out of the car
and felt my way to his car. My mother lit a coal-oil lamp and held
it in the window of the house and we drove toward that."

He tells another story about all that dust in those days. "My mother would hang wet sheets over a frame on our bed to keep the dust out of our lungs when we went to bed. The neighbors all around us lost children because they didn't take the precautions my mother did."

And two more stories of those days of poverty:

"One of the happiest days of my life—I was about in the seventh grade—we were farming in Kansas and I was trying to plow with a team of horses, walking behind, trying to keep the plow straight. My dad came home with wheels and a seat for the plow. I'll never forget it.

"When my mother had to have work done on her teeth we had no money, so I went to the dentist and offered to work for him in exchange for the work she needed. I washed his car and I did such a good job he hired me to work around the office. I washed the floors and the windows, cleaned the bathroom—anything he wanted. He said I was the best help he'd ever had, and he gave me the keys to the office so I could come and go when I wanted. I told him my mother taught me to clean house."

A neighbor had a John Deere tractor in need of an overhaul. He asked Charles whether he could handle the job. In fact, Charles had never worked on a John Deere, but that didn't discourage him. The neighbor's wife drove him to town to buy the parts. He took the tractor apart, installed the new parts, and put it back together again.

"I had a wonderful dad, but after any of us children got to a certain age we started working and never kept a paycheck. It all went into the family kitty. I could find a job at age fifteen when my father couldn't. I just had natural skills. I got a job cutting broomcorn by hand. The rows were a mile long. The boss told the other men that if they couldn't keep up with me, they could leave. My dad couldn't keep up, so I'd cut his row, too."

His father was having a more difficult time on his own farm, according to Briscoe. "We planted wheat five years straight and only one year the crop came in. We got twenty-five bushels an acre and sold them for twenty-five cents a bushel."

By the time Briscoe was high school age, the family was living on a farm thirty-five miles from Arkansas City, Kansas, where his sis-

Charles Briscoe, junior college, 1938

ter was teaching school. He wanted to complete his studies, so he hitchhiked to town to attend the high school. "I studied in the city library until they closed it," he said, "and then I would pick up an abandoned newspaper and go to an abandoned house. I'd sleep on the newspapers. My main meal was salted peanuts because you could get them for a nickel. That went on for three weeks until we sold a pig. Then I could rent a room for a dollar and a half a week."

After graduation Briscoe left for California, where he enrolled in a sheet metal school, learning the ways of this new trade that blended perfectly with his eye for design and his instinct for a job well done. He returned to Wichita, Kansas, in 1940 with his new craft, for a job at the Stearman Aircraft Division, a branch of Boeing. The plant was already gearing up for the possibility of war, turning out light training planes and working on a supersecret project: the development of the B-29, the Superfortress, the long-range bomber the Army Air Corps desperately needed.

Briscoe knew the mission was urgent. "We knew the B-17s and B-24s didn't have the range to get to Japan. We had to have the B-29 to win the war and get the men home from over there. We worked seven days a week, often twelve to fourteen hours a day." He says Boeing tried to find farm boys for their workforce "because we were used to long hours. Out on the farm we got up at four A.M. to milk the cows and then milked them again at eight-thirty that night. So hard work wasn't anything." There was another dividend for Boeing in hiring farm boys at a time when the aircraft industry was in a do-or-die creative phase. Farm boys were inventive and good with their hands. They were accustomed to finding solutions to mechanical and design problems on their own. There was no one else to ask when the tractor broke down or the threshing machine fouled, no 1-800-CALL HELP operators standing by in those days.

My father, Red Brokaw, was a blue-ribbon member of that fix-it generation. My mother learned not to say aloud that she needed, say, a new ironing board, because my father would immediately build her one. She liked to buy something from the store occasionally. When I was a young man in need of spending money I mentioned that I could mow many more lawns if I had a power mower. I had a snazzy new model from Sears Roebuck in mind. My father went to his workshop and built a mower using an old washing machine motor, welded pipes for handles, a hand-tooled blade, and discarded toy wagon wheels mounted on a plywood platform. He painted it all black and it was a formidable machine. At first I was embarrassed, but then as it drew admirers I was proud of its homespun place in a store-bought world.

During the war, Red and his pals made all of our Christmas toys. Later in life, when I took our daughters home for a Christmas visit, it snowed hard and we were determined to go sledding. By then my parents had gotten rid of all of our childhood sleds, so Grandpa Red took my daughters down to his workshop and turned out a wooden sled in less than an hour. It went down the hill as swiftly as any Wal-Mart model. My daughters, grown now, treasure the memory.

My father and his friends were like Charles Briscoe. They loved to make things work, and although they were not formally trained they had an instinct for design. Briscoe worked in tool design at Boeing. "I had to learn it all on the job because I had no experience like that whatsoever," he says. "We couldn't always get the materials we needed, so we'd make some tools out of Masonite or maple wood. They didn't last long, but then we'd make another one using just a band saw."

Briscoe's parents were also used to hard work, so he got them jobs at the Boeing plant. His father was sixty-five at the time and his mother was in her late fifties.

They were all part of a team effort to build the new, long-range airplane. Nothing like it in aviation had ever been undertaken before. Just four years earlier, Boeing had produced a total of one hundred airplanes from its Seattle and Wichita plants. Now the military wanted more than five thousand a year, including this new, long-range bomber—the first mass-produced, pressurized heavy bomber. It had a wingspan almost fifty feet longer than a modern 737. It would be the single greatest airplane program during World War II.

It was America at its inventive best. "Today you have to have FAA approval," Briscoe says, "but on the B-29 the engineers were drawing plans and we were making parts before it was approved by anyone. Some of what the engineers gave us were just pencil sketches— not even blueprints.

"We started putting beds in the B-29 because we figured the pilots would be in there a long time—but then we decided there wasn't enough room, so we had to redesign and take the beds out."

In February 1943, a prototype B-29 was tested near Seattle with tragic results. It caught fire and crashed, plowing into a building near Boeing Field. All twelve crew members and nineteen people on the ground were killed.

In June 1943 the first production B-29 rolled off the Wichita assembly line. Briscoe will never forget the moment. "All of us went out to the front of the hangar to watch the new B-29 take off, and as it took off, smoke started coming out! We thought we'd lost everything. But it turns out they'd left an O-ring off one of the oil lines.

"The next day it took off and it was beautiful. We knew we had a successful airplane. It looked as big as an apartment house—and I had built it."

What he did not know at that moment was that the B-29 Superfortress would be the means of delivering the bomb that would bring Japan finally to its knees. It was a B-29 called the *Enola Gay*, named after the mother of the pilot, Colonel Paul Tibbets, who dropped the atomic bomb on Hiroshima—the beginning of the end for imperialist Japan.

Charles Briscoe was not on the job the day the news came of the bombing of Hiroshima. He was in the Navy. "I was twenty-nine years old and I had two sons and I wanted the world to be safe for them, so I volunteered for the Navy in 1945. I was in for just nine months before the war was over. I definitely knew it had to be a B-29 carrying the bomb, because that was the only airplane we had that could make it that far. I was thrilled. I realized it was sad that all those Japanese died, but how many Americans would have been killed without the atomic bomb?"

After the war and his short-lived Navy career Briscoe returned to Boeing and spent the rest of his working life there, helping develop parts for the new airliners that were rapidly filling the skies around the world. Briscoe was an invaluable troubleshooter for Boeing. Going back to the time when they were inventing the B-29 day by day, he had developed a knack for designing and producing airplane parts. After he retired at sixty-seven, Boeing brought him back at the age of seventy to work on special projects. The company tried to bring him back after his eightieth birthday as well, but there he drew the line.

He's proud of the work he did on the Boeing 737, the world's most popular airliner. The skin of the 737 was first formed by two sheets of metal that met the thickness specifications but exceeded the weight restrictions. So Briscoe and the Boeing experts designed a series of waffle-shaped cutouts on the inside to reduce the weight. It was one of many challenges the former farm boy relished during his long career at Boeing.

It's been a much better life for Charles Briscoe than he expected when he was moving around the Dust Bowl with his parents as a teenager. What he learned then, however, served him well. He learned to work. As he says, "If you've got a job, there's a way to do it. As a farm kid I didn't have anyone to ask; I just had to figure it out. So when I went to Boeing, that's just what I did."

It's a way of life for him. Now in his eighties, Briscoe is still fixing what's broken. "I buy run-down houses and remodel them and rent them. Anything that needs to be done, I do it—the plumbing, the electrical. I roof 'em, I do the Sheetrock, patch the holes, all of that."

Briscoe teaches his children and grandchildren by example. "The kids nowadays," he says, "their parents buy them fancy cars and depend on someone else to keep them running. When all my grandchildren wanted cars I bought five hail-damaged cars—we get a lot of hail in Kansas. I got them for about three thousand dollars each instead of ten thousand or fifteen thousand dollars. I welded a finishing nail in each of the dents, bent it over, ground it smooth, and filled it in with body putty. By the time we finished, the cars looked brand-new. I had my grandchildren help me so they'd learn that if you want something badly there's a way to get it."

DOROTHY HAENER

"A number of my men friends said it wasn't a place for women. They said I'd be too nice. I had to fight them."

I N OTHER FACTORIES converted to wartime production, other children of hard times were finally making a good wage. Many of them were women, able to take their place on the factory floor only because the men were needed in uniform. One of them was Dorothy Haener, a strong-willed young woman from a hardscrabble Michigan farm run by her single mother. Dorothy says she developed a sensitivity at an early age to how women were treated in the workplace. Recently she told a niece "how disturbed I was when my eighth-grade teacher was fired because she had been married the year before." That was not an uncommon practice in small-town America and in the rural areas. Teaching jobs were reserved for single women and men who were "heads of household." In the reasoning of the time, a married woman would not qualify as a head of household.

Once Haener graduated from high school, she went to work at a Ford Motor Company plant in Willow Run, Michigan, where production was already underway on the B-24 bombers that would be so critical in the war in Europe. Haener makes it clear she was not motivated by patriotism alone. "What people forget now is that people went to work because they wanted to live. Years later, when the women's movement came along, I heard people talking about work that was 'meaningful' to them. I consider myself lucky that eventually I found work that was meaningful, but I was always willing to work for just wages."

It was while working as a B-24 parts inspector at Willow Run that Haener began to reevaluate her life. Until then, she says, "I had always expected to get married and raise a family, something modern women's organizations don't like to hear me say, but that's the way I was raised." Working nine-hour days, six days a week alongside men in the plant, however, made Haener realize she could have an independent life. She was proud of her work and happy with the money she was earning.

In the summer of 1944 that life ended for Dorothy Haener. She was laid off when Kaiser–Frazier Industries took over the plant to prepare for the postwar years. It had no room for women. Kaiser declared it would hire the best of the returning servicemen—and who was going to argue with that? Haener thought there was room in the plant for men *and* women. After all, she'd done her job well. Why should she be penalized?

Her efforts at getting hired back at her old wage were unsuccessful. She went to work in a toy factory for much lower pay. She assembled cheap toy guns and plotted to return to the Willow Run plant and her old salary.

In the fall of 1946 she was hired back at Kaiser–Frazier but in a clerical position at a lower wage than what she had earned during the war. She quickly found a new calling: union activist. It was the beginning of the glory days of the United Automobile Workers union under the enlightened leadership of Walter Reuther, and Dorothy Haener became an eager acolyte.

She began by organizing the office workers and engineers, motivated by her anger at having been demoted summarily from parts inspector to secretary and by the wage gap between those on the production line and those working in the offices. "I can't speak for why the engineers organized," she says, "but for the women it was simply a matter of money."

Haener's success as an organizer of her colleagues and her passion for fairness won her a following within the ranks, and soon she was elected a trustee of her UAW local. She'd also gotten to know Walter Reuther, who admired her skills so much that he brought her into the national headquarters as an organizer of engineering and office staffs around the country.

Although Reuther was an articulate and committed champion of equality across all lines—race and gender—not everyone in the labor movement shared his philosophy. Haener learned that she was most successful when she didn't single out women as an issue. She says women had to be smarter and better dressed to hold their jobs, but "if you played the equality thing too much," she says, "you turned off men. The message played best when I focused on better pay and control of the workplace."

At headquarters she was also an important force in raising the place of women within the UAW at every level, including the establishment of a separate women's department for the union. Irving Bluestone, then an administrative assistant to Reuther, is now a professor of labor studies at Wayne State University and he remembers, "Dorothy was actively outspoken and put pressure where pressure needed to be placed."

Sometimes she did that by personal example, often meeting resistance from her male colleagues in the labor rank and file. She decided to run for the powerful bargaining committee within the UAW, the elite group that goes head-to-head with management in hammering out the terms of a new contract. Many of her male colleagues opposed the idea of a woman on that critical committee. It was the labor movement equivalent of a woman in the cockpit of a fighter jet.

"A number of my men friends said it wasn't a place for women. They said I'd be too nice. I had to fight them. Finally I won in an open-caucus vote and I lost some male friends over that. They wanted women around but they didn't want them to have any responsibility." It still hurts Haener to discuss personal attacks leveled against her by her male colleagues. They raised questions about her morality and whispered slanderous rumors about her personal life. When she asked a union lawyer for advice, he told her to ignore them and devote all of her energies to her union commitments.

Later, one of the men in the anti-Haener movement came to her and apologized for his role. That eased the pain some, but the larger lesson for Dorothy was that women would have to go through those kinds of experiences if they wanted an active role in the union movement. That's what she wanted, and she was devoting her life to it.

Haener never married for largely that reason. "By the time the war ended," she says, "I was too independent to get married."

Haener met Betty Friedan, the author of *The Feminine Mystique*, when Friedan was touring the country for President Kennedy, assessing the issues of women and equality. As a result of those early meetings Haener became a founding member of the National Organization for Women, NOW. She's no longer on the board, and while she does feel that NOW has filled a need in promoting equality for women, she believes that it and other women's organizations have come up short in pushing hard for equal pay.

"We've made some improvements," she says, "but we still have a long way to go. So many of the younger generation don't know how far we've come. . . . They don't realize that what's given to them in the law can be taken away when the law isn't enforced."

Dorothy Haener got into the labor movement because she felt cheated on the job and in her paycheck when the war came to an end. It's what keeps her going now. "Wages affect women more than anything else," she says. "Take child care. We pay women who take care of children less than we pay people who take care of animals."

The war years gave Dorothy Haener a chance to earn a good wage, to contribute something to her country, and to learn a good deal about herself. She not only became a seminal figure in the postwar women's movement, she also chaired the Michigan Civil Rights Commission in the eighties and testified several times before Congress on the issue of equal pay for equal work.

She's now retired but she hasn't given up her long fight; she volunteers to walk picket lines in the Detroit area when needed and discusses with her nieces the continuing need to make sure women are treated fairly on payday. She's confident they understand. After all, one of them is now an engineer at General Motors and a mother. Dorothy's niece has maternity leave and child-care benefits. The bitter experience of her aunt Dorothy more than fifty years ago and how it changed her life paid off for Dorothy's niece, and for thousands of other women who are just now beginning to take their place alongside men in the workplace and at the pay window.

HEROES

———————— • ————————

"Hero" is a description tossed around lightly these days—like "star" or "celebrity"—another significant difference between the closing days of the twentieth century and the century's middle years, World War II. During the war the use of the phrase "You're a hero" was likely to bring on the quick rejoinder, "No, I'm not; I'm just doing my job here—like everyone else." The fighting men and women were so dependent on each other and shared so many common experiences they were embarrassed to be singled out.

Some acts of heroism, however, were so breathtakingly conspicuous, so daring and vital to the military mission, they could not be overlooked or turned aside. In many instances they changed forever the lives of those who were decorated. Others who were decorated returned to the lives they would have had without the medals and the attention.

If there is a common thread among the major medal winners, it is the same modesty expressed by Army nurse Mary Louise Roberts Wilson when she received the Silver Star. Almost to a person they have said to me, "I didn't *win* this medal. I merely accepted it for all the people who were with me." Nonetheless, they *did* win it, and the very qualities that led them to take great risks to save others served them well once they returned home.

Bob and Wanda Bush, wartime portrait

BOB BUSH

"Everyone should learn the meaning of that famous little four-letter word—work."

B OB BUSH has been married to his high school sweetheart, Wanda, since 1945, when they were both eighteen. They have three grown children and the comfortable lifestyle that goes with Bob's great success in the lumber and building supply business in the state of Washington. He has one blind eye to remind him of that day on a ridge on Okinawa. He went to the aid of a gravely wounded Marine officer that day, one of the deadliest days in the fight for control of the Pacific, for the planned invasion of Japan.

He has something else to remind him of that day: the Congressional Medal of Honor, the nation's highest commendation for battlefield valor "beyond the call of duty." There were 440 Medals of Honor awarded during World War II, 250 of them posthumously.

When Bob Bush earned his medal he was fulfilling a promise to his mother. As he left for basic training as a Navy medic the year before, when he was seventeen, he told her, "Mom, I'm going into the service to help people, not to kill them." Bob knew that was important to his mother, a single woman who worked as a nurse in an Oregon hospital. They had already been through so much together, mother and son.

They lived in the basement of the hospital in which Bob's mother worked and money was very scarce. But at an early age Bob had a flair for commerce. As a teenager, when he saw how hot and sweaty it was for the men working in the holds of the ships in the harbor at Raymond, Washington, his hometown, he brokered a deal with a local grocer to supply the workers with cold soft drinks. It was a profitable enterprise and Bob learned lessons early in how to fill a need, arrange credit, and most of all, provide good service.

By 1943, however, when he was in high school, the war was raging and he wanted to be a part of it. So he dropped out of school to join the Navy medical corps. He reported for basic training in Idaho, and less than a year later he was on an amphibious assault vehicle loaded with Marines, going ashore at Okinawa for what everyone knew would be a long, brutal battle against the Japanese forces dug in on the island. It was a critical piece of geography for the Allies, as they made their way toward the Japanese mainland.

Bush now remembers shouting at one of the Marines to tell their landing-craft driver, "Slow down! We don't have to be the first onshore!" Getting ashore, however, wasn't the problem. Gordon Larsen, the man who made me laugh when he fixed our furnace, was an eighteen-year-old Marine on Okinawa and he recalls that landing day was the first of April. As he says, "I thought it was an April Fool's joke. There were no Japanese to fight us."

The main Japanese force had retreated from the advance to the south end of the island, where they were well armed and holed up in caves, prepared to make this a very costly campaign for the invaders. As the Americans moved south toward the Japanese positions, the fighting became so fierce and so unrelenting that it has a special place in the storied history of the U.S. Marines.

Thirty-two days into the campaign to take control of Okinawa, on May 2, 1945, Bob Bush was attached to a rifle company of Marines on the attack over a ridge against heavily fortified Japanese positions. Bush was constantly on the move, going from one downed Marine to another to patch them up and get them evacuated.

Then he was called to help a Marine officer gravely wounded and lying in the open on a ridgetop. Bush didn't hesitate. He went directly to the officer's side and began administering plasma just as the Japanese attacked the position. His Medal of Honor citation describes what followed:

Bob Bush, wartime portrait

Bob Bush and company

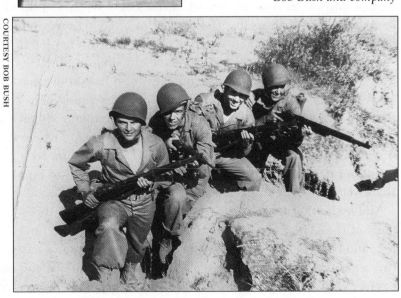

In this perilously exposed position, he [Bush] resolutely maintained the flow of life-giving plasma. With the bottle held high in
one hand, Petty Officer Bush drew his pistol with the other and
fired into the enemy ranks until his ammunition was expended.
Quickly seizing a discarded carbine, he trained his fire on the
Japanese charging point-blank over the hill, accounting for [the
deaths of] six of the enemy despite his own serious wounds and
the loss of one eye suffered during the desperate defense of the
helpless man.

Bush finally drove off the Japanese and made arrangements for
the evacuation of the Marine officer. He refused aid for himself
until he collapsed from his wounds as he walked off the ridgetop.
More than a half century later, he told me in a cheerful tone, "I remember thinking as the Japanese were attacking, 'Well, they may
nail me but I'm going to make them pay the price.' "

Bush was shipped to Hawaii for treatment of his injuries and as
soon as he was patched up, he was sent home. He'd been in the
service just one year, six months, and twenty-two days but he'd
seen enough of war to last a lifetime. He'd earned his right to get
on with his life. As the Navy plane carrying him back passed over
the Golden Gate Bridge, Bob Bush made a pledge to himself. "I
was going to put everything west of there behind me. I was eighteen. I had to get back to school in the fall. I had the girlfriend
back home in Washington." He knew a lot of young men were interested in Wanda and he wanted to get back to win her hand.

Wanda Spooner, a petite beauty, was eighteen as well when they
were married that summer. She quickly got a notion of what life
would be like with the charming and ambitious young hero back
from the war and ready to take on the world. Their honeymoon was
the long cross-country train ride to Washington, D.C., where Bob
was to receive his Medal of Honor from Harry Truman, who had
been president just a few months, following the death of Franklin
Roosevelt.

Suddenly, these two love-struck teenagers were on the south
lawn of the White House, surrounded by the president, his cabinet, and the legendary military leaders of the day. Wanda was getting a lot of attention from the generals and the admirals, and one
of the White House organizers told Bob as they went on to a re-

Bob Bush shaking hands with President Harry S Truman

Bob Bush on the job

ception at the Mayflower Hotel in Washington, "Don't worry about Wanda. The admiral will keep his eye on her." Bob recalls saying, "Yeah, but who's going to keep an eye on the admiral?"

Wanda was excited because after the Washington ceremonies they were scheduled to go to New York for a parade and an all-expenses-paid tour of the Big Apple. "But Bob told me we were skipping that. We had to go back home so he could finish his schooling and get on with his business plans." A frivolous weekend in New York, however tempting, just was not in Bob Bush's plan for life.

Once back in the Northwest, Bob finished his high school requirements, enrolled in a few business classes at the University of Washington, and talked to his friend Victor Druzianich, another veteran, about buying a small lumberyard. Bob figured that with all of the veterans coming home it could be a promising business.

They named their company Bayview and they were off to a fast start in southwest Washington, buying lumber directly from the many sawmills in their area and selling it to contractors and the growing number of homeowners with money to remodel or expand. In fact, business was so good they were working seven days a week and figured they could prosper even more if they could somehow add an extra day.

They had learned in their military training how long they could go without sleep and still function, so they developed a plan. Every other week one of the partners would work a full twenty-four-hour day, driving through the night to Portland to pick up an extra truckload of lumber. That demanding schedule went on for seven years.

It was the essence of one of Bob's favorite expressions: "Everyone should learn the meaning of that famous little four-letter word—*work*." He also lived by the credo of his favorite high school football coach: "Practice as you play." To Bob Bush that meant pursuing his business goals full-time, all the time. It was the rigorous schedule pursued by so many World War II veterans. In the service they had learned the importance of identifying an objective and pursuing it until the mission was accomplished. Also, they felt they had to make up for lost time. These were children of the Depression, with fresh memories of deprivation, and the postwar years were abundant with opportunities to make real money. They didn't want to miss out.

At home, Wanda was in charge of raising the family—three boys and a girl. They later lost one of their sons in a car accident. The surviving children, Mick, Rick, and Susan, say Bob was often an absentee father, but he would tell them he was working so hard to make their lives better than his had been. Now that they have their own grown-up responsibilities they have a better understanding, but the boys still point out that their dad missed a lot of their Friday-night football games.

Summer vacations often consisted of Bob's dropping the family at a cabin on a lake and then returning to work.

Bob also put the children to work in the rapidly expanding Bayview business empire at an early age. Mick laughs now when he says, "If I put my kids in the situation he put us in, I'd be in jail." As soon as they were teenagers the boys were learning to drive forklifts and trucks in the lumberyards. Susan was always Daddy's little girl to Bob, but he didn't spare her his favorite four-letter word, either. As a teenager she had to work cleaning the toilets and other public facilities in the stores.

Wanda was the indulgent parent. She was up before everyone in the morning to get breakfast on the table, pack the school lunches, do the laundry, and act as the court of last resort if Bob refused to back down from "no," his favorite initial response to most requests. That division of family responsibility and the lines of authority were not unusual in the households of veterans across the country.

There were moments of tension in the Bush family, but Wanda smoothed them over and, besides, the kids were the beneficiaries of Bob's wartime heroics. He almost never talked about those awful days on Okinawa, but he belonged to an elite club and the family would be visited by other Congressional Medal of Honor winners, including the famous flier Jimmy Doolittle or the Marine Corps ace Joe Foss, later the first commissioner of the American Football League.

When Rick was in the eighth grade he began to become more fully aware of his father's wartime heroics, but when he asked Bob about what it was like on Okinawa he remembers his father saying only, "Well, you know, it was very difficult. We had to dig foxholes. Hygiene was terrible. We had hair lice but we had a job to do, and mine was to help people hurt in the war. I was happy to do it." Period.

As the business flourished and expanded into mobile homes, golf course construction, and ready-mix concrete—as well as the seven lumberyards and building supply stores—Bob began to relax a little. He took Wanda and Mick to the inauguration of John F. Kennedy, the first member of his generation to be elected president. It was notable for mother and son for two entirely different reasons.

Bob laughs when Wanda, to this day, gets a kind of dreamy expression as she describes meeting JFK at a White House reception. "He looked right into my eyes," she says, "and even though I didn't vote for him, I certainly thought he was handsome and charming."

Mick remembers another reception for the Congressional Medal of Honor winners. Former president Harry Truman was the speaker. Mick was just ten years old but he could hardly believe what he was hearing. Truman was recalling his favorite Medal of Honor recipient. The former president said it was a young man from the West Coast who had promised his mother that he was going into the service to help people, not to kill them. Mick knew Truman was talking about his dad, but Bob did nothing to draw attention to himself, not even when he introduced Mick to Truman as the reception was winding up.

Rick was also struck by the modesty of the Medal of Honor winners. He noticed something else about those common men who acted with uncommon valor. "For them," he says, "responsibility was their juice. They loved responsibility. They took it on head-on, and anytime they could get a task and be responsible, that was what really got 'em going."

Nonetheless, Rick struggled for a time as a teenager when he realized what he'd have to live up to with Bob as a father. He acknowledges they clashed over lifestyle and values for a while, but he always tried to understand what his father had been through in the Depression and the war. As he puts it, "I try to assimilate his values but I also try to show him the difference." Bob has another way of describing it. "Rick," he says, "is a Porsche and I am a Volkswagen."

Now that the children are in their forties, with kids of their own, and Bob and Wanda are in their seventies, they have a new Bush generation as common ground. Bob manages to work into almost every conversation the success of a granddaughter who graduated from Pepperdine College and immediately got a high-paying job with a Fortune 500 company. Or another granddaughter, a star basketball player, who's also going to Pepperdine on a scholarship from the Medal of Honor Society, an organization made up of all living recipients of the coveted decoration. His daughter, Susan, a schoolteacher married to a building contractor, says, "Dad is all about family now. He built an extra-large house in Palm Springs so he can take care of all the grandchildren."

The boys, Mick and Rick, also have a keen appreciation of Bob's business skills. They followed him into the company, but on Bob's terms. He sold each of them a lumberyard and building-supply store so they could be independent. As he put it, "I'm not going to give you the business. I am going to give you the opportunity." He financed the purchases but they've had to make the payments.

He's also available for advice, including the Bob Bush rules for operating a successful business. He told the boys that when they're asked how the business is going, answer "Good," never say "Great," because your customers will think you're doing too well. Don't say "Terrible," because they'll think you're about to go broke. He also told them to stay away from personal relationships with women who work in the business, and from stating their personal opinions about politics and religion in the office.

For their part, they've gotten him to relax a little more. As Rick says, "He'll now play nine holes of golf. In the past he'd only play six holes before rushing back to the office." Susan thinks she's helped him lower the emotional walls a bit. She says, "He is a lot more loving and he hugs more than he used to, he's a lot more emotional and openly affectionate." Bob listens to all of this with a mixture of pride and bemusement.

So does Wanda, sitting just off to the side, looking a little wan. She's going through a difficult bout with cancer and the prognosis is not encouraging. Bob is spending all of his time with her, consulting with doctors, trying to make her comfortable. She remains the light of his life. Besides, he agrees with their children when they say, as Mick put it, "My mom is the bravest person in this family today." And Susan adds, "And Dad wouldn't be where he is without my mom." Rick chimes in, "I'll second that." Bob, the wartime hero and tough-guy businessman, looks at Wanda adoringly and smiles.

Bob Bush was awarded the Congressional Medal of Honor for conspicuous valor on Okinawa, but it was the thought of Wanda that got him home alive. Together they have had memorable moments as a result of that medal, and certainly the prosperity that came with Bob's business success was a dividend, but it is their enduring love for each other and for the family they had together that is their greatest accomplishment.

———————— • ————————

JOE FOSS

"Those of us who lived have to represent those who didn't make it."

NO ONE would ever accuse Joe Foss of slowing down. Even now, at the age of eighty-two, he inhales life in big, energetic drafts. He is in many ways the quintessential World War II hero. He grew up poor on a farm in South Dakota at the height of the Depression. He lost his father when he was a teenager. He was inspired to fly when he saw another midwesterner, Charles Lindbergh, on a barnstorming tour. He worked at a gasoline station after high school to earn money for college and flying lessons. After playing football and graduating from the University of South Dakota, he enlisted in the Marine Corps in 1940. He quickly became one of the Marines' most gifted pilots, and when war broke out he spent a year working at Pensacola as an instructor.

In the fall of 1942, Foss shipped out to Guadalcanal as the executive officer of a squadron of Marine F4F-4 Wildcat fighter planes. Foss remembers they were at sea, with their planes on a carrier, "wondering what it would really be like to finally be in the war." They found out quickly enough when they were aroused from their berths in the middle of the night with the news that Japanese submarines were in the area and the pilots would have to launch their planes early.

Foss, who now lives in Scottsdale, Arizona, remembers that once the squadron was off the carrier and headed for Guadalcanal, "I

Tom Brokaw with Joe Foss, Two for the Money *game show, 1957*

knew what war was going to be like. As we came in low to Henderson Field on Guadalcanal, we could see bomb craters all around and the antiaircraft guns were firing at Jap planes overhead. When we landed, the Marines on the ground gave us a big reception, cheering and everything." Those Marines were happy to have the help. They had been fighting steadily since August just to gain control of the field and hang on to it.

Foss said to one of the Marine fliers who had been there awhile, "Well, I guess you veterans will show us around." Foss says the Marine answered, "Oh, you'll be veterans, too, by tomorrow." Actually, it took a week. On October 16, 1942, Foss shot down his first Japanese Zero. By November 19 he had shot down twenty-three, an extraordinary number, but the skies over the Pacific were filled with fighter planes and bombers as the United States and the Japanese battled for control of the air and the sea lanes leading to the mainland of Japan.

In fact, on the day he shot down his first Zero, Foss was nearly shot down himself. In those days, aerial combat was practically face to face. Foss and the other pilots didn't have laser-guided weapons and sophisticated computer systems telling them when to shoot. Those aerial battles were accurately called "dogfights," two snarling high-powered fighter planes twisting and turning, each trying to get the advantage, the pilots hitting the buttons to fire the machine guns, while they continued to fly at speeds of up to 300 miles an hour at altitudes ranging from just a few feet off the ocean surface to high in the clouds.

The F4F-4 Wildcat was not as quick or as responsive as the Japanese Zero, so when Foss's plane was hit, he knew he was in trouble. He had three Zeroes on his tail as he went into a steep dive and then a big, wide turn, trying to get back to Henderson Field with a dead engine and his propeller free-wheeling. "The Zeroes stayed right behind me," he says, "and as I cleared the hill to land at Henderson they unloaded all their lead at me." Foss landed the plane at full speed, with no flaps and little control in what is called a "dead stick" landing. The F4F-4 careened across the runway and skidded to a stop just short of some palm trees. Later his ground crew counted more than two hundred bullet holes in the plane. Foss, then twenty-seven years old, sat in his cockpit, badly shaken, thinking,

Why did I ever leave the farm? Suddenly he heard the cheers of the ground crew, "kids eighteen and nineteen years old who had watched it all," he recalls, "and I said to myself, Well, you're a leader, Joe. You're in it all the way now, and from that point on I was just a full blower."

By January 1943, Foss had shot down twenty-six enemy planes, equaling Eddie Rickenbacker's record from World War I. He had been shot down and forced to ditch at sea, swimming through the Pacific waters for twelve hours until he was rescued by island natives in a dugout canoe. Two days later he was back in the air.

His exploits included a breathtaking maneuver in which he dove directly toward a Japanese battleship to deliberately draw fire and make it easier for other American planes to torpedo the vessel. As he started his dive he radioed to the rest of the squadron, "Keep it steep, girls, keep it steep." He figured a plane coming straight down would be a difficult target for the battleship guns. He was right, but it was an extremely risky maneuver. When Foss pulled out at the last moment, he was so close to the ship he could see the Japanese officers on the bridge.

He was indestructible. Though he was knocked off the flight line for six weeks by a bout of malaria, he came back to fly again. Foss, who had learned to shoot pheasants and ducks on the wing as a boy on the South Dakota prairie, was a warrior of the old school, mourning the losses of friends from his squadron but never crying. He carried a Bible and a pair of dice in his flight-suit pockets, wore a leather helmet, and chewed on a cigar when he was on the ground. He had a Marine's vocabulary and a bellowing voice. One of his squadron members would say of him, "All the balls of any man who ever walked the earth."

In the spring of 1943, the Marines decided Captain Foss had done his share and brought him home to a hero's welcome, less than a year after he had shipped out. He was awarded the Congressional Medal of Honor and was put on the cover of *Life* magazine, the ultimate press accolade during the war. He had a hero's swagger but a winning smile to go with his plain talk and movie-star looks. Joe Foss was larger than life, and his heroics in the skies over the Pacific were just the beginning of a journey that would take him to places far from that farm with no electricity and not much hope north of Sioux Falls.

Before the war ended, he returned to the Pacific for another tour, and he was invited to Australia to brief a squadron of British Spitfire pilots. He had just started his talk when he noticed the Englishmen were not much taken with this rough-hewn Marine with the barnyard style of speaking. So, typically, he just confronted them in his direct, take-it-or-leave-it way. "I said to them, 'I know what you birds are thinking right now. You've been up there in Europe flying against the Germans, and you don't need any advice from me. Lemme give you a tip: You're going to underestimate the Zero, and when you do you're going to land on the deck.' Well, they didn't pay much attention," Foss said, "and when they went up against the Zeroes over New Guinea, seventeen or eighteen of them were killed, including their best flier." It was a moment that crystallized Joe Foss's philosophy of skill over style.

When the war was over, Foss went home to South Dakota and opened a charter flying service and a Packard car dealership before getting involved in Republican party politics, first as a state legislator and then as governor in the mid-1950s. Whatever their politics, South Dakotans like me were proud to have such a blue-ribbon war hero as the state's chief executive. We could count on our largely anonymous state getting more attention with Foss in charge.

Besides, Foss, for all of his acclaim, was a South Dakotan through and through. He loved to hunt and fish and he still knew his way around a farm. His speeches were usually rambling affairs, filled with Marine or prairie colloquialisms. For example, he still likes to remind audiences, "Hey, if we hadn't put up a scrap back there during the forties, you'd be living under the Japs or the Germans and I don't think you'd like that very much."

It was during his terms as governor that I got to know Foss personally. When I was seventeen, I was elected governor of Boy's State, a weeklong program organized by the American Legion to expose honor students to the structure of government and the challenges of politics. As governor, Foss came to a lunch in my honor and we hit it off. Later that summer, he invited me to become his partner on a national quiz show that wanted to cash in on his war heroics.

It was a very generous gesture from this nationally famous figure, to reach out to an obscure teenager and offer a spot by his side on *Two for the Money,* starring Sam Levenson, live from New York. All of the questions were about American politics, and we won $612 apiece, a small fortune in the preinflationary days of the fifties.

It was my first trip to New York, and when the show was over Joe asked what I was going to do. I explained I had to fly back early the next morning, but there was so much I wanted to see. He said, "I think you should stay a few extra days. I'll get in touch with your parents when I get back and tell them it was my idea." When I called home later that night to tell my folks that the governor thought I should stay a few days more, there was a long pause at the other end of the line. Finally, my father said, "Well, I think you should. You'll probably never get to see New York again."

Now that I've lived in Manhattan for more than twenty years, I often think of that night and the days that followed, when I went to Ebbets Field to see my beloved Dodgers in their final summer in Brooklyn, the trips to Greenwich Village, to the Statue of Liberty, and to the top of the Empire State Building, walking by Carnegie Hall, listening to Dixieland jazz from the sidewalk in front of the old Metropole Café at Times Square. By the end of my stay, I had a better understanding of what appealed to me and what I could handle. I knew somehow that this time my father was probably wrong. I would see New York again. Maybe Joe Foss knew that, too, as he encouraged me to stay.

In the fifties, Foss was busy on several fronts. In addition to his duties as governor, he was still flying as a senior officer in the Air National Guard and he was in demand at Marine reunions and other military gatherings around the country. But there were other challenges outside the public limelight. He had married his South Dakota girlfriend when he returned from the war, but they soon discovered that it was not a perfect union. Foss not only was gone a good deal on political or military trips, he was also an avid sportsman, so he had many invitations to far-off safaris and other hunting expeditions.

The marriage lasted longer than many troubled relationships because one of the Fosses' children suffered from cerebral palsy, another from polio. Although these challenges temporarily united the couple, they also served to put strains on their marriage. In addition, Foss's wife suffered from diabetes, a condition that would eventually take her life. The demands of their life became too much for the couple to endure, so they decided to separate.

The public by and large was not aware of the fissures in the Foss marriage. In those days the private lives of public officials remained just that, unless a scandal became too large to ignore. There was no scandal here, just a troubled marriage. Because Foss was active in the establishment of a children's hospital in Sioux Falls to treat the handicapped, and was also the national president the Society of Crippled Children and Adults, an organization dedicated to the welfare of polio victims such as his son, it was a surprise to many in his home state when the Foss divorce became public knowledge.

By then Foss had left politics, having lost a race for the U.S. House of Representatives to another South Dakotan with a distinguished war record, George McGovern, who had won one of the military's most coveted awards, the Distinguished Flying Cross, as a B-24 bomber pilot in the European theater. McGovern, a history professor, was as self-effacing as Foss was bold, but he was a much better politician, with a strong sense of his political beliefs and an ability to articulate them.

McGovern, who rarely mentioned his DFC or wartime service, went from the U.S. House of Representatives to the Senate before becoming the 1972 presidential nominee of a badly fractured Democratic party. As he campaigned hard for his prairie populist beliefs, against the Vietnam War, and for a liberal economic agenda, Richard Nixon and company portrayed him as a captive of the hippie left. McGovern was crushed in the general election, but his warnings about Vietnam and a budding scandal called Watergate proved to be prophetic. He remains one of the country's most decent and thoughtful public servants. The DFC McGovern won for landing a crippled bomber and saving his crew is much more telling about his courage and patriotism than any whispered innuendo from the crowd that saw their president resign in disgrace.

After losing to McGovern, Foss went on to become the first commissioner of the fledgling American Football League, often appearing at games in a white cowboy hat with a bolo tie around his neck, exuding enthusiasm and sharing war stories or trading hunting tips with the eager men of his age and interests.

When, by mutual consent with the owners, he left the AFL in 1966, Foss went on to a variety of other jobs, including a starring role in his own television series, *The American Sportsman*. His primary role, however, remained that of being Joe Foss, war hero, or, as he liked to say, "bull in the woods." He was a restless sort, so he liked to keep moving.

Money wasn't all that important to him. He turned down $750,000 for the screen rights to his story in 1956, a veritable fortune at the time. He remembers the final meeting in the Polo Lounge of the Beverly Hills Hotel, what Foss called "that little café just off the lobby. I was in a booth with John Wayne on one side of me and the producer Hal Bartlett on the other. Wayne was to get a million dollars to play me. They asked me how I liked the script. I said, 'Fine—except for that romance baloney. If you're going to do a story on Joe Foss, you gotta take that out.' " The screenwriter, who had contrived a love story to go with the combat, said, "We need that to make a show for the public." Foss explains, "I just turned them down flat. It wasn't me at all."

After all, Foss knew that what he had been through in the skies over the Pacific wasn't a love story. It was kill or be killed, pure and simple. Or, as he once said, "Combat is dangerous. It tends to interrupt your breathing process."

Foss's breathing process was once almost interrupted in a freak incident, this one connected to his love of the outdoors. In the sixties, he suddenly became very ill, practically paralyzed and steadily losing weight. No one could figure out what was wrong until, finally, his condition was accurately analyzed as arsenic poisoning, probably from chewing on insecticide-soaked weeds while filming his television show.

That experience, and his second wife, DiDi, led him to a life-changing experience. Joe Foss became an enthusiastic born-again Christian. For an old whiskey-drinking, cigar-smoking master of profanity who had been an absentee father and husband for much of his first marriage, it was a complete makeover. As a fundamental Christian who takes the Bible as the literal truth, Joe Foss had found a theology to match his personal philosophy: There is no middle ground in his life.

As president of the National Rifle Association, he was proud to appear on the cover of *Time* magazine with crossed six-guns. He believes fervently in the Second Amendment to the Constitution and thinks "that crew that wants to take the Constitution a section at a time has got it all wrong. The only piece of paper that's outlasted the Constitution is the Bible. They both mean what they say."

In Gary Smith's riveting 1989 profile of Foss in *Sports Illustrated,* the journalist said that if Foss were "a traveling campfire, men would form a circle around him and warm themselves by the flame that men have always sought—certainty. And nudge each other in the ribs and grin and whisper, 'Isn't he a pisser.' Because even if they thought he was wrong, he was still that rare thing, an original, himself."

Foss has the same unapologetic attitude toward his religious beliefs. He told me his embrace of the Lord is "the greatest decision I ever made. I made it for eternity. In every speech I give I mention the Lord. I always end with, 'In Jesus' name, Amen.' Now there are those who take me aside and say, 'Joe, maybe you ought to leave Jesus out.' 'No, sir!' I tell 'em."

He simply can't understand the shadings of modern life. President Clinton's lawyers arguing about the meaning of his answers under oath triggered strong memories for Foss. "Folks now just don't have an appreciation for what an oath means. When we took the oath when we were sworn into the Marines, it was a contract! That's what we went out there to defend. I can still see my pals sitting around when we weren't flying, guys like Casey Brandon and Danny Doyle, a couple of baseball players from Minnesota, talking about what we were going to do when we got back from the war. Well, they didn't get back. I lost half my squadron. We all knew what an oath was about."

Foss, for all of his strong feelings, isn't a bitter old man. He still roars to life shortly after dawn on the Arizona desert, ready to fly off to give a speech at a Marine base change-of-command somewhere, or share with others what his embrace of Christianity has meant to him. He was pleased recently when a schoolboy member of his church asked him to come to his school for a day set aside to honor American heroes. Joe chuckles when he says, "Well, I got there and I was the only living hero. All the rest were George Washington and those guys. But at least the school was studying history and thinking about heroes."

When I asked him if he thought more about those World War II days now than he did a few years ago, Foss said, "Yes, more people seem to be bringing it up. People seem to realize how the world would be different if we hadn't put up that scrap." When I ask if he missed the old days, he answered quickly, "Oh, no. I'm not a guy who missed anything from anywhere. I've always been a guy who just gets up and goes."

It's probably that quality that made him such a cool, daring, and effective fighter pilot. It's also what makes him so engaging as a man. His unalloyed views on everything from guns to God to education to right and wrong may not match your own, but you know that he's arrived at them honestly. And if you don't agree with him, Foss, now in his eighties, may think of you as a "bird" or a member of "that crew," his all-purpose mild epithets, but he won't take time to hate you. He's too busy for hate.

As he says of his World War II experience and what it should mean to others, "Those of us who live have to represent those who didn't make it."

LEONARD "BUD" LOMELL

"We were trained so well I didn't believe anything could kill us."

Leonard "Bud" Lomell hasn't been an active-duty U.S. Army Ranger in more than a half a century, but in his heart and in his mind he still wears the distinctive patch of the elite military unit that had the most dangerous assignment on D-Day. He led his men up the sheer cliffs at Pointe-du-Hoc while German forces dropped grenades on them, kept up a steady stream of fire, and even cut the ropes the Rangers were using to scale the precipice. We met when Lomell was one of the veterans featured in NBC News's documentary on the fortieth anniversary of the invasion.

By then he was a sixty-four-year-old lawyer from Toms River, New Jersey, but as we rode together in a small motorized rubber raft just offshore from Pointe-du-Hoc, talking about that day decades earlier, I could almost see the tough, young First Sergeant Lomell directing his men as they landed under the withering fire of the German forces.

They had been getting ready for this mission for more than a year, undergoing training that was so grueling that many of the Rangers said they were looking forward to combat to escape the rigors of preparing for it. They had endured long speed marches with full packs, nighttime landing exercises in the cold waters of the Atlantic, hand-to-hand combat training, climbing slippery rock cliffs

Leonard Lomell,
wartime portrait

Charlotte Lomell

and rappelling down again. They were young men, between eighteen and twenty-four, and superb athletes, their bodies sinewy with muscle after months of the most demanding forms of physical exercise.

Bud Lomell had volunteered for the elite Ranger Corps after enlisting in the Army following college. He was the adopted son of Scandinavian immigrant parents who took him into their family when he was just an infant in Brooklyn. Later they moved to the Jersey shore, where Bud grew up, pampered by two older sisters and a big brother in the poor and hardworking family.

He remembers that the night he graduated from high school his father bought him some ice cream. As they sat at the family's kitchen table, Bud was stunned when his dad burst into tears and said, "I am broke. I don't have any money. I can't help you go to college. I wish I could, but I can't." Bud had never seen his father cry. He recalls, "I went over to him, put my arms around him, and told him not to worry. I could make it on my own."

Bud knew the family was poor. His dad was a housepainter, and at the height of the Depression no one in their working-class community was spending money to paint their home. Bud always had after-school and summer jobs to help pay the way, and he figured his athletic prowess would help him get a college education.

It did. He enrolled at Tennessee Wesleyan College on a combination athletic scholarship and work program, earning letters in football and participating in Golden Gloves boxing. He was also editor of the school newspaper and president of his fraternity before he graduated in 1941.

He returned to New Jersey, where he was able to get a job as a brakeman on a freight train, often working sixteen-hour shifts on the runs up and down the Atlantic seaboard. He knew, however, that before long he'd be in uniform, so he enlisted in the Army.

Three years later he was a first sergeant in charge of a platoon of Rangers as they ran their LCA ashore at the base of Pointe-du-Hoc. Lomell was commanding the platoon because his lieutenant had been reassigned just a few days before.

As they were landing, Lomell felt a sharp pain in his lower back. He was sure another Ranger with whom he had been arguing the day before had hit him. He turned and gave the guy a whack. Lomell still laughs when he recalls how the other Ranger was stunned, saying, "What's that's all about? I did nothing to you!" Lomell didn't realize until later that, in fact, he'd been shot through the right side. He kept going despite the wound.

The 2nd Rangers had a specific mission on Pointe-du-Hoc. They were to knock out five 155mm German coastal guns Allied intelligence figured to be just atop the cliffs. When Lomell and his men got to the top, however, there were no major German guns on the emplacements. Lomell and another sergeant, Jack E. Kuhn, found a dirt road leading inland and they began to follow it.

By now their daring mission is well known to students of that chaotic and vitally important day. Stephen Ambrose and many others have recounted what the two sergeants accomplished. They found the five 155mm guns heavily camouflaged, well back from Pointe-du-Hoc and aimed at Utah Beach, another landing spot for the Allies on D-Day. The guns were not manned, but Lomell and Kuhn could see German troops about a hundred meters away, apparently forming up to get the guns operational.

Lomell instructed Kuhn to cover him, saying, "Give me your grenades. . . . I'm gonna fix 'em." He ran to the guns and attached thermite grenades to critical parts and smashed the sights of all five guns with his rifle butt. The two sergeants withdrew to get more grenades and finished off the gun emplacement by disabling the remaining weapons. Mission accomplished.

It was just nine A.M. D-Day morning and Sergeants Lomell and Kuhn had already performed so heroically they would later be awarded the Distinguished Service Cross and Silver Star, respectively. It was also the beginning of a long war for both men, as they fought their way across Europe in all of the major campaigns, including the Battle of the Bulge.

That morning and in the days following the heavy fighting on and around Omaha Beach, First Sergeant Lomell came face-to-face with the worst of war. "When I saw my dead Ranger buddies laid out in rows," he told me later, "their faces and uniforms caked with dirt and blood, I couldn't believe it. I wanted to yell at them, 'C'mon, get up!' We were trained so well I didn't believe anything could kill us."

Before the war was over Lomell would be wounded twice more and would receive a battlefield promotion to second lieutenant. In

Charlotte and Leonard Lomell

Lomell family portrait,
taken at the Lomells' fiftieth wedding anniversary, June 6, 1996

1945 he was ready to come home, and when he did, he led other uniformed veterans from his hometown in a victory parade down the main street of Point Pleasant, New Jersey.

He had not been home long when his mother began to talk to him about that nice girl he had been seeing before he enlisted, Charlotte Ewart. She had been training to be a nurse at a hospital in Long Branch, New Jersey, in the summer of 1941, right after Lomell's college graduation. He was already working seven days and nights a week so there wasn't much time for courting. When they were together, however, the mutual attraction was strong. Charlotte remembers, "I thought he was very handsome and very self-confident. That was important to me. He knew what he wanted."

Before long, however, Lomell had enlisted in the Army and, typically for him, he then turned all his attention to his military training. He called Charlotte occasionally when he was home on leave but he didn't write, and soon they drifted apart.

After the war, when he took his mother's advice and called, Charlotte was enrolled in a public health nursing program at the College of Seton Hall. They arranged to have dinner and as Lomell says, "She was just the most impressive girl I had ever known. The rest didn't have a chance. We just picked up where we left off."

A year and a half later they were married, on June 6, 1946, two years to the day after Sergeant Lomell was fighting his way up the cliffs at Pointe-du-Hoc, a bullet wound in his side, determined to find and knock out a battery of German guns. As Charlotte says now, laughing, "Every wedding anniversary we share with the surviving Rangers, because it is also the anniversary of D-Day."

The GI Bill was Lomell's ticket to a career he could not have expected to have before the war. It allowed him to enroll in law school, at LaSalle University and Rutgers University. By 1951 he had passed the state bar exam and been admitted to the New Jersey bar.

The Lomells continued to make their home in southern New Jersey, and by 1957 Bud had founded his own law firm in the growing community of Toms River, about halfway between Philadelphia and New York. It quickly became one of the largest in Ocean County. As Bud likes to say, "I ran it with Ranger discipline." As the father of three daughters he was especially sensitive to the idea of sexual harassment before it became a popular workplace issue. Over the years, "I had to fire a couple of young lawyers for violating the rules in that area," he says. "Paid 'em off and got them out of there. I'm proud that my firm is known as the 'league of nations.' We've had several women and men of different ethnic backgrounds, sixteen lawyers in all and about thirty other employees."

Charlotte and Bud were a team at home and in the law firm. She kept the books and looked after the maintenance in the law offices, and together they made family decisions. They were raising three daughters of their own when Charlotte's sister died, leaving a teenage son and daughter. The Lomells simply brought them into their family as their own and sent all five children to college.

Through it all, Bud kept a close association with his Ranger buddies from the war. When they were younger, the Lomell daughters—Georgine, Pauline, and Renee—were so accustomed to Ranger veterans from Bud's old outfit dropping by, they just considered them "uncles." Renee—Bud and Charlotte's youngest daughter—a schoolteacher, considers those visits to be an important part of her education. "You really didn't see the military side," she says. "It was just a bunch of good men from a variety of backgrounds who cared about each other a lot."

They rarely talked about the worst of the war, she says. "They talked about the fun times during training or whatever, never about the fighting."

Renee also remembers as a teenager in the sixties how her father adapted to the idea of young men with long hair and unusual wardrobes. "He worried a lot more about our safety than he did about the length of hair," she says. He had essentially the same attitude toward the war in Vietnam. He supported it at the beginning, but when he saw it was poorly planned and executed, a terrible waste of young American lives, he turned against it.

Most of all, what the Lomell daughters remember is their parents as a perfect team. Bud, the energetic and outgoing lawyer with a soft touch for his daughters, always consulted Charlotte, who ran the family finances and preferred quiet evenings to large social gatherings. They were divided politically, Charlotte as a Democrat and Bud as a Republican, but that rarely caused any real rifts. "Our parents are a team," one daughter said, "and they made the family a team."

As a lawyer Bud did have certain rules to protect his feelings about his family. If he took on a divorce case he would never discuss it after three o'clock in the afternoon because he didn't want to be upset by someone else's family dispute when he went home to his own family. He often attended juvenile court on Fridays, and the girls remember that when he came home those nights his warnings about the dangers they could encounter took on new meaning.

Daughter Georgine is an Episcopal priest and chaplain at a long-term-care facility in Louisville, Kentucky. She says of her dad, "He walks his talk. He's all about fairness and justice. When my sisters and I were teenagers we looked younger, so when we went to the movies we could have gotten in on the kids' prices, but Dad would never do that. From him we learned how to be straight arrows."

One of Bud's protégés is Judge Robert Fall, who sits on the New Jersey state appellate court. Fall was in a local grammar school when Bud came to speak, and he made an indelible impression. Later, when Fall was in law school, Bud hired him, first as an intern and then as a member of the firm. "He was just the epitome of a leader in that firm," Fall says. "The lines were drawn very clearly between right and wrong, and with Bud you just didn't cross the line. I learned so much about integrity from him."

Fall says Bud didn't talk about his war experiences, but there were occasions when the old Ranger training spilled over into firm activities. "Every year we went as a firm—lawyers and spouses—to the Princeton–Rutgers football game," the judge remembers, chuckling. "We'd have to meet at the offices at a fixed time, travel in a convoy of cars to the game, eat a tailgate lunch at a specific time, and meet for dinner at a fixed time and place later. Bud ran it all with military precision."

As time went on, Bud Lomell became much better known in Toms River for his civic contributions than for his war record. He was a director of a local bank, president of the county bar association, a member of the local school board, president of the local philharmonic association, and, as a lawyer, always available to do pro bono work for local firemen, policemen, juveniles, and churches.

Judge Fall says that in his role on the bench, he thinks about Bud Lomell every day, and he is guided by the lessons he learned from him about right and wrong. Although Fall has known about Bud's war record since he was a grade-school student, he remains in awe of the raw courage he demonstrated on D-Day and beyond. "You wonder," Judge Fall asks, "could I reach down and do that? I guess I'll never know."

As for Bud, he still goes to his law offices a few times a week, even though he's been retired since the mid-1980s. He's survived two heart surgeries and he still has a military command style. As we were sitting in his comfortable waterfront home along the Jersey shore, preparing to do an interview on his reaction to the Steven Spielberg film *Saving Private Ryan,* a gardener started up a power mower outside. Bud turned to Charlotte and said firmly, "Tell that lawn mower to move out and come back later."

Bud had been a special guest at the Hollywood premiere of *Saving Private Ryan.* He was impressed that Spielberg had been able to re-create the chaos and the bloody conditions of the D-Day landing so effectively, but he had lots of problems with the rest of the film. Tom Hanks as a Ranger captain, he said, "should never be walking around with his men, all talking loudly in broad daylight. That would only bring in German mortars." Also, Bud noted that Hanks and his men were much older than the soldiers had actually been. "We were all eighteen or nineteen years old; I was one of the older ones at twenty-four," he points out.

Bud Lomell is now in his late seventies and he counts his long, happy marriage to Charlotte and the lives of their three daughters as the most meaningful events in the lifetime that began in the poor, immigrant neighborhoods of Brooklyn and took him to the heights of military and professional success.

Charlotte and their daughters recognize that Bud will always have another family as well. The men of the 2nd Rangers who landed with him on D-Day and fought their way across those beaches and the rest of Europe, those who lived and those who died, are in Bud's heart forever. Bud still leads Ranger tours back to those battlefields, but when they come to the American cemetery on the headland overlooking Omaha Beach in Normandy, he stays in the back of the bus. "To walk up to one of my Ranger graves there gets to me to the point I can't do it anymore. I know he knows I've been by—so I'll just go sit in the bus."

WOMEN IN
UNIFORM
AND OUT

———————— • ————————

The transformation in the life of Dorothy Haener as a result of
World War II was distinctive and highly visible, but millions of
other women were experiencing their own unique odysseys at
home as a result of the gender climate changes brought on by the
demand for men in fighting jobs. In fact, there were 350,000
women in uniform and an estimated 6.5 million at work in war-
related jobs on the home front. Harder to measure but equally important were the contributions of the women who stayed home,
raised the children, taught school, clerked in schools and banks,
kept the fabric of society together. At night they went to bed wondering if their sons or husbands were safe in those far-off places
where they were fighting for their lives every day. All these experiences—for the women in uniform, for those assembling airplanes
or ships, for the women who kept families and communities together—shaped that generation of women as much as combat
shaped the men of their time. To this day they are living the lessons
of those difficult and instructive times.

Colonel Mary Hallaren,
Tokyo, September 1947

Jeanne Holm,
Women's Army Auxiliary Corps,
1942

COLONEL MARY HALLAREN

"You don't have to be six feet tall to have a brain that works."

GENERAL JEANNE HOLM

"Did you ever see an ugly general?"

THE FACE OF WAR is almost always one of a man. The familiar images of World War II are no different: FDR as commander in chief; Eisenhower directing the D-Day invasion; MacArthur wading ashore in the Philippines; Patton astride a tank, pearl-handled sidearms prominently displayed; General Jimmy Doolittle, his smiling face poking out of a cockpit; Marines raising the flag on Iwo Jima; B-24 pilots, their caps at a jaunty angle; Navy chiefs at their battle stations; GIs in a foxhole. The male was in his historic role as warrior.

Early in America's war effort, however, it was clear there were not enough men to do all the fighting and to fill all the support jobs such a massive military undertaking required. There was a desperate need for military clerks, drivers, telephone operators, medical technicians, cooks, and couriers. The Women's Army Auxiliary Corps was created to help fill the need. It was the beginning of a radical change for America's military services that continues to this day.

Mary Hallaren was a natural for the WAAC. She was a junior high school teacher in her home state of Massachusetts when Pearl Harbor was attacked. Her brothers all enlisted immediately and she was not far behind. "To me," she says, "there was no question but that women should serve." The Army recruiter wasn't so sure, especially when he sized up Mary Hallaren, who's only five feet tall, by asking what someone so short could do in the Army. She answered, "You don't have to be six feet tall to have a brain that works."

The idea of enlisting in the war effort was really just an extension of her adventurous ways. She was a schoolteacher who, during summer vacations, went on long hitchhiking trips across Canada, Mexico, Europe, and even China—a highly unusual undertaking for women in those days. During a visit to Munich in the thirties she had been present at a Hitler rally. At the time, he was getting little notice in the United States. She was struck by the buildup preceding his arrival, but as for her, "He just didn't make such a strong impression." Little did she know then that he would change the course of history, and of her life, forever.

Jeanne Holm, another woman with a taste for the unconventional life, was living at the other end of the country from Mary Hallaren—in Oregon—when the Army formed the WAAC. Jeanne was working as a radio technician for the U.S. Forest Service, the tomboy daughter of a widowed mother. Her brothers were already in the Navy. She signed up for the WAAC, never guessing that her life's course was taking a new and rewarding direction. "At the time," she says, "the only reason women went into the military was to serve the country; we wanted to help America win the war and come home. No one thought of a career."

Holm began as an Army truck driver but was quickly accepted to officers' candidate school and assigned to Fort Oglethorpe, Georgia, where she rose to the rank of captain and spent the war training WAAC recruits. One of her brothers, John Holm, a Navy officer, wasn't impressed when she enlisted, but when Jeanne returned to their Oregon home on leave wearing her captain's bars, their common experience of military responsibility was a leveling influence. "I found I really admired her," he said. "She was a person in her own right and very bright."

Other men were no doubt coming to the same conclusion in their one-on-one experiences with women in the military, but it remained a world dominated by men.

It was the world Mary Hallaren was determined to alter. Given her self-confidence and worldliness at such a young age, it was little wonder the Army promoted her swiftly once the women's corps was founded.

Newsweek

MAY 21, 1951 **20c**

Wac Col. Hallaren: Boss of the Ladies' Legion

Colonel Mary Hallaren, 1951

She commanded the first battalion of women sent to England and immediately began a lifelong campaign for women to be taken seriously in the military. "At first," she says, "they only allowed the women to be clerks, telephone operators, cooks, drivers, but by the end of the first year women were filling more than two hundred jobs, including the job of cryptographer. The men discovered the women were very quick to pick up new things—they could do many jobs."

During the war Mary served in England, France, and Italy and so impressed the brass that when the fighting ended Dwight Eisenhower asked her to oversee the upgrade of the Women's Army Auxiliary Corps to the Women's Army Corps, which would give women a permanent part in the military establishment for the first time. It was a hard sell in the House of Representatives, especially in the Armed Services Committee.

Mary, who was put out front by General Omar Bradley and other returning heroes of the war, remembers the House Armed Services Committee wanting to rename the bill The Reserve Act of 1948. "They felt," she said, "the cost of integrating women into the service would be prohibitive—because when women reached menopause they'd be worthless!

"We organized men who were now out of uniform to lobby the committee members. After a few weeks I got a call from a staff member of the committee and he said, 'Call off this lobbying and letter-writing campaign. We can't handle it all.'" The committee finally agreed that women should become a permanent part of the military as WACs (Army) and WAVES (Navy). "That was a major step toward the role of women in the military today." It was a profound change for the place of women in American society, not fully appreciated at the time and not fully accepted by military traditionalists even now.

By then Jeanne Holm was back in Oregon, attending Lewis and Clark College on the GI Bill, still uncertain what she wanted to do with her life. A letter arrived from the newly named Defense Department, informing her of the Women's Armed Services Integration Act and inquiring whether she'd like to be considered for regular duty. She left immediately in her car for Fort Lee, Virginia.

"I was flat broke," she says, "so as I drove across the country I had to sleep in my car for two or three nights. When I got to Fort

Jeanne Holm, AIRSOUTH, NATO, Naples, Italy, 1957

Promotion to major general, 1973

Jeanne Holm, at the White House with President Ford

Lee for the physicals and exams, I remember that first night listening to the bugle calls and Taps and realizing how much I missed the military."

Mary Hallaren was promoted to colonel and took charge of the new branch of the U.S. military, the Women's Army Corps. She was called the "Little Colonel" because of her diminutive stature, but when it came to promoting a wider role for women in the military she was a towering figure, a godmother to the women who continued to struggle to find their places in the male-dominated military establishment. Her assistant, Mary Lever, recalls visiting WACs stationed abroad. "Wherever we went she'd get a standing ovation—the enlisted people adored her."

Mary Hallaren was the first American woman to achieve the rank of colonel, but under the 1948 legislation that was the highest rank for women in the military, so she decided to retire in 1960. Her seminal work for women in the U.S. military, however, cleared the way for the eventual dissolution of the WACs and WAVES in the 1970s and the integration of women into all branches of the service.

By then, Jeanne Holm was well on her way to a distinguished military career, having served in Germany during the tense time of the Berlin airlift in 1948. She had been assigned to the Air Force, and she was the war plans officer at Erding Air Force Base near Munich, responsible for determining how Erding's massive supply depot would be protected if war broke out with the Soviet Union. She was the first woman selected to attend the Air Force Air Command and Staff College.

Major Holm represented the Air Force at the Army's mustering-out ceremony for Mary Hallaren, and they began a long, deep friendship that grew out of their shared sense of adventure, duty, and commitment to an equal role for women in the military and the civilian worlds.

Mary was leaving the military but that did not mean the end of her service to the nation or to women. After her retirement, she heard from a friend about a new organization called Women in Community Service, WICS. It grew out of the civil rights movement of the 1960s, when women's organizations found common ground and common strength in the fight for equal rights for black Americans. Why, they wondered, don't we have a common cause for women?

Representatives of the National Council of Catholic Women, the National Council of Jewish Women, Church Women United, the National Council of Negro Women, and other organizations began to meet secretly to see what could be done. About that time President Kennedy's brother-in-law, Sargent Shriver, was trying to recruit women for the new Job Corps, one of Lyndon Johnson's War on Poverty projects.

Shriver approached the women who had been trying to find a new crusade and asked them for help. They decided it was exactly the kind of mission they had been trying to define, so they helped organize WICS, which became the recruitment wing of the Job Corps. Mary Hallaren was the first executive director.

"I moved right into it," she said. "The military was good training. I liked the challenge." One of the officers of WICS has a vivid memory of her first encounter with the Little Colonel. "I heard this sound. I thought, 'Is there a loudspeaker in here?' It was Mary. She was saying, '*Atten-shun!*' in that military voice. She looks like a cute schoolmarm with those braids, very cute, but when she barks an order she can stop you in your tracks."

Mary agreed just to get WICS off the ground. She thought she'd stay for six months; in fact, she stayed for thirty-four years, leading WICS through its formative years, when the primary role was to attract young women into the Job Corps, and into the modern era. WICS is now a full-service organization for women in trouble: it is one of the great success stories to grow out of the War on Poverty of the Johnson years. It's a vibrant organization headquartered in Arlington, Virginia, where it coordinates a national network of local chapters and their work with poor young women who desperately need help developing job and child care skills.

More than six thousand volunteers work in the WICS centers, some of them graduates of the very programs they now help staff. In the Pacific Northwest they work with women about to be released from jail. In San Diego WICS is a sanctuary for young women who want to get out of the southern California gangs' way of life and into the mainstream. The New Orleans chapter has a program for moving women from welfare to self-sufficiency.

Mary Hallaren got all of that started. One of her successors as executive director said, "For an organization that was putting together a really radical coalition in 1965, Mary was able to articulate the value of putting all those resources together." And, in a tribute to Mary's military training, she added, "And mobilizing; she knew how to mobilize resources for poor women. She's a big-picture person."

This five-foot dynamo, after a lifetime of helping women—first in the military and then in the inner cities across America—was inducted into the National Women's Hall of Fame shortly before her ninetieth birthday. She reacted with her characteristic modesty. "I just happened to be fortunate enough to have been with two organizations that really did a terrific job for women." In fact, those two organizations—the WACs and WICS—were fortunate to have Mary Hallaren in the forefront in their formative years. One more example of how World War II, in ways no one could have anticipated, elevated the place of women in American society.

While Mary left the service, Jeanne Holm continued to find her challenges in uniform. She returned from Europe to work in the Pentagon as personnel director for the director of the women in the Air Force. The Air Force allowed her to return to Lewis and Clark College so that she could complete her degree.

Still a major, she then spent four years at NATO headquarters in southern Europe as director of manpower. She loved her work, but in the back of her mind she knew there were limits to how far she could go. There were quantitative and qualitative quotas written into the 1948 legislation accepting women into the military. They could represent no more than 2 percent of the total armed forces, and there was that clause restricting their top rank to colonel.

Holm began to bang up against the ceiling when she finished another Pentagon tour and asked permission to attend the Officers College to study management. "No woman had ever been considered and when I asked the two-star general in charge he said, 'You have no future in the Air Force. I'm not going to waste a quota on you.' Well, I thought, that's it for me."

Instead, someone higher up in the chain of command had a better idea. Holm was appointed director of the women in the Air Force and immediately set out to make some long overdue changes. She worked to overturn the Air Force policy of automatically discharging women with children, arguing that the Air Force had no right to make a judgment about a woman's ability to raise her children by pointing out, "We do not meddle in this fashion in the private affairs of male personnel." She made sure married WAFs (Women in the Air Force) received the same pay and housing allotments as their male counterparts.

"It was 1965," she says, "and the women's movement was beginning to hit the fan. What was going on in the country was beginning to be reflected onto the women in the military. Even the smallest gain was an effort; I had two-star generals laugh at me." For a time Holm was so discouraged that she almost retired, but then she got a new boss, Lieutenant General Robert Dixon, who rescinded the standing discharge orders for Air Force mothers.

Holm went to Vietnam and argued with base commanders to accept women in support roles. "Some of these commanders had such a paternalistic attitude. They kept saying, 'What if a woman gets hurt?' But they ran out of nurses, so the first Air Force women to go over were nurses."

There was a breakthrough for women, however. In 1968 President Johnson signed legislation lifting the restrictions from the 1948 act integrating women into the service. For the first time women were not restricted to a numerical quota, and the lid was off on promotions. "It opened up opportunities to women that had been arbitrarily closed before, but no one took it seriously as a threat to the generals and admirals," Holm recalled.

Nonetheless, Holm was on a fast track to that most coveted rank, general. By 1971 she was the Air Force's first female one-star, a brigadier general. Two years later she was director of the Air Force Personnel Council and received her second star: Major General Jeanne Holm. "It meant one of the male one-stars wasn't going to be promoted. For the most part, I got a lot of letters congratulating me, but there were a few guys who were ruffled."

She was also developing a new generation of women officers for the Air Force. Wilma Vaught, now a retired brigadier general, remembers, "When I went into the service in 1957 I was told, 'Don't try to influence your assignments, just do as you're told.' What I didn't realize was that General Holm was up there looking out for me and for several other women with good records. She made sure we got the assignments and schools that would help us move up. She was always so happy to see women promoted and succeed. She was always on the front lines, making speeches and addressing women's concerns when other people would not."

When General Holm retired in 1975 she wasn't out of uniform long before she was called to duty again. President Ford asked her to come to the White House to work on women's issues. Her primary assignment was to prepare an initiative instructing the Justice Department to review all federal laws and policies that discriminated against women.

After her White House assignment she became a familiar figure on Capitol Hill as a member of the Defense Advisory Committee on Women in the Services. General Holm was a vigorous advocate of assigning women to combat roles, pointing out that modern wars require brains more than brawn. She posed the questions "To what extent can and should women be involved in defense?" "What are women's rights and obligations?" "Should they be allowed to fight?"

Holm testified on the issue of sexual harassment in the military. This from a woman who was once asked if her good looks didn't contribute to her success in the military. She'd responded, "Did you *ever* see an ugly general?" In her appearance before the House Armed Services Committee in 1992 General Holm opened with a defense of the qualities of the men and women serving side by side in the military. This was after Operation Desert Storm, when so many women served with such distinction in every kind of role, including critical assignments in the combat zones.

She then went directly after those who, in her words, "still haven't gotten the word or just don't want to get it." That included a Navy admiral who'd attended the infamous Navy fliers' Tailhook convention in Las Vegas, where sexual harassment was a crude corridor sport for many of the men in attendance. She recounted how twenty years earlier women in the service were forced to handle similar situations on their own, knowing that if they reported them, they'd be branded as troublemakers.

Now she said, "To change people's behavior requires strong, committed leadership at the top, conveying a message to everyone that sexual harassment or other improper conduct will not be tolerated. It requires more than publishing high-sounding phrases such as 'zero tolerance.'" She went on. "It requires setting standards of conduct and enforcing those standards vigorously."

Mary Hallaren fully supports that judgment. She believes the problem is not with the troops, but with leadership.

General Holm continues to monitor the issues affecting women in the military and to celebrate their achievements. Their role remains a work in progress, but Holm is persuaded that the demands of modern warfare will only enhance the place of women in the service of their country. General Holm finds that possibility as exciting and rewarding now as she did more than a half century ago, when she left her home in Oregon to become a truck driver in private's stripes.

Mary Hallaren, at the age of ninety-two, still follows the struggles of women in the various military establishments closely. She was pleased when the Supreme Court forced the Virginia Military Institute to accept women. Referring to VMI's leaders, she said, "They'll grow up after a while. They're afraid of the competition. The women will teach them a few things. Give them a little time and there will be no question about that."

The Little Colonel, ninety-two years old, knows something about what women can do when given the chance. She went into the military to serve her country during a war, and when that fight was finished she began anew, this time serving her country in a new capacity, as the godmother of women in the American military.

Marion Rivers (extreme left), wartime fashion show

Three Women
and How They Served

MARION RIVERS NITTEL

"A full-blown spirit of patriotism was in every heart."

CLAUDINE "SCOTTIE" LINGELBACH

*"I want to tell my grandchildren I was more than
a pinup girl in the Great War."*

ALISON ELY CAMPBELL

"You had to do your part."

M ARION RIVERS'S LIFE was centered on her family, her job, and her small city of Attleboro, Massachusetts, until the war caught up to America. Then the company for which she worked, General Plate Division of Metals and Controls Corporation, was immediately forced to convert from making rolled gold plate for jewelry to producing technical instruments for military purposes.

She remembers the pride of all the employees when the company was awarded a large E for excellence and the Army and Navy organized a ceremony to present a banner to be flown outside the plant. "I can still see that flag," Marion says, "snapping on the flag-pole whenever I entered and left the building." She believes it was the last time "in the history of our country when a full-blown spirit of true patriotism was in every heart."

CLAUDINE "SCOTTIE" SCOTT shared that spirit of patriotism dur-ing her freshman year at the University of Kansas in the autumn of 1940. "It was a fun, exciting time," she says, "but by the following fall, the campus had changed considerably. All of the boys were gone." Scottie decided to enlist in the Navy's female auxiliary, the WAVES (Women Accepted for Volunteer Emergency Service), and when the student newspaper, *The Daily Kansan*, asked why, she re-called a cartoon of two WACs walking down the street, one saying to the other, "I want to tell my grandchildren I was more than a pinup girl in the Great War."

Scottie wanted to be in on the action as well. As she says, "My generation was highly patriotic. Back when I was in junior high the words ENTER TO LEARN, GO FORTH TO SERVE were carved at the en-trance to the school. Those words affected me in many ways. I served."

She applied for a commission in the WAVES. Not only was she commissioned, she was assigned to the prestigious duty of serving on the staff of the Joint Chiefs of Staff. She was an administrative assistant and a courier, delivering highly classified papers to the White House every day. "I went to a basement room—the War Room—and they'd open the door only six inches to take the report from me. It was a log of the fighting going on all over the world."

ALISON ELY was doing graduate work in California. She was from a prominent Oregon family, and when Pearl Harbor was attacked her parents wanted her to return to Portland. She had other ideas. She got a job at an Oakland, California, shipyard, saying now, "You had to do your part."

IN ATTLEBORO, just outside her company's plant, Marion Rivers came to know the war effort through the troop trains that often

ABOVE: *Claudine "Scottie" Lingelbach, wartime portrait*

LEFT: *Claudine and Dale Lingelbach, c. 1945*

BELOW: *Scott, Scottie, and Coach Roy Williams—the inscription reads, "Scottie, you're special and always will be to me"*

stopped on a nearby siding, headed for Camp Myles Standish, a major point of embarkation for Europe.

When the trains stopped, the women in the plant would be summoned to a conference room to assemble baskets of fruit, candy, gum, and cigarettes for the GIs. Marion and the others would first head for the ladies' room "to remove our silk stockings, which were as scarce as hen's teeth—shredding those stockings would have been catastrophic." Bare-legged, they scuttled up the cinders on the steep railroad bed. The GIs, she remembers, cheered as she and the other young women distributed the baskets, laughing and waving at the young men who were headed for the unknown. "Later we'd be back in the office, covered with coal dust," Marion says, "but we loved it."

America in the forties was a nation of railroad tracks and trains. Railroad stations in small towns and cities were crowded with men in uniform, their wives and sweethearts giving a last embrace before the trains departed for a distant port and for the war in Europe or the Pacific. Later, those same trains returned with the young men, now greatly changed. They brought home the wounded and they bore the caskets of those who didn't make it. Marion remembers later in the war, when the trains materialized again in Attleboro, this time headed in the opposite direction. These trains had no troops cheering. The young women didn't scramble up the steep embankments with baskets of fruit and candy. The shades were drawn on the returning trains. "They didn't stop," Marion recalls. "These were the wounded coming home."

ON THE WEST COAST, Alison Ely was getting an entirely different view of the war. In the shipyard, she was assigned to the administrative offices, but that was boring and tedious. This highly educated daughter of Oregon affluence asked to go to work on the assembly line and stuck with her request even though the executive in charge grumbled, "All she'll ever do is get married."

She was assigned to work on the urgent construction of huge oil tankers. Her job was keeping track of the welding process, which meant mastering a complicated set of blueprints and diagrams. Her training was cursory at best. Forced to improvise her under-

Alison Ely Campbell,
wartime portrait

Alison Ely Campbell,
July 1998

standing, she often took other women workers into the ladies' room, where they labored together over the schematics until they figured out the intricate requirements.

IN WASHINGTON, Scottie's interest in the fighting went well beyond the messages she carried from war room to war room. Her boyfriend from the University of Kansas, Dale Lingelbach, was a second lieutenant with the Army's 9th Infantry in England. She knew he was scheduled to be part of the Normandy invasion.

Because she knew the plans for D-Day, when she was asked if she'd ever like to attend a White House press conference, she chose that day, June 6, 1944. She remembers it was in the Oval Office and President Roosevelt's little Scottish terrier, Fala, was running free through the small crowd assembled there. She also remembers FDR, then in the last year of his life, "dressed in all white, with white hair and a very ruddy complexion."

Earlier that day FDR shared with the nation his prayer for the success of D-Day. In a radio broadcast he said, "In this poignant moment I ask you to join with me in prayer; Almighty God: our sons, pride of our nation, this day have set on a mighty endeavor, a struggle to preserve our Republic, our religion, and our civilization, and to set free a suffering humanity. . . . They will need Thy blessings. Their road will be long and hard. For the enemy is strong. He may hurl back our forces. Success may not come with rushing speed, but we shall return again and again; and we know that by Thy grace, and by the righteousness of our cause, our sons will triumph. They will be sore tried, by night and by day, without rest—until the victory is won."

It was a long and heartfelt prayer and it is difficult in this day of instant communication from the battlefield to appreciate fully the absence of information about just what was happening there on the beaches of Normandy. Perhaps it was just as well, for D-Day was chaos, a bloody hell. The anxieties of those at home were high enough just listening to the somber and candid prayer of the president and the stream of news bulletins on the radio.

My mother remembers going to a hairdresser that morning and finding the young woman distraught, near collapse in tears. Her fiancé, she explained, was a paratrooper and she was sure he was taking part in the invasion. In fact, he was, and he survived. Several weeks later he sent her his parachute and told her to have a wedding dress made from it.

About the same time, Scottie was notified that her boyfriend, Dale, had been seriously wounded by German artillery as his unit pushed across Europe. When he was shipped home, they were married in September 1945, at the Richmond, Virginia, hospital where he spent two years recovering from his wounds. Scottie had loved her wartime assignment in Washington, but she wanted to be married and raise a family.

In MASSACHUSETTS, Marion Rivers and her friends spent long hours at the factory and then joined the rest of Attleboro in providing a home away from home for the troops from nearby Camp Myles Standish. They invited them to their homes for holidays or a Sunday meal; occasionally there would be an ice skating party on a local pond. "Once a week several buses filled with young women and our ever present chaperones would take us to wonderful dances on the base. Big-name bands on their way overseas to entertain the troops would play," Marion remembers.

On one occasion a familiar young man insisted on dancing with Marion, all the while saying, "Betcha don't know who I am." Of course she did. It was Mickey Rooney.

Other memories linger in a darker corner. Once at a dance the young women were asked how many could type. Marion volunteered. "We were taken to the camp hospital where all the beds and stretchers were filled with the wounded. They were being shipped to hospitals near their homes and we rolled typewriters from bed to bed, taking information off dog tags, talking to the men, placing phone calls for them. I have never forgotten the sight of so many broken bodies. I wondered how many of them had been on those trains going off to war when we ran up the railroad banks with our baskets of fruit and candy. That evening turned into twenty-four hours, and I think I remember every moment."

ALISON ELY married midway through the war and left the shipyard to follow her husband, John W. Campbell, to training camps before he shipped out for the Pacific. It was the beginning of a life of learning to fend for herself, including getting to the hospital on her own when their baby was due, with no other family around.

WHEN SCOTTIE'S HUSBAND, Dale, was released from the hospital, they moved to Schenectady, New York, where he had a job with General Electric. Before long they decided they wanted to return to the Midwest. They moved to Carthage, Missouri, a small, quiet town, and he went to work for the Smith Brothers company, the famous cough drop concern.

It was a pleasant, prosperous life. They had two children: a girl, Cynthia, and a son, Randy. Dale was promoted to vice president. The future looked bright, but at the age of forty-five, Scottie's carefully ordered world came apart. Dale contracted melanoma and died. Scottie faced a world not very friendly to single women.

She had difficulty obtaining credit after Dale died simply because she was a widow. Sears gave her a hard time. So did a pharmacy where she tried to open a charge account. She was stunned and angry. She learned not to tell businesses of her marital status. "I pulled myself up by my bootstraps. You can give up or decide to do something with your life. I had a degree in business administration but I knew I would never rise higher than secretary, so I thought, Where can a woman make the most money?"

This was 1968. Job opportunities for women had yet to catch up with the rising tide of feminism. Like many women of her generation, Scottie is strong and self-reliant but a little reluctant to be closely identified with the women's movement. She speaks for many in her age group when she says, "I'm not a radical person because I believe that has done more to turn people off." At the same time she's quick to add, "But I've always believed in equal access to jobs." Still, she was practical enough to realize that her choices were limited to what were considered to be women's jobs in a community the size of Carthage.

So Scottie went the traditional route and qualified for a teacher's certificate. Besides, it was where she could bring to life that junior high motto from so long ago, "Enter to learn, go forth to serve."

She became a civics teacher at a high school in nearby Neosho.

She set out to bring to the children of the sixties and seventies the values that marked her generation. Patriotism. Respect for the presidency. Love of country. She felt a special obligation to tell them about World War II, the war of their parents. It was the beginning of the social upheaval of the sixties and seventies, but at Neosho High she could still get the attention of the kids by staging mock political conventions. When she taught a section on the Roaring Twenties she came to class dressed as a flapper. Now, ruefully, she doubts she could have the same success.

It was hard enough, she says, to talk to the young people during Watergate. At first she believed in President Nixon and said so. When she realized he was lying, however, she shared her change of heart with her students. "It was hard, because I was trying to teach respect for the presidency." As for President Clinton and the Monica Lewinsky scandal, Scottie says, "Watergate was hard enough, but what do you tell the students today?

"I don't think my teaching would be the same now," she says. "I learned about patriotism through my school and family and I don't think you can get those values across in schools now. It's a little square to say you're patriotic. I would like to think that if the United States were attacked we'd band together, but I'm not sure." If there's a common lament of this generation, that is it: where is the old-fashioned patriotism that got them through so much heartache and sacrifice?

MARION RIVERS, WHO married Karl Nittel after the war, wonders about that when she visits cemeteries to decorate graves on Memorial Day. "They never found my husband's brother, who was lost at sea. For many years I kept his gold naval wings in my jewelry box. Recently I gave them to his daughter, who was just two months old when he died. She never knew him. The war never ends; there are so many memories." Marion's husband keeps his World War II Army uniform hanging neatly in his closet wherever they live, a mute reminder of a time when he answered the call to duty.

Marion and Karl stayed in the Attleboro area, raising a son and a daughter. In 1968 she went back to work and developed a successful career as a writer for a technical company, the first woman in that firm to head a department. Nonetheless, she worries that too many women these days are more interested in work than they are in their family, simply because they want to have more things. As a child of the Depression, Marion doesn't remember that being a bad time because "all the neighbors got together to help each other. At Christmas they would go into the basements of their homes to make the gifts. No one has time for families anymore."

Marion's connection to the war years was brought painfully home when her daughter died of cancer at the age of forty-three. She then knew the full force of losing a child, and she thought of all those parents whose sons didn't return from the war. She was middle-aged when her daughter died, and it was a difficult flashback to the time that was at once so exciting and so difficult.

ALISON CAMPBELL had a similar midlife challenge. Her husband left her when she was fifty-five. She had not worked since the war. "That experience made me fairly tough. I took unfamiliar steps then, and I could do it again." She was also reading Betty Friedan's seminal book on the place of modern women, *The Feminine Mystique*. It spoke directly to her own conflicted life. Here she was, a highly educated woman, and yet when she had to go back into the workplace she took secretarial classes because she was so stuck in the strictures of her generation.

She got a secretarial job, but she moved up steadily before retiring as a technical writer and editor for IBM. Now she volunteers at a women's center, where they often refer to her a new generation of women who suddenly find themselves alone. Alison shares her stories of the war years, the husband abroad, the midlife divorce, and the lessons she learned.

AFTER FIVE YEARS as a teacher, Scottie Lingelbach studied for a real estate license and started still another career. "The war made me self-reliant," she says. "I went to Washington not knowing anyone. My parents helped shape me. My father was very stern. He said, 'I'll educate you but then you're on your own.' When he gave me money to pay my way to officer's training, you can bet I had to pay it back."

Scottie stayed in real estate for eleven years, until the downturn in the eighties, but then she grew restless again and decided it was time to return to her origins. She moved to Lawrence, Kansas, where she had begun her adventurous life as a KU freshman in 1940. When she returned, the world had changed, but Scottie's values had not.

One of her daughters is divorced, a fact of modern life Scottie still finds unsettling. "Never did I realize it would happen in my family. Divorce was so uncommon." Not just uncommon, a bit of a scandal for Scottie's generation. That's not all that troubles her.

"What concerns me most about the future is the breakdown of the family. We were willing to make sacrifices so that I could stay home with the children. Now couples both work so they can be more affluent. We would rather delay gratification to ensure that our children had a nice home environment."

ALISON CAMPBELL SHARES similar sentiments. "During the war . . . we learned to deal with deprivations—rationing, being away from our husbands and families. I look at my daughter's generation and their big influence was television—and that's created a tremendous demand for material goods. My brother and I used to play and build things but my grandchildren don't build things, they only buy them!"

And there are other memories of that time when her life took a sharp turn from the conventions of her upbringing. She has an indelible photograph in her mind "of getting to the shipyard at seven A.M., when it was still dark in the west, and the stars would be out and there would be these giant cranes, which looked like dinosaurs against the sky, and sparks flying from the big machines." It was a daily reminder that her world of Oregon affluence and California graduate school was forever altered.

These days, Scottie keeps busy as a docent at the Spencer Museum on the KU campus and as a student at the Citizen Police Academy three nights a week. She's also started discussing her experiences as a WAVE with her grandchildren and with students at elementary and middle schools in the Lawrence area—about what America was like during World War II.

And when Scottie comes home at night after a trip to one of

those schools, or after a meeting of one of the committees she serves on at KU, or after a round of golf—she now rides nine holes and walks nine—she can, at the age of seventy-five, look back on a life of service and self-reliance, a life of strong values and of an unapologetic love of country.

When she goes into her modest kitchen in Lawrence, Scottie is reminded of that long-ago time when she began her life of service. When she was leaving the WAVES in 1945, the staff at the Joint Chiefs of Staff allowed her to take from the metallic war maps a handful of the tiny magnetic airplanes used to mark battles around the world. Then, they were symbols of terrible battles in distant places, of the powerful struggle to preserve freedom. Now, they keep in place on her refrigerator Scottie's reminders of what's coming up next in her long, rich life.

MARGARET RAY RINGENBERG

"My father said, 'I didn't get to serve and I don't have any boys, so I guess you'll have to do it.'"

ALL OF the military and political leaders of World War II were white males, sharing the attendant attitudes characteristic of their gender at the time. A woman's place was not in the military. A manpower shortage, however, and some clever visionary women forced them to correct their myopia.

A famous woman pilot of the era, Jacqueline Cochran, persuaded the legendary Army Air Corps general Henry "Hap" Arnold that if women were permitted to handle the domestic flying duties, he could send more male pilots into combat overseas. A few women were already working as military ferry pilots, shuttling planes from base to base or from factory to training site. General Arnold decided to expand the operation, so he authorized the formation of the WASPs, the Women's Air Force Service Pilots.

More than twenty-five thousand women applied, and the requirements were tough: candidates had to have a pilot's license and a minimum of two hundred hours in the cockpit. They had to pass rigorous physicals and submit to a series of interviews. In the end, only a thousand were assigned to Army Air Force bases around the country. They received their orders through the military chain of command but technically they were civilians, so when the war ended they received no veterans' benefits, even though thirty-eight of them died in the line of duty.

Margaret Ray, wartime portrait

Margaret Ray of Hoagland, Indiana, was an original WASP. She was raised on a farm but at the age of seven she had an experience that changed her life. "We were going for a ride south of Fort Wayne when we saw a small plane landing in a field. My dad was the curious type so we approached the pilot—and he offered us a ride. My mother said, 'No!' She was sure we were going to die but when we all crawled in, she did too. I remember the instruments on the panel. I was fascinated. I decided I had to fly but I thought I couldn't be a pilot because I was a girl, so I decided to become a stewardess."

When she graduated from high school, Maggie, as she was called, had a change of heart about being a stewardess because she didn't want to go through nurse's training, which was required for flight attendants. She went back to her original goal: to fly.

In 1940 she started taking lessons at the local airfield and earned her license by the time she was twenty-one, just in time for the Army Air Force to recruit her for the WASPs. "I was flabbergasted," she remembers. "What an opportunity. My father said, 'I didn't get to serve and I don't have any boys, so I guess you'll have to do it.'"

After six months of rigorous training in a wide variety of military aircraft in Sweetwater, Texas, Maggie was sent to Wilmington, Delaware, the 2nd Ferrying Division, assigned to testing and transporting the planes used to train young men for combat flying.

"I was a copilot on the bigger planes because I was only five foot five and you had to be five six to be a pilot on those. It was very exciting and very demanding. We worked seven days a week, sunup to sundown, but only when the weather was good because some of the planes didn't have radios yet. We'd fly a plane to Kansas, for example, turn right around and come back for a few hours of sleep before heading out again."

She piloted the PT-19, a single-engine, open cockpit training plane; the AT-6, an advanced training plane; and the C-45, a small passenger and light cargo plane; she copiloted the B-24 and the four-engine C-54. Many of the planes she flew were new designs, right off the assembly line. At first the male pilots didn't know what to think about this invasion of their territory.

Somehow word got around that these WASPs were a bunch of rich women who were taking the safer domestic flying jobs, forcing more men into the line of fire overseas. The latter half of the rumor was true, but these were no privileged princesses of the air. They were crack pilots and, at eighteen hundred dollars a year, they were underpaid as well as underappreciated.

Their missions were often dangerous. Some of the WASPs piloted radio-controlled low-target planes. They sat in the cockpit while a mother ship guided the target plane through a series of low-level maneuvers by radio control. If the radio signals failed, they were there to take the controls. Other WASPs towed practice targets for antiaircraft batteries and airborne gunners to shoot at, and more than once a WASP pilot returned to the base with more bullet holes in her plane than in the target.

Maggie had a harrowing experience ferrying a worn-out plane to the boneyard, a remote airfield where aircraft with too many hours on them were parked. She lost an engine and radioed her superiors with the information. She was told to get out, to parachute to safety. Maggie knew getting out of that cockpit was a difficult proposition, and besides she was confident she could nurse the plane down. It was a tense but successful landing. Everyone was full of praise except the commanding officer who had ordered her to jump. He chewed her out for not following his orders.

When a WASP died in the line of duty, there were no military honors, even though they were performing vital and dangerous military assignments. As civilians they did have the option of resigning, but few did. In fact more than nine hundred were still flying when the Army decided in December 1944 that it no longer needed their services. The combat ranks were full and the manufacturing of new military aircraft was dropping off. The WASPs were told to go home.

Maggie couldn't believe what was happening to her. "Here I was, this farm girl with this new life, and it was so exciting. And now I'm going home knowing all of my girlfriends have married or moved away. During the war I had more in common with the guys than with the girls who were getting their hope chests ready."

She was determined to keep flying. She decided to get her flight instructor's rating. "I thought, 'I have all this military experience. I'll start teaching.' Well, I got my instructor's license, but who wanted to take flying lessons from a girl? No one!" Instead she took

Margaret Ray and other WASPs

Margaret Ray

a desk job at the local airfield, worked on the sidelines directing and fueling planes, and waited for her chance.

"If a flight instructor didn't show up I'd give the lesson. Once I got them in my plane I usually kept them. My method was different than the men. In the early days it was a rough business. Men used a lot of swear words and intimidated the students. My idea was to tell you what to do and let you do the best you can. It's sort of a mother's instinct."

It was also very successful. Marvin Berger was also a pilot by the time he signed up with Maggie for instrument training. "She lets you fly the plane," he says, "and when you think you're doing pretty well she'll say simply, 'What are you doing?' That's a wake-up call. She never took the wheel from me but she never let me get in trouble."

Maggie did have one final World War II experience before going full throttle into her civilian flying and teaching life. She was at her desk job in August 1945 when the local radio station called to say it appeared that Japan was about to surrender. The local newspaper was on strike and people weren't near their radios during the day, so the enterprising station had an idea: a news drop, so to speak. It hurriedly printed up thousands of leaflets with the news of the impending surrender and hired Margaret to drop them over Fort Wayne. "I got to fly right over Main Street," she says. "Over the factories. I was flying real low—at only about a hundred feet, almost below the tops of some of the buildings." It must have been some sight in that small Indiana community. A small plane piloted by a woman at treetop level, papering the town with the news that the war was over.

That memorable flight was just the beginning of another life and another aviation career for Maggie. The following year, even though she hadn't paid much attention to her hope chest, she was married to a local banker, Morris Ringenberg, a veteran of the combat Army Corps of Engineers in World War II. They settled into a comfortable life in Grabill, a small town in the middle of Amish country just north of Fort Wayne. They raised a daughter and a son. They also had a compact: whenever he wanted to go golfing, she didn't complain. Whenever she wanted to go flying, he didn't complain. She also changed from Maggie to Margaret, explaining, "I thought it was more dignified for a banker's wife"—one of her few concessions to convention.

In the mid-fifties she discovered a new dimension to her flying: the Powder Puff Derby, a cross-country air race for women pilots. For the next twenty years she was a competitor in the Derby, later named the Classic Air Race. She won it in 1988 and finished second six times. That was a warm-up for her big race.

In 1994 Margaret Ringenberg, the former farm girl who fell in love with flying at the age of seven and learned in the WASPs that she could hold her own against the best of the best, decided to compete in a race around the world. Twenty-four days in a small, twin-engine plane, a Cessna 340, more than a hundred hours in the air. She was seventy-two years old at the time, the oldest entrant.

Her daughter, Marsha, had grown up with her mother in the cockpit. "I just accepted it as normal. When I flew with her I read comic books in the back. But later, when people began making a fuss over her, I thought, 'Maybe this is a big deal.'" Then Marsha saw the plane her mother would pilot around the world. "My heart just dropped. I thought, how could she go around the globe in such a tiny plane?"

Margaret remembers the consternation among her family members, including her ten-year-old granddaughter's getting everyone in her Sunday-school class to pray for her. She wasn't worried. By then she had more than forty thousand hours in a cockpit. "A lot of sitting" is her understated way of describing that estimable record. The 'round-the-world race went off without a hitch. She didn't win, but then she wasn't in it for the trophy. She has a roomful of those already, testimony to her place as one of the most skilled and experienced small-plane pilots in the world today.

When she flies out of the Fort Wayne airport, the flight controllers take an almost reverential tone when speaking with her. "Notice the difference?" she asks. "I think they talk different to a woman pilot." She's at the controls of her single-engine Cherokee and we're going for a short ride over the prosperous Indiana countryside. For my part, I think they use a different tone of voice for her too. I notice they call her "Mrs. Ringenberg."

In the cockpit, Margaret settles her matronly figure comfortably into the small seat and her eyes run easily over the control panel.

This is where she belongs. She crooks one hand behind the yoke, or steering wheel, of the small plane and guides it up to twenty-five hundred feet, then lets me take over for a short lesson in the Margaret Ringenberg school of flying. I try to keep the plane headed in a straight line and at a level altitude as we look down on the large, new homes and golf courses that have replaced the farmland where her father struggled to make a living while working in the nearby GE factory. Her instructions are specific but parenthetical: "Yes, I never thought I'd see so many houses here—you're drifting left a bit, try to get back to a zero reading; use a light touch. Good. Oh, look, there's Smith Field, where I soloed more than fifty years ago." Actually, it was almost sixty years ago, but as she looks down at the small airstrip she says she can almost see herself taking off on that memorable day that changed her life.

Her passion about flying is matched by her generous ways. A Fort Wayne friend remembers how she flew him to the Mayo Clinic in Rochester, Minnesota, several times so he could be treated for cancer. "She was upset that I even tried to pay her," he says. She's a family friend of former Vice President Dan Quayle and flew him around Indiana during his first campaign for the Senate.

These days she's come to appreciate her standing as a role model for young women. She's especially proud of the women pilots in the military. They're still trying to work up to full-combat roles, of course, but the women of the WASPs were not even treated as veterans until an act of Congress changed that in 1979. It wasn't until 1984 that the surviving WASPs were awarded medals signifying their participation in the war effort. Margaret follows the place of women in the military and she's convinced they could hold their own in the combat flying of high-performance jet fighters.

For her part, Margaret was so hurt by the abrupt way her service ended, as she put it, "I came home and put all of my WASP stuff in the back of the closet." Then she was asked to represent the WASPs in a Fort Wayne Memorial Day parade. It reawakened the old pride. Now she gives motivational speeches at the Air Force Academy and serves on a scholarship committee for low-income female Academy cadets. It's a little late, of course, but she says, "Oh, how I would love to be a cadet at the Air Force Academy."

She also works with Indiana schools on giving youngsters direction in their lives. It's a stark contrast, the difference between her generation and this one. "A few months ago I went with an eighth-grade class to the airport. I showed them around the hangar and talked about flying. On the way back to the car I thought, 'Oh, why am I doing this? It takes so much time.' Then on the car radio I heard the news about that school shooting in Arkansas. I realized if I could just reach one child it's worth it." Margaret puts it in perspective. "Everything that happened in my life came from one phone call from the Army. I can't believe what an opportunity I had as a twenty-one-year-old who loved to fly. I was from the country, but going into the service I found I could keep up with others."

Mary Louise Roberts (left) and fellow nurses, Anzio, 1944

MARY LOUISE ROBERTS WILSON

"I don't much like tents anymore."

THERE ARE SO MANY impressive numbers connected to World War II that it's difficult for one or two to catch your eye. Here are a few that caught me by surprise: more than sixty thousand women served in the Army Nurse Corps. Sixteen died as a result of enemy action. Sixty-seven nurses were taken prisoner of war. More than sixteen hundred were decorated for bravery under fire or for meritorious service.

One of them was Mary Louise Roberts, who was a long way from her Mississippi childhood the day German shells started ripping through the operating tent on the Anzio beachhead in Italy where she was working to save young American lives. But then her life never had been easy.

Mary Louise had just graduated from high school in 1930 when her father died, leaving behind Mary Louise, her five younger siblings, and their thirty-four-year-old mother. The Depression was setting in and the Roberts family had no money, so the family moved from Texas back to Mississippi to be near their grandparents. Mary Louise, a precocious child, graduated from high school early and went to work in a laundry. When the owners discovered she was just sixteen, however, they let her go. The family couldn't lose the income, so her mother took the job and Mary Louise stayed at home to care for her brothers and sisters.

Two years later, Mary Louise entered the nurse's training program at Hillman Hospital in Birmingham, Alabama. "I really wanted to do something to help my family," she says. "I didn't have any aspirations to be a nurse—I just needed to make a living for my family." She was just eighteen.

After graduating, Mary Louise worked at several hospitals in the South before landing a job at Dallas's big Methodist Hospital. After a year she was promoted to operating room supervisor. It was 1941. By then one of her brothers was in the military and two of her siblings had died from childhood diseases. She invited her remaining family—her mother, a brother, and a sister—to live with her in a one-bedroom apartment in Dallas. Mary Louise supported them all on her eighty-five-dollar-a-month salary. That's twenty-one dollars a week for four people.

Mary Louise admits it wasn't easy, but she credits her mother's frugality and the family's willingess to share for their survival. In those difficult times that was the code of survival for an untold number of other families across America. Everyone in the family tried to earn something and they all shared it, however little it might have been.

When the United States entered the war, there was an obvious and urgent need for people who could treat the wounded and comfort the afflicted. Mary Louise Roberts volunteered. "I guess it was a matter of wanting to do my part," she says. "I thought it was my patriotic duty to do it. I know it sounds corny because there's not much of that feeling anymore."

Because of her age—she was almost thirty when she enlisted—and her experience, Mary Louise was made the operating room supervisor with the Army's 56th Evacuation Unit. She trained in Louisiana and Texas for surgery under wholly new conditions—in the field and in combat. By Easter Sunday, 1943, she was ashore at Casablanca and assigned to follow the 36th, 88th, and 91st infantry divisions of the Fifth Army.

The women of the Army Nurse Corps wore helmets, fatigues, and boots. They lived in tents, used latrines, and had to guard their privacy constantly. They were often targets for air raids, and yet they were almost always thought of as girls out of place.

One of them, June Wandrey, wrote lively, newsy letters home regularly and later had them published under the title *Bedpan*

Three Army Nurse Corps officers presented with Silver Star decorations for heroism (left to right): Mary L. Roberts, Elaine A. Roe, Rita Virginia Rourke

Surgery at Nocelleto: Mary Roberts, second from left

Commando, the derisive nickname a male soldier had shouted at her. In it she describes several occasions when drunken soldiers invaded the nurses' private space. On one occasion, near the front lines, a German soldier wandered into their latrine. He was gone by the time they summoned help.

Fighting in North Africa was intense but it was only an overture for what lay ahead: Anzio, the beginning of the mainland invasion of Europe from the south. Mary Louise Roberts and her medical unit landed five days after the invasion. It was still a combat hot zone. She remembers, "At one point our commanding officer got the nurses together and asked whether we wanted to be evacuated. It was pretty bad, but we decided if the infantry was going to stay, we were going to stay." She also remembers a male officer who was eager to get the hell off the Anzio beachhead. "But he said there was no way he was going to leave until at least one nurse agreed to go—so he stayed, too."

It was a brave decision. The war was all around them and the workload was draining. "We got patients straight from the battlefield," she remembers. The men were terribly wounded, bloody, and dirty. "In the course of the day we had twelve-hour shifts and eight operating tables, with teams assigned to each table. We had all kinds of injuries, from neurosurgery on down. But there were times when I thought, 'How long can this go on?'"

In one of her letters home, June Wandrey, the proud bedpan commando, wrote from "Somewhere in Italy. . . . I am too busy and too tired to write but we must keep in contact; it's all that keeps me sane. We're working twelve to fifteen hours a day now, never sitting down except to eat." Then she describes her ward, filled with

such young soldiers . . . nineteen years old. . . . They're so patient and they never complain. I won't be able to write . . . often and here are the reasons why:

• Bed 6, penetrating wound of the left flank, penetrating wound face, fractured mandible, penetrating wound left forearm.

• Bed 5, amputation right leg, penetrating wound left leg, lacerating wound of chest, lacerating wound right hand.

• Bed 4, massive penetrating wound of abdomen. Expired.

THE GREATEST GENERATION / 177

She ended another letter home, after describing a long, terrifying night trying to hook up with her hospital unit on the front lines
of the march to Rome, by saying, "This field-nurse business is not
for the faint of heart."

There was another role for the women of the Nurse Corps. They
were surrogate mothers. Wandrey writes of working in a shock
ward in Sicily and seeing an eighteen-year-old who was just
brought in from the ambulance. "I went to him immediately," she
said. "He looked up at me trustingly, sighed, and asked, 'How am I
doing, nurse?' I was standing at the head of his litter. I put my
hands around his face, kissed his forehead, and said, 'You're doing
just fine, soldier.' He smiled sweetly and said, 'I was just checking
up.' Then he died.

"Many of us shed tears in private," she continued. "Otherwise
we try to be cheerful and reassuring." She said she saw doctors
working for hours only to have their young patients die on the
table. "Some doctors," she said, "even collapsed across the patient,
broke down, and cried."

The nurses were not immune to death, of course. All of the
nurses were traumatized by the death of one of their own, Ellen
Ainsworth, killed by a German artillery shell—one of six nurses to
die at Anzio. Mary Louise said they were all tempted to begin to
think, " 'It could be me,' but then in the heat of battle you don't
really have time to mull things over." On February 10, 1944, the
heat of battle was very hot.

As Mary Louise Roberts supervised several operations under
way, German shrapnel started ripping through their surgical tent.
She says, "We had patients on the table and we wanted to at least
get them off. I said something like, 'Maybe we can keep going before this gets to be too bad.' It went on for thirty minutes or so. We
just kept on working." Her superiors were so impressed with her
coolness and inspirational personal conduct they recommended
her for the coveted Silver Star.

Mary Louise and two other nurses were awarded the medal, but
because she had senior rank she went forward first and thus became the first woman to win the Silver Star. It was, she says, not
an auspicious occasion. "We went to the ceremony in our operating clothes. It took twenty minutes. It was a quickie because we

were needed back at work. Certainly I am proud of it, but others deserve credit, too. Everybody in our group deserved the medal." That's another common reaction from the World War II generation. Those who won medals often say, "I didn't *win* the medal. I just accepted it for all who deserved it."

Later, Mary Louise would also say of that particularly harrowing day, in her understated fashion, "I don't much like tents anymore."

Her unit advanced north through Italy, following the Fifth Army, setting up operating facilities, repairing the wounded, or when they were severely wounded, patching them up enough so they could be transported to more sophisticated medical facilities. Mary Louise remembers the day the good news came. She was in Bologna, Italy. "We had just set up and we were treating patients when we got word the war in Europe was over. Oh, Lord, everyone was so excited. I thought I'd be glad to get home and get a bath, a long, uninterrupted bath."

Her sense of duty had kept her overseas for twenty-nine months, and she says during that time her unit treated 77,025 patients. Mary Louise isn't the first or last veteran of those days to say, "I wouldn't trade it for a million dollars but I wouldn't give you two cents for another day of it. I learned an awful lot about people and how they react under pressure. The war gave me an appreciation for life."

She returned to Dallas in October 1945, and by January the following year she was back at the familiar post as operating room supervisor, this time at the Veterans Administration hospital. She went back to school at the University of Texas medical school and got a degree in nursing service administration. The VA wanted to promote her to a chief nurse's position but she wasn't interested. She wanted to stay in the operating room.

In 1961, at the age of forty-six, she married another veteran, Willie Ray Wilson, a pilot with the 9th Artillery Corps during World War II, assigned to ferrying high-ranking officers from headquarters to the battlefield and back. Wilson, a computer programmer after the war, had three children from an earlier marriage.

Mary Louise Roberts Wilson, who got into nursing to send money to her family, came to love the profession for the opportunity it provided to care for others, but she retained the lessons of those difficult early years. She stayed with the VA because the chances of promotion were excellent and it had a substantial pension program. She also joined the Army Reserves and served as chief nurse for the 94th General Hospital unit, retiring as a lieutenant colonel.

She keeps her Silver Star in the bottom of a cedar chest, rarely bothering to take it out. Since her husband died in 1993 she's tried to keep busy with Bible studies, church, reading programs for children of Spanish-speaking families, and an art-appreciation course at a local junior college. Mary Louise, who had to be so tough so many times in her long life, now admits that in her eighties, with her husband gone, her nights can be "awfully lonely."

She remains a taciturn woman, tempered by her difficult childhood and the ordeal of combat nursing duty. She doesn't volunteer much when asked to reflect on her life and all that she's seen and done. She simply says, "In some ways I feel I accomplished a great deal. In other ways I feel I've done nothing. I really don't have anything to show for it. I am just an ordinary person."

An ordinary person who as a teenager supported her family, became a highly skilled nurse, won the Silver Star, and lived an exemplary life. In her modesty she typifies so many women of her generation.

SHAME

The World War II years will forever be testimony to America's collective and individual resistance to tyranny, its awesome and ingenious industrial machinery, and what may be its greatest strength, the common values of its richly varied population when faced with a common threat. Any celebration of America's strengths and qualities during those years of courage and sacrifice, however, will be tempered by the stains of racism that were pervasive in practice and in policy. As it was an era of great glory for America and its people, it was also, indisputably, a time of shame.

One does not cancel out the other, but any accounting of the war years is incomplete without the stories of those who were serving their country while fighting to protect their individual rights and dignity. What they experienced would be shocking enough if the acts of prejudice had been simply the work of a few misguided bigots, but the most shameful acts of discrimination and oppression were officially sanctioned by the highest officials in the land.

Black Americans were called Negroes or Colored in polite company and official documents, but the hateful epithet *nigger* was a common expression, even when referring to black Americans in uniform. They had few champions of racial equality outside their own ranks. Eleanor Roosevelt spoke up for them, but her husband, the president, the great champion of the common man, was mostly quiet on the subject.

Japanese Americans were subjected to even greater discrimination during the war. Their fundamental rights were swept aside in a campaign organized by some of the most distinguished figures in public life. The relocation of Japanese American citizens from their homes and businesses on the West Coast was upheld by the U.S. Supreme Court in the name of military security. In a contemporary review of that decision, the current chief justice, William Rehnquist, concludes that civil liberties are not expected to have the same standing in wartime as they do in peacetime, but he does believe the courts in the future will review more carefully the government's arguments for curtailing fundamental rights.

Past practices and court decisions aside, the most compelling arguments against the wartime racism and official acts canceling civil liberties can be found in the lives and attitudes of the people who were the victims of those shameful episodes.

MARTHA SETTLE PUTNEY

"I knew when World War II approached it would be a terrible thing, but afterward I was so grateful. . . . It provided opportunity."

THE FACES OF AMERICAN WOMEN in the thirties ranged from the classic Yankee beauty of Katharine Hepburn, the strong-willed movie star, to the haunting, defeated expressions of the migrant worker mother in Dorothea Lange's photographs documenting the terrible toll of the Great Depression. There are, however, very few black women in our album of memories. Lena Horne, yes, but her beauty and talent were so blinding she seemed to occupy a universe of her own.

Imagine, then, the world of Martha Settle Putney, now a retired history professor after a distinguished teaching career at Bowie State and Howard universities, the latter her alma mater. In the thirties, Martha was one of eight children of Oliver and Ida Settle; she was an ambitious young black woman in Norristown, Pennsylvania, an industrial town where most black women could find work only as domestics. That was not for her, but how to find a way out?

Her county was a Republican stronghold even during the height of FDR's popularity, so when she heard a Republican candidate for Congress speak, she offered to help him get out the vote of the black community. She kept her word, but she didn't tell her political patrons she wasn't voting Republican. She was for President Roosevelt and for Martha Settle. Nonetheless, when the Republican congressman got to Washington, he agreed to help her get an academic scholarship to Howard University.

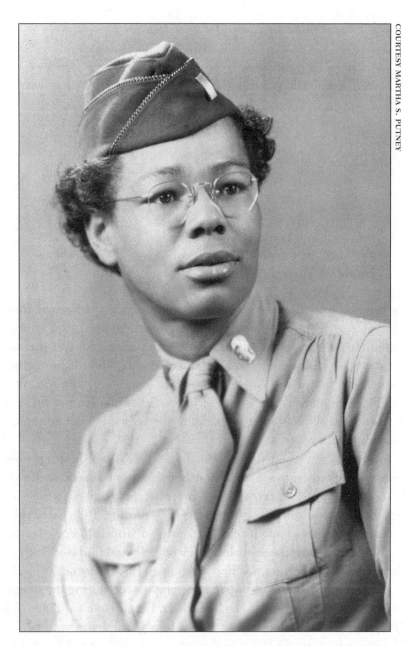

Martha Settle in WAC uniform

Martha earned a master's degree in history and applied for a teaching job in Washington, D.C. She says political cronyism dominated the school system, however, so she went to work as a statistical clerk for the War Manpower Commission, where she quickly encountered the institutional racism endemic to the nation's capital in those days. So, in frustration, she resigned and volunteered for the newly formed Women's Auxiliary Corps—the WACs, women in the Army.

It was not an idle choice. As a student of history, Martha understood that the war "was the turning point of the century. When it was over the world would change. And I wanted to profit from it." She also wanted to be an officer and told the WAC official she would accept nothing less than a commission. It was an elite group: the Army had agreed to recruit blacks, but no more than their representation in the population. In other words, a quota. Forty black women were selected after they had been personally approved by Mary McLeod Bethune, the founding president of Bethune-Cookman College and the formidable president of the National Council of Negro Women.

Bethune was a friend of Eleanor Roosevelt and she saw the WACs as a great opportunity for young black women. Through the war she closely monitored what she called "my WACs," especially when it came to racial slights and worse.

Martha Settle was exactly the kind of young black woman Bethune had in mind, and after a six-week training course she was shipped off to Des Moines with her new lieutenant's bars.

She helped train women recruits, but her duties were confined to teaching calisthenics and drills, the kinds of assignments reserved for blacks. There were other forms of discrimination, some shocking even during that time of racial apartheid in America.

Martha remembers to this day the anger she felt when a group of German officers, who were POWs at a garrison in the Des Moines area, were invited into the Fort Des Moines officers' club while the black officers were barred. She also remembers there was nothing she could do about it.

Black musicians were routinely banned from the base band, so they formed their own—maybe the first all-black, all-female military band in the world. Martha recalls that Army officials in Washington sent word to Des Moines: "We don't need two base bands. Get rid of the black band." Martha, who normally kept her objections in race matters to herself, raised the band issue with her superior officer, although she acknowledges now that she did it in a low-key way since it might have jeopardized her chances for promotion. Others got involved as well, including the musicians' guilds, and eventually word reached the White House and Eleanor Roosevelt. Not long after, the black band was back in business.

Martha does believe she was personally responsible for the integration of the base swimming pool. Black WACs were to swim on Fridays only but Martha says, "After every Friday they would clean the pool! It didn't make me angry because I expected it." All of the units at the base were segregated by color except one. It was made up of recruits who were struggling with basic training and it contained a half dozen black women. Since the swimming schedule was organized by unit, Martha saw her chance. She took the black recruits aside and said, "Swim with your unit." After that, she says, "The pool rules became more relaxed and people more or less swam when they wanted to. I don't know if that would have happened at the men's camp. I think the women had a little more fellowship."

That was never more clear to Martha than when she applied for additional specialized training. She wanted to avoid the plight of most blacks, being sent to the "unassigned pool," which generally meant menial tasks. So she asked for and received permission to go to the Army's adjutant general school to train as an executive officer or administrative commander.

En route to her new assignment in Texas, it was clear that other passengers on the train didn't want to share their car with a black woman, but Dr. Putney remembers how her fellow officers, all white, rallied to her side, making sure they sat in the same car with her all the way to Houston. Later, as she was returning from Texas to the Midwest, there was a much uglier incident.

The train conductor refused to accept her Pullman car tickets and directed her to a freight car at the rear of the train. She protested but then started for the rear before deciding, "No, I won't do this." She stood between two cars, refusing to move. The conductor, quite angry now, called the Military Police. Dr. Putney

Martha Settle Putney

chuckles now when she remembers that when the two MPs arrived, they saw her lieutenant's rank and saluted her as the conductor watched, astonished. She was courteously escorted back to the base, where other officers hurriedly arranged for her to make the trip to Chicago and her new assignment in a military plane. She was heading for what she called "choice assignment," the Women's Army Corps Hospital in Chicago. Before she could begin work, however, she had to endure yet another uncomfortable round of discrimination.

Her all-black unit of medical technicians was to be housed near Gardner General Hospital, not too far from Chicago's tony Lake Shore Drive. The Army had built a barracks for the WACs, but several local residents protested. They wrote city officials, demanding that black WACs be moved to another neighorhood. Local civil rights organizations heard about the protests and sent word to the War Department in Washington not to buckle. Dr. Putney remembers it took the War Department a while to do the right thing, and when it did, it said, in effect, "We'll send you to that neighborhood, but if anything happens, we'll move you out of there."

Lieutenant Settle spent the rest of the war supervising medical technicians at the hospital with no difficulties. It was an assignment that she remembers with pride to this day.

After the war Martha returned to her old assignment as a statistical clerk with the Manpower Commission, work that is now a part of the Labor Department. She met her husband, Bill Putney, in Washington and they were married in 1947. They had one child, Bill Jr., now a product engineer with Ford in Detroit. Her husband died in 1965.

By then Martha's ambitious intellect had kicked in again, this time prompting her to take advantage of the GI Bill and enroll in a doctoral program in history at the University of Pennsylvania. She earned her PhD in European history and was hired by Bowie State College, a mostly black institution in Maryland.

She stayed for sixteen years and then went on the faculty at Howard for another nine years. Martha attributes her success in life to the opportunities she would not have had without the war. "I knew when World War II approached it would be a terrible thing, but afterward I was so grateful. . . . It provided opportunity. The army has a way of teaching personnel, and it sticks. At Bowie they had a book on teachers the students passed around. Under my name it said, 'Don't take her unless you want to study.' "

Dr. Clifford Muse, Jr., now a professor at Howard, did his graduate work under Dr. Putney, an experience he remembers well. "She worked me to death. I really learned from her. She tried to prepare you for discrimination in the sense you had to be very good to be accepted." In fact, that was how Dr. Putney had always dealt with discrimination, and she was determined to pass along to all of her students the lessons of her own life.

William Missouri, another former student, recalled, "I was in Dr. Putney's African American history class and, let me tell you, it was tough." Missouri, now a circuit judge in Maryland, dreaded the days he arrived in class unprepared. "She would bring you up short in front of the class. She wouldn't chastise you, but she'd say, 'How can you be an African American and not *want* to learn African American history?'

"She'd say, 'Work hard. If you fail, don't look around for others to blame. Look in the mirror. You have to accept responsibility for your own life.' " When Dr. Putney did discuss her military experience it was always in that context: she felt she had to do extra well because she was so conscious that she was representing other black women with her success. In her conversations with Dr. Muse, Judge Missouri, and her other students, she used her life during World War II as a teaching tool for them.

Since retiring from Howard, Dr. Putney has been volunteering at the Smithsonian and working on her histories of the role of blacks in the armed forces. She's already written *When the Nation Was in Need: Blacks in the Women's Army Corps During World War II*. She's also been working on a history of blacks in combat from the Revolutionary War through Operation Desert Storm.

For all of the changes she's witnessed, for all of the successes she's enjoyed personally, Dr. Putney is saddened by the recent turn against affirmative action in California and other states. She knows what can happen when government programs provide opportunity. "We still have honor in America within a basic core of people. . . . But you can't make all people [share that sense of] honor unless you respect them. If you push them around they're not going to respond."

She's persuaded she was accepted for graduate work at the University of Pennsylvania because of her whole life, including the military, and not just because of how well she performed on tests. Dr. Putney is convinced more emphasis must be placed on essays and backgrounds rather than SAT scores for college admission or the situation will not change much.

Dr. Putney and her husband were in Washington the day Dr. Martin Luther King, Jr., made his "I Have a Dream" speech. "I really thought it was going to be a new day after that. There has been a lot of progress but I have been disappointed. People need to be accepted on their merits and their character. Not everyone gets the same opportunity."

Martha Settle, a working-class black female from a tough town in Pennsylvania, didn't have affirmative action when she was coming of age. She had a national crisis in which the need for the bright and able was so great she could take advantage of opportunities that would not have been available otherwise. Racism was still the order of the day, but it gave way just enough for Dr. Martha Settle Putney to remind everyone that the premise was false and the consequences were unworthy.

JOHNNIE HOLMES

"It is my country right or wrong. . . . None of us can ever contribute enough."

JOHNNIE HOLMES was born in Ohio in 1921, but his family moved to the Chicago area after a few years because there was, well, opportunity: an aunt was involved in the Al Capone bootlegging empire and Johnnie's father could get a job as a driver and deliveryman.

They settled in the suburbs, in Evanston, home of Northwestern University, and life was good. His father had steady work and Johnnie, one of the few black students in Evanston High School, has no memory of any racial discrimination.

At an early age he became enthralled with the military way of life. For a time he even considered joining the French Foreign Legion. So by the time the United States was attacked at Pearl Harbor it had a ready volunteer in Johnnie Holmes, even though the U.S. military was hardly friendly territory for black Americans.

It's not that black Americans were not represented numerically. There were 1.2 million in uniform during the war, almost 10 percent of America's black population at the time. Most were confined to the service areas of the military, however. They were ship's stewards or worked in the quartermaster corps or served as drivers for transportation outfits. Ten percent saw combat. Those who did had distinguished records, but the myths remained. The military establishment was reluctant to acknowledge that black Americans were fully capable of taking their place in the front ranks.

Johnnie Holmes, wartime portrait

Holmes was blissfully unaware of what awaited him. As he put it, "I went into the Army to become a man. I told my momma, 'I'm not going to let it break me. I'm going to let it make me.'"

He began his military career at Fort Custer in Michigan but it wasn't until he shipped out to Fort Knox, Kentucky, that he encountered real, bitter racial hatred and segregation for the first time. All of the noncommissioned officers were white southerners, as Holmes remembers it, and they made the trials of basic training all the more difficult for the all-black outfits. Among other indignities, Holmes is persuaded that Fort Knox dentists experimented on the black soldiers. He remembers being strapped in a dentist chair and getting his teeth drilled with no novocaine.

At the end of basic, Holmes was sent on to Camp Claiborne, Louisiana, to begin his training as a tanker. By now Holmes and the other black soldiers had weekend passes, but even though they wore the uniform of the United States Army and even though they were prepared to give their lives in defense of their country and for the cause of freedom and against the fascist juggernaut rolling across Europe, the racial wounds deepened. Whenever they accidentally strayed into all-white neighborhoods they were met with anger and derision: "Hey, boy, what you doin' here? Git outta here, nigger."

When a black soldier friend of Holmes's was found dead on railroad tracks near an all-white neighborhood in Alexandria, the other black soldiers were not fooled by the official story that he'd gotten drunk, stumbled onto the tracks, and been run over by a train. They were sure he'd been beaten to death, and they were furious. They were by now combat-trained and they were prepared to go to war against Alexandria. They rounded up their tanks, machine guns, and grenades, but Colonel Steele, their commanding officer, reasoned with them and they backed off.

It wasn't long, however, before there was another racial flare-up, this one at the PX. A black soldier was cheated at the cash register by a white clerk. When the soldier protested, racial slurs started flying, and again the Louisiana base was at a racial flashpoint. Holmes recalls with pride that not long after that the PX staff was integrated.

If anything, life as a black soldier became even more intolerable when Johnnie Holmes and his units transferred to Fort Hood,

Texas, to begin the final phase of their preparation as an armored unit. Fort Hood was also home to a stockade full of German prisoners of war. It is one of the little-remembered curiosities of World War II that German and Italian prisoners were often shipped to remote places in the American West to await the end of the war, with more comforts than they would have had at home.

Johnnie Holmes remembers, however, just as Martha Putney remembers. He remembers the German POWs were allowed to go to the PX when Holmes and his friends could not. He remembers white officers saying, "If you boys don't behave we'll have those Germans guard you." What he remembers most of all was an incident involving his platoon lieutenant, a recent graduate of UCLA, where he had starred in three sports. His name was Jackie Robinson.

One weekend Holmes, Robinson, and some of their friends went to Temple, Texas, on a weekend pass. They weren't in town long before Holmes felt a piercing pain in his chest. He didn't know it at the time but it was pleurisy, an inflammation of the thorax membranes that can be debilitating. He could barely walk.

Lieutenant Robinson helped his young soldier onto a bus headed back to the base, stretching him across the front row of bus seats. The white driver would have none of it, telling Robinson to get Holmes to the back of the bus and get there himself. As Holmes remembers it, Robinson said no, he would not move Holmes to the back of the bus and he sure wasn't going there himself. Holmes recalls that they were arrested by MPs back at the base. I was unable to find references to this in biographies of Jackie Robinson, but given the time and place, it may have been too common to warrant attention.

In many other accounts of his life, another Robinson bus incident involved a light-skinned black woman who was the wife of a fellow officer. When Robinson was told by the bus driver to stop talking to her and move back, Robinson refused and was court-martialed. He was subsequently found not guilty and left the service not long after, suffering from bone chips in his ankle from his college playing days.

Holmes and his fellow black tankers shipped out for Europe as the 761st Tank Battalion. They were quickly in the thick of battle in the final drive across Europe toward the heart of Germany.

Johnnie Holmes

Johnnie Holmes, with 761st Tank Battalion

They were in combat for 183 straight days, including the worst of the Battle of the Bulge, the ferocious fight through the winter of 1944–45 in the forests of Belgium. They were praised by General Patton and the other commanders of the infantry units they were supporting, but they could not fully escape the racial insults, not even there. Holmes remembers coming back from battles, their tanks battered and bloodied by the loss of their comrades, and hearing white soldiers tell Belgian villagers, "Those niggers ain't up there. They're just bringing the tanks up for the white boys to use."

In fact, Holmes and the others in the 761st were face-to-face with death every day. One of Holmes's chilling memories is running through the woods, on attack, when he spotted a German sniper. He opened fire, killing the sniper immediately, realizing that if he had not seen him, just by chance, Holmes would have been shot in the back as he ran past.

There was a widespread belief that the black soldiers weren't up to the job. Dale Wilson, a retired Army major and now a military historian, said, "The African American was fighting a war on two fronts. He was fighting racism at home—Jim Crow, segregation—and he was fighting for the opportunity to fight. . . . Here's a guy who has to beg to get into combat."

General George S. Patton became a hero to the black tankers when he appeared before the 761st. Holmes thought he was "the most dashing thing you ever saw—standing on a half-track with those two pearl-handled pistols." Patton said something to the effect of "You guys are a credit to your race. You're here because I asked for the best. Now go out there and kick some Kraut ass." Yet there's also evidence that Patton had his private doubts about the ability of blacks to perform as well as whites in the military.

The record of the 761st, however, was exemplary. Those black soldiers earned 8 Silver Stars, 62 Bronze Stars, and 296 Purple Hearts, according to Trezzvant W. Anderson's book *Come Out Fighting: The Epic Tale of the 761st Tank Battalion, 1942–1945*. The historian Dale Wilson has no doubt about the effectiveness of the 761st. "This unit saw action with eight divisions, so it was making a significant contribution during the war. It performed in an outstanding manner. I think there are clear-cut cases where guys should have been recognized, if not with an award he didn't receive, then with a higher award than what was given."

Doubts about the fighting ability of the black soldiers were not confined to the American side. Holmes remembers vividly a conversation with a German prisoner of war, a Nazi major who had been born in Chicago before returning to the fatherland. The major, stunned when he saw Holmes, a black man in uniform, said, "What are you doing here? This is a white man's war."

Holmes and his buddies thought otherwise. They thought it was America's war. One of the veterans of the 761st said more than fifty years later, "When you get over there and the nation's in trouble you ain't got no black and white. You only got America." A simple and profound declaration from a man who, before he went into combat, trained at bases in American communities where the water fountains and toilets said WHITES ONLY.

Holmes's daughter, Anita Berlanga, a Chicago businesswoman, has a different set of sensibilities about discrimination, and she still finds it hard to believe what her father went through. What saddens her most is that racism probably kept him from pursuing a legal career or a career as an artist after the war. As she says, "I learned from my father . . . how ridiculously hypocritical this country is. They took good, honest men and treated them poorly before and after the war."

They haven't talked about it much but Berlanga says, "I don't know what my father's real expectations were but there was this sense of bafflement: 'Why couldn't I have done that?' The war gave him a sense, for the first time, of what he could do. He was given a job to do and he did it extraordinarily well. Then to come back and find out that didn't count—that was disappointing, but he kept going. He believed in the essential goodness of man, so coming home to racism was disheartening to him."

In the rage of combat Holmes often made a deal with God: Get me out of this and I will be a better, decent person. God didn't have to worry about Johnnie Holmes, but he might have spent a little more time with some of the people who were back in Chicago, far from the front lines. One of them was working at the Foot Brothers factory when Holmes went looking for work, now a twenty-five-year-old battle-scarred veteran, down to ninety-eight pounds as a result of lingering problems from injuries suffered when he was hit by shrapnel from land mines. It was Johnnie Holmes's first stop after getting out of uniform. As soon as he entered the office, he remembers vividly to this day, the woman in charge of hiring looked up and said, "What are you doing here? We don't hire niggers. Get outta here."

Welcome home, Sergeant Holmes.

Shortly after that, however, he heard about a company that maybe had openings for machinists. He went early the next morning and was startled to find a black personnel director at Doehler Jarvis Corporation. Holmes had never seen a black man in a white-collar job. The personnel director said he didn't have anything at the moment but that Holmes should leave an application and he'd get a call if a job opened up. Johnnie didn't leave it to chance. He showed up early again the next morning and again the morning after that, politely refusing to accept the personnel man's assurance that he would call when a job developed. When it was clear Holmes would do this until he got a job, the personnel man looked at Holmes, sighed, and said, "Okay, report here Monday morning."

Holmes worked as a machinist until the factory closed in 1951. Then he went to work for the city of Chicago in a variety of jobs until his retirement in 1985. It was a good life, he says; he was treated well on the job.

Johnnie Holmes and his fellow black veterans, however, were still living a lot of their days as second-class citizens. Holmes married a white woman during his days at Doehler Jarvis and they stayed married for thirty-eight years, until she died in 1985. It was not always easy, being a racially mixed couple in Chicago. Johnnie can remember many occasions when he sent his wife, Louise, into a restaurant to bring the food out to the car rather than risk the wrath of some bigot who wouldn't approve of their loving but black and white relationship.

For all of his combative ways, Johnnie decided he wouldn't personally bow to the inherent frustration of discrimination. As he puts it today, "If I let all of the negatives intervene, I would have never achieved anything. I kept focused on what I wanted to do, which was to make money, provide for my family."

Holmes, however, did support the civil rights movement through his church and he recalls with pride meeting Dr. Martin Luther King and joining him in his Chicago marches.

He also set out to advance his station in life his own way, as a real estate investor. His speciality was low-income rental apartments in buildings in black neighborhoods. At one time he owned as many as three buildings divided up into rental units. It was as a landlord and as a black man who had overcome so much on his own that he came to hate the welfare system that grew so fast in the fifties, sixties, and seventies. "It just killed ambition," according to Holmes. "I had all of these tenants who in their late twenties had never worked a day in their life. They just waited around for that government check. No incentive."

Holmes speaks of the welfare system in the same tone of voice that he uses to describe his son's cocaine problems. Disdain. He's plainly disgusted that his son, who makes good wages working in the oil drilling business in Louisiana, gave in to drugs, leaving behind a child in Chicago. Holmes wants nothing to do with his son; he's no longer welcome in his home. What Holmes went through during the war and after strengthened his already tenacious character and he sees no need to compromise his standards for anyone, even family members.

Although Johnnie Holmes's unit, the 761st Tank Battalion, was not involved in the liberation of the notorious concentration camps at Buchenwald and Dachau, according to its own official records it was in the area. There's been some confusion about that over the years and it lingers to this day. The 761st did participate in freeing the fifteen thousand Jews from a branch of Mauthausen, another concentration camp in Austria.

So the 761st soldiers did have firsthand knowledge of the depravity of the Third Reich's racial attitudes. As indefensible as America's attitude was toward blacks, Germany's ultimate solution took racial hatred to its darkest levels. Who better to put all that in perspective than Johnnie Holmes? So he's always willing, when asked by Jewish organizations or schools, to speak about the horrors he saw in World War II.

In his seventies, however, he may be mellowing some. He's much more inclined to help out at his church or take his Lincoln Town Car on long driving trips than to sit around and remember the bad old days or speak of the two-front battle he was forced to fight, Germans in front of him, racial bigots at his back.

Now he can say with pride and confidence, "I am proud of the way I live my life. I was a good soldier. I served my country. It is my country, right or wrong. I'm still waiting to find out what God really wants me to do. None of us can ever contribute enough."

LUIS ARMIJO

"I live a good life. Not with riches or money. I love to teach. I love to help people."

IN 1939, NEW YORK was the site of the World's Fair, a glittering exposition in Queens, a half hour from midtown Manhattan, near where La Guardia Airport and Shea Stadium are now located. The theme was the future, and it was a dazzling exhibition of the fantastic possibilities about to be realized—including television, mass airline travel, and superhighways—spread out over 1,216 acres along a backwater of the East River. The industrial giants of the age, General Motors, Westinghouse, and General Electric, constructed elaborate exhibitions to demonstrate the possibilities of travel, electrical power, and communication. In his evocative book *1939: The Lost World of the Fair,* David Gelernter makes the persuasive argument that the fair was a metaphor for a nation infused with the idea of a future full of grand possibilities. He wrote in his epilogue, "The future was a tangible, tasteable, nearly corporeal presence in your life." For many Americans, precisely. Much of the country was living more in the past than in the future, however.

As a child in the forties I recall visiting farm families still living with kerosene lamps and outhouses. In our tiny home on the Army base the only heat came from a coal-burning stove in the front room. Many years later we went back to the now abandoned base with our children and my parents. My father found the foundation of our home and walked it off with our youngest daughter, Sarah. She was astonished to learn that her New York bedroom was larger

Luis Armijo, wartime portrait

than the small house that was home to five of us by war's end. And, as my mother reminds me, we were living better than many families still struggling to escape the deprivations of the Great Depression and dealing with the acute housing shortage brought on by the war.

In 1940 only about 54 percent of the homes in America had complete plumbing—running water, private bath, and flush toilet. Almost a quarter of the homes had no electrical power. Economists estimate that most American homes in 1940 had only 1,000 square feet of living space. In 1998, they estimate, new single-family homes have more than double that, a little more than 2,100 square feet of living space.

In the rural American Southwest in 1940 the past and the future were joined on the same desert landscape, rudimentary and surreal forces coexisting in the sagebrush and cactus. A new age of infinitely greater power and peril than anything history had known was about to begin in a remote corner of New Mexico—the development and the detonation of the first atomic bomb, the ultimate weapon of mass destruction. The manipulation of the atom was intended to produce nuclear power, first for war, then for peace, but always in reserve for war.

Not too far from where J. Robert Oppenheimer and America's keenest scientific minds were racing to build and test a bomb so lethal not even they could imagine the full magnitude of its power, Luis Vittorio Armijo was growing up in the traditional fashion of his family. He was the son of a Spanish Basque father and an Apache mother. The family lived on a cattle ranch originally acquired by his Apache grandmother in a government land grant. It was located in the heart of the Apache reservation in southwestern New Mexico.

Armijo had an unusual childhood, even by the standards of that time and place. His parents and both sets of grandparents lived in the big house. The children—three boys and three girls—lived in a bunkhouse. Armijo recalls how the melding of the Apache and Basque cultures made it a lively household. "We spoke Spanish, French, and Apache," he says. "We were self-sustaining—with the cattle herd and big gardens. We went to town only about once a month."

Armijo didn't get his first name until he was about ten years old because first he had to perform certain Apache rites. "Grandpa took me out to kill my first deer," he says. "I had to drink some of the blood, then get the deer home, skin it, tan the hide, and make moccasins and other things." A family friend suggested the name Luis and his grandmother said his middle name would be Vittorio, which Armijo was told was also the name used by Geronimo as a young man.

As a young man Luis spent a lot of time with his father, who, though Spanish, identified with his wife's Apache ways. Luis remembers now, sixty years later, how his father taught him endurance. "He said, 'If you can walk three miles, you can walk four.' I learned how to track animals—how to tell a buck from a doe. I learned the medications from plants. White people take aspirin. We took the bark from the wala wala tree. I rode my horse three miles to the school bus and then took the bus ten more miles to school.

"I was just following the patterns of my parents. I thought I'd continue the same life. I knew nothing of the outside. On the maps in school, Colorado was in red and Arizona was in yellow, so I really thought when I got to those states they would be those colors. But when I got to high school and traveled with the basketball team to other towns, I realized I could do other things. I didn't have to depend on the four winds like my grandfather—the ground that gives you nutrients, the air you breathe, the sky that goes from light to dark and back, and the rain."

In 1942, his senior year in high school, Luis received his draft card and signed up for Army Air Force cadet training. A month later he was inducted and shipped to Fort Bliss, Texas, where he had an unexpected lesson in racial stereotyping. They said they wanted to use Southwestern Indians to speak their native language, as code talkers, to pass along vital military information.

"They called my name and I said, 'I'm not a full-blooded Indian; I can talk the language but you can find better people—I'm supposed to be a pilot.' The guy said to me, 'Hey, Apaches don't become pilots. They're not smart enough.'" Armijo says people think that American Indians aren't smart because they don't talk a lot. But, he says, Indians are always thinking.

In the 1940s, Native Americans were an invisible population for most of the nation. It was thirty years before they began to

Luis Armijo, wartime, in restored Japanese car

THE BEARER HAS CEASED RESISTANCE
TREAT HIM IN ACCORDANCE
WITH INTERNATIONAL LAW.
TAKE HIM TO THE NEAREST
COMMANDING OFFICER.
C-IN-C AMERICAN FORCES

TRANSLATION OF TEXT

LIFE SAVING LEAFLET
1. The American Forces will aid all who follow the instructions given in this leaflet.
2. Good treatment—food, clothing, tobacco, medical treatment, etc., will be accorded in conformity with International Law.

HOW TO USE THIS LEAFLET
1. Come slowly toward the American line with your hands raised high above your head, and carry only this leaflet.
2. Come one by one. Do not come in groups.
3. Men must wear only pants or loin cloths. Sufficient clothing will be provided. Women and children may come dressed as they are.
4. Do not approach American lines at night.
5. This leaflet may be used by anyone—Japanese, Korean, Soldier, Civilians, etc.
6. Those who do not have leaflets may advance to the American line if they follow instructions as if they had a leaflet.

Life-saving leaflet dropped over Japan

208 / TOM BROKAW

demand—through AIM, the American Indian Movement—more autonomy from the federal government's paternalistic system. When the war broke out, they were still largely confined to their reservations or the fringes of their native lands throughout the American West—but they were prepared to be warriors again. Moot Nelson, a Lakota Sioux, was working as a clerk in a western South Dakota draft board when the Japanese struck Pearl Harbor. Recalling the morning after, he said, "Here was a line of them already at eight A.M., Indian boys, twenty of them." His supervisor told him, "Get ready, Moot, the boys are fighting mad." That was true at reservations across the country.

In the Southwest, Armijo was sent to infantry basic training in California, but in the final week he heard about another test for the air cadet program and signed up again. He passed and was assigned to Truax Field, in Wisconsin, to train in ground communications. He wasn't going to be a pilot, but he wasn't disappointed. "I was just happy to be going places. I had never been on an elevator before, and here I had been in Texas, California, Wisconsin, and Illinois in a few months. I saw sailboats on a lake! I went to my first big basketball game. I couldn't wait to go to the towns and see the people, the lawns, the churches. If I heard a siren, man, that was really something."

At Chanute Field in Illinois, Armijo began an intense course in aviation electronics and communications. He learned navigation and, especially, how to guide a plane in when it was foggy. "We didn't know it then," he says, "but we were being trained to guide B-29s that would be landing on Pacific islands after bombing Japan."

He became a member of General Curtis LeMay's 20th Air Force, and early in 1945 he left San Francisco for a tiny island a little less than six hours by bomber from the heart of Japan. "We were a team of sixteen communications specialists. Our job was to tell the pilots how to land in the foggy conditions."

As the summer wore on, Armijo and his friends began to suspect something big was up. A plane called the *Enola Gay* was practicing landings and takeoffs with two other planes following it. It finally took off with two other B-29s early in the morning of August 6, 1945, and arrived over Hiroshima at 31,600 feet at 8:15 A.M. Nuclear warfare was born in an enormous explosion that unleashed a towering mushroom cloud and triggered a firestorm that destroyed Japan's

Luis Armijo

eighth-largest city and killed more than eighty thousand of its residents. Back on Tinian Island, Armijo and his friends heard about the mission as Colonel Tibbets headed home. Armijo remembers, "As they were returning, the *Enola Gay* radioed it had been a success. Word quickly got around what they were talking about."

Luis Armijo, who three years earlier had been riding a horse to a school bus, was there for the beginning of this moment that, more than any other during the war, defined the perils of the future. He had no qualms about the attack on Japan, however, citing the ferocity with which Japan had waged war and the forecasts of hundreds of thousands of American dead, if not a million or more, if an invasion of the mainland became necessary.

For Armijo, the moment had a certain symmetry. His family was a little more than an hour's drive north of the White Sands testing range where America's newest weapons were exploded, some of them blowing out the windows in the family home.

About two weeks later a typhoon hit Tinian, taking Armijo's tent and throwing him hard onto the ground. He cracked four vertebrae and had to be shipped home for treatment. The war was over, and Luis Armijo was eager to begin a new life.

Despite his service, however, when he returned it was "back to the same old thing." Racism. "Before the war," he says, "we were treated as bad as black southerners. We couldn't have a business in town. The movie theater was segregated—minorities sat on one side, the whites on the other.

"During the war it was different. You signed papers and the Army didn't say you were Hispanic or an Indian. The papers just said, 'Hey, you're an American soldier.' If we got captured, we were just Americans. We were in a war.

"Once you got back," he says, "you went back into the same old hole. I thought, 'Hey, how can I make them understand me?' " A Veterans Administration counselor suggested a sitting job because of his back condition, so Armijo signed up for accounting courses at a New Mexico state teacher's college. While there, the ways of his family awakened another interest: teaching. "Being the eldest in the family, whenever I learned something I was expected to teach my siblings. That was my grandfather's way. So I got a degree in education with specialties in business and physical education."

Armijo was hired immediately by the high school in Socorro, New Mexico, to teach typing, shorthand, business, and accounting. "I could see how eager these kids were to learn. To them, I knew more about the outside world than anyone. I said to them, 'You don't have to finish high school and go right back to the ranch. You can become a doctor, a nurse, a typist.' " That same message was heard in high schools across America. Returning veterans who went into the classroom brought a new worldliness and sense of adventure to the small-town kids they were standing before.

Armijo got a master's degree and set out for California where, he heard, teaching jobs were plentiful. He was quickly hired at Fullerton Union High School in what was then rural Orange County, California. It was the beginning of a mutual love affair between teacher and kids.

"My philosophy," he says, "is if you have a kid who leaves the house and comes to the school, that parent is saying, 'Take care of my child as I would.' I helped them make the right decisions. I kept money in my desk for those who didn't have enough for lunch. They could just take their lunch money out of my petty cash and pay it back later. They didn't have to leave their names. At the end of every year I always had more left over than what I started with. I made out a check to the company that provided the class rings. I wanted to be sure the kids who didn't have the down payment at the time got to order theirs with everyone else. They always paid me back. You have to show them trust."

The students, who liked Armijo, quickly came up with an affectionate twist on his name: Army Joe. They also knew that Army Joe didn't miss much. If students were missing from class on a sunny day he'd drive to a popular beach and catch them there and administer a fatherly talk about the importance of education. He was a master at knowing when schoolyard fights were about to break out, and would step in at the last moment to offer mediation over Cokes or coffee. One time he forgot to duck, however, and one of two girls in a ferocious fistfight landed one on Army Joe—and he wound up with a black eye. Remarkably, one former student remembers, he didn't lose his temper and the fighting coeds were filled with remorse.

A friend who has traveled with Armijo has been witness to his effect on his students. "Everywhere we'd go," he says, "we'd run into one of his students. They'd run up to him, throw their arms around him, and say, 'Mr. Armijo!' And he always remembered them and told you all about them. It happened wherever we would go."

There have been many changes in recent decades, however. "When I first started teaching," Armijo says, "parents were behind you a hundred percent. When you called home they would take your advice. They'd come to school if there was a problem. When I was teaching you could always find one parent at home. Not anymore."

Armijo likes the four-winds concept of his youth. He says a school has four sides: the students, the parents, the teachers, and the community. "And the parents are not holding up their part anymore. I think the home has gotten away from the parents."

Armijo also thinks the new generation of teachers, however, has to share the blame. "When I retired in 1987 the superintendent said, 'He always wore a coat and tie to school.' Today's teachers wear sports shirts. If their first class is at five past eight they arrive at eight. When I had an eight-thirty class I would be in the classroom at seven, opening the windows to get the air circulating, preparing the lessons. If you did an excellent job on a paper I'd make a small, complimentary remark, to be encouraging. Today so many teachers don't take the time."

Joe Yuddo remembers how Mr. Armijo, as he still calls him, always took the time. By his own description, Yuddo was a teenage rebel in the fifties, when he was a student in Armijo's high school. Yuddo says, "I had a wonderful father, but in high school there's always that conflict between parents and kids. Mr. Armijo was always the buffer that brought the kids back into line."

Yuddo was seriously injured in a motorcycle accident as a teenager, and for nine months Armijo came to his home to keep him abreast of his Spanish studies. It was the beginning of a lifelong friendship. Yuddo says, "I lost both my parents, and Mr. Armijo is the closest thing I have to a mother and father."

In his role as friend, Armijo takes a special interest in Yuddo's son, who has cerebral palsy. Armijo accompanies the Yuddos to physical therapy, and lately he's been helping them evaluate special-care facilities for the child in the event something happens to the parents. Yuddo says his counsel is always welcome because "sometimes you may not want to hear the truth, but you're always going to hear it from Mr. Armijo."

One of Armijo's granddaughters, Shantelle Westbrook, has her own unique connection to his personal generosity. "I really needed money for college," she says. Her father had abandoned the family so Shantelle went to her grandfather. He had a plan. He would begin selling Indian jewelry at swap meets on weekends. Shantelle was impressed. "He could have just retired, stayed inside, but instead he went out into the hot sun every Saturday to try to make money for my college fund."

Armijo doesn't see anything exceptional about his helping hand. "I buy from the various tribes," he says, "and since I am part Indian I can get a license for resale. I go to the swap meets from six A.M. to five P.M. every Saturday and Sunday. I put the money in a bank account under her name. She's starting her junior year in college and now I am doing the same thing for my younger granddaughter and grandson. I do it because I believe if you want to achieve a goal, you have to have an education."

Armijo is a good Samaritan to those well beyond his circle of friends and his family. Once he retired from teaching, Armijo became an enthusiastic member of the local Lions Club. He immersed himself in the Lions' many causes for the blind. "I collect glasses and turn them in. I organize drives to collect glasses. I organize raffles for the blind. We park a bus outside schools to screen kids for seeing problems. I'm in the bus, directing them to the different booths." He was so dedicated and efficient in his work for the blind that Armijo won the Melvin Jones Award, the Lions' highest honor, named after the club's founder.

William Rosenberger, the Fullerton businessman who invited Armijo to join the Lions, said he did so only because his son pestered him so much. It turns out another member had considered inviting Armijo into the club, but he was afraid he couldn't afford it on his schoolteacher's salary. Rosenberger says, "The Lions almost missed a golden opportunity. He turned out to be a real asset."

This humble man from another time and another place who went across the Pacific and was witness to the flight that changed warfare forever still rises every morning at five for a two-mile walk before attending Mass, every day, at a local church. Now in his late seventies, he says simply, "I live a good life. Not with riches or money. I love to teach. I love to help people."

Nao Takasugi, June 1941

Norman Mineta

NAO TAKASUGI

"The relocation centers were not yet ready, so we were taken to the Tulare county fairgrounds in central California. Our entire family was housed in a converted horse stable. We shared one stall."

NORMAN MINETA

"This is your home. You are all Americans."

I T WAS A FINE SPRING DAY in May 1998 at the Presidio in San Francisco, the former Army post in a bucolic setting of conifers and manicured lawns next to the San Francisco Bay. The Honorable Nao Takasugi arose to address the National Japanese American Historical Society. He was a familiar figure to those in attendance. A member of the California State Assembly, he'd also served as a city council member and mayor of his hometown of Oxnard, just north of Los Angeles on the California coast. His family had been there since 1903, well-established members of the Nikkei, the name Japanese Americans use to describe themselves as an ethnic group.

When Takasugi's grandfather first arrived from Japan he was unable to apply for citizenship because of his Asian ancestry but he thrived by opening a small store, the Ashai Market, a popular store renowned for its seafood. He personified the American immigrant experience as thoroughly as the Irish Americans of Boston or the East Europeans of New York's Lower East Side or the Scandinavian farmers of Wisconsin and Minnesota. It was his grandson,

Nao Takasugi, who was at the Presidio at the age of seventy-six in 1998, a testimony to the achievements of the Nikkei in America.

By then Takasugi was an elder statesman in California's ever growing Asian American community. As always, he was proud of his ancestry. He was a Nisei, as the second-generation Japanese Americans were called. But, foremost, he was in his heart, his mind, and by virtue of his birth, an American citizen.

In his remarks at the Presidio he reflected on his long life in California, paying tribute to his family and their culture. Referring to his office in the California legislature, he said, "Upon my return to Sacramento on Monday I will again take my place in the very legislative chamber that fifty-six years ago voted—with but one dissenting vote—to endorse the issuance of Executive Order 9066."

Executive Order 9066. One of the most shameful documents in American history. It was signed by President Franklin Roosevelt on February 19, 1942, to begin the forced internment of one hundred twenty thousand residents of Japanese ancestry—seventy-seven thousand of them American citizens. There were no hearings, no appeals. Executive Order 9066 was the codification of racism. Moreover, it was defended at the time by major figures in American civil liberties, including newspaper columnist Walter Lippmann and Supreme Court Justice William O. Douglas.

Some didn't attempt to justify the relocation for security reasons. A California organization of white farmers, the Grower-Shipper Vegetable Association, stated back then in *The Saturday Evening Post*, "We've been charged with wanting to get rid of the Japs for selfish reasons. We might as well be honest. We do. It's a question of whether the white man lives on the Pacific Coast or the brown man. They came into this valley to work and they stayed to take over."

Italian and German aliens living in California coastal areas were ordered to move in early 1942 but by June of that year the order had been rescinded, and there was no major relocation for those groups. Italian and German immigrants were picked up and questioned closely; they may have had some uncomfortable moments during the war, but they retained all their rights. Not so for the Japanese Americans.

Nao Takasugi was a junior studying business at UCLA when the Japanese bombed Pearl Harbor. Suddenly, because of his ancestry,

Nao Takasugi, graduating as Oxnard High School valedictorian, and Joe Kawata

Nao and Judy Takasugi on the floor of the California State Assembly, Sacramento— March 23, 1998, their forty-sixth wedding anniversary

he was subject to a strict curfew: he couldn't be out before six A.M. and after six P.M. He couldn't go five miles beyond his family home in Oxnard, which ruled out UCLA, more than fifty miles away. Then, in his neighborhood, came the posting of Executive Order 9066. "Here I was," he says, "a nineteen-year-old college student full of ambition and ideals. All of that just came crashing down."

The Takasugi family—the parents, four daughters, and Nao— were told to prepare whatever personal possessions they could carry in their hands and report to the railroad station in Ventura. An old family friend, a Mexican American named Ignacio Carmona, went to Nao's father and offered to take care of the market while they were away. Takasugi recalls his father handing him the keys, shaking his hand, and saying, "Whatever you make is yours."

The Takasugi family was driven to the railroad station by another friend, the branch manager of the Bank of America. Nao remembers this man saying, "I can't believe I am being asked to do this."

The railroad station was bristling with armed guards. The train was a collection of ancient passenger cars with the blinds drawn. The Takasugi family, just days before a respected and productive family of American citizens, boarded for an unknown destination, their most fundamental rights stripped in the name of fear.

THERE WERE small acts of cruelty to go with the larger violations of constitutional rights. Norman Mineta, later a congressman from California, was just ten years old when his family was loaded onto a train in the San Jose freight yards. He was wearing his Cub Scout uniform and carrying his baseball bat and glove, the American-born son of a prominent Japanese businessman who had lived in the area for forty years. Several of young Norman's schoolmates came to the tracks to say good-bye, just in time to see the armed guards confiscate his baseball bat because, they said, it could be used as a weapon. It was a world turned upside down for these law-abiding, productive, and respectable families.

NOW, MORE THAN a half century later, Nao Takasugi recites from a journal of memory. "The relocation centers were not yet ready, so

Assemblyman Nao Takasugi and family

Nao Takasugi (front row, extreme left) and family

we were taken to the Tulare county fairgrounds in central California. Our entire family was housed in a converted horse stable. We shared one stall."

There were fifteen thousand people in the "temporary" assembly center. They were there for three months. "The people running the camp organized schools, and teachers were brought in from the outside. I was a teacher's aide in the high school, teaching business and Spanish, my subjects in college." Typical of the equanimity that served him so well during his long life, Nao praises the quality of the camp drinking water that originated in the nearby mountains. "One of the nicest things I remember," he says. "It was excellent water."

After their extended stay in Tulare the Takasugi family was again loaded onto a train with the blinds drawn. They were not told their destination. "That was very scary," Takasugi says.

When the train stopped they were in the middle of the Arizona desert, at the Gila River (Pima-Maricopa) Indian Reservation. Their relocation center was still under construction. It was a bleak and foreboding place and it would be home for the Takasugi family and other men, women, and children of Japanese ancestry for the next three and a half years.

It was one of ten camps established in remote locations, most of them in the West. The Gila River camp, forty-five miles southeast of Phoenix, had a population of more than thirteen thousand, making it the fourth largest of the camps. It was operated from July 1942 until November 1945.

Among those interned in the Gila River camp were some cousins of Nao, four brothers who all volunteered for the 442nd Regimental Combat Team, the Army unit made up of Japanese Americans. One of his cousins, Leonard Takasugi, came to see his family before he shipped out after basic training. Nao says, "Here was my American-born cousin, in his Army uniform, leaving to fight for his country, yet he had to wait at the barbed-wire fence to get a security clearance to visit his family." It was for Nao Takasugi the ultimate irony of what Japanese Americans were experiencing during the war. They were good enough to defend their country, but they were always under a cloud of suspicion.

That cousin, Leonard, was killed in action in Italy on April 5, 1945—Nao's birthday.

In camp, Takasugi resumed his teaching job for which he was paid sixteen dollars a month. Then, an unexpected opportunity. A representative from the American Friends Service Committee in Philadelphia, the Quakers, visited the camp to urge those who had been in college to apply for a security clearance so they could resume their studies.

Takasugi was encouraged to apply to the business studies program at Temple University in Philadelphia. The Quakers would help with the costs and they helped him with the application process. He was accepted for the February term in 1943 for the class of 1945.

"Thank God for the American Friends," he says. "This was a shining light. . . . In four and a half years they sent more than four thousand young Nisei to school."

During a long, lonely train trip that took him across parts of the Deep South, Takasugi saw for the first time the signs designating WHITE and COLORED, the separate water fountains and separate public toilets. By then, of course, he had his own deeply personal understanding of discrimination. When Takasugi arrived in Philadelphia, his first real trip out of California, he was worried about how he would be treated but quickly realized that with the deep tan he'd acquired in the Arizona desert most people mistook him for a Puerto Rican.

He did so well at Temple, getting his BS in business in the spring of 1945, that he was accepted for graduate work in business at the prestigious Wharton School at the University of Pennsylvania. "I didn't even know what a famous school this was until later," he says. "I studied business and accounting and once I got my master's degree I pounded the streets of Philadelphia, applying to all the top accounting firms." They all said the same thing. "You have excellent credentials but we can't take a chance hiring you because of the war situation." Japan had surrendered the year before, but America remained deeply suspicious of anything Asian.

By then the families in the internment camps had been released and Nao's parents were back in Oxnard, where they had resumed operating their market. They needed Nao's help. "Being the only son," he said, "I had no choice." Besides, once back in California, he was relieved to discover that his old neighbors had no animosity left over from the war.

Their family friend, Ignacio Carmona, had operated the store as the Los Amigos Market, substituting *chorizo, pan dulce,* and *menudo* for the Asian products of the Takasugi reign. Carmona didn't disturb the locked storerooms, explaining to the *Los Angeles Times* later, "We knew that was their private property. . . . We knew eventually they would take back the store."

When that time came, Carmona simply said to the Takasugi family, "Welcome back. Thank you for letting us run the store." And he handed back the keys.

Takasugi was involved in every aspect of the market. "One day," he says, "one of my Wharton classmates came to visit and found me behind the meat counter. He said, 'You've got a degree from Wharton!' I said to him, 'MBA—master of butchering arts.' " Under Nao's stewardship, the market was flourishing. He wanted to expand, and he thought a new sign would help.

The city, however, denied the request. When Takasugi complained to his city councilman he was told there was an opening on the city planning commission. Would he like to serve? Takasugi says, "I thought they needed a businessman's perspective. That was the beginning of my civic career."

He had found his calling. He ran for the city council and was elected to two terms. Halfway through the second, the mayor's job opened and Nao had three good offers for the family market. He decided to sell and go for the top job at city hall. "I was a little sad," he says, "because the market had been in the family since 1907. But selling the store freed me up to do a good job as full-time mayor." Nao Takasugi was Mr. Mayor in Oxnard for ten years.

He had an important ally in the Mexican American neighborhood called La Colonia. His old friend Ignacio Carmona was a community leader who stayed in close touch with the mayor's office. Carmona said of Takasugi, "He always made it a point to represent the Mexican community. And he speaks good Spanish."

Takasugi kept his end of the bargain. He improved lighting, the roads, and police protection in La Colonia. In the rest of Oxnard, which had been called the doormat of Ventura County, he was successful in encouraging additional businesses, including a shopping center and an auto mall.

By 1992 Takasugi was ready to move up the political ladder. He ran for the powerful California Assembly, the state legislature, as a Republican from a district where there were few Asian Americans, and he won easily. He was the first Asian American in the California Assembly in a dozen years.

Takasugi was seventy when he arrived in Sacramento, an age when most men are retired, but he quickly established a reputation as an energetic and pragmatic lawmaker. One of his first acts was to challenge the established way of doing business by proposing that the legislators lose part of their salary, *and* pay a fine, if they didn't get the budget prepared on time.

His party boss, Governor Pete Wilson, did not have Takasugi's support when he sponsored the controversial statewide initiative to restrict the rights of immigrants. As Takasugi put it, "I am just one generation away from the immigrants coming to California, so I have to be very, very sensitive."

In 1988 Congress passed an act calling for an official apology and reparations of twenty thousand dollars to each of the survivors of the internment camps. The congressional action came after a commission held twenty days of hearings with testimony from more than seven hundred witnesses who had lived through the ordeal of Executive Order 9066. It was a deeply troubling reminder of a time when, as the commission concluded, "The broad historical causes that shaped these decisions were race, prejudice, war hysteria, and a failure of political leadership." In signing the congressional action, President Reagan admitted that the United States had committed a "grave wrong."

THERE WERE other wrongs to be corrected. While most Japanese Americans were sent to camps, many young Japanese American citizens were relocated to Japan against their will. Didn't they also deserve an apology and reparations? In 1996 the California Assembly was debating whether to pass a resolution encouraging Janet Reno to pay the extra reparations. Republicans were largely against the idea. Then, on their side of the aisle, Takasugi took the floor and all were quiet as he said he would support the resolution.

He told his fellow legislators the memories of his own internment would never be erased. "They may fade, but they will never go away. We lost . . . liberties you can never repay with twenty thousand dollars." He called the proposed payment "a small bit of redress, of fair play . . . for these kids." He concluded, "I urge your aye vote."

The resolution passed 62 to 0.

IN HIS SPEECH at the Presidio, Takasugi said, "One of the phrases that saw my family through the internment . . . is *shikata ganai*—it cannot be helped. Unlike yesterday, the phrase *shikata ganai* must not be the answer to the question of whether tomorrow's children have . . . a full understanding of the Japanese American experience."

Continuing, Takasugi reminded his audience, "America must never again fall prey to the temptation to count its citizens by color." It is a lesson, he said, that can be passed on to future generations.

Takasugi has had serious heart problems in the past year and for the first time he's talking about retiring. He's proud of what he's accomplished. He offers another Japanese phrase as his motto: *gambate*. Work hard, never give up.

He refuses to be bitter, telling audiences, "I find that I am compelled to remember the best—not the worst—of that time. To focus not on the grave deprivation of rights which beset us all, but rather on the countless shining moments of virtue that emerged from the shadows of that dark hour."

That bitter experience was the beginning of a new place for the Nisei, the second-generation Japanese, in American life. When they returned to their homes following the war they knew they had to reach out beyond their own communities and develop political muscle.

NORMAN MINETA was one of the leaders of the congressional action on reparations—that San Jose youngster who had been forced to give up his bat in 1942 because it might be a weapon. He was now California Congressman Norman Mineta; earlier he had served as mayor of San Jose. During the war his family had been relocated in a camp at Heart Mountain, Wyoming, a long way from the temperate climate of the Bay area. While in the camp Mineta had struck up a lasting friendship with a visiting Wyoming youngster who shared his interest in Cub Scouts. The boy's name was Alan Simpson, and when he grew up he became a powerful senator from Wyoming. Mineta was a Democrat and Simpson a Republican, but on the issue of internment they had a common point of view. The United States government had made a terrible mistake and it owed everyone involved an official apology.

MINETA RETURNED to San Jose after his odyssey through the camp in Wyoming and, later in the war, a more normal childhood in Evanston, Illinois, where the family moved when his father was recruited to teach Japanese to Army personnel at the University of Chicago. Back in San Jose, Mineta quickly became active in student politics, getting elected president of the San Jose High School student council seven years after he had been sent out of town on a train with the shades drawn and armed guards.

He went on to the University of California at Berkeley and stayed active in student politics while majoring in business administration. After a stint in the U.S. Army he returned to California to join his father in the family insurance business, which had recovered from the forced interruption of the internment.

The Mineta family had long been active in civic affairs but always within the Japanese community. Norman decided to expand their horizons. When he ran for the San Jose city council his father warned him, "You're going to be like a nail sticking out of a board. You know what happens to that nail? It gets hammered. Are you ready to get hammered?"

Apparently he was, for within four years he was elected mayor of San Jose, the first Japanese American to head a major city on the mainland. He was an instant success, a rising star in the Democratic party and a leading advocate of new approaches to old urban problems. In California's polyglot population he knew the feelings of an outsider, so he reached across invisible lines and brought in those who had not been represented in the seats of power, including Mexican Americans.

He was also the beneficiary of the local Japanese American community's determination to get a piece of the political power base. First, they had to get the attention of established political leaders, and the most expeditious route went through fund-raising dinners. Mineta said a patriarch in his community figured out a system. He knew that most Japanese American families were rebuilding their lives and couldn't afford the fifty- or hundred-dollar-a-plate cost of a dinner, and so, Mineta says, "he collected a dollar here and there until he had the price of two tickets and then he'd designate who would attend the dinner." Mineta was often one of those to represent the community.

It was the beginning of a political network for the ambitious young businessman, and after he'd worked his way up to mayor he decided to run for Congress in the election following Richard Nixon's resignation over Watergate. It was a banner year for Democrats, and Mineta was one of the beneficiaries.

He quickly became one of the stars of what was called the Watergate class in Congress. He also knew he wanted to do something about what had happened to his family and thousands more during the war. Executive Order 9066, that awful stain on a society of laws, had been allowed to fade away. By the 1970s internment had become a footnote to the war years; younger Americans had only a vague awareness of its implications. Older Americans, through discomfort or an eagerness to remember only the glories of those years, had pushed it to the far corners of their memories.

Mineta and three other Asian Americans in Congress, Senators Dan Inouye and Spark Matsunaga of Hawaii and Congressman Robert Matsui, also of California, decided they had to begin by sharing with their colleagues their personal stories. They also proposed a commission to prepare an independent study of the policies.

When the commission finished its research it concluded the internment was the result of race, prejudice, hysteria, and a failure of political leadership. The commission's work also generated a number of newspaper and magazine articles, television news reports, and documentaries. When the American public was forced to confront the truth of what had happened, Mineta and his friends were able to get through the Civil Liberties Act of 1988, which called for the apology and reparations for every family of twenty thousand dollars, an amount that was more symbolic than financially fair.

Mineta remembers the day it passed: September 17, 1987, the two hundredth anniversary of the signing of the U.S. Constitution. "House Speaker Jim Wright designated me as the speaker pro tem for the day so I could sign the bill for the House," he said. "I still have a copy of the legislation hanging in my office."

That legislation may have helped heal old wounds and it was certainly an uncomfortable reminder to the rest of society of how hysteria can overrun the basic laws and decency of a nation, but it didn't eradicate stereotyping. Mineta recalls speaking at a ceremony for Toyota and General Motors. When he finished, one of the GM executives congratulated him on how well he spoke English and wanted to know how long he'd lived in America!

It has been a long American journey for the ten-year-old in the Cub Scout uniform who once got on a train for an unknown destination. Before they got on the train that day in May 1942, Mineta's father called them all together—three girls and two boys—to say, "I want you to remember 545 Fifth Street. This is your home. You are all Americans."

A great deal has changed in the life of Norman Mineta, who is now a vice president of Lockheed Martin Corporation after serving twenty years in the House of Representatives. One part of his life remains the same. The Mineta family still owns that house at 545 Fifth Street in San Jose, California.

LOVE, MARRIAGE, AND COMMITMENT

The World War II generation shares so many common values: duty, honor, country, personal responsibility, and the marriage vow: "For better or for worse . . ." It was the last generation in which, broadly speaking, marriage was a commitment and divorce was not an option. I can't remember one of my parents' friends who was divorced. In the communities where we lived it was treated as a minor scandal. My age group, which preceded the Baby Boomers, retained that attitude, but it did begin to unravel. At my fortieth high school reunion, second marriages were not unusual and there were a number of third marriages.

There were divorces before and immediately after the war, of course, but the laws governing the dissolution of a marriage were much tougher, and society was not as tolerant as in later years. Of all the new marriages in 1940, one in six ended in divorce. By the late 1990s, that number was one in two.

Although divorce has been a common fact of life in America since the sixties, World War II couples have not fully adjusted; they're still unsettled by its popularity, especially when it occurs in their own families. Many of the couples I talked to would recite matter-of-factly, even cheerfully, the travails of their lives during the Depression and the war. But when I asked about the divorce of one of their children, their voices dropped and they struggled for words, saying something to the effect of "We still can't get used to it."

At reunions of various World War II outfits, almost all the veterans show up with their first wives; if they're with a new mate, it's because the first one died. Those marriages, I believe, are more than a reflection of the expectations of society at the time the vows were exchanged. These relationships were forged when the world was a dangerous place and life was uncertain. Couples were forced to confront the profound emotions—and passions—that come with the reality of separation and the prospect of death. If their relationships could withstand the turmoil and strain of the war years, it should only get better after that.

They were also part of a generation accustomed to sharing and working together toward a common good. So many of these couples came from homes or conditions where life was a team effort. In the face of severe economic deprivation, illness, or unexpected death, the preservation and common welfare of the family was the collective goal. It was a conditioning they carried over to their marriages.

It is a legacy of this generation seldom mentioned with the same sense of awe as winning the war or building the mighty postwar economy, but the enduring qualities of love, marriage, and commitment are, I believe, equal to any of the other achievements.

JOHN AND PEGGY ASSENZIO

"The war helped me love Peggy more, if that's possible."

JOHN AND PEGGY ASSENZIO have been married since a month after Pearl Harbor. He was twenty-three; she was two years younger. They've known each other even longer—since they were youngsters in Bensonhurst, Brooklyn. Peggy remembers, "When I was eleven, I was on my porch reading. John threw a football to get my attention. I threw it back. That was it."

Shortly after their marriage, John was heading for basic training at Camp Pickett, Virginia. He was trained as a medical technician and assigned to the 118th Combat Engineers, the men who went in with the first wave to clear the minefields, bust through any defensive barriers, and start a network of roads and bridges for additional troops and supplies. It was vital and dangerous work.

At home, Peggy was a teacher in the Brooklyn Roman Catholic Diocese middle school system during the day and often volunteered at the Red Cross in the evening. She says, "I never went to sleep until I wrote John a letter. I wrote every single day. I wouldn't break the routine, because I thought it would keep him safe. You bet I got to know the men in the post office." Peggy also followed the progress of John's outfit through the newspaper and kept an elaborate scrapbook of everything connected to his part in the war, including newspaper clippings and his draft notice.

In the Pacific, John was on the move so much he didn't get his mail regularly. He saw action in five different campaigns over twenty-three months. His memories of Okinawa, one of the most

John and Peggy Assenzio, wartime

ferocious battles of the Pacific war, still come to him in Technicolor. "We were down on our bellies and I saw one guy—his arm flying through the air; it had been blown off. I jumped up and put a tourniquet on the stump and got him evacuated. I don't know whether he survived."

John still breaks down when he recalls one excruciating close encounter. "I was on a scouting mission, crawling, when I came face-to-face with a Japanese soldier. He looked at me and I looked at him. I fired first. He went down. It was a horrible, horrible experience."

It's all the more important to John that he won the Bronze Star for saving lives, not taking them. On November 12, 1944, at Dulag, on the Leyte Gulf, the Japanese sent a fleet of kamikaze planes to attack U.S. ships anchored in the bay. There were hundreds of casualties. John and another volunteer were on the beach, where they loaded a small boat with medical supplies and rushed out to help the stricken ships and wounded sailors for the next seven hours.

His breaks from combat were rare, so when he arrived in New Guinea there were fifty-eight letters waiting for him, most of them from Peggy. He read them in the order they'd been written, and he remembers to this day that in one of them he learned his grandfather had died. When he had left for basic training, his grandfather had assured him, "You'll come back, but I won't be here," and then he had kissed John.

What John experienced was characteristic of the personal turmoil in the lives of young people at the time. While the men were in strange and hostile places, thousands of miles from home, relatives died, wives and sweethearts were left to fend for themselves, children were born, and Dear Johns were written. Sometimes it would be weeks or even months before the men would get the news, however disappointing, sad, or joyous.

John's outfit was dispatched to Japan following the surrender. They were assigned to the port city of Kure, just southeast of Hiroshima. He was stunned by what he saw in the ruins of the first target of an atomic bomb. "Hiroshima," he says, "was the most horrible thing you ever saw . . . just twisted steel, complete devastation." Assenzio is firmly convinced the decision to drop the bomb was appropriate. Like most veterans of the Pacific, he believes the

Japanese would not have given up and there would have been an untold number of casualties during an invasion.

One small moment during John's stay in Japan is a poignant reminder that wars are made from the top down and that the people at the bottom, were it left to them, would likely find other ways to settle whatever differences exist. John says he was under strict orders: "No fraternization with the locals." But one day he and a friend passed by the home of the postmaster of Kure. He invited them in for tea. "The postmaster could speak English. You should have seen his garden. His little son took out a geography book and pointed to New York, because that's where we were from.

"We had the most delicious tea—never had tea that delicious. We were going against fraternization orders . . . I still had my rifle . . . but they were so nice."

Days before, the two nations represented by the four people at that party had been in a vicious war with each other. The Japanese family was living in the shadow of the wreckage of Hiroshima, the single most destructive act of war ever. They were entertaining two young Americans, men who were lucky to have survived the deadly intentions of the Japanese as they fought their way across the Pacific. Now they were enjoying each other's company and a pot of wonderful tea.

"I finally got back to New York on December thirtieth. I missed Christmas, but I got a temporary discharge so I could spend New Year's at home. I rode the train into Brooklyn with a rifle over one shoulder and a souvenir samurai sword over the other. I looked so strange."

When they were courting, John and Peggy had developed a special signal so they could always find each other in crowded places, like Coney Island. It was what John called his "love whistle," a sweet, melodious whistle in four beats he used only when he wanted to get Peggy's attention. When John arrived at the bottom of the steps leading to her family's home in Bensonhurst on December thirtieth, a great deal had changed in his life, but he remembered how to do the love whistle. When Peggy heard it, he says, "She came running out and almost took my head off." Her memory: "I had just finished making a big WELCOME HOME sign and I was talking to John's uncle when I heard the whistle. I just ran down the steps and hugged him."

John Assenzio (extreme left) in Kure, Japan

The Assenzios' Western Union telegrams—"They speak for themselves"

MGM couldn't improve on that for a love scene, and as corny as those black-and-white movies about love and marriage during the war years may seem now, they were a reflection of what was happening to couples across the country. Newly married couples didn't have an opportunity to adjust slowly to the complexities of suddenly sharing a life.

And then they were separated, often for years. Husbands were living in an intensely male environment, trying to deal with the stresses and dangers of war, while young wives were left at home, staying with relatives or living alone in strange cities, working when they could or caring for a child conceived before the father shipped out and born while he was away.

Still, John and Peggy Assenzio were typical. When he came home, they simply resumed their life together. They loved each other. They wanted to have a family. They were faithful Catholics. They were true to the way they had been raised. They were grateful the only lasting effect of the war on John was nightmares. When he went through a difficult time, thrashing around in their bed, sometimes knocking over a table lamp, occasionally sleeping on the floor to avoid hitting Peggy as he flailed out at the dark memories, she was always there to comfort him, to remind him just by her presence that they would get through this together. John says, "The war helped me love Peggy more, if that's possible. To appreciate her more."

John went back to his old job as a salesman for an import-export firm. Peggy had saved some money from her teaching job during the war. They couldn't find an apartment in their families' neighborhood, so they bought a home on Long Island, thus becoming part of a fundamental alteration of American life, the rise of the suburbs and the subsequent diffusion of the family.

They raised a family—two sons. Their firstborn, John Jr., a schoolteacher, died of cancer a few years ago, and they've established a scholarship in his name. Another son, Rich, is a production manager with NBC Sports.

John and Peggy are proponents of women's liberation, but they worry that in trying to have it all—a career, marriage, and children—too many young women put their careers ahead of their families. Peggy, who had been a schoolteacher during the war, resumed teaching once the boys were in school themselves. She worries. "The morals have changed tremendously. The way you're told to raise your kids now—there's no discipline."

Divorce is another issue they worry about. Peggy says young couples these days "don't fight long enough. It's too easy to get a divorce. We've had our arguments, but we don't give up. When my friends ask whether I ever considered divorce I remind them of the old saying 'We've thought about killing each other, but divorce? Never.' "

John and Peggy Assenzio are not unique within their generation. They can look back on a love affair that began in the Great Depression, was consummated at the outset of World War II, survived combat and separation, and flourished in the postwar years. They were just twenty-one and twenty-three when they were married and they could not have imagined what strains the world would put on their commitment to each other, but they believed their wedding vows were not conditional. Now, in their fifty-seventh year of marriage, that belief has not diminished for John and Peggy. If anything, it has been strengthened by John's recurring memories of the horrors of combat. They come to him less often now, but Peggy is always there for him. As he says, "I relive it sometimes, but with the help of my wife—and the love she has for me—that's how you get over it."

These marriages and the values the men and women brought to them may seem curiously old-fashioned to modern young couples. They may have a difficult time relating to a love affair forged by sacrifice and separation, faith and commitment. They may not know how to measure the tensile strength such marriages bring to a society. In an age of divorce, pagers, cell phones, and fax machines, they may never know the sweet sound of a love whistle.

The Dumbos, Halloween party, 1949

THE
DUMBOS

*"Expectations were different: We had a higher regard for
marriage. You just didn't divorce."*

OTHER WORLD WAR II marriages became part of larger groups.
Veterans formed such close associations with their wartime
buddies that they became friends for life, and their wives learned
to care for each other as well. In some cases, the wives were the
catalysts for postwar friendships. Their husbands returned home
to find their wives had gotten through the ordeal with the help of
other women in similar straits. They were sisterhoods that did not
end with the war. With the men back, it became an extended family, a gathering of couples who had shared experiences and common values.

In the small South Dakota city of Yankton, four wives with husbands in the service met to play bridge: my mother-in-law, Vivian
Auld; her sister, Lois Gatchell; their friends La Verne Hubner and
Joyce Hagen. Vivian's husband, Merritt, was an Army doctor who
was overseas for five years, seeing heavy action in North Africa and
Italy. Don Gatchell was in the Marines. Roland "Doc" Hubner, another physician, was a flight surgeon. Joyce's husband, Clarence
(everyone called him "Hack"), was an officer aboard a heavy
cruiser in the Pacific.

Joyce remembers that it was a mutual support group. All of the
women were in their early to mid-twenties. Vivian, Joyce, and La
Verne had infants at home, conceived before their husbands
shipped out, born while they were abroad. It was an uncertain time

in the lives of these young women with their husbands so far away, many of them in the line of fire. Joyce's anxiety for Hack only heightened when word came that her brother had been killed in action.

Now, however, more than a half century later, she remembers the solidarity of the little circle of women. She laughs when she says, "If any of the serviceman husbands came home, he had to take us all out to dinner. We'd save gas rations and drive to Sioux City [a small city with more restaurants, about sixty miles away from Yankton] and have a big dinner. Then we'd wait for the next husband to come home."

The separation anxieties were not confined to the wives. Meredith, my wife, can remember seeing her father only once during her first five years, when Merritt managed a short home leave between the North African and Italian campaigns. Meredith lived with her mother at the home of her grandparents, not an unusual arrangement for war wives, especially those with small children. Nonetheless, she didn't have a father around during what we now call the bonding years. It must have been equally awkward for him. He returned home to find a five-year-old stranger as his daughter.

As a result their relationship evolved slowly; as she was growing up, it was more distant than it might have been if he had been home in the early years. By the time she was an accomplished adult, they were very close. How many other World War II fathers and children must have experienced the same early strains in their relationships?

Hack Hagen received word of their firstborn just after his ship, the heavy cruiser *Salt Lake City*, had been shot up in a raging naval battle in the North Pacific. It was welcome news after what he'd been through—almost four hours of intense exchanges with a Japanese armada twice the size of the American flotilla. In his definitive study of the naval battles during World War II, the distinguished Harvard historian Samuel Eliot Morison described how the *Salt Lake City* "received almost all of the enemy's attention" as the Japanese tried to sink the cruiser with shells fired from twelve miles away. They were almost successful. It took four major hits before the ship was forced to a stop after a battle that ran for almost a hundred nautical miles.

Joyce and Clarence Hagen, 1942

*Joyce and Clarence Hagen's fiftieth anniversary, 1991,
with the entire Hagen family, Le Mars, Iowa*

Several crew members were killed near where Hack was a gunnery officer, but as he says, "We just kept going." Finally, the *Salt Lake City* was dead in the water. The engine room had taken a hit, killing the power and causing some serious leaking. It appeared Hagen and the crew were doomed, but for some reason the Japanese broke off the attack and retreated. Morison figures that "smoke concealed . . . *Salt Lake's* plight" and that the Japanese worried American fighter bombers would arrive at any time.

The *Salt Lake City* managed to make it back to San Francisco for repairs, and Hack went on to South Dakota for a reunion with Joyce and their new son, Christopher. Before long, however, he was back on the high seas, once for three months without seeing land. He did have a way of letting Joyce know his whereabouts, however. In his weekly letters he made reference to a time of day, which she could then convert into latitude and longitude. As he says, "It was good for her to know and it was a comfort to me to know she was following along."

Those letters, which took a long time to get back to South Dakota, did get special treatment from the mailman. Joyce recalls, "If a letter arrived from a brother or a husband, no matter what the time of day, the mailman got it to our house and dropped it through the mail slot. It was an extra kindness."

Most of the war news came from the big cabinet radios that were a fixture in every living room. Meredith remembers the nightly ritual in her grandparents' home, when everyone would gather and remain absolutely still as they listened to the news from the front. With so much action on so many fronts and the filter of military censorship, they were getting only the big picture. For long stretches of time they had no idea exactly where their husbands were or how they were doing. There were millions of these young wives, women in their twenties, their lives in a state of suspension as they awaited the return of their husbands, always dreading that the unexpected knock at the door would be a telegram or their minister with news that he wouldn't be coming back.

There were other sources of information if you were in the right place. Lois Gatchell was living in San Francisco before she returned to Yankton. Her husband, Don, was a Marine officer on the USS *Ticonderoga* when it was attacked and almost sunk by two

Four generations of Hagens (left to right): Torger Hagen, George Hagen, Clarence Hagen, Christopher Hagen— Webster, South Dakota, 1945

Meredith, Merritt, and Vivian Auld

Japanese kamikaze planes. He says to this day, "I can still see them—two Japanese planes headed right for us. It was a mess." Lois remembers her friends who were Navy wives knew almost instantly what had happened, well before the news became public. "It was an incredible grapevine," she says. "They knew before anyone." It was not until the ship returned, however, that she knew Don was okay.

As a result of these harrowing experiences, the young women became emotionally mature beyond their years, just as their husbands were learning to grow up fast with the responsibilities and duties that came with military service. In the nineties, young men and women often talk of using their twenties to find themselves, to explore the options of life. Their grandparents at the same age found themselves in a hurry.

It wasn't always perfect, of course. Couples who were just getting started in their relationship were living with the strain of protracted periods of separation, the absence of timely communications between the wife at home and the husband abroad, the anxieties brought on by the everyday life-and-death dangers of war.

When Meredith's father returned after five long years away, he brought with him a letter from his mother-in-law, Nan Harvey, written in June 1945. It was a poignant yet firm plea for him to come home. She was worried about his wife, her daughter Vivian.

Nan couldn't believe that the Army was insisting Merritt stay on awhile longer even though the war was over. She said that Vivian was "on the verge of the breaking point after hearing you can't get home. . . . The long separation for you and Vivian has been *too* long for you both and it does worry us." Nan went on to relate Vivian's worry that the continuing separation diminished "the chances to finish life together happily." Plainly, the brave front put up by Vivian and millions of other wives at home was often just that, a front. Who could blame them for their anxieties?

Merritt apparently got the message, for he came back to Yankton not too long after that, and his marriage to Vivian was long, happy, and productive. They had five children and regularly took in young women who came from troubled homes.

In fact, when the war was over, *all* the husbands of the women in the weekly bridge game returned home safely and went swiftly into their civilian careers. Auld and Hubner joined a medical practice in Yankton. Gatchell entered the insurance business, and Hack resumed the teaching career he had started before the war.

The wives decided not to give up what had been so important to them during the war—their regular meetings and, by now, very deep friendships. They decided to organize a dinner club and monthly bridge game. They named it Dumbo for one of those silly reasons: the dinners would be jumbo, with everyone bringing food, and someone laughingly suggested, "Dumbo Jumbo, that's us."

The monthly dinners and bridge games went on for the next thirty-five years, and the friendships only deepened as time went along. Hack and Joyce Hagen were absent for a time while he got a degree in optometry, financed in part with a loan from one of the Dumbo members. He set up practice in LeMars, Iowa, just sixty miles from Yankton, and they resumed their regular attendance at Dumbos.

For the women it was not an easy time, for it was very much a man's world in the immediate postwar years. In Yankton, married women were not hired as schoolteachers, and in Dr. Auld's medical partnership his own sister, a pediatrician with a thriving practice, was paid half of what the male partners earned. There were no women lawyers or business owners. It wasn't fair, especially after all the contributions women had made during the war, but for most of the wives there were other immediate priorities. Children were coming in waves and homes were being bought or expanded. Husbands were working long hours, trying to catch up after their years of military service. Given the current place of women in American life, it is difficult to imagine that time. It is equally difficult to appreciate the urgency of young couples to get on with their marriages after the uncertainties of the war years. It was, as they say, a different time, and it made possible what was to come.

Considering what they had all been through, they emerged from the war with a remarkable appetite for public service, for "doing good," as so many of them now describe it. It was a natural extension of the patriotism and training of the war years, but it was not a short-term phenomenon. It was the ethos of the time. Get married, have a family, stay married, do something for your community.

The Dumbos and the other World War II couples in Yankton were in the forefront of every community-improvement project. The two doctors, Hubner and Auld, served terms as president of the local school board, pushing through reforms to get equal pay for women teachers and to raise the place of girls' athletics in a state where boys had the only games in town. Vivian Auld became a force in building a new public library.

It was a generation of joiners. They belonged to the Masonic Lodge or Knights of Columbus, the VFW and the American Legion, the Elks, the Rotary, Kiwanis, and Toastmasters International. The wives were in PEO, a popular women's service organization.

As children of the Depression, they managed their new prosperity carefully. Within the Dumbos an extravagant purchase, a fancy new car or a boat, would trigger a round of sharp kidding. As couples, they all shared a natural resistance to conspicious consumption. Moderation in spending was as important to them as faithful marriages, well-behaved children, and church.

They were all active in their various religious faiths well beyond regular attendance at Sunday worship. As Episcopalians, the Aulds and the Gatchells helped start the 20-40 Club for adults over twenty and under forty. They raised money for St. Mary's, a local school for girls from the Sioux reservations. Later Hack Hagen became active in national Lutheran church efforts to counsel conscientious objectors during Vietnam. As a World War II veteran, far from being bitter toward those who chose not to serve in Vietnam, he says, "I learned about compassion."

Don and Lois Gatchell, who now live in Tulsa, Oklahoma, remember life revolving around family, friends, church, and community, and all of the couples approached it as a team effort. Well before the phrase "extended family" came into vogue, these couples were just that. They vacationed together, celebrated birthdays and holidays together, and supported each other during difficult times. I remember them to this day in tandem: Vivian and Merritt; Doc and La Verne; Hack and Joyce; Lois and Don.

That was not unique to this group or just to Yankton, of course. Moreover, it's not that these values were absent before the war. However, America had never been subjected to an explosion of marriages, births, prosperity, and population shifts of this magnitude. The landscape was being transformed in every conceivable way and the place of marriage and the family was critical to the management of it all in an orderly fashion. What makes it all the more remarkable in contemporary terms is that the couples were so young. It was not unusual for a young man and woman to have three children, mortgage payments, and expectations of a lifelong career in one company by the time they were thirty.

Lois Gatchell believes their marriages were strengthened by those months and years of difficult, often frightening separation in the early stages. "I believe we were all determined to make it work as a result of that," she says. Don adds, "Expectations were different. We had a higher regard for marriage. You just didn't divorce." And if they hit a bump in their relationship, they worked it out between themselves. They were too busy putting their lives back together, too grateful that they had emerged from those difficult years alive and together again, to dwell on the occasional hitches in their relationships.

Outside of our own families, to those of us growing up in Yankton at the time, these World War II couples were emblematic of the values that shaped our lives. In many respects, their marriages and the way they conducted them were a form of community service.

Gaylord Nelson

Carrie Lee Nelson, 1945

GAYLORD AND CARRIE LEE NELSON

"We didn't have much, and we didn't expect much. . . . We struggled, but we kind of liked the struggle. We had love and friends, and our aspirations were right, so it was a good time."

GAYLORD NELSON, later the governor of Wisconsin and a U.S. senator from that state for three terms, was the son of a small-town physician when he enlisted in the Army, a self-confident and fun-loving bachelor who already had a law degree. He was headed back to Wisconsin after the war to pursue a career in politics, hoping to follow in the footsteps of his boyhood hero, Senator Robert La Follette.

Carrie Lee Dotson came from markedly different circumstances. She was the ninth child of a couple in Wise County, Virginia, the heart of Appalachia's coal country. When she was just three years old, her father died and her mother was forced to place her in a home for poor children run by the Masonic lodge in Richmond, Virginia. Two of her brothers were already there.

Carrie had big dreams as well, although hers were rooted more in fantasy than reality. After all, she was a poor, overweight child in a foster home. Nonetheless, she looked at pictures of dashing, famous women like the flier Amelia Earhart and the glamorous tennis player Alice Marble and thought she could be like them. Of course, she says now, she had no idea what that truly meant, as she didn't have access even to a newspaper, much less to flying or tennis lessons. Instead, when she was eighteen, she went to nurse's training, a popular choice among young working-class women who couldn't afford to go to college. Carrie Lee also considered that if she couldn't be Amelia Earhart, she could still become a flight attendant.

Instead, at the end of her nurse's training, she qualified for Officer Candidate School within the U.S. Army Nurse Corps, and after basic training she put on her second lieutenant's bars and reported to Fort Indiantown Gap, Pennsylvania, where a blind date would change the direction of her life forever.

It was near the end of the war, in the spring of 1945, when a friend asked her to double-date with a couple of young Army officers. Carrie Lee's date was Gaylord Nelson, and her first impression was mixed. She thought he was cute and funny but that "Gaylord" was a dumb first name. They had a nice time at the movies, and later, over a few drinks at the Officers Club, Gaylord told her about his Wisconsin upbringing, but there were no sparks flying. At the end of the night he put her on the bus back to her nurses' ward.

She was a little surprised when the next day there was a phone call for her from a general. It was, in fact, "General" Nelson, and this was Carrie Lee's first encounter with Gaylord Nelson's deep streak of mischief. They continued to see each other until it was time for him to ship out. Carrie Lee admits she was smitten, but she didn't expect much from Gaylord because he'd made it clear he didn't write to anyone, not even his mother. So, as Carrie says, "That was the end of that—for that time." And as Gaylord says, "I never expected to see her again."

Gaylord Nelson had the unusual experience—particularly unusual for a young man from Wisconsin—of commanding a company composed entirely of black soldiers. The son of the president of Liberia was his first sergeant, and he was the highest-ranking "Negro," as blacks were called in those days. This was for Gaylord a very personal experience with racial discrimination. "Every post I was on," he says, "the black troops were assigned to World War I barracks. The white troops got into the brand-new barracks with central heating. They stuck the black troops in barracks heated by

Gaylord and Carrie Lee Nelson meeting Harry S Truman

coal stoves. I began to see—in a minor way, of course—how it was to be a minority and be discriminated against."

Nelson and his soldiers were assigned to Okinawa after the fierce battle for control of that island, and they were there when the war ended. He fully expected just to kill time there and get back to whatever life had in store for him in Wisconsin. Little did he know that someone else was also headed to Okinawa.

Carrie Lee had made the long journey to Okinawa to work as a replacement nurse in a hospital that was being deactivated. She was not happy about the assignment—most of her friends were going to the Philippines—but as she came ashore she encountered a young Army lieutenant checking off the nurses' assignments. Carrie Lee remembers that the lieutenant said, "Hmph, Dotson. Weren't you at Indiantown Gap?" When she said yes, he went on, "Didn't you go out with Nelson? He's on this island." Carrie Lee says that in those days she didn't say things like "No shit, Joe!" but she might as well have. When the lieutenant said, "I'll have to tell him you're here," she replied, "Yeah, do that, will you?"

When Gaylord was told that Carrie Lee was on the island, he decided to look her up. By then he was a captain, but again he mischievously told the guard at her barracks, "Tell Lieutenant Dotson that General Nelson is here." When she came out to greet him, he exclaimed, "Jesus Christ, you're skinny." She responded, "Jesus Christ, you're not a general." As she says now, more than a half century later, "So we found each other."

The Okinawa courtship proceeded apace. Carrie Lee had to stay on the island until the spring of 1946, so Gaylord extended his assignment as well. By the end of their time there Gaylord had given her "a little silver band that one of his soldiers had made—took quarters and pounded them into rings."

Eventually Gaylord went back to Madison, Wisconsin, to open a law practice, and Carrie Lee returned briefly to Virginia before agreeing to move to Wisconsin. She became a nurse at the University of Wisconsin while they continued their engagement. They were married in November 1947.

Gaylord was a popular and hardworking young lawyer, but he wasn't making much money; looking back, Carrie Lee believes it's just as well. "We didn't have much, and we didn't expect much," she says. "We had spaghetti dinners with jugs of red wine. We struggled, but we kind of liked the struggle. We had love and friends, and our aspirations were right, so it was a good time."

When Gaylord got more deeply involved in politics, Carrie Lee wasn't as happy, but it never occurred to her to demand that he give up his boyhood dream, not even when she felt like a single parent as he campaigned and she stayed home with their children.

When Gaylord became the first Democrat elected governor of Wisconsin in fifty years, Carrie Lee, the child of Appalachia and a Masonic home for children, was suddenly the best-known woman in the state. It was an honor she didn't cherish. She describes her role as first lady: "I tolerated it. I never liked all the scrutiny. I had a miscarriage during Gaylord's first term, and I resented it when the press wrote about it. I felt the same way when our third child was born—why my pregnancy had to be in the news, I don't know."

Nonetheless, she rarely complained. In turn, Gaylord never asked her to change her ways, not even when some of his political advisers warned against her easy use of mild profanities. Her maverick ways appealed to his own bold sense of humor. He gave her space and she did the same for him. They had mutual friends, but they also had separate friendships, and they didn't impose one set on the other.

When Gaylord was elected to the U.S. Senate and they moved to Washington, it didn't get any easier for Carrie Lee. The capital was a city of protocol alien to her background in the Masonic home. The Nelsons had only Gaylord's Senate salary to support their family of five, so though Carrie felt pressure to maintain an expensive wardrobe, there was very little left over for her to indulge herself with fancy dresses, even if she had been so inclined. As Carrie Lee says, "We'd never been in debt, and we didn't intend to start now."

Gaylord's trips back home to Wisconsin to tend to his political base meant that Carrie Lee had an expanded role as a single parent. She admits that this "strained the marriage," but there was never a thought of divorce. Her sense of isolation was more than offset by the love she felt for Gaylord and their family. It was, she says, "a wonderful dream to have that family after my childhood."

Because of their refreshing independence, the Nelsons quickly became one of the most popular couples in Washington. At the peak of Gaylord's power as a senator, Carrie Lee was an equally dynamic presence whenever they entered a room—not always the case with political wives. But then she didn't play by the rules. She was wholly at ease with herself and her background, cracking jokes, deflating big egos with a well-aimed verbal dart or a slightly profane comment. She was comfortable with the men and women of the power circles.

Looking back, Carrie Lee is certain that despite their vastly different childhoods, her and Gaylord's marriage worked so well because they had confidence in each other. Even when they disagreed, they worked to find common ground, and they never fought in front of their children. She says now that if she were to do it over, she'd be more assertive about Gaylord spending time with the family, but all in all, she is grateful that she was on the right boat and in the right line when she reported for duty in Okinawa. Otherwise, she might never have run into "General" Nelson and traveled a world far beyond the Masonic home for children in Richmond.

As for Gaylord, whose ancestors are Norwegian, he likes to tell the story of Ole, the stereotypical Norwegian, who once confided to a friend, "It's all I can do to keep from telling the kids how much I love their mother."

JEANETTE GAGNE NORTON

"When the war was over everybody was honking their horns and yelling ... but I couldn't really join. ... My heart wasn't in it."

DAPHNE CAVIN

"I didn't have riches but I had love."

WOMEN HAD SO MANY ROLES in World War II, from serving on the front line as nurses to taking the place of men on the assembly lines. They were also the wives and sweethearts of the fighting men, and in that role they were the moral support back home and the reason many men said they were so determined to stay alive.

Jeanette Gagne Norton of suburban Minneapolis was just seventeen when she met Camille Gagne, a native of Quebec, as the war was getting under way. They had a six-month courtship and decided to marry in June 1942, because Camille knew his draft number was coming up. Jeanette became pregnant shortly after they were wed and he left for basic training that autumn.

Following basic, Camille volunteered for the 82nd Airborne, which meant additional training at Fort Benning, Georgia. He had hoped to get a furlough after Airborne training, but the Army wanted his unit to ship out immediately. He called Jeanette with the bad news shortly after she had gotten home from the hospital with their newborn son.

Jeanette said, "Tears welled up in my eyes. I said, 'I guess you won't be able to see our boy.' And he says, 'Well, I wish I could hear him cry.' I had a little gold necklace on and just then the baby caught his finger in it and really started to cry. So I was glad Camille could leave knowing at least he'd heard his son cry."

Raymond Russell Kelley,
last picture in France, 1944

Raymond Russell Kelley with
Daphne Cavin, wartime

The inscription on the back reads
"I love you darling"

Camille had one other request of Jeanette. He said, "Whatever you do, don't name him Camille." Jeanette promised she wouldn't. In Canada that name—Camille—wasn't unusual for a boy, but in the States it was. Jeanette decided to call their boy Robert—Bob.

Jeanette had to grow up fast. Married, a mother, and her husband off to war—all of that happened before she was twenty. "When they placed that baby in my arms I changed from being a kind of giddy, goofy teenager to being a real responsible person. . . . It seems like I matured overnight."

Her husband was going through his own maturation process. His outfit went from Fort Benning to North Africa for additional training, and then into battle in Sicily and Salerno. Camille was injured, although not seriously, when a landing went bad on one of his jumps, so he was sent to England for recuperation and was kept there to train for the D-Day invasion in the spring of 1944.

He wrote when he could, and Jeanette remembers the letters sometimes arriving five or six at a time. She shared them with the women at Honeywell in Minneapolis, where she had gone to work assembling automatic pilot instrumentation for warplanes. Her mother moved in to care for the baby when Jeanette got the job at Honeywell. "When I'd go to work I'd say I got a letter from my husband today and I'd share that. They'd say, 'Yeah, I got one, too,' and they'd share it. It was real close."

Jeanette's mother, however, was having a hard time keeping up with the newborn back home, so after about nine months they switched roles and Jeanette stayed home with the baby while her mother worked.

Still, she was an energetic young woman and spending all her time with a toddler was not easy, so she wrote Camille, asking his permission to attend the weekend dances at nearby Fort Snelling. As she recalls now, "He wrote back to say okay but just don't get too interested in someone."

Jeanette and two or three friends would ride out to the Fort Snelling armory in streetcars and dance the night away. "I would dance with just about every branch of the armed forces, I guess," she recalls. "Of course some of the questions were 'I guess you must get pretty lonesome,' but I just said, 'I'm married and I have a baby and I just enjoy being here dancing.' It was fun, but it was hard because some of them were out of small towns for the first time and missing their families—so I felt like I was helping the war effort."

Jeanette says Camille didn't have anything to worry about. "I didn't want to do anything to upset my marriage—and being where he was at the time, it wouldn't have been right. I was so glad to have our son, because every time I looked at him it would be like part of my husband was there, especially when I'd hold him and hug him."

Camille stayed in the thick of battle. He survived his D-Day experience, one of the lucky members of the 82nd Airborne to land near his objective, the village of Ste. Mère-Église, and not get killed or wounded. When his unit was returned to England following the Normandy operation Camille wrote to Jeanette, saying, "I'm going again; after Normandy I have one more battle and then I'll be headed home."

The objective was Nijmegen, on the border between Germany and Holland, a critical crossing of the Rhine River. The operation, under the direction of Britain's Field Marshal Montgomery, was code-named Market Garden. In another unit of the 82nd Airborne, Thomas Broderick, the former Merchant Marine, was sent into battle at Arnhem. Camille jumped into battle September 19, 1944, and he was immediately in a ferocious fight for control of a bridge at Nijmegen. His outfit was greatly outnumbered, fighting against the well-fortified German forces, part of Hitler's desperate attempt to counter the losses that began with the D-Day invasion.

BACK HOME, young Bob was just seventeen months old. Jeanette was home with him when there was a knock at the door. It was a Western Union man. Jeanette remembers every detail to this day. "He says, 'Are you Mrs. Gagne? I have this telegram for you. Are you going to be okay?' I said, 'Oh, sure, I'm okay.' When I opened it, I thought it would say 'Your husband was wounded,' but when it said, 'We regret to inform you your husband was killed in action'— Oh, boy—I picked up our little boy and started crying real loud."

The bridge at Nijmegen was captured by the Allied forces against great odds. The preeminent British military historian of World War II, John Keegan, called it "a brilliant success." Camille Gagne was an important part of that success. Operating from a

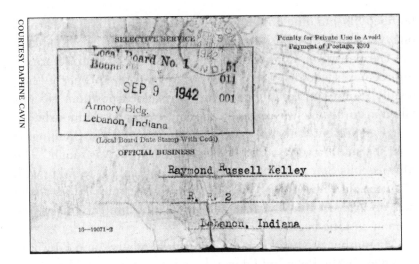

Raymond Russell Kelley, notice of classification, September 8, 1942

Children gathered at the grave of Raymond Russell Kelley, June 1997

bombed-out building on the western bank of the Rhine and armed only with light weapons—bazookas and grenades—his squad kept the Germans from counterattacking across the bridge. Before reinforcements could arrive, the Germans rolled up one of their deadly 88mm guns and opened fire on Gagne's position. He was killed instantly. He was awarded the Silver Star posthumously.

It was presented to Jeanette in ceremonies at Fort Snelling. It was, she says, "a very sad, sad day. . . . Oh, boy, it was rough." The Minneapolis *Star and Tribune* took a photograph of Jeanette with two-year-old Bob wearing the Silver Star won by his father—who had never seen him. It was the end of one life for this young woman and the beginning of another.

"My mother was working," Jeanette remembers, "and I'd watch Bob play on the floor and I'd wonder what was going to happen to us. Would I ever marry again? I wondered if I'd find a man who would be good to my boy. I used to sit and wonder a lot what would happen to me."

Her future was uncertain, but she was grateful for one thing: young Bob resembled his father so much she knew Camille would live on through him. When she met another man and fell in love a second time, they agreed he would not adopt Bob, so the Gagne family name could be continued.

Her second husband, William Norton, was the only real father Bob had ever known and he met the test of loving him as his own son. In fact, Jeanette says, Norton considered it an honor to raise the son of a World War II hero, and there was never any resentment when Camille's name came up.

When Bob was a teenager he announced to his mother that one day he'd go visit his father's grave in Holland. Jeanette didn't think much about the promise since she was busy with her new life. She had three daughters with William Norton, and they led a happy existence in a Minneapolis suburb.

When Norton died of a heart attack in 1993 after forty-five years of marriage, Jeanette was, as she says now, alone with her thoughts and they took her back to World War II and Camille. By now Bob, an engineer with a major Twin Cities radio station, was also determined to fulfill his teenage pledge to visit his father's final resting place.

His mother and stepfather had always kept his father in his life, reminding him of Camille's birthday, discussing his heroism when

Camille Gagne

Jeanette Gagne,
wartime portrait

news of World War II would come along. Bob decided it was time to somehow try to connect to the father he'd never known.

When he arrived at the American cemetery in the village of Margraten, near Maastricht in the Netherlands, he was not prepared for the full impact on his emotions. As he says of his father, "Here was a young guy who basically had his whole life in front of him. He had a young wife in the States and a son he had never seen. He was in a strange country. But he continued to fight with valor for his country. Tears came. . . . Yeah, I did feel a kinship with him people would have a hard time understanding. But I feel closer to him than I would have otherwise."

Bob brought back a videotape of his father's headstone, the cemetery, and the chapel to share with his mother and his three stepsisters. It was an intensely emotional experience for all of them. The younger people felt an association with the values of their parents' time and generation that might have eluded them before. Jeanette was reminded of her first love, the father of her first child, a man she knew for less than a year before he went off to war. The soldier-husband who gave her permission to attend weekend dances and told her in letters how he longed to be home and hold her and their son.

Now in her seventies, Jeanette remembers when the telegram came and her world came apart. She remembers how she worried that she could not love again. She did love again, of course, and gave birth to sisters for Bob. She enjoys her life in a senior citizens complex, reading Christian novels and crocheting, participating in communal dinners. It's a far more serene time than those years between 1942 and 1945, when she was just a teenager and experiencing enough passion, joy, fear, and grief to be remembered for a lifetime.

DAPHNE CAVIN has a thick scrapbook from the World War II years. She calls it *Lost Love Remembered*. She discovered it a few years back, and it opened a torrent of memories, many of them difficult. But it also reminded her of a young man and a time in her life when she was certain they would be together forever.

She met Raymond Kelley in August 1941 at a Sunday-school party. "It seemed like there was some chemistry from the begin-

COURTESY JEANETTE GAGNE NORTON

Jeanette Gagne Norton, receiving her husband's posthumous Silver Star

COURTESY JEANETTE GAGNE NORTON

Jeanette Gagne Norton with baby Robert

ning," she says. "I thought he was quite a handsome person." The romance started quickly and by the following June they were married. Daphne was twenty-one and Raymond was nineteen. By November of 1942 he was off to basic training. They had been in love for a little more than a year.

Daphne kept busy as a beautician in their hometown of Lebanon, Indiana. Just as Jeanette Gagne was filling her days in Minneapolis with work and movies, Daphne and many other young war wives were doing the same. But there were the constant underlying anxieties. As Daphne says now, she didn't want to tell her customers in the beauty shop about her fears for Raymond, who was fighting in France, because they all had husbands or brothers or boyfriends away for the war effort as well. "You were lonely in a crowd" is the way Daphne explains it.

She wrote to Raymond every day, and the postman made sure she received prompt delivery when a letter arrived from overseas. "He would bring my mail just inside the door at my shop and joke and chat with us." In one of the letters, Daphne learned that Raymond had been wounded in Italy and was being treated. She didn't know the full extent of the injuries but hoped he'd be shipped home. He wasn't. He was patched up and sent back into action.

In June 1944 Raymond Kelley, twenty-two years old, was killed by a German artillery shell in France. Daphne was helping her sister clean her home when their mother and the family minister suddenly appeared at the front door. Daphne says, "I knew immediately what it was." Daphne was in a daze. Her world changed instantly. The postman no longer stopped to chat and joke. Now he quietly slipped beneath the door of her beauty shop the returned letters she had written to Raymond.

She recalls, "In our little town, when you walked through, you would see stars in the windows. A blue star meant there was someone in the service. A silver star, you would know he had been sent overseas. A gold star meant you knew he wouldn't be coming back. I had all three stars."

Daphne decided she wouldn't marry again, and she had to support herself, so she purchased her own beauty shop and named it Daphne Ray Beauty Salon after their two first names. She had a natural flair for business and a good head for numbers, so the beauty salon flourished, but her life was on hold. After about four years her mother encouraged her to become socially active again. Raymond's mother, with whom she kept close ties, seconded the idea. Daphne agreed it was time to move on.

One of her clients had a son, Marvin Cavin, a veteran who had worked in Army hospitals during the war. They courted for a year or so, and then married and settled into a comfortable life on a farm in the middle of Indiana. They raised a family—two girls and twin boys—and over the years Daphne decided not to tell them much about Raymond, for fear it would hurt Marvin's feelings. Her own memories of her first love began to fade.

Once the children were grown she went back to the hairstyling business; she renewed her license and learned the new fashions. Shortly after that, her work became more urgent. Marvin was diagnosed with terminal cancer. Daphne would once again know the heartbreak of losing a husband.

She also had to make a living, so she purchased her own beauty shop again, and when Marvin died, in the mid-seventies, she went back to work full-time. Daphne was surprised when Congress passed a law that made her eligible for Raymond's military pension, even though she had remarried. She laughs now when she says, "I had two men taking care of me."

Daphne continued her business until 1987, when she decided it was time to retire. Then, unexpectedly, her life took another turn back toward Raymond, her first love. Her sister found the scrapbook she had assembled during the war years. It was thick with memories and poignant reminders of Raymond.

Daphne had saved the wallet Raymond was carrying when he was killed. His driver's license and Social Security card were in it. The scrapbook also preserved their wedding license, a photo of their wedding day, a scratchy recording of a message he sent to her before shipping out, the telegram notifying her of Raymond's death, a letter from President Roosevelt expressing sympathy, and Raymond's combat infantryman's badge.

As the state of Indiana prepared to build a memorial to the Hoosiers who served in World War II, word of Daphne's scrapbook reached *The Indianapolis News* and the paper featured her in a long story called "Lost Love Is Still a Comfort." Daphne opened the scrapbook for a reporter, smiled, and said, "This is a love story."

Going on, she added that when her sister discovered the scrapbook, "It was hard for me . . . yet it opened up a lot of memories. . . . We put on a lot of false gaiety during the war."

Raymond was buried in the Allied cemetery at Épinal, France, his grave marked with one of those white marble crosses. Daphne has not been there, but when a group of students from a nearby Indiana high school went to Europe as part of their French language training they visited the cemetery and found Raymond's grave. They posed for pictures and brought them home for Daphne.

She's added the pictures to the scrapbook's final pages. There's a powerful symbolism in the snapshot of a young Hoosier's final resting place framed by innocent young teenagers from his home state. His death, and millions more, gave those Indiana teenagers the world they have today. In Daphne's scrapbook there's another equally compelling symbol of their relationship and his sacrifice. When he was killed, he was carrying a poem from Daphne entitled "When You Come Home." The paper on which it is written is stained with the blood of his mortal wounds.

When You Come Home

When you come home once more to me,
It is unlikely, dear, that I shall be
Articulate; the words I've wanted so
To say, I'll try in vain to speak, I know
I shall reach blindly for you, stricken dumb
With swift and aching joy when you have come,
Or if my tongue find utterance at all,
It will be commonplace and trivial.

But you will understand. And, oh, once more
I'll feel your hand laid lightly on my hand
As was your wont, smoothing it again
And yet again. You'll lift my face and then
We shall forget all else. You'll hold me fast
When you come home, come home to me at last!

Raymond would not be coming home, of course. But Daphne keeps him in her heart. As she says, "He would be seventy-five now. He was twenty-two when he was killed, and that's how I think of him."

FAMOUS
PEOPLE

One of my favorite pictures from the World War II era is of Jimmy Stewart standing with a group of ordinary young Americans, his right hand raised, being sworn into the Army Air Corps. It was everyone's war, from the impoverished North Dakota farm kid to the Ivy League scion, the Hollywood star, the sons of the rich and powerful. Theodore Roosevelt Jr. landed in Normandy on D-Day. FDR's boys were on duty in the South Pacific when their father died, and only Elliott was able to get home for the funeral. Jack Kennedy and his brother Joe were in uniform and in harm's way.

Others we came to know later: George Bush, Richard Nixon, and Gerald Ford, all Navy officers, later presidents of the United States. Ben Bradlee, the most celebrated newspaper editor of his time, was another young naval officer in the Pacific. Art Buchwald, a foster child from the Bronx, joined the Marines at seventeen and emerged to become a universally beloved columnist. Johnny Carson, the master of the television medium, looked like a skinny twelve-year-old in his naval officer's uniform. Julia Child, America's favorite woman in the kitchen, was in the OSS. Byron "Whizzer" White, an All-America football player and Rhodes Scholar, was turned down by the Marines because he was color-blind but was accepted for the Naval Intelligence School. He met John Kennedy in England, and when Kennedy became president, White was his first appointment to the Supreme Court.

Kennedy was just one of scores of World War II veterans to enter the political arena. Their fame grew out of their place in the great public policy debates of their time and the offices they occupied.

The themes of war have long been the stuff of great literature, and once World War II ended, a new generation of American writers emerged. Some are still at work today. Norman Mailer, Kurt Vonnegut, William Styron, William Manchester, James Jones, Paul Fussell, Shelby Foote, and Joseph Heller all served in uniform during World War II.

So did Pierre Salinger, JFK's press secretary and, later, ABC News correspondent. Al Neuharth, founder of *USA Today*, was a combat infantryman. Andy Rooney, of *60 Minutes*, wrote for *Stars and Stripes* during the war.

William Webster has been a distinguished federal judge, the director of the FBI, and director of the Central Intelligence Agency. During the war he had an unremarkable time as a Navy lieutenant; he was not involved in combat, yet he credits the discipline and organizational skills he learned from the Navy with helping him when he took over the formidable job of reorganizing the FBI after the chaos of the Watergate years.

Cyrus Vance embodies the best of his generation as a private citizen and public servant. Vance, a small-town native of West Virginia who earned Ivy League credentials at Yale as an undergraduate and law student, was a junior officer in the Navy during World War II. He left the military in 1946, but in a manner of speaking, he's never left the service of his country. Now in his seventies, he's still at the top of any list when there's a need for a skilled and tireless diplomat in trouble spots such as Bosnia or Africa. For more than half a century he has moved gracefully and effectively between congressional staff jobs, a thriving New York law practice, and as secretary of the Army during the John Kennedy administration, a major player on Lyndon Johnson's diplomatic and national security team, and, for three years, Jimmy Carter's secretary of state.

World War II, like the Civil War but so distinctly different in origin, locale, and time, was the common denominator and the defining experience in the lives of millions of young Americans, whatever their status before the first shots were fired. Later accomplishments, however grand or notorious, cannot diminish the place of their service in the war years.

GEORGE BUSH

"I learned about life."

WORLD WAR II and the demands it made on all parts of the country was the quintessential American melting-pot experience. It was a great unifying force, requiring sacrifice and imposing new disciplines across the many layers of American society. In a way, America came to know itself better through this common experience.

George Bush was a child of privilege when the Japanese attacked Pearl Harbor. His father had accumulated a fortune on Wall Street and was a member of the U.S. Senate. His mother presided over a large home in Greenwich, Connecticut; she sent her children off to the best private schools and camps in chauffeured limousines, but when they returned home she preached modesty and public responsibility.

So it was only natural that on the day he turned eighteen George Bush volunteered for the Navy. He didn't wait for his draft number to be called. His father, the powerful senator Prescott Bush, didn't attempt to arrange a safe job for his son in the War Department. George volunteered for a relatively new branch of the service, the Navy Air Corps. He wanted to be a combat pilot.

By now, after all of his years in public life, his combat experience is well known. There's even a home movie of him being fished from the sea after his plane was shot down during a bombing run on a Japanese target. He rarely talks about the experience personally; he is more likely to recite his mother's admonition "Don't brag." When he was running for president, he was asked what he thought

George Bush as a young officer

about as he drifted in hostile seas after being shot down, and he answered in that clumsy but endearing way of his, "Oh, you know—the usual things, duty, honor, country." As a political answer it was a groaner. Nonetheless, it was probably very close to the essence of George Bush.

For a man who spent so much of his life in the public arena, President Bush was curiously inarticulate about those defining moments. He was battle-scarred in a way that the man he served as vice president, Ronald Reagan, was not; but next to Reagan, Bush always looked a little like the younger kid, wide-eyed with hero worship.

Even when invited to expand on his thoughts about how World War II shaped him, President Bush is a reluctant witness. Yes, of course, he considers his years as a Navy combat flier an important experience. He often thinks about the day he was shot down, but when he does, he's more likely to think about his two buddies who were killed. Could he have done more to save them?

When he returned home and plunged into a college education at Yale, sharing very crowded quarters with his wife, Barbara, and other couples in a New Haven home hastily converted into an apartment building, Bush didn't look back. He played varsity sports, got his degree, and headed west, to the oilfields of Texas and the opportunities they presented. Did combat make him more willing to take those kinds of risks?

"I do not believe my combat experience was in any way responsible for my coming to Texas," he reflects now, adding, "The Navy sent us all over . . . so a move away from a home base was not so traumatic." In that regard, George and Barbara Bush were like many young Americans in their postwar migration to other parts of the country. Kids from the Great Plains who joined the Navy returned to settle down hard by the sea in California. Young black veterans headed north to the good factory jobs in Detroit. World War II rearranged more than the political landscape of Europe and Asia; it was a major catalyst for the shifting population patterns of the United States in the fifties and sixties.

As for business, President Bush agrees that, yes, "both military training and experience were helpful to all of us as we tackled various businesses. Maybe, just maybe," he concludes, "having taken risks in the service, we were less concerned about taking risks in business."

Overall, however, responding to questions about his youthful trials in combat, President Bush likes to invoke what was drummed into him at home even before he enlisted: honor. As he says, his service in the war was "a duty, yes, but truly an honor." He also feels strongly it was an obligation of citizenship that requires no additional reward. "What are we 'owed'?" he asks. "Nothing. Not one damn thing."

However, it is clear President Bush did gain something personally from the war that he would not have experienced if he had gone directly to Yale and then on to, say, a career on Wall Street or even a political career from his home in Connecticut. He saw the other side of life through the eyes and some very private thoughts of his comrades from other classes back home.

As an officer on a carrier, even though he was only nineteen or twenty at the time, one of Lieutenant Bush's jobs was to read the mail of the enlisted men before it went out so no sensitive military information would be inadvertently compromised. As Bush recalls, "As I did my duty and read the other guys' mail, I learned about life—about true love, about heartbreak, about fear and courage, about the diversity of our great country. The sailors would ask about the harvest or fishing or the heat in the cities." Bush goes on, "When I would see a man whose letter I had censored, I would look at him differently, look at him with more understanding. I gained an insight into the lives of my shipmates, and I felt richer."

As a young man at the controls of a TBM Avenger, flying off carrier decks, dropping torpedoes on enemy targets, and getting back safely, Bush was a long way from those days of privilege in Greenwich. What he learned went well beyond his own involvement, however. He remembers vividly standing on the carrier deck when another plane made a bad landing. As the pilot tried to take off again, the plane veered out of control and its propeller cut a crew member in half. As Bush stood there, stunned, staring at a severed leg, a salty chief petty officer "rallied the shocked sailors. 'Goddamnit, get back to work. Swab the deck, clear the deck, get ready for the next plane.' " More than fifty years later that Navy chief stands out in the mind of President Bush as a man who, under

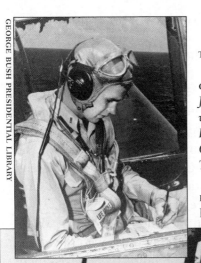

TOP: *George Bush as a Navy pilot*

CENTER: *Fort Lauderdale Naval Air Station, July 1943, Flight 44: (top row) Bill Donovan, Ralph Cole, Mort Landsburg, George Bush, Louis Grab; (bottom row) Mike Goldsmith, Leslie Mokry, Bill Shawcross, Tom Campion, Tex Ellison*

BOTTOM: *George Bush, in his plane* Barbara III

great adversity, took charge, rallied the men, got the job done—did his duty.

By his own admission George Bush is not a reflective man. It may have to do with his mother's constant counsel not to draw attention to yourself. Work well done and a life lived honorably were reward enough. As a former congressman, ambassador to the United Nations, director of the Central Intelligence Agency, vice president, and then president of the United States, George Bush represents an unequaled record of public service within his generation.

He insists he is owed nothing. In fact, he believes that World War II was such an overwhelming threat that those who served did so out of an obligation that should not require special treatment forevermore. He believes some veterans' organizations are wrong to keep asking for more and more benefits. As he says, "Serving in World War II, I was a tiny part of something noble."

George Bush, presidential portrait

Ben Bradlee

BEN BRADLEE

"It separates those of us who were in the war from those who never had that kind of experience."

BEN BRADLEE, the son of a prominent Massachusetts family, was a Greek major at Harvard when war broke out. Eager to become involved, he made arrangements to fulfill his degree requirements in an abbreviated time so he could get into uniform. In his bestselling autobiography, *A Good Life,* he describes August 8, 1942, as a "day that has defined hectic for me forever." I should think so. He was awarded his Harvard degree at ten in the morning, commissioned as a Lieutenant, J.G., in the U.S. Navy at noon, and married that evening in a small chapel across from the Boston Common to the daughter of one of Massachusetts's most prominent families.

No doubt other young men across the country were undergoing similarly life-changing days that summer, but few could match the Harvard degree–Navy commission–society wedding trifecta of Benjamin Crowninshield Bradlee. It was a portent of the life he was to lead for the rest of the century.

Bradlee was assigned to a destroyer, the *Philip,* in the South Pacific. He was in the middle of the action in what is called "The Slot," a stretch of water bisecting the Solomon Islands, islands that were bloody killing grounds for the U.S. Marines. It was in The Slot that the fight for control of the seas between the U.S. Navy and the Japanese Navy was both critical and ferocious.

It was there that Ben Bradlee, who had been tutored in French as a child and sent only to the best schools, began to learn about the real meaning of personal responsibility. "I remember," he says, "the first day I was made officer of the bridge. I was twenty-one years old. I was in charge of the ship. I am driving this goddamn thing. It was a tremendous responsibility, and at twenty-one it was good to see what you could do."

Bradlee was also able to see what others, those who lacked his pedigree, could do. He laughs and says, "They were all a guy named Joe with an unpronounceable last name. *They* could fix the radar, and *you* couldn't. I learned a tremendous amount about how excellence had nothing to do with class."

One long night off Saipan, Bradlee had a lesson in excellence and courage that sticks with him to this day. He was working in the ship's command and control center, directing the shells the *Philip* was booming toward the island. His partner on shore was an anonymous Marine forward observer. "Often when he hit his radio to talk," Bradlee says, "we could hear the Japanese yelling in the background. They were that close to our guy."

After hours of this harrowing duty, the forward observer said he could use a break, that he'd like to get off the island and out of danger for a while. Bradlee radioed right back: " 'Sure, we'll come get you, give you a decent meal and a night's sleep.' My God, when he got onto our ship he looked about thirteen years old. He was tiny and so heroic. I get all excited even now thinking about it. We kept him for two nights, scrubbed him up and sent him back. I know I learned a lot from those experiences."

What Bradlee learned, he says, is that there are no tests or psychological profiles that can compare to the experiences of war when it comes to determining what capabilities people have within them. "The war took the cockiness out of you. You couldn't bullshit your way out the first time you were under fire." It also gave this Greek major from Harvard an early lesson in what would become a defining characteristic of his personality. "I had not been a big leader before the war," Bradlee acknowledges, "so the idea that you could persuade people to do things was awesome. Not only that you could, but that you had to—and it was fun and, my God, you were good at it."

It also prompted Bradlee to think of a life outside the constraints of his establishment background. Before the war, Bradlee thought

Ben and Jean Bradlee

Constance Bradlee, John La Farge, Jean and Ben Bradlee, 1945

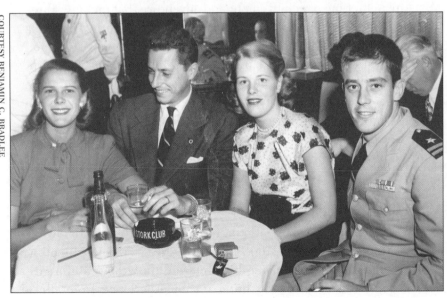

he'd probably wind up a stockbroker, working for a friend of his father, like so many of his peers. Then, World War II started and, in his words, "I had a sense of what was possible: how many different lives and professions were out there—how many exciting prospects in the world."

In his own privileged way, Bradlee was as provincial as any enlisted man from a small town in West Texas. He'd known only one way of life, and suddenly he had options. Bradlee remembers that once the war was over he led group discussions on his ship about what the men would do next. "I remember," he says, "people were interested in public service; teaching got a big call. We were determined not to make the mistakes of earlier generations. I was hustling journalism as a way of righting wrongs."

Ironically, about that same time, another young naval officer in another part of the Pacific was thinking about his future. He was going home to California, where shortly after the war he got involved in politics. His name was Richard Nixon, and thirty years later he and Bradlee would be on a historic collision course. Bradlee's vision of journalism as a means of righting wrongs was never truer or more important than when he was directing two young reporters, Bob Woodward and Carl Bernstein, in their coverage of Watergate.

After a lifetime of achievement and adventure that includes three wives; four children; six years abroad (most of them in Paris as a *Newsweek* correspondent); a close personal friendship with his fellow Harvard graduate John F. Kennedy; the editorship of *The Washington Post* during Vietnam, the Pentagon Papers, Spiro Agnew, Watergate, and the fall of communism; his dazzling marriage to Sally Quinn and their large, comfortable homes in Georgetown, on the Chesapeake Bay, and in the Hamptons; Bradlee was a little surprised how vivid his recollections of the war were and how important they seemed to him in his seventies, when he was writing his autobiography.

Nonetheless, they remain stories and memories for his own satisfaction; he seldom shares them, not even with the two fellow officers from his destroyer, the *Philip,* who live in the Washington, D.C., area. As he was raising his children, three boys and a girl, Bradlee would occasionally bring up an experience from those days. When he did, the kids would say, "Uh-oh, here comes the Big Two." Bradlee would like to go to a reunion of the men and officers of his ship, but he laughingly concedes that he hasn't been to one because his wife, Sally, has no interest, even though she's the daughter of a distinguished Army general.

It's probably just as well. Bradlee's life since those exciting days on the *Philip* has taken him to places and heights far removed from the lives of the other men on board. They shared a time and a place in their late teens and early twenties that could never be duplicated, and Bradlee has reserved a special corner of his memory for that distinctive experience. While a reunion might be fun, it's hard to imagine it could add to the original experience.

There are times when Bradlee doesn't hesitate to bring up the war years and the pride he has in his service record: when people question his patriotism, a not uncommon blasphemy leveled at journalists, especially one running the preeminent newspaper in the nation's capital. As Bradlee puts it, using one of his many favorite profanities, "I have a special reaction to those who impugn my love of country, especially those f——s on the Hill." But Bradlee also believes it gives him a special bond with people like Senator John McCain, the Arizona Republican, Naval Academy graduate, and POW in Vietnam.

He thinks of the experience of World War II as being as important to his life as overseeing the Watergate reporting when he was editor of *The Washington Post*. He says, "It separates those of us who were in the war from those who never had that kind of experience—the teamwork, the danger of dying, the self-confidence we gained. I don't feel superior as a result of those days. I just know I learned a helluva lot from being there."

He also believes this is true for almost everyone who served in the military, whether they saw combat or were heroes. "It wasn't just about throwing grenades or jumping into the water to save someone's ass," he says. "God, my ship went from the coast of Massachusetts through the Panama Canal, forty days to Guadalcanal. When we started, I was the lowest cog in the machine. By the time we got there, I was really a part of something."

Art Buchwald, wartime portrait

---- • ----

ART BUCHWALD

"People are constantly amazed when I tell them I was a Marine."

IT'S HARD TO IMAGINE a greater contrast to Ben Bradlee's family, Harvard education, wartime service, dashing appearance, and general rakishness than his old friend Art Buchwald, the lovably teddy-bear humorist and columnist who may have been the most unlikely Marine in all of World War II. In his autobiography *Leaving Home,* he wrote with endearing candor, "People are constantly amazed when I tell them I was a Marine. For some reason, I don't look like one—and I certainly don't act like one. But I was, and according to God or the tradition of the Corps, I will always be a Marine."

At seventeen, Buchwald was running from a troubled childhood and the heartbreak of a failed summer romance. He persuaded a street drunk to forge his father's signature on the permission form needed to enlist in the Marine Corps. That he survived basic training on Parris Island was a minor miracle. He was always in a jam for his bumbling ways, terrorized by his drill instructor, Corporal Pete Bonardi of Elmhurst, Long Island.

Buchwald spent the war in the South Pacific, attached to a Marine ordnance outfit, loading ammunition onto the Marine Corsairs that were dueling with Japanese Zeroes in the skies over places like Guadalcanal, Okinawa, and Midway. He was on a tiny island called Engebi.

Buchwald was not much more competent on Engebi than he had been at Parris Island. Loading a large bomb onto a Corsair, he hit the wrong lever and it dropped onto the tarmac, sending his buddies scattering, convinced they were about to be blown up. Finally Buchwald's sergeant assigned him to work on the squadron's mimeographed newsletter and to drive a truck, reasoning he couldn't do much harm to himself or others in those jobs. His sergeant told him later, "You had the ability to screw up a two-car funeral. Anything you touched ceased to function."

He also learned more than he wanted to know about anti-Semitism. Many of the small-town boys he served with had never known a Jew, and they were quick to repeat the bigotry of their upbringing. Buchwald, much more a man of wit and words than fists, nonetheless found himself in numerous fights after some reference to a "kike" or "Christ-killer." But then he decided it wasn't worth all the anger and bruises, so he just responded "Stuff it" and walked away. Now, on reflection, he says, "I can't maintain people picked on me just because I was Jewish. They picked on me because I was an asshole"—followed by that familiar Buchwald laugh.

Buchwald's life after the war began at the University of Southern California, where he enrolled under the GI Bill even though he didn't have a high school diploma. In the crush of veterans registering in 1946, the admissions office simply didn't check. By the time he was found out, Buchwald was a fixture on campus and accepted as a special student.

At USC, Buchwald began to hone the gentle, mocking style of humor that would make him one of journalism's best-known columnists and a high-priced public speaker. He wrote for the campus newspaper and a humor magazine. He was friendly on campus with Frank Gifford, the All-America football hero; David Wolper, later one of Hollywood's most successful producers; and Pierre Cossette, who became the man behind the televised Grammy Awards. It was a fantasy come true for this funny little man from a succession of foster homes in New York.

His Walter Mitty life took an even more romantic turn when he learned the GI Bill was good in Paris as well as in the United States. Determined to become another Hemingway or Fitzgerald, Buchwald hitchhiked to New York and caught an old troop ship for France. He lived the life of an expatriate on the modest stipend the GI Bill provided him for classes at the Alliance Française, drinking

Art Buchwald

Pernod late into the night in Montparnasse, stringing for *Daily Variety* back in the States, and hanging out with new friends who would later become famous writers: William Styron, Peter Matthiessen, James Baldwin, Mary McCarthy, Irwin Shaw, and Peter Stone. As he recounted in *I'll Always Have Paris,* Buchwald loved the life. "We had come out of the war with great optimism," he said. "It was a glorious period."

It became even more glorious when Buchwald talked himself into a job at the glamorous *International Herald Tribune,* the English-language newspaper that was distributed throughout Europe and served as a piece of home for American tourists. In 1949, just seven years after he'd been rejected by his summertime sweetheart and joined the Marines in a desperate attempt to find a new life, Art Buchwald had talked his way into one of the most sought-after jobs in journalism. "Paris After Dark," Buchwald's column, quickly became one of the most popular items in the paper, and it led to the byline humor column that made him the best-known American in Paris. He was the city's most popular tourist guide for visiting stars such as Frank Sinatra, Humphrey Bogart, Lauren Bacall, and Audrey Hepburn.

His books became bestsellers, and when he came home, sixteen years later, he was an even bigger star in Washington, with his own table at the most popular restaurant in the capital and lecture fees now at five figures, often with a private plane for transportation. He was practically an uncle to the various Kennedy offspring. When he went to Redskins games, he sat in the owner's box. He summered on Martha's Vineyard with pals Katharine Graham, Mike Wallace, Bill Styron, and Walter Cronkite.

However glamorous his life had become, he never forgot he was a Marine. When Colin Powell was preparing to leave the military and enter civilian life, Buchwald offered to advise him on what lecture agencies would serve him best. Powell's assistant called Buchwald, inviting him to lunch with the general at the Pentagon. Buchwald said, "Lunch? Don't I get a parade? I was in the Marine Corps three and a half years and I never had a parade." When Buchwald arrived at Powell's office, the general said, "Follow me." He took Buchwald into a large room where Powell had assembled fifty of his staff. As Buchwald entered, they all came to attention and gave him a salute. After all those years of people not believing he had been a Marine, Buchwald had a parade, with the Chairman of the Joint Chiefs at his side, in the Pentagon.

He laughs now when he thinks of how much attention he received from Marine brass once he moved to Washington. "They said I was a great Marine. I was a *lousy* Marine. But at the last Marine Ball I attended, colonels were coming up to have their pictures taken with me. I loved that."

Buchwald's feelings go well beyond the attention he gets at Marine ceremonies. "I had no father to speak of, no mother. I didn't know what I was doing. Suddenly I'm in the Marines and it's my family—someone cared about me, someone loved me. That's what I still feel today."

Despite his lovably rumpled appearance, Buchwald also maintains certain habits he learned at Parris Island. He keeps his personal effects neatly arranged, just as he did in his footlocker during basic training. His shoes are always shined to a high gloss. He always has an extra pair of socks, just as the Marines taught him.

During the Vietnam War, he was caught between conflicting emotions. He was against the war, yet when the Marine Corps asked him to record some radio commercials for their recruiting efforts he happily complied. He was flattered, in fact; after all, he was a Marine. He realized that his old loyalties and his current thinking were in conflict only when friends began to point out the inconsistencies of his behavior. He stopped recording the commercials.

Buchwald has written about his Marine Corps experience so often that fellow leathernecks often approach him to compare notes, inevitably saying, "You think *your* drill instructor was tough. *Mine* was the toughest in the Corps." Buchwald never concedes. He *knows* Pete Bonardi was the toughest.

In 1965, *Life* magazine asked Buchwald to return to Parris Island for a week of basic training, to recall the old days. He agreed, if he could take along his old drill instructor, Pete Bonardi.

He found Bonardi working as a security guard at the World's Fair in New York and arranged for him to get the time off work. Bonardi remembered Buchwald from basic training, saying, "I was sure you'd get killed," adding warmly, "You were a real shitbird."

In his book, Buchwald recalls that they had a nostalgic week at Parris Island and that nothing much had changed. He may have been famous, but he was still a klutz. On the obstacle course, Bonardi was still yelling things like "Twenty-five years ago I would have hung your testicles from that tree." At the end of the week, they shook hands and parted friends.

A quarter century later, Buchwald received a call from a mutual friend telling him Bonardi was gravely ill with cancer. Buchwald telephoned his old drill instructor, whose voice was weak as he told Buchwald he didn't think he could make this obstacle course.

In *Leaving Home,* Buchwald describes taking a photo from their *Life* layout and sending it to Bonardi with the inscription "To Pete Bonardi, who made a man out of me. I'll never forget you." Bonardi's wife later told Buchwald that the old D.I. had put the picture up in his hospital room so everyone could read it.

Bonardi also had one final request. That autographed picture from the shitbird, the screw-up Marine he was sure would be killed, little Artie, the guy he called "Brooklyn" as he tried to make a leatherneck out of him? Corporal Bonardi, the toughest guy Buchwald ever met, asked that the picture be placed in his casket when he was buried.

I confess that I weep almost every time I read that account, for it so encapsulates the bonds within that generation that last a lifetime. For all of their differences, Art Buchwald and Pete Bonardi were joined in a noble cause and an elite corps, each in his own way enriching the life of the other. Their common ground went well beyond the obstacle course at Parris Island.

ANDY ROONEY

"For the first time I knew that any peace is not better than any war."

ANDY ROONEY, the resident curmudgeon of *60 Minutes,* might have difficulty with the sweep of my conclusion. Indeed, he's challenged my premise that his was the greatest generation any society could hope to produce. He believes the character of the current generation is just as strong; it's just that his generation had a Depression, World War II, and a Cold War against which to test their character. When I counter that his generation didn't fumble those historic challenges, that they prevailed, often against great odds, and moved quietly to the next challenge, he listens but I am not persuaded I've won him over.

I wanted to talk to Rooney because his splendid book *My War* is a compelling personal account of his odyssey from a privileged background in Albany, New York, through a phase of pacificism as a student at Colgate, to his years as an adventurous sergeant working as a correspondent for the Army's newspaper *Stars and Stripes.* Beyond Rooney's book, one of the lasting impressions I have of the fiftieth anniversary of D-Day is Rooney's reporting on the *CBS Morning News.* He had covered Normandy for *Stars and Stripes,* and a half century later he was back in Normandy, conveying to CBS viewers what it had been like during that muddy June in 1944. As he led the camera through the hedgerows where the fighting had been so fierce, he seemed to be walking and talking ever faster, trying to stay ahead of his emotions. He talked about the young American troops—just boys, really—who had such a terrible time

Andy Rooney, wartime portrait

there, about how so many died and how the fighting was at close quarters.

Rooney was drafted out of college at Colgate, where he played football and wrestled some after a comfortable upbringing and a private prep school education in Albany. His disdain for convention and authority, now so familiar to viewers of 60 *Minutes,* was already well established by the time he arrived at basic training with an infantry outfit.

Regimentation was not his favorite way of life. Besides, during college he had had an infatuation with journalism, so he applied to become a reporter with *Stars and Stripes.* This was the Army's enterprising newspaper that kept troops in the field informed and entertained with dispatches from the front lines, gossip, and Bill Mauldin's incomparable cartoons of the lives of the dogfaces, the combat infantrymen.

Rooney was a daring and resourceful young reporter, writing first about the exploits of the crews of the 8th Air Force flying B-17s and B-24s in bombing raids out of England, across the Channel, and into the heart of enemy territory. When he went on one of the raids for a firsthand account, his plane was shot up and Rooney helped save the life of a crew member. This incident got him a page 1 byline in *Stars and Stripes* and a glowing testimonial in his hometown newspaper, *The Albany Times Union.*

He went ashore at Normandy shortly after the invasion and stayed close to the advancing American infantry and armored units as they fought their way from hedgerow to hedgerow and village to village. He went into Paris with French forces the day the City of Light was liberated, finding himself beside Ernest Hemingway at one point as the remaining German forces tried to slow the entry with artillery fire.

For Rooney, August 25, 1944, the day Paris was liberated, "was the most dramatic I'd ever lived through." When he returns to Paris even now, he rents a car and drives the same triumphal route. Rooney, who is not given to emotional gestures, says simply, "It thrills me still."

He crossed the Rhine with the first American troops and unwittingly took a prisoner of war when a hapless German soldier insisted on surrendering. He still has the German's pistol. He went to Buchenwald to see for himself what had been only rumors as the Americans advanced across Europe. When he arrived, he was stunned by what he encountered, and embarrassed. "I was ashamed of myself for ever having considered refusing to serve in the Army," he wrote. "For the first time I knew that any peace is not better than any war."

All the while, he was working alongside some of the most gifted names in journalism: Ernie Pyle, the peerless war correspondent who was later killed in the Pacific, the legendary Homer Bigart of *The New York Times,* and Edward R. Murrow, the godfather of broadcast journalism. One of his colleagues became a lifelong friend and a coworker at CBS News: Walter Cronkite, at the time a correspondent for United Press. As Rooney says now, "It was a three-year graduate course in journalism I couldn't have duplicated in twenty years without the war."

As you might expect, Rooney is not an emotional romantic about the war and what came later. He regularly gets in trouble with veterans of armored units for his caustic comments about the place of tanks in the war. He took a lot of flak from old bombardiers when he wrote that their job didn't require much skill. He said they just dropped the bombs when they were told to and often they missed their targets.

Rooney is willing to take on the American Legion and the Veterans of Foreign Wars, pointing out that most veterans belong to neither organization. He says the Legion and the VFW expect too much. In Rooney's view, the only veterans deserving of special treatment are those who were disabled or seriously wounded.

He figures about 90 percent of the men in uniform didn't get anywhere near the fighting, so he doesn't believe the country owes them anything extra. "I'm not sure I even like the word *veteran,*" he says.

That is not to say that Rooney is cold-hearted about the war and the men who fought on the front line or in the cockpits of the B-17s and B-24s on their daring and dangerous bombing raids. He relishes his own adventures across the European battlefields and, briefly, in India and China when it appeared the war would go on longer there. Obviously, Rooney's wartime experience served him well once he returned home and turned to writing for a living.

Oram "Bud" Hutton, Charles Kiley, Andy Rooney

His wartime experiences nurtured his youthful skepticism and disdain for authority, two of the refreshing characteristics of the Rooney voice on 60 *Minutes* and in his newspaper column. He says now he believes the U.S. Army was successful in part because officers and men weren't afraid to question authority. "They often improvised, they came up with their own plan, they reacted to what was happening in the field instead of just blindly following orders like the Germans. That's one of the reasons the Germans lost."

Nonetheless, despite his challenges to the premise of this book and his inherent resistance to any thought on the sunny side of skepticism, I think Sergeant Rooney carries more of the war with him than he lets us know. He told me that when he returns to France now he always goes to Normandy, to drive the back roads between the hedgerows, taking a different route each time, remembering when he was there a long time ago.

In *My War*, Rooney describes how he has been to Omaha Beach and the nearby cemetery five times. "On each visit I've wept," he writes. "It's almost impossible to keep back the tears as you look across the rows of crosses and think of the boys under them who died that day. Even if you didn't know anyone who died, the heart knows something the brain does not—and you weep."

Exactly.

JULIA CHILD

"I didn't have anything but an eagerness to help."

ANOTHER FAMILIAR FIGURE on American television had the course of her life changed by World War II. More than anyone else, Julia Child brought the idea of French cuisine onto the American table through her television shows and her popular cookbook *Mastering the Art of French Cooking*. Anyone who has seen her on television, all six-foot-two of her, a formidable and commanding figure, may be surprised to learn that during the war she was a sort of spy. She worked for the Office of Strategic Services—the OSS—the precursor to the CIA.

It was an unlikely turn in the life of this product of a comfortable home in Pasadena, California, who after graduating from Smith College in 1934 worked in New York as an advertising copywriter. When the war started, she went to Washington and tried to enlist in the WAVES, the women's branch of the Navy, but she was rejected because of her height. How that could have affected the duties of a WAVE is not clear.

She was so eager to serve that she signed up as a clerk typist, one of an army of women who came to the capital from across America to help with the daily mountains of paperwork generated by the war in those precomputer days. Child hated the job. It was drudgery. "All I did was type little white cards," she says. "Finally, through some friends, I managed to get into the OSS."

She quickly became a senior clerk, supervising forty people, securing office equipment, hiring other clerks, setting up office financial systems and security. This was a big step for her: "I had no

Julia Child, wartime

Julia Child

training for anything whatsoever. In the mid-thirties a woman was expected to become a teacher or a housewife, take care of the children, and do the laundry. I didn't have anything but an eagerness to help."

She also had ambition. She'd been a clerk about a year and a half when she heard the OSS was going to send people to the Far East. As she recalls, "I knew that someday I would get to Paris and Europe, but not to the Far East." She signed up and, with a dozen other women from the home office, headed for the unknown in Asia.

They sailed on a troopship for India. Child says, "The trip was quite jolly. There were not very many women and lots of boys." They arrived in Bombay just as another ship caught fire and drifted into a nearby ammunition ship, causing a tremendous explosion. Child was a long way from typing little white cards in a Washington office.

As it did for so many women, the war liberated Julia Child. Before going to work for the OSS and setting off for exotic locations, she had no plans for her life. "I wasn't thinking in career terms," she says. "There weren't many careers to have. There wasn't anything really open."

If there had been no war, what would have become of Julia Child?

She's in her late eighties now, but she hasn't lost her sense of the plain thought. She answers, "Who knows? I might have ended up an alcoholic, since there wasn't anything to do."

Gertrude B. Elion and George Hitchings, Tuckahoe, New York, 1948

GERTRUDE BELLE "TRUDY" ELION

"She's improved the human condition. . . . Trudy was a role model for women but she was a role model for men, too."

THE MANPOWER DEMANDS of the war effort created opportunities for women that were unexpected. For example, America's scientific community, which was almost exclusively a male domain, was desperate for qualified people of either gender once the shooting got under way. Gertrude Belle "Trudy" Elion was a major beneficiary and, in the end, so were the rest of us.

She had graduated from high school at fifteen and college at nineteen, *summa cum laude,* with a major in chemistry. She had a goal: the death of her grandfather made her determined to find a cure for cancer. She went on to earn a master's degree and set out to find laboratory work. It was a discouraging process. "They told me," she said, "they didn't want a woman in the lab. They said, 'We think it would be a distraction.'"

Trudy refused to give up, but to earn a living she would have to teach high school chemistry. There were no other jobs for a woman with her credentials. Then came Pearl Harbor, and America was at war. More than a million men would go into uniform immediately, including many from the scientific laboratories of the country.

Trudy started getting calls from panicked personnel officers looking for someone with her credentials. Her first job was with the big supermarket chain A&P as a quality-control officer. "I tested the acidity of the pickles, the mold in the frozen strawberries; I checked the color of the egg yolk going into the mayonnaise. It wasn't exactly what I had in mind but it was a step in the right direction."

She got out of the egg yolk business and into what she wanted when Johnson & Johnson opened a small research laboratory. That lab didn't survive, but it did give Trudy the opening she'd been waiting for: she was hired as a research assistant for the distinguished scientist Dr. George Hitchings at Burroughs Wellcome, the giant pharmaceutical company.

At the time Elion was hired, Hitchings was Burroughs Wellcome's lone biochemist, and he said later that even though Trudy didn't have a PhD she was far and away the most knowledgeable and intelligent of the prospects. She was hired for fifty dollars a week. It was one of the most fortuitous pairings in the history of modern medical research.

Hitchings and Elion began a forty-year collaboration that was at once astonishingly prolific and inventive. Before he died a few years ago, Hitchings told the *Los Angeles Times,* "When we started, it was all trial and error. You'd develop a compound and then take some kind of target—usually a mouse—plug it in, and see what it did or didn't do." Hitchings and Elion began to rewrite the how-to manual for medical research.

Simply put, they developed a scientific rational approach to the problem of understanding how a disease affects the human body. They started with how cells reproduce in their various stages. The differences in what is called nucleic acid metabolism led Hitchings and Elion to develop a series of drugs that blocked the growth and reproduction of cancerous cells and other harmful organisms, without destroying the normal human cells. It is difficult to overstate the lasting impact of their new approach in medical research. It is at the heart of cancer and antiviral research today.

Over the years, they developed drugs that were effective in fighting childhood leukemia, the treatment of rheumatoid arthritis, gout, and kidney stones. Trudy's research in the antiviral area also led to the development of the most effective treatment for herpesvirus infections. So the range of her work with Dr. Hitchings was impressive—from life-threatening diseases to socially embarrassing and physically painful cold sores. Moreover, their approach led to the development of the most effective early AIDS treatment, the drug AZT (azidothymidine).

As their joint projects broke through one scientific barrier after another they remained laboratory partners in every sense of the phrase. They shared credit equally, and they were jointly dedicated to the idea of work, work, work.

They stayed on at Burroughs Wellcome when it moved from New York to the Research Triangle in North Carolina outside of Raleigh–Durham in 1970. It was later bought by the British pharmaceutical giant, Glaxo. By then they were established stars and had a research staff of fifteen hundred. Trudy Elion was a department head and a mentor to a new generation of scientists, including many women.

Karen Brion, who now heads the department of virology at Glaxo Wellcome, says, "I learned so much from her because she was a leader—an excellent scientific mentor, and not just a role model for women. In one sense Trudy is atypical because she didn't marry or have a family, but she made such a difference just by being a woman and showing she could assume the level of responsibility, be an effective manager and scientific leader, and have the credibility she does in the scientific world."

Trudy gave up on the idea of marriage when her fiancé died in the early forties. That loss, she says, reinforced her devotion to science and research. Besides, she points out, it wasn't "an option open to women with careers. If a woman got married, she was often fired; if she had a child, no question—out she'd go. There was no such thing as maternity leave."

Trudy goes on to say, "I'm supposed to be a role model for girls. I don't know about that. What I like to do is encourage young women, and I think I succeed at that. I do tell them you can have both [motherhood and a career], but not a hundred percent of both. You can have maybe eighty percent of each."

For her part, Trudy created an extended family. She notes that her brother, Herbert, a physicist living in California, "had the foresight to have four children." There are also the graduate students she advises at Duke University Medical School and all those scientists who have worked with her over the years.

One of them, Dr. Thomas Krenitsky, who now has his own pharmaceutical company, is in awe of Trudy. "You have to remember," he says, "when Trudy and Hitchings and their team started working with nucleic acids [in cells], we didn't have any idea they were the chemical basis for heredity—that discovery came ten years later. They were way ahead of their time.

"She's improved the human condition. Before, if you had leukemia—tough, you died. If you had kidney stones, if you had gout, if you had herpes—tough, you suffered. Trudy was a role model for women but she was a role model for men, too.

"She and George were more than just brilliant scientists—they were humanists. They were interested in the human condition—they weren't out just for themselves."

In 1988 George Hitchings and Trudy Elion, a team born out of the manpower shortage of the war years, won the Nobel Prize for Medicine, but it was not the ultimate recognition for their work. They both have said their greatest gratification comes from people whose lives were saved or whose suffering was relieved because of their devotion to the use of science to help people.

Still, Trudy wonders. "I don't know if I would ever have gotten into a research lab without the men being gone." So it is one of the many ironies of World War II. It was a terrible time of great suffering that also produced, in its own way, one of the great humanitarian scientists of the second half of the twentieth century.

CHESTERFIELD SMITH

"No man is above the law."

N O MAN is above the law." That was the simple and direct opening of a statement issued by the new president of the American Bar Association on the Sunday after the infamous Saturday
Night Massacre, when Richard Nixon fired the Watergate special
prosecutor, Archibald Cox, prompting Attorney General Elliot
Richardson and his number one assistant, William Ruckelshaus,
to resign. Nixon's ambush of Cox was a startling and deeply troubling event. It did seem that this nation of laws was in a precarious
state given the desperation and the power of the man in the White
House.

I remember standing on the White House lawn that night, participating in a White House special report, when my colleague the
late John Chancellor remarked, with chilling effect, "There seems
to be a whiff of the Gestapo in the air of the nation's capital
tonight."

Chesterfield Smith, a gregarious and prosperous Florida barris-
ter, had been president of the ABA for only a month when Nixon
rattled the country and the legal establishment with his imperious
action. Outwardly, Smith appeared to be the quintessential establishment lawyer. His entrepreneurial ways had turned his law firm
into a powerful money machine in Florida. He was a Democrat,
but he had voted for Nixon over McGovern. After serving as presi-

Chesterfield Smith, Camp Phillips, Kansas, October 1943

dent of the Florida Bar Association and chairman of that state's constitutional revision commission, he had risen to the presidency of the ABA in record time.

Smith, however, was a leader in reforming the legal establishment. He was quick to recognize the greatly expanded enrollment of women in law schools in the late sixties and early seventies. He began recruiting them for his firm, reasoning, "It would be better to get a smart woman than a dumb man, right?" Smith grew up in the segregationist South, and yet he was among the first to recruit minorities for a mainstream firm. He installed pro bono legal work as a fixed part of the firm's practice. In his unpaid role as chairman of the Florida constitutional revision commission, he took on what was called "the Pork Chop Gang," canny legislators from sparsely populated north Florida who had controlled state politics for most of the twentieth century by beating back attempts to install one-man one-vote reforms. Smith won and helped make it possible for Florida to become a modern political state.

Smith believed so deeply that the law should always be viewed first as an instrument of public good and then as a means of making money that he refused to endorse his own firm's largest client when the man was running for governor. One of Smith's partner's says, "We lost the client, but I guess Chesterfield just thought the other candidate was better."

Nonetheless, it was a long journey for Chesterfield Smith, from an itinerant boyhood in central Florida to his role as the conscience of the nation's leading legal organization on the weekend when the president of the United States, hunkered down in the White House, seemed to be sweeping aside the Constitution in his rage against his investigators. Curiously, Smith and Nixon had come of age in similar circumstances. They were two bright and ambitious men from families of modest means—one in Florida, the sunny land of promise on the southeast coast, the other in California, the warm-weather anchor of the West Coast. Smith and Nixon were both World War II veterans with law degrees. Each in his own way rose through the common and trying experiences of his generation to become prominent in his chosen field.

Smith says his father "had an up-and-down life." He was a schoolteacher for a while, then ran an electrical appliance shop near the town of Arcadia when power first became available to the remote cattle ranches in central Florida. When Florida went through a boom-and-bust period in the twenties, Chesterfield's father went out of business and on the road, looking for steady work. Eventually the family returned to Arcadia, where Smith finished high school at the top of his class without making much of an effort. He enrolled at the University of Florida as a prelaw student, but he'd stay only a semester at a time, dropping out to make money and raise a little hell. His childhood sweetheart, Vivian Parker, who was his wife for forty-three years before she died of cancer, was quoted as saying of Smith in those days, "He was just a poker-playing, crap-shooting boy who wouldn't settle down." Smith agrees that this is a fair and honest description.

By the time Smith was twenty, America had passed the Selective Service Act, and rather than wait to be drafted, Smith enlisted in the Florida National Guard, which was mobilized for active duty in November 1940. Smith finished his basic training in Florida and was then shipped out to Officer Candidate School at Fort Sill, Oklahoma, where he trained as an artillery officer. He became part of the new 94th Infantry Division, and after marrying Vivian Parker at Camp McClain in Mississippi, he was sent to join General George Patton's 3rd Army in northern France about six weeks after D-Day. The poker-playing, crap-shooting boy from central Florida was in the thick of the war until the end, fighting across France and Belgium, participating in the Battle of the Bulge, then moving into Germany, the Ruhr Valley, and ultimately into Czechoslovakia.

By the time he was discharged, in the fall of 1945, he had been in the service sixty-one months, more than five years. He held the rank of major and had been awarded a Purple Heart and a Bronze Star. The circumstances of the wound that won him the Purple Heart are more dramatic than the injury. His outfit had paused along a major road en route to the Rhine River after the Battle of the Bulge. The men were out of their vehicles, resting, when suddenly never-before-seen airplanes appeared in the skies, the first jet fighters developed by the Germans.

Smith recalls, "They came roaring down the roads, strafing armored columns and people. I was one of the dummies. I remember being so amazed at seeing a jet plane I didn't run, and my left

Chesterfield Smith,
wartime portrait

Chesterfield Smith,
ABA president, 1973

shoulder got clipped by a machine-gun bullet. It didn't hurt, but I did have to file a report, and that meant I got the Purple Heart. When VE Day came and they were sending people home on a point system, that little ol' nick was worth ten points."

When he did get home, Smith also had a new outlook on life. His wife said later, "Something happened to Chesterfield's attitude in the war. I don't know just what, but he was a serious man when he returned." He had not given up all of his old ways, however. He won $4,000 playing craps on the twelve-day voyage home. When he added that to his $3,500 in saved military pay, he had a comfortable start for his postwar life.

Smith was eager to start anew. "The way I was going before the war, I don't think I would ever have made it through law school," he says. "But after the war I felt I had something invested in my country—five years of my life. I said to myself, Boy, you've got to settle down and make something of yourself, otherwise you ain't ever going to 'mount to nothing."

Smith applied his military discipline to his law-school and family schedules. "I was very regimented about my duties," he remembers. "I worked from seven A.M. till noon." Then, not completely forgoing his past, he played golf every afternoon, returning home around four o'clock to be with Vivian and their firstborn through dinner. In return for his golf time, he did the baby's laundry; Vivian played bridge in the evening when Smith returned to his studies between nine o'clock and midnight. That was his schedule seven days a week. It paid off. Smith says, "I worked three hundred and sixty-five days a year and graduated in two years."

"I was paid $115 a month under the GI Bill, and you could get by on that, but after about six months, when I got high grades, I became a student instructor and got another $90 a month. And we had almost $8,000 left over from the war—so we were doing fine. It was a methodical life, but we were men, not boys anymore."

Smith graduated from law school with honors and was widely recognized as the class leader. He was a man in a hurry. "Hell," he says, "here I was, almost thirty years old—I wanted to get that law license and get into a practice and make myself some money." He returned to Arcadia, his hometown, and joined a small firm. Two years later he joined Holland, Bevis, and McRae, a larger firm in nearby Bartow. His new employers could not have known that hiring the handsome young veteran from Arcadia would change the destiny of their modest firm.

One of the firm's leading clients worked with Smith shortly after he arrived in Bartow. He was impressed and went to the Holland, Bevis, and McRae partners with a message: "I've been your client for many years, but lately I've been dissatisfied. I like young Smith, however, and if you give him all of my work, well, I'll stay with you. If not, I'm taking my business elsewhere."

Smith was made a partner in record time. He was a primary force in getting the firm into the lucrative and growing business of representing central Florida's phosphate industry; this proved to be a legal gold mine. At the same time, Smith was attracting a wide band of admirers. He was elected president of the Florida Bar Association, and that in turn led to his chairmanship of the state constitutional revision commission.

Simultaneously, Smith was becoming more involved with his profession through the American Bar Association. He met and became close to Lewis Powell of Virginia and Ruth Bader Ginsburg of New York, future justices on the U.S. Supreme Court. He says, "Powell appointed me to a committee called Availability of Legal Services. We made sure people who needed legal representation and didn't know where to turn or couldn't afford a lawyer, that those people could get a lawyer." It was a radical idea at the time, but it changed the face of American law, leading to more pro bono work within established firms, legal ombudsmen, and the Legal Services Corporation.

Those were active years for Smith in his firm and in public service. He received no compensation for the sixteen months he directed the rewriting of Florida's antiquated constitution. Besides establishing one-man one-vote, Smith installed provisions for periodic citizens' review of the constitution and language that would make it impossible for a willful minority to amend the state's fundamental laws for narrow, self-serving purposes. His law firm was thriving during Florida's big-growth years, but Smith saw even more opportunity in a merger with a substantial Tampa firm, Knight, Jones, Whitaker, and Germany. The new firm became Holland and Knight, a veritable colossus of the law, one of the largest and most prosperous legal establishments in the country. It now has 734 lawyers in eighteen offices around the United States and in Mexico City.

In addition to its lucrative practice, Holland and Knight, under Smith's sure hand, became a model of diversity. He is characteristically modest about his contributions. "It was the firm willing to do it," he says. "I think the people at the firm learned that African Americans, that women, that Cubans, Israelis, Japanese, Koreans, could all make a contribution—not because of their race or gender but because they were smart and worked hard. Once we learned that, we didn't have trouble with discrimination anymore. For example, I get a little more credit than I deserve for helping women. I was really kind to *talented* women. If they could help me, I could help them."

One of those talented women is Martha Barnett, the first of her gender hired in the firm; she is now a partner in Holland and Knight. She remembers when Smith came back to the firm after his term as president of the ABA. He asked her to become his associate, to work solely with him. "It made all the difference in the world," she says. "I was the first woman in the firm and there were some rocky times, but having Chesterfield select me . . . that was a statement to everyone that 'I am going to make this work.' He would introduce me to his colleagues around the country as *his* lawyer. That was a message that 'This is a person I value.' It gave me credentials."

There's another quality about Smith that Martha Barnett and others who know him volunteer, unprompted. "He's the most gregarious person I've ever known," Barnett says. "He invests his personal time and commitment to making people's lives better. I don't know how he finds the time. I am convinced he spends hours every day thinking of ways to make my life better. There are probably a thousand people who are convinced he spends his time trying to make *their* lives better."

Bill McBride, now the managing partner of Holland and Knight, is one of Smith's protégés. "I used to say that for the first two years I was with the firm I was convinced the first thing Chesterfield did every day while shaving was say, 'What can I do for Bill McBride's career today?' The joke around here is that I'll fire someone and they'll hate me and hate the firm forever, but they'll name their grandchildren after Chesterfield Smith."

McBride grew up professionally at Smith's side. They were in Chicago the weekend of the Saturday Night Massacre. "I was sort of his assistant—ran for Cokes, carried his briefcase, that sort of thing," McBride says. "Mr. Smith, the morning after the Saturday Night Massacre, asked me if I wanted to join him at a Chicago Bears game. Of course all the talk that morning was about the events the night before."

That talk went well beyond the Chicago headquarters of the American Bar Association, where Smith had been in office as president for only a month. In the nation's newspapers, on the Washington talk shows—wherever people gathered—the stunning firings and resignations overwhelmed all other topics. Nixon and his staff were convinced they were well within their rights, that they could persuade the nation that Archibald Cox was a liberal Harvard lawyer bent on getting the president at all costs. It was a serious misreading of the public sentiment. I've always thought that that weekend was the moment when whatever public support Nixon had retained began inexorably to crumble. His actions seemed so desperate and self-serving that it was hard to believe he was acting only to preserve the integrity of the office.

Smith and McBride went to the game, the Bears against the Boston Patriots in Soldier Field, a world unto itself on autumn Sundays in Chicago, a place where Bears fans were single-minded about football, shutting out the rest of the world in their lusty cheers for "da Bears."

Chesterfield Smith was in his seat, but his mind was on the events in Washington. Bill McBride watched his mentor closely. "You could tell his mind was somewhere else," he recalls. "I think he said something like 'I've decided what I've got to do.' So we got up and left during the first half." They went back to ABA headquarters and began gathering people. Smith was on the phone to prominent lawyers around the country, discussing the situation and describing what he was about to do. He wasn't seeking consensus. McBride says, "He'd basically taken the position that the job was to be a spokesperson for what was right rather than what the establishment wanted. Most ABA presidents would have spent weeks debating that sort of thing. Not Mr. Smith."

As Smith remembers that afternoon, "Lawyers—Republicans and Democrats—were calling me, saying, 'What are you going to do?' I started drafting a statement I still like. It began, 'No man is above the law.' The next day it was on the front page of *The New York Times* and about eleven other major papers. We were the first large voice of a substantial organization that called for Nixon's impeachment."

Elliot Richardson, the attorney general who resigned rather than fire Cox, said later, "We, the people, at the end of the day had the final voice in what happened—we were given that voice by the leadership of the Bar, which itself was embodied in Chesterfield Smith."

Smith then led the effort, through the ABA, to get an independent counsel to investigate Nixon. He became concerned, however, "when I learned that Leon Jaworski, a dear friend and a drinking buddy of mine, had gone to the White House and was to be appointed special prosecutor. I opposed it. Leon was a man I loved and cherished, but I believed that a special prosecutor should not be appointed by the man he's investigating."

In the end, of course, Smith's drinking buddy did a superb job. He marshaled an airtight case against the man who had appointed him and took it to the Supreme Court. The Court ruled unanimously against the president's arguments for executive privilege, and within a week Nixon was forced to resign.

Once his ABA term had run out, Smith returned to Florida and the demands of Holland and Knight. Ever the visionary, he expanded the firm's practice nationally and internationally. He retired as chairman at age sixty-five, but he still goes to the office every morning, advises younger partners, deals with clients he's had over the years, travels and gives speeches on the place of the law in modern society. Ron Olson, Warren Buffett's lawyer and one of the nation's top litigators, speaks for his generation of lawyers when he says, "Smith is the best president of the ABA we've ever had, period."

Smith has not lost his passion for justice. He's argued for gay and lesbian rights before the Florida Supreme Court, simply because he was persuaded it was the legally appropriate thing to do. He's now active in a campaign to repeal the independent-counsel statute that he was so instrumental in establishing. "Despite its good intentions," he says, "it has created an incentive for zealotry."

His lifetime of good works and enterprise as a lawyer have earned him the nickname "Citizen Smith." He attributes a great deal of his success to the lasting influences of his service during World War II. He remembers his poker-playing, crap-shooting days before the war, but what he remembers after the war is his determination to make something of himself. The war gave him a personal focus and an understanding of what was important in his life, his profession, and his country. He emerged from the service a fully formed man with a matchless passion for family, hard work, the irreducible strengths of a just society, and, most of all, his belief that no man is above the law.

In his Miami office, Smith has a memento of his military service. It's a framed silk map of France, about two feet by a foot and a half. Smith says, "They allowed us to sew these inside our battle jackets so if we ever got lost we'd have a general idea of what France looks like. I never had to use it, but I wore it in the mud and the rain, I even slept in it. When I got home, my wife had it sent to the cleaners and framed for my office." It's a small, elegant reminder of another time and another place in the long, productive life of Chesterfield Smith. It's also a reminder to him and to the thousands who have known him that Citizen Smith had a map but really never needed it. He always knew where he was and where he was going.

Al Neuharth, wartime portrait

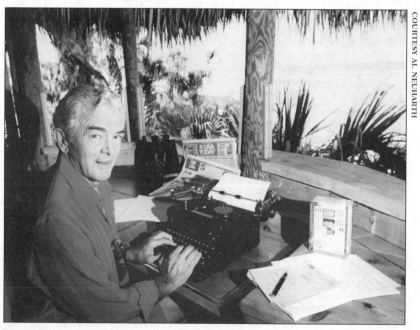

Al Neuharth

AL NEUHARTH

"If you separate what you did right from what you did wrong, you can learn a helluva lot more from failure than from a big success."

MAURICE "HANK" GREENBERG

"We don't wait until the bridge is built and a couple of tanks go across. We want to be the bridge builders."

IT'S CURRENTLY FASHIONABLE for celebrities to invoke a difficult childhood as a means of getting attention, attracting sympathy, or excusing outrageous behavior. In some instances, to be sure, the stories are authentic and troubling, but so many seem to be either exaggerated or inconsequential. In contrast, the World War II generation, with its roots in the Great Depression, is almost a case study in how to succeed despite a childhood of deprivation.

Consider Al Neuharth, the flamboyant founder and publisher of *USA Today*, and Maurice "Hank" Greenberg, one of the most powerful figures in American business, the tireless boss of an international insurance empire. Both men grew up in rural areas in poor families, and both lost their fathers at an early age.

Neuharth wears a large, gaudy ring signifying his role in changing the face, if not the nervous system, of American newspapers. He has reason to be proud of his vision. *USA Today* is now firmly fixed in the national consciousness, and its enterprising journalism is finally receiving the respect of competitors.

When *USA Today* was launched, there were cries of anguish from newspaper traditionalists. Neuharth was derided as a self-promoting maverick who lived to tweak journalism's brahmins at *The New York Times* and *The Washington Post*. In fact, Neuharth didn't shy from publicity, and he did relish his reputation as a rogue. And as president and CEO of Gannett, the highly profitable national chain of mostly smaller newspapers, he was confident of his place in publishing's front ranks.

Neuharth dressed entirely in black and white. He traveled the world in a luxurious corporate jet outfitted with a private office and shower. He had a taste for white stretch limousines and large hotel suites. His oceanfront home in Florida is a sprawling compound he calls Pumpkin Center.

He now runs a news think tank called The Freedom Forum, which is richly endowed with hundreds of millions of dollars realized from the sale of Gannett stock and placed in a foundation once operated by the company. The Freedom Forum has well-appointed offices in Arlington, Virginia, and New York City, and Neuharth regularly leads tours to world capitals for the Forum trustees to discuss press practices.

It is a life well beyond his surroundings in December 1941, when he was the son of a single mother in the Great Plains hamlet of Alpena, South Dakota. His father had died in a farm accident when he was three, and it had been a hard life for young Al, his brother, and their mother. She took in sewing and laundry. The boys worked in the grocery store, for the butcher, and at the soda fountain. Between the three of them, in a good week, they made less than twenty dollars.

Al was always ambitious and self-confident. He thought he'd grow up to be rich and famous as a lawyer—after all, the one lawyer in town had the biggest house. When Al won a scholarship to a local state college he took prelaw courses, but he knew he'd be drafted soon, so in the fall of 1942, just before the end of the quarter, he enlisted in the Army, knowing the college would give him credit for the full term.

Al Neuharth was assigned to the 86th Infantry Division, trained in intelligence and reconnaissance in Texas and California, and shipped to Europe to join General George Patton's 3rd Army racing toward Germany. He was involved in combat on several occasions and won the Bronze Star, which he now dismisses as a common decoration. "Hell, everyone got the Bronze Star," he says. "More importantly, we all got the Combat Infantryman Badges, which I think we're more proud of than anything."

Neuharth returned to South Dakota following the war, and after marrying his high school sweetheart, he enrolled at the University of South Dakota. The prospect of spending seven years in pursuit of a law degree, however, was not very appealing: he was a young man in a hurry, and he'd already given up four years of his life to the military.

So, as he says, "What's my next interest? Journalism, because of my high school newspaper work. What's likely to be the easiest curriculum? Journalism was also at the top of that list."

Neuharth breezed through the journalism courses at the university, and after graduation he persuaded a friend to join him in a newspaper startup, *SoDak Sports,* devoted almost entirely to high school athletics, a major interest in that rural state. They raised fifty thousand dollars, "begging, borrowing, and stealing" all they could, as Neuharth now says, laughing. After all, that was a lot of money in the early fifties, especially in a state just a few years out of the Great Depression.

They lost it all in just two years. The weekly newspaper was a big hit with the schoolboy athletes who could read their names in print every week, but when it came to advertising, the paper had a hard time competing with well-established local newspapers and the arrival of local television. Still, as Neuharth says, "I mismanaged it, but I learned the greatest lesson of my life. In the first place, I would not have taken that risk if I had not gone off to war and seen the world. I wanted to be a rich entrepreneur. I thought that because I was such a brilliant sportswriter . . . it would automatically mean the paper would be a success. I found out that wasn't the way it works in business."

Neuharth also learned, however, that "if you separate what you did right from what you did wrong, you can learn a helluva lot more from failure than from a big success." So, with those lessons in mind, he and his wife packed everything they had into a small moving trailer and headed for Miami, where he had lined up a job at *The Miami Herald.*

It was there that he began his climb to the top.

Neuharth moved up fast. Not only was he a deft rewrite man and a resourceful reporter on the streets, but he was a cunning inside operator, working just as hard at sizing up his competition and currying favor with his boss as he did at getting the story. When he got the opportunity, he rarely fumbled.

Years later he titled his autobiography *Confessions of an S.O.B.* It was a how-to manual describing how he'd outwitted his co-workers, adversaries, and even, in some instances, his patrons. He also let his ex-wives and his son offer critical commentary on his style and personality.

He quickly rose from the lowest position in the *Miami Herald* newsroom to executive city editor to assistant managing editor, and then he moved on to the *Detroit Free Press,* because he'd been spotted as a comer by Jack Knight, the owner of the Knight newspaper chain.

Making his mark in Detroit but frustrated by the more conventional managers following in the footsteps of the dashing Knight, Neuharth was approached by Gannett, a chain of small-city newspapers. The rest, as they say, is history. He made a big impression when he launched a new newspaper in the Cape Canaveral area, where the space program was fueling a business and residential building boom as well as flights to the moon.

Before long he was expanding Gannett from a group of what even he called "shitkicker" newspapers into the largest chain in the country—and one of the most profitable. He dismissed critics who said his papers' popular style and breezy look defiled journalistic tradition. That kind of talk played right to his anti-establishment genes.

Besides, no one could fault his personnel practices. Neuharth built a company on the reality, not just the promise, of equal opportunity. He had more blacks and women in senior management positions than any other comparable company. He attributes this to his World War II experience, and calls it his single greatest achievement during the fifteen years he ran Gannett. "I learned largely because of World War II . . . that the strongest possible organization is made up of decision makers who understand people. I used to say, 'Our leadership should reflect our readership.'

"When I first went in the infantry, I met people from Brooklyn who talked funny and people from Texas who you couldn't understand at all. I realized for the first time that the world is not made up of the white Germans and Scandinavians who settled my part of South Dakota. While it was a shock initially, I got to like it."

It was also not a bad lesson for the man who forty years later started the country's most successful all-purpose national newspaper, again to the jeers of traditional newspaper advocates. USA Today is now such a fixture in American life that it's hard to remember when it wasn't there. Although it still has its critics, it also has more than a million readers every day and some of the newspaper business's most imaginative investigative reporting of domestic social issues.

Al Neuharth, the self-confessed S.O.B., was always bright and ambitious, so it's likely he would have been a success in whatever field he chose, but his experiences as a combat infantryman taught him he could manage risks. He failed at some, but he always succeeded when the big risks were in play. There is no greater example of this than USA Today, in its way another unexpected dividend of World War II.

HANK GREENBERG is another titan of American business who started life with more brains and ambition than promise. He grew up poor on a farm in the Catskills, often getting up in the middle of the night to check his trap lines for mink and muskrat in hopes of making some extra change, then walking four and a half miles to school every day.

Greenberg dropped out of school at the age of seventeen to join the Army. He was assigned to the Signal Corps, and then, on June 6, 1944, he was attached to the U.S. Army Rangers storming Omaha Beach on D-Day. He fought from there across Europe to the end of the war, but it is next to impossible nowadays to get him to talk about what he went through. It simply is not the Greenberg way. He's too busy moving on to his next objective.

In fact, when I tell his Wall Street friends and business journalists that Greenberg landed with the first wave on D-Day and was later recalled to serve in Korea, they're astonished. Most of them have never heard him mention his wartime exploits.

Now in his mid-seventies, a billionaire, Greenberg will admit that he learned the importance of discipline, focus, and loyalty while in the service. When he emerged from World War II, he was determined to get an education and a job. First, he had to finish high school, and he was accepted at the Rhodes School, an elite private academy in midtown Manhattan. Greenberg remembers now that he lived more than thirty blocks away, in a room on West Twentieth Street that rented for nine dollars a week. "I walked to school rather than spend the ten cents on subway fares," he says. "Now there's an expensive men's clothing store near where the school was located, and when I go in there I am reminded of the old days. That was a tough nine months for me; I almost went back in the service."

In fact, Greenberg did stay in the Army reserves so that he could make extra money. So when he finished law school on the GI Bill, he was recalled, this time for service in Korea. He went back into uniform first as a lieutenant and then as a captain.

In Korea, Greenberg quickly earned a reputation as a highly effective defense lawyer for GI's accused of stealing government property. "No one ever prosecuted officers accused of stealing," he explains. "Why should the enlisted men be the only ones punished?"

It was in another legal capacity, however, that Greenberg had his most memorable—and educational—Korean experience. He was sent to Koje-do, a harsh island off the coast of Korea. It was a POW camp ostensibly run by the U.S. Army and the South Koreans, but the North Korean and Chinese prisoners had all but taken over. By night they were killing prison guards, including American soldiers, and holding kangaroo courts for prisoners who didn't participate in the mutiny.

Greenberg says of Koje-do, "We could have been in the middle of hell." He organized an investigation of the murders and managed to place informers among the ringleaders. It was a dangerous, deadly business. "Any one of the prisoners who didn't cooperate with the ringleaders was thrown up against the fence and killed," Greenberg says. It was anarchy of the most primitive kind, but eventually Greenberg's investigation paid off with more than enough evidence to punish the guilty.

And yet, the trials never took place. Someone higher up put everything on hold because peace talks were about to get under way at Panmunjom, and the Chinese were threatening retaliation if there were prosecutions at Koje-do. Justice was set aside for other priorities. As Greenberg said later, "War brings out the worst in everyone; no matter how honorable you are . . . things happen that you feel ashamed of later on."

He took from Koje-do a comprehension of how to deal with the Asian culture later in his life. "Our understanding of Asia at the time was very bad," he says. "Americans viewed Asians as little brown brothers and as subhuman, and in return we were not loved."

Greenberg came out of Korea determined to make his mark—and his fortune—in business, but he had no clear notion of what area suited him best. He got into the insurance industry by accident, but in typical Greenberg fashion. After rude treatment at the hands of the personnel officer of Continental Casualty Company, a large insurance concern, he accidentally ran into Continental's president and raised hell about the treatment he'd received. He was hired on the spot.

His reputation as a tough, resourceful manager who was willing to take calculated risks and make them pay off soon attracted the attention of C. V. Starr, a flamboyant Californian who had established a worldwide insurance empire called American International Group—AIG. It was a privately held firm, and already a success by the time Greenberg arrived in 1960.

Now it is a colossus, and Hank Greenberg—nicknamed, by the way, after the famous Detroit Tigers slugger "Hammerin' Hank" Greenberg—is only the second chief executive officer in the history of AIG, a far-flung insurance and financial-services company he has built into an $88 billion megapower around the world.

When Greenberg took AIG public, he made a fortune for himself, but he continues to run the company, as one observer put it, "like a one-man Lloyds of London." He's famous on Wall Street for his gutsy moves and penny-pinching ways, his demanding management style and his tireless personal schedule. Greenberg, calling on his military experience, has said, "We don't wait until the bridge is built and a couple of tanks go across. We want to be the bridge builders."

AIG insures oil platforms and drilling platforms, cargo ships and a subway system in Hong Kong, as well as a wide variety of industrial pollution risks—not exactly your run-of-the-mill home or car insurance business. It is a complex network, with more than three hundred subsidiaries, and Greenberg manages to keep track of all the layers.

One of his managers was not exaggerating when he said, "We'll send a man in a dugout canoe up a river in the Philippines to sell some insurance."

This former Catskills farm boy follows a physical regimen that would exhaust a man twenty years younger. He's within a pound or two of his World War II weight, and he's an expert skier, a tireless tennis player, and a nonstop traveler.

But then, he also personally does business in 130 companies around the world, including in China, where he's on a first-name basis with the notoriously secretive Chinese leadership. He works hard at understanding the future of the Asian societies that were once mistreated, as he put it, as "little brown brothers." He speaks knowingly of the financial and political culture in Indonesia, Singapore, and Malaysia, and then switches easily into a discussion of the Russian ruble.

What he does not talk about is his retirement, a subject of much speculation on Wall Street, where the analysts love his company but fear the repercussions if anything takes Hank Greenberg out of the captain's chair. He's likely to snap something like "I enjoy what I am doing. Besides, no one's offered me another job."

Hank Greenberg and Al Neuharth, two smart, ambitious, and demanding business entrepreneurs, built highly profitable empires a long way from their humble origins. While doing so, they never lost touch with the lessons of those earliest years, when they worked so hard for so little, when they volunteered for dangerous duty as they came of age and returned home with a new sense of the possibilities for their lives.

THE ARENA

—— • ——

"Let the word go forth from this time and place, to friend and foe alike, that the torch has been passed, to a new generation of Americans, born in this century, tempered by war, disciplined by a hard and bitter peace."

—From John F. Kennedy's inaugural speech, January 1961

Given the ambitions of his father and family, John Kennedy's decision to pursue a public life was not wholly altruistic, but in his eloquent inaugural speech he gave voice to his generation on the issues of peace and war, and also on the importance of entering the arena beyond the battlefield. In the postwar years, politics was a noble calling and a natural extension of the lives of the men and women who had made so many sacrifices and learned so many lessons during the war. Their ideologies and their ambitions spanned a broad spectrum, but they came to the public arena determined to have their say in the future of the country and of the world.

Some, such as Wisconsin senator Joe McCarthy, a tail gunner in the Marine Corps during the war, emerged with a dark and twisted view of what was necessary to advance the cause of liberty. Others drew entirely different lessons from their common experiences. John Kennedy, the scion of a rich and powerful Boston family, a decorated Navy veteran, ran as a Democrat against Republican Richard Nixon, also a Navy veteran, the son of a poor Quaker family from California. Senators Barry Goldwater and George McGovern were both pilots from western states during the war, and when they landed in the U.S. Senate they were at opposite ends of the political field. Strom Thurmond and Ernest "Fritz" Hollings, both World War II veterans, represent the same state, South Carolina, in the U.S. Senate. They're equally colorful and canny, politicians with Old South manners and rich accents, but one is a Republican and the other a Democrat.

From Eisenhower through George Bush, all but one American president was a veteran of World War II. The exception was Jimmy Carter, a Naval Academy graduate who was commissioned as an officer just as the war ended. From the fifties through the seventies, the halls of Congress were dominated by World War II veterans. Senator Paul Douglas of Illinois, a classic liberal, had been a lieutenant colonel in the Marine Corps. Senators Gaylord Nelson of Wisconsin, George McGovern of South Dakota, Edmund Muskie of Maine, Jacob Javits and Daniel Patrick Moynihan of New York, Warren Magnuson of Washington, George Smathers of Florida, John Tower of Texas, John Glenn of Ohio, Mark Hatfield of Oregon, Frank Church of Idaho—all World War II veterans.

State capitols were the fiefdoms of governors such as Orville Freeman in Minnesota, who still carried a prominent scar on his jaw from a gunshot wound he'd received while serving in the Marines. Governor John Connally of Texas saw considerable action in the Pacific with the Navy, but his most serious wounds came when he was riding in a limousine with fellow Navy veteran John Kennedy on November 22, 1963. William Scranton, governor of Pennsylvania, was a World War II pilot. Governor Harold Hughes of Iowa was an Army infantryman. George Wallace was a defiant symbol of segregation as governor of Alabama, but he had a notable combat record as a crewman on Army Air Corps bombers in the Pacific.

They came out of the same war to their political posts, but they were not in lockstep in their ideologies. Their varied views on social, diplomatic, and military questions were another affirmation of the independence and skepticism that Andy Rooney so admired when they were men in uniform. They emerged from the war with those qualities intact and reenforced. They took them to the political arena along with their hard-won understanding that the world is a large and complicated place, a personal self-confidence gained in the most trying circumstances, and their determination to influence the fate of their time.

They were immediately faced with a new war, a Cold War that would go on for forty years and threaten the entire world with nuclear destruction of a far greater magnitude than Hiroshima or Nagasaki. An ally turned foe, Joseph Stalin, had a voracious appetite for power and a nuclear arsenal to back it up. The day he died in 1953, a refugee from eastern Europe living in our South Dakota community said to my mother, "They're stoking it up down below for old Joe today."

Stalin had galvanized the West into forming a new military alliance, NATO. China under Mao Zedong and communism set off a wave of other fears, leading to another shooting war, this one on the Korean peninsula.

Then there were the unresolved issues at home, particularly of race and broader economic opportunity. There were great public-works projects to construct. The men and women of this generation moved from the problems of war to the problems of peace with alacrity. They were not always correct in their approach, but they were not intimidated. They also had a deeply personal understanding of the consequences of war as an instrument of national policy. They were the young men another generation of old men had sent to war. Now they had in their hands those same decisions for another generation of young Americans, this time in Vietnam.

The Vietnam War deeply divided not only the country but the World War II generation as well. The leading hawks and some of the most eloquent doves were from that generation. The new war also created a cultural schism. Those in political life who publicly supported the war effort while wrestling with private doubts had a visceral antipathy for the long hair, language, and flag-burning ways of the antiwar demonstrators. Then, too, they knew that in the working-class neighborhoods and on the farms, there were no deferments and little access to alternative service.

No two politicians symbolized the differences with greater clarity than two friends in the U.S. Senate, both members of the Republican party: Bob Dole of Russell, Kansas, and Mark Hatfield of Salem, Oregon. One the son of a small-town jack-of-all-trades, the other the son of a railroad blacksmith. One an infantry lieutenant, the other a Navy ensign.

Mark Hatfield

MARK
HATFIELD

"I could almost feel the hate leaving me. It was almost a spiritual experience."

S ENATOR MARK HATFIELD of Oregon is a politician whose central political philosophy was defined by the interlocking experiences he had as a young man raised in a strongly religious family and by what he saw as a Navy ensign in the Pacific, particularly at Hiroshima. Consequently, he was always a unique member of the Republican party in the U.S. Congress. While other members of the GOP were aggressive defenders of American involvement in Vietnam, he was an early critic of that war. He also voted against his own Republican presidents, Reagan and Bush, when they sent American troops to Grenada and the Persian Gulf.

Hatfield, a teetotaler and devout member of the Baptist church, also split from his party on the issue of gun control and the death penalty, although he did support the antiabortion views of the vast majority of his fellow Republicans. Despite the differences on some of the major litmus tests of the GOP, Hatfield's place in Oregon politics was always secure.

Following the war, he earned a master's degree at Stanford and returned to his alma mater, Willamette University in Salem, Oregon, to teach political science and serve as dean of students. He served in the state legislature, as secretary of state, and in two terms as governor before winning the first of his four elections for senator in 1966.

Before Pearl Harbor, Hatfield said his family had been strongly isolationist, explaining, "My father had been in the Navy in World

War I. . . . We were very patriotic . . . but you didn't want to become cannon fodder for European wars. We thought we were protected by the oceans. Why should we get involved? Pearl Harbor changed all of that."

Hatfield was a freshman at Willamette when Pearl Harbor was attacked. He immediately joined the Naval Reserve and accelerated his studies so he could be in training by the winter of 1943. He remembers it was a jolt to go from the mild winters of the Pacific Northwest to the harsher ones in upstate New York, where he trained to become first a midshipman and then an ensign, assigned to amphibious landing craft duty.

However, he was such a novice that when he was told to report to Coronado Beach, California, for assignment as a wave commander, he remembers his first reaction "was that I was going to do a lot of close-order drills for WAVES [the newly formed women's branch of the Navy]. I found out that wasn't the waves they were talking about. They meant ocean waves to hit the beaches in those flat-bottom boats."

After additional training in Hawaii, Hatfield participated in the invasions of Iwo Jima and Okinawa, two of the most critical and costly battles of the war in the Pacific. As is often the case with veterans of combat, he remembers the comical and the tragic equally well.

Recalling the landings at Iwo Jima, he said, "Our boat was taking on water and we had to bail. We had two buckets. The first bucket load . . . they threw the bucket overboard with the water. . . . It wasn't going to work with that bucket down in the water, so it just came to me, 'Take off your helmets and use them—and hang on to them!' It broke the tension and gave everyone an opportunity to laugh."

There weren't many other laughs on Iwo Jima or in Ensign Hatfield's experience there, however. He was too busy making the runs from the mother ship to shore with fresh Marines, and returning with wounded Marines. The Navy maps failed to show that the approach to the landing zone was a steeply pitched beach, so many of the larger vessels were partially sunk or wrecked. That made maneuvering the small landing craft a tedious and even more hazardous affair.

It was a dangerous assignment that Hatfield repeated again and again, always aware that he could be killed at any moment, but like

Mark Hatfield, wartime

Mark Hatfield, senatorial portrait

so many his age and in these conditions, he had what he remembers as a "certain feeling of fatalism. There is nothing you can do
about it. You become oblivious to the death and wounds all around.
You become a detached person, viewing it from a distance, even
though it is going on right at your feet."

There was something else for Hatfield: his faith. "I was raised in
a very strong Christian home," he says. "I suppose that was also
part of my armor, in the sense if I got hit, I knew where I was
headed. I had confidence in my faith."

Hatfield was on the beach at Iwo Jima the day one of the most
symbolic acts of World War II occurred. He remembers, "One of
the guys said, 'Hey, look!' At the top of the rock—Suribachi—we
saw the American flag being raised. It was a thrilling moment.
When we saw that flag go up it really did give us a sense of victory,
even though we still fought on for some time."

The future senator from Oregon had a close-up look at other
momentous occasions in the Pacific war. After participating in the
Okinawa invasion, his unit was sent to the Philippines to prepare
for the invasion of Japan. When the United States dropped the
atomic bombs on Hiroshima and Nagasaki, forcing Japan to surrender, Hatfield suddenly had an altogether different assignment:
he was part of the fleet that accompanied Douglas MacArthur into
Japan to begin the occupation.

"We sailed by the USS *Missouri* as the Japanese diplomats were
going aboard to sign the terms of surrender. Quite a moment.
MacArthur had instructed the Japanese to place a white sheet in
front of every gun emplacement, so when we were coming into
Tokyo Bay it was like a checkerboard on all sides of us. We would
have been caught in a murderous cross fire in the invasion. It would
have been terrible, terrible, invading Japan," Hatfield concludes.

In September 1945, Hatfield had a one-day experience that
would affect his life and his political behavior forever. "I was part
of a crew of people that went into Hiroshima," he says. "This was
about a month after the bomb had been dropped. There was a
smell to the city—and total silence. It was amazing to see the utter
and indiscriminate devastation in every direction, and to think just
one bomb had done it. We had no comprehension of the power of
that bomb until then."

Hatfield says as the American party sailed into the canals, Japanese parents and their children watched silently. "When we landed, the little kids saw we weren't going to kill or shoot them, so they began to gather around. We realized they were very hungry, so we took our lunches and broke them up and gave them to as many kids as we could."

In that moment, Hatfield came to realize something that stays with him to this day. "You learn to hate with a passion in wartime," he says. "If you don't kill your enemy, they'll kill you. But sharing those sandwiches with the people who had been my enemy was sort of a therapy for me. I could almost feel my hate leaving me. It was almost a spiritual experience."

When he made his way to the U.S. Senate, Hatfield brought with him not only what he calls "an unshakeable anti-nuke" philosophy, but also a firsthand understanding of what motivated Ho Chi Minh and his forces. In addition to seeing the flag raised on Iwo Jima, the USS *Missouri* when the surrender ceremonies were getting under way, and the devastation of Hiroshima, Hatfield saw a future battleground, Vietnam.

"We were sent to Haiphong to pick up Chinese nationalist troops and transport them to northern China, where they would fight the Communist forces of Mao Zedong." In Vietnam, Hatfield visited Hanoi, where Ho Chi Minh, who had been an American ally against the Japanese, was organizing his forces for independence. "Seeing the terrible misery imposed on the Vietnamese people by the French affected my position on the Vietnam War from the very beginning," Hatfield says. "I never could buy the idea that America somehow had a national interest out there, or was threatened."

Hatfield became one of the most persistent and articulate opponents of the Vietnam War as soon as he was in the Senate, often joined by fellow World War II veteran Senator George McGovern of South Dakota, another product of a religious family who had learned to abhor war during his heroic service in the Army Air Corps. They were among the earliest congressional critics of the war, often mocked by conservative voices as being somehow soft on the question of how to face down communism.

At least McGovern had support within his own party. Hatfield was often alone within the GOP ranks, but it did not deter him. Simultaneously he devoted a good deal of his energies to checking the growth of nuclear weapons and power. "I was persuaded," he says, "that the genie was out of the bottle, but somehow we had to try to put it back in. I devoted myself to stopping underground nuclear testing and controlling the military spending on nuclear weapons. Also, I was opposed to the use of nuclear power for electricity. That, to me, is the greatest environmental problem that we have."

Through the years Hatfield remained a consistent foe of nuclear weapons and war in general. In addition to his persistent stand against Vietnam, one of the reasons he wound up on President Nixon's infamous "enemies list," Hatfield also opposed Ronald Reagan's invasion of the tiny Caribbean island of Grenada, and he was even more critical of President Bush's plan to go to war in the Persian Gulf. He says, "Why, I couldn't believe the American people approved the . . . war in the Gulf. To me, it was nothing but an oil war." Hatfield was one of just two Republicans to vote against approving Operation Desert Storm. He also criticized the dispatch of an American peacekeeping force to Bosnia, wondering aloud what American troops could do to reverse eight hundred years of history.

As time went on, Senator Hatfield was increasingly isolated within his own party, and not just because of his views on war and nuclear power. He had cast the vote that defeated the proposed amendment to the Constitution requiring a balanced federal budget. At the time he was chairman of the mighty Senate Appropriations Committee, so his negative vote was a powerful statement— and unacceptable to the class of aggressively conservative younger Republicans who had been elected to the Senate in the Republican Revolution. They wanted to strip him of his chairmanship or find some other way to punish him. Hatfield was astonished. He'd even offered to resign his seat rather than be forced to vote against his conscience. As Hatfield told *The Washington Post,* "I said what I would do from the beginning. I at no time got any indication that I was going to be chastised or disciplined for voting my conscience."

Hatfield stood his ground and won the day, garnering praise primarily from older senators who recognized that instances of individual courage in their chamber were rare. But Hatfield also knew it was time to go, after four terms in the Senate. In his last election, his margin of victory had fallen after an embarrassing and surprising development. "St. Mark," as he is sometimes called, had been formally rebuked by the Senate Ethics Committee for not reporting gifts and loans from friends and lobbyists. Now he was plainly much more out of step with his party on the issues that defined the GOP agenda in the nineties.

So in 1996, Mark Hatfield retired and returned to his beloved Oregon to teach and share in the benefits he had brought to his state during thirty years in the Senate. He left as he arrived, a man of strong, independent convictions and still a member of the Republican party, despite the changes in the DNA of the GOP in recent years.

Commenting on the Republican newcomers, Hatfield told a reporter, "There are those who think we should be of one mind. They feel, perhaps, that diversity in the party is a weakness, not a strength. I'm an Old Guard Republican. The founders of our party were for small business, education, cutting the military budget. That was our platform in 1856 and I think it's still a darned good one."

Some of the newer Republican senators, with their strict conservative dogmas, may never understand a man like Mark Hatfield, but then they've never shuttled Marines ashore under heavy fire at Iwo Jima or Okinawa. They've never looked out on the unworldly landscape of nuclear devastation and shared their lunch with a starving Japanese child.

*Bob Dole, platoon leader, 10th Mountain Division, December 1944
(Dole is in the third row, extreme left)*

———— • ————

BOB
DOLE

*"I have a daily reminder of the war because of my disability.
It changed my life."*

THE WARTIME EXPLOITS of Bob Dole are well known by now.
He was a young lieutenant out of Kansas when he was gravely
wounded as he led his squad from the 10th Mountain Division
against a fortified German position in the Italian Alps. He almost
died before he was evacuated to the United States for a long series
of operations and excruciating therapy in what turned out to be the
impossible task of completely saving the use of his right arm. The
terrible wound came in a flash of enemy fire on an Italian hillside.
The recovery took three years and three months in America, during which he almost died from infections and other complications.

For part of his recovery period he was in a hospital ward with
two other wounded veterans, Daniel Inouye of Hawaii and Philip
Hart of Michigan. Later the three friends would serve in the U.S.
Senate at the same time. Although they represented different political philosophies, that common experience of the war and
wounds was a bond that transcended partisan considerations.

Dole still remembers how Hart, whose injuries were not so
grave, would leave the hospital to arrange baseball or concert tickets for the men's rare nights out. "We'd talk about who was the
worst off, when we were going to get out of that place, but then
you'd look around and see someone who really had a problem."

Dole's experience in the war and the sacrifices of his working-
class parents and friends from the small, hardscrabble town of Rus-

sell, Kansas, to help him recover from his injuries were appropriately familiar themes in his political career, especially in his campaign for president against Bill Clinton. It was always touching when this complex, proud man, so private and even abrupt when it came to other personal matters, talked about that time in his life, choking up as he described how his father, with so little means, struggled to make the train trip from Kansas to Chicago to see his badly injured son; how his mother, even though she hated smoking, held his cigarettes for him as he lay in a hospital bed, barely able to move either arm in the early going; how the people of Russell set up cigar boxes in businesses along Main Street and labeled them THE BOB DOLE FUND, raising eighteen hundred dollars for his medical fees, mostly through quarters and a half-dollars. One of his neighbors was as poor as the Doles, but he wanted to do something, so, the Senator remembers with an affectionate chuckle, "He brought me a duck. Couldn't afford anything else, so he brought me a live duck!"

It may be difficult for current generations to understand just how much poverty there was across America, even after the war. Working-class families lived right on the margins with very little left over. They were used to it, as it had been that way since the beginning of the thirties, especially in rural America. Indeed, after the Depression, joining the Army was a step up for many Americans. Dole remembers, "It was a good deal; you got a good pair of boots, three meals a day, new clothing, a new rifle. It was the most many young Americans had ever had."

One of Dole's fellow Kansans, Walt Ehlers, who won the Congressional Medal of Honor as a sergeant with the Army's 1st Infantry Division in Normandy, was a poor farm boy when he enlisted, and he still remembers the breakfasts at the Presidio, the Army base in San Francisco. "We had cereals on the table and they had bacon and eggs over easy . . . or whatever you wanted. That lasted for about three months!"

Senator Bob Kerrey, who won a Congressional Medal of Honor in Vietnam, has commented on the old black-and-white photographs of young men lined up for their draft physicals. "About half of them look as if they were malnourished or had rickets," he said.

James DeVane grew up in rural North Carolina during the Depression. As a combat infantryman, he was captured by the Ger-

Bob Dole:
1961 freshman term

Bob Dole:
rehabilitation, 1946

mans during the Battle of the Bulge and spent three harrowing months in a prisoner-of-war camp. Still, he believes what he and his family went through during the thirties was more difficult and more meaningful to his life. They lived in a simple log cabin, heated by coal and a wood stove, with no plumbing or electricity. DeVane carried a shotgun to school every morning so he could shoot game birds along the way for the kitchen table. His father raised pigs and goats and sold his catch of shad from the Cape Fear River. His mother organized local friends to gather mistletoe from the nearby woods and sell it to New York merchants. Together, DeVane's parents managed to keep the family together, which so impressed their son that he's able to say, "I know it was less stressful to fight as a soldier with only yourself or your squad to look after than it was to care for, feed, and raise children in the Depression." DeVane, who now has a successful printing business, concludes, "We World War II infantrymen came from a background of heroes."

Bob Dole wouldn't argue with that. Although he has been gone from the neighborhoods and the economic constraints of Russell, Kansas, for a long time now, those early experiences still shape his attitudes. In his richly appointed office in Washington, D.C., he keeps a picture of his father dressed in his Key-brand overalls, explaining that that's what his dad wore to work every day. For all of his power, celebrity, and prosperity, in his emotional makeup Dole isn't that far removed from his Great Plains roots and formative experiences.

The financial deprivations of his childhood, however, were not enough to prepare him for the terrible price he paid in the war. Dole admits he was bitter at times, that he felt sorry for himself. Even now he occasionally goes back over the fateful day he was hit.

The assault had been delayed for a day because of the death of Franklin Roosevelt, the beloved president and commander in chief. Dole was greatly saddened by Roosevelt's passing, but he sometimes wonders, "What if he hadn't died *that* day? What if we had moved out on schedule? Would I have been wounded?"

After the war, when he fully understood that he would never be completely the same again, that he couldn't turn back the clock, he decided to make up for lost time. By his own admission, he hadn't been much of a student before the war. He had been a good-time fraternity boy at the University of Kansas. But his life had since been changed forever. He'd spent five years either in uniform or in hospitals, and as soon as he was able, he took advantage of the GI Bill and headed for Washburn Municipal University law school. There, the government provided him with a left-handed typewriter, a recording machine so he could take notes, and a car with a left-handed gearshift. As he says now, fifty years later and having spent an adult lifetime in politics, "Talk about a generous government."

It did not, however, make Dole a champion of government-spending programs for other needs that were more social in character. He says the lesson of the GI Bill was that it provided self-reliance.

Dole was not particularly ideological when he was asked by both the Democrats and Republicans in his home county to run for Congress. He was pragmatic, however, figuring the Republicans gave him the best chance of success, so that's where he wound up. He went from the U.S. House of Representatives to the U.S. Senate in 1969.

In his maiden speech in the Senate on April 14, 1969, Dole appealed for a presidential commission on people with disabilities. He described the disabled as a group no one joins by personal choice, saying "the requirements for membership are not based on age, sex, wealth, education, skin color . . . political party, power, or prestige. . . . It's an exceptional group I joined on another April 14: 1945."

It was the beginning of his personal crusade to make life easier for the more than forty million disabled Americans. By 1990 he had moved Congress to pass the Americans with Disabilities Act, a sweeping piece of legislation that mandated changes in public buildings, accommodations, and transportation to make it easier for the disabled to function in American society.

For Dole, it was his greatest legislative victory. Yet it was also a classic example of the two sides of Bob Dole. Although he was a champion of this federal directive that imposed on states and businesses rigid requirements that were costly and, in some cases, little used, he was also known for advocating a reduced role for the federal government.

On some issues Dole was much more single-minded. The Vietnam War was the most taxing time for him. He hated the flag-burning, noisy protests, the in-your-face lectures from long-haired students protected from the draft by deferments or influence. As chairman of the Republican National Committee under President Nixon, Dole made some very harsh speeches, all but accusing antiwar protesters and the news media of treason.

As President Gerald Ford's running mate in 1976, Dole's intolerant side would show through. In a famous moment, during a debate with his vice-presidential opponent, Walter Mondale, Dole blamed the Democrats for World War II. Later, in 1988, when he lost the New Hampshire primary to George Bush in the race for the Republican presidential nomination, I had both candidates on the air simultaneously. Bush, flush with victory, said he looked forward to seeing Dole at the next stop on the campaign trail. When I asked Dole if he had anything he wanted to say to Bush in return, Dole snarled, "Yeah, tell him to stop lying about my record." It was a self-wounding act for Dole, and even he seemed to know it.

He's much more mellow now, content to be an elder statesman. But looking back on his political career, he cannot forget those days when antiwar protestors would come to his office or show up at his speeches. This man who endured so much personal pain and whose life was so altered by his time in uniform can now recall thinking during those confrontations, Why am I sitting here all banged up for this ragtag operation? Is this what America is all about? Then, answering his own question, he says in that cryptic Dole style, "I guess that's what it is all about—freedom. But sometimes it's a stretch. I remember being glad when they were gone. Besides, kids are better now."

As a product of his time and a proud but private man, Dole was an anachronistic candidate for president in the last election before the turn of a new century. He seemed to be playing by old rules and values as he made his way across the country, raising questions about Bill Clinton's facile form of governing by asking, "Where's the outrage?" He invoked his World War II experience and the lessons of his wounds repeatedly, but they were lessons lost on a new generation of voters who were barely aware of Vietnam.

The earlier flashes of dark rage that characterized his initial years on the national stage were gone, but the sharp humor, one of Dole's most endearing characteristics, remained. It was Dole who once remarked that America had three living ex-presidents, "Jimmy Carter, Gerald Ford, and Richard Nixon." Without missing a beat, he went on, "Speak No Evil, Hear No Evil—and Evil." But as a man who wanted the presidency for himself, he simply could not win the hearts and minds of enough American voters.

In his campaign, however, there were moments that gave him a lift. He'd be on a stage somewhere, preparing to give another speech, another stop in a long campaign that simply could not get traction. He'd look out into the audience and lock eyes with a white-haired man or a group of them in their American Legion or Veterans of Foreign Wars caps, sometimes in windbreakers with their military units spelled out. They would nod quietly to one another, the candidate and the men of his generation who had been to war and back. It was a silent ritual played out hundreds of times across America, a valedictory salute between a generation and one of its own.

Bob Dole, the man from Russell, Kansas, who grew up in the basement of his family home so that his parents could rent out the upstairs, is now a prosperous elder statesman in Washington, often cited as a prospective intermediary in vexing political problems. He's undertaken special presidential missions to Bosnia and Kosovo.

He's also commander of a national campaign to build a World War II memorial in Washington, D.C. The $100 million fund-raising drive became the primary focus of his life following his loss to Bill Clinton in the 1996 presidential election. President Clinton unveiled the design for the memorial on the same day he awarded Dole the Presidential Medal of Freedom, the nation's highest civilian award. Typically, Dole had a quip for the occasion, saying he had originally hoped to be there that day to accept the key to the front door of the White House.

Then, as he has in recent years, he became emotional as he talked about the meaning of World War II. Dole believes the memorial, which is to be located on the Mall at the Washington Monument end of the reflecting pool, is necessary to remind the world that just men and women can prevail. He wants it to be a backdrop for World War II's unrealized ideals, a platform for America's children to speak out for freedom, decency, and human democracy.

In his White House remarks that day, Dole was particularly eloquent. He said, "I've seen American soldiers bring hope and leave
graves in every corner of the world. I've seen this nation overcome
Depression and segregation and communism, turning back mortal
threats to human freedom."

He was describing his own life and the monumental legacy of
his generation in a few well-crafted words. It was just a moment in
the life of this complicated man from the Kansas prairie, his right
arm dangling at his side, those dark and flashing eyes filled with
emotion, but it was a moment to savor, for it represented the many
sides of Bob Dole. Public servant, wounded veteran, proud patriot,
elder statesman.

Dole, now in his sunset years, misses the action of the Senate,
the urgency of public discourse and political maneuvering on the
critical issues of the day, but he's found a new calling in his determination to get the World War II memorial finished. He lives by
the lessons he learned when he was bitter and recovering from his
combat wounds. "For a while," he says, "I subtracted five years
from my life, but I caught up. People move on. That's the way it is
in America. Don't just dwell on the past. Gotta look ahead."

DANIEL
INOUYE

"The one time the nation got together was World War II. We stood as one. We spoke as one. We clenched our fists as one."

WHEN BOB DOLE of Russell, Kansas, got to know Danny Inouye of Honolulu in that rehabilitation hospital in Michigan after the war, they had a good deal in common for two young men from such distinctly different backgrounds. Both were trying to learn to live without the use of an arm as a result of combat wounds suffered as Army lieutenants in the mountains of Italy. As a result of their injuries, both were forced to give up dreams of becoming physicians after the war. They also shared a direct style of dealing with people and an ironic sense of humor.

However, Inouye's route to that hospital took a few turns not imposed on the young man from Kansas. Inouye was a Japanese American, raised in Hawaii and named after the Methodist minister who had raised his orphaned mother. On December 7, 1941, Inouye, who was just seventeen, was preparing to attend church when he heard a hysterical local radio announcer exclaim that Pearl Harbor had been attacked.

He rushed outside the family home in Honolulu. In the distance he could see great volumes of smoke. "Then," he remembers, "three planes flew over. They were gray with large red dots. The world came to an end for me. I was old enough to know nothing would be the same." The land of his ancestors, the nation his grandfather had revered, had attacked the United States and, by extension, Danny Inouye, U.S. citizen.

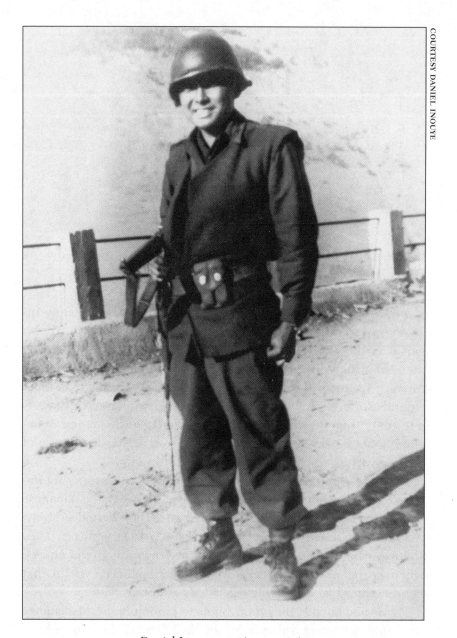

Daniel Inouye, wartime portrait

Young Inouye was enrolled in a Red Cross first-aid training program at the time, so he went directly to the harbor and began helping with the hundreds of casualties. In effect, he was in the war from the opening moments. He stayed on duty at the Red Cross medical aid facility for the next seven days.

In March 1942, the U.S. military repaid Inouye by declaring that all young men of Japanese ancestry would be designated 4-C, which meant "enemy alien," unfit for service. Inouye says, "That really hit me. I considered myself patriotic, and to be told you could not put on a uniform, that was an insult. Thousands of us signed petitions, asking to be able to enlist."

The Army decided to form an all–Japanese American unit, the 442nd Regimental Combat Team. Its shoulder patch was a coffin with a torch of liberty inside. The motto was "Go for Broke." Before the war was over, the 442nd and its units would become the most heavily decorated single combat unit of its size in U.S. Army history: 8 Presidential Distinguished Unit Citations and 18,143 individual decorations including one Medal of Honor, 52 Distinguished Service Crosses, 560 Silver Stars and 28 Oak Leaf Clusters in lieu of a second Silver Star, 4,000 Bronze Stars and 1,200 Oak Leaf Clusters representing a second Bronze Star, and at least 9,486 Purple Hearts.

The regiment trained at Camp Shelby in Mississippi, and Inouye remembers that he and the other Nisei (second-generation Japanese American) soldiers didn't know what to expect. "We'd only heard about the lynchings," he says, "but to our surprise these people were very good to us. We were invited to weekend parties and picnics, and for the first time in my life I danced with a white girl."

Back at the base, Inouye says, other troops were not as welcoming, but "the problems were minimal because they could see we had a whole regiment!" Besides, the treatment by Mississippi civilians, the famed Southern hospitality, gave the young men of the 442nd new confidence after their original classification as "enemy aliens."

Inouye's experience in Mississippi was a reflection of the racial schizophrenia loose in America. The Magnolia State was the epicenter of discrimination against black citizens, treating them as little more than paid slaves, and yet it made the extra effort for

Japanese American soldiers at the same time the U.S. government was shipping their families off to internment camps.

Inouye and his buddies went from Mississippi directly into combat with the 5th Army in Italy. They were out to prove something. "I felt that there was a need for us to demonstrate that we were just as good as anybody else," he says. "The price was bloody and expensive, but I felt we succeeded."

After three months of heavy fighting in Italy, during which Inouye was promoted to sergeant for his outstanding traits as a patrol leader, the 442nd was called upon to perform one of the legendary feats of the war: rescue 140 members of a Texas outfit that had been caught in a German trap in the French Vosges Mountains. Another Texas division had tried and failed to get their fellow Lone Star Staters out, so the 442nd was sent in.

Inouye remembers, "We only had two thirds of our regiment after the Italian campaign. We had to fight hard for four straight days. We knew this was *the* test. We knew we were expendable. We knew it would have been unheard of to call on another regiment to rescue us. They were asking these brown soldiers to rescue these tall Texans. Our casualties exceeded eight hundred, but we rescued them."

Inouye's role was so impressive that he was awarded the Bronze Star and won a battlefield commission as a second lieutenant. The 442nd also won the admiration of commanders throughout the Army. "After that," Inouye says, "we were in demand."

They were sent back to Italy to continue the long, bloody battle for control of southern Europe. In the Po Valley, Lieutenant Inouye was leading an assault against heavily fortified German positions in the mountains when he was hit by a bullet that went through his abdomen and exited his back, barely missing his spine. He continued to charge, gravely wounded, making a one-man assault on a machine-gun nest that had his men pinned down. He threw two grenades before the Germans hit him with a rifle-launched grenade. His right arm was shattered. He pried a third grenade from his right hand and threw it with his left. He continued to fire with his automatic weapon, covering the withdrawal of his men. Finally, he was knocked out of action by another bullet in the leg, but by then the German position was

Daniel Inouye, senatorial portrait

neutralized. Twenty-five Germans were dead, and Inouye took eight as prisoners of war.

Inouye was awarded the Distinguished Service Cross for his gallantry, and many believe that if he had not been a Japanese American he would have won the Medal of Honor. He was shipped back to the United States to begin treatment for his extensive injuries, and it was in the hospital that he met Bob Dole.

As the two became friends, Dole often talked about getting a law degree and going into politics back home in Kansas, maybe running for Congress. Inouye thought that wasn't a bad plan for the future and began to think about law school and politics as a possible career for himself.

He spent twenty months in hospitals before his discharge as a captain. On a layover in Oakland, California, on his way back to Hawaii, he decided he wanted to get, as he puts it, "all gussied up so when I got home Mama and Papa would see me in all my glory. I went into an Oakland barbershop—four empty chairs—and a barber comes up to me and wants to know if I'm Japanese. Keep in mind I'm in uniform with my medals and ribbons and a hook for an arm. I said, 'Well, my father was born in Japan.' The barber replied, 'We don't cut Jap hair.' I was tempted to slash him with my hook, but then I thought about all the work the 442nd had done and I just said, 'I feel sorry for you,' and walked out. I went home without a haircut."

Remembering the plans of his friend from Kansas, Inouye utilized the GI Bill to get a law degree from George Washington University. He returned to Hawaii and became active in local politics, serving as a prosecutor and in the territorial legislature before Hawaii became a state.

When Hawaii was admitted to the Union, Danny Inouye was a natural choice to become the state's first congressman, and he was elected overwhelmingly. It was an arresting moment in the well of the House of Representatives when Sam Rayburn, the larger-than-life Speaker, intoned, "Raise your right hand and repeat after me . . ." Of course, the new congressman from Hawaii had no right hand. Danny Inouye raised his left and took the oath of office, the first U.S. representative from his state and the first Japanese American in Congress. As another congressman said later, "At that moment, a ton of prejudice slipped quietly to the floor of the House of Representatives."

After just one term in the House, Inouye was elected to the Senate in 1962, and he's been successfully reelected six times. He's highly regarded on both sides of the aisle for his middle-of-the-road Democratic party principles and his measured, almost stately style. When a *Washington Post* reporter asked him how he reconciled his laid-back demeanor as a senator with his record as a fearless, hard-charging member of the 442nd, he answered with a shrug and a laugh: "I was young. I was eighteen, first time leaving Mama. I had no strings, no sweetheart."

Inouye's reputation for fairness has served him well on the Senate Watergate Committee investigating the Nixon White House and as chairman of the Senate committee that investigated the Iran-*contra* scandal during the Ronald Reagan administration. Former senator Lowell Weicker of Connecticut, a Republican and not an easy judge of other public figures, has said simply, "There is no finer man in the Senate."

Inouye also knows how to make a point. He was a lead sponsor of the bill to get reparations for the Japanese American families interned during the war, and there were very few senators who could look at this quiet man with the Japanese surname, valorous military record, and empty right sleeve and vote no.

On another occasion, the Senate was considering a bill to place a limit of $25,000 on rewards "for pain and suffering" in product liability suits. It was a hot issue in the Senate Commerce Committee, where Republicans were determined to rein in corporate exposure in lawsuits. Then Senator Inouye spoke up, saying, "It's easy for those who have not been the victims to set the caps." End of argument. End of bill.

Daniel Inouye, "Danny" to all his fellow senators and his friends, has just finished his sixth term as a U.S. senator. In September 1998, he turned seventy-four. He was a teenager when he saw those Japanese planes, "with pilots that looked like me," and knew that his world was changed forever. What he did not know at the time was how much he would shape the new world through his bravery and his commitment to public service and the end of discrimination.

What he does know now, as he looks back, is that this country has been divided at critical times in its past, during the Revolutionary War and the Civil War; but, as he says, "The one time the nation got together was World War II. We stood as one. We spoke as one. We clenched our fists as one, and that was a rare moment for all of us."

CASPAR WEINBERGER

"Young man, you go where you're sent in the Army."

THE PUBLIC ARENA was not reserved only for those who ran for elective office. Some of the most distinguished and influential public servants to emerge from the World War II generation were men who moved easily in and out of the private sector to take assignments in public life. They are as well known now as their fellow veterans who chose elective office.

Caspar Weinberger is one of them. He was an important adviser to Ronald Reagan during Reagan's first term as governor of California. He served in the Nixon administration, and when Reagan went to the White House, Weinberger went to the Pentagon as secretary of defense. That appointment was the apotheosis of a lifetime of deeply held conservative personal and political beliefs, a passion for public affairs, and the lessons learned by an eager young lieutenant in the U.S. Army during World War II.

Weinberger grew up as the bookish youngest son of a prosperous San Francisco couple. His father, a lawyer, was Jewish, and his mother was Episcopalian. Young Caspar was raised in his mother's church, although his last name often subjected him to anti-Semitic insults.

The future defense secretary was so interested in public affairs that he subscribed to the *Congressional Record* before he reached high school, and he remembers his father telling him stories of the American constitutional convention at bedtime.

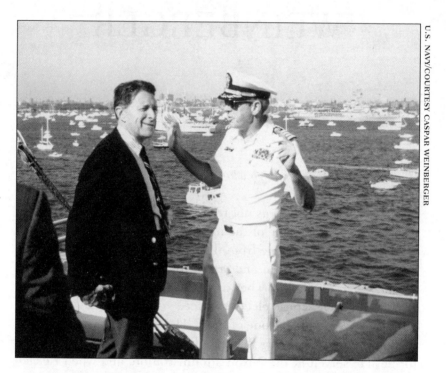

*Secretary of Defense Caspar Weinberger and Captain John A. Moriarty,
commanding officer of the aircraft carrier USS John F. Kennedy,
touring the ship during the International Naval Review
celebrating the centennial of the Statue of Liberty*

Weinberger went to Harvard in the autumn of 1934, but as a product of a California public high school he was not naturally a member of the inner circle at the venerable academy that, for many of its students, was the natural extension of their prep schools and family pedigrees.

However, Weinberger did find a place at Harvard. When he was not pursuing his studies in English literature and political science, he was a tireless worker at the *Crimson,* the school's highly regarded student newspaper. Students of the contemporary *Crimson* may be surprised to learn that at the height of the New Deal and the first term of Franklin Roosevelt, the newspaper was very conservative, a perfect fit for young Weinberger.

When he was elected president of the *Crimson,* he found an outlet for his anti–FDR and anti–labor union views. He was an unapologetic, take-no-prisoners editorialist, firing off scathing memos to *Crimson* staff members who questioned his judgment and fairness. His position as president of the newspaper has been a point of pride his entire life.

Weinberger maintained his interest in journalism, later writing columns for California newspapers and, when he retired from politics, serving as a publisher and commentator for *Forbes,* the conservative business magazine.

Weinberger stayed at Harvard to get a law degree, and then, in August 1941, he enlisted in the Army. He was accepted for Officer Candidate School and shipped out to Australia as a second lieutenant. His training experience would later help shape his views as secretary of defense. "We were trained with wooden rifles and little blocks of wood painted to look like grenades," he remembers. "We did little live fire, because there wasn't enough ammunition."

Weinberger was not one of those children of the Depression who saw the Army as a step up in their lifestyle, as Bob Dole did. As Weinberger puts it, "I had been very pampered and very carefully brought up. I have always been extremely ashamed of myself because I complained about the food at Harvard. When I got in the military, I saw *that* was really something to complain about."

The future defense secretary also benefited, he believes, from having been both an enlisted man and an officer. Forty years later, when he ran the Pentagon, "it gave me a certain resolve to do something about two things: improve the food and the mail service, which are the two biggest factors in morale."

In Australia, Weinberger also learned something about chain of command. He protested when he was pulled from an infantry outfit and assigned to intelligence on General Douglas MacArthur's staff. "I wanted to stay with my division. They were on the eve of an invasion," Weinberger says. "I was very gung ho . . . very much the crusader. I thought this was a just war." When he appealed to a general who was running operations, he had a very short hearing. Weinberger says he was told, "Young man, you go where you're sent in the Army."

So Weinberger reported to MacArthur's headquarters in Brisbane, where he was a very junior officer on the staff of the legendary general. Nonetheless, he saw enough to have a full appreciation of MacArthur's brilliance. "I saw the plans for the invasion of Japan," Weinberger says, "the breadth and scope of his military genius. With very few troops, a couple of understrength divisions, and some Australian militia forces, he accomplished an enormous amount in the Pacific."

The young intelligence officer also learned directly from MacArthur something about judgment and decision making. Weinberger was on duty one night as the American forces were moving on a small island, lightly occupied by the Japanese, to take it for a radio base. Suddenly, there were reports of a Japanese ship and Japanese aircraft in the vicinity. Weinberger thought he'd better take this information directly to MacArthur. "So I walked the two blocks to his hotel," Weinberger remembers. "I got through the various security and gave him the message. He came out in his bathrobe, looking just as erect and as imposing as he did in full uniform, that magnificent posture, deep voice. He looked the message over carefully and said, 'Well, Lieutenant, what do you think?' I said, 'General, I think it's a coincidence they're there. They don't seem to have hostile intent. I would go ahead with the landing.' General MacArthur said, 'That's what I think, too. Good night.'" Weinberger walked back through the night to his post "in fear and trembling—to see if I was wrong or not. Fortunately, it worked out."

· · ·

Caspar Weinberger, chairman, Forbes *magazine*

WEINBERGER came home from the war to a successful law practice in San Francisco and a continuing passion for conservative causes. He was elected to the California Assembly in 1952 and became active in California and national Republican party politics. In 1966 he worked for one of Ronald Reagan's opponents in the Republican primary for governor. Later, however, he became a key adviser to Reagan on the state budget. When Reagan was elected president in 1980, one of his first appointments was Weinberger as secretary of defense. The former first lieutenant had moved to the top of the military chain of command. If Douglas MacArthur had still been alive, he'd have been reporting to Caspar Weinberger.

Weinberger immediately set out to repair what he believed was the damage inflicted on the military by the cutbacks of the Jimmy Carter presidency. He went on a military spending spree that lasted seven years and added up to a price tag just shy of $2 trillion. This was about much more than memories of wooden blocks painted as grenades and stick rifles when he was in basic training. Secretary Weinberger was on a crusade with his boss, President Reagan, to persuade the Soviet Union that it could not win and could not keep up.

He was—and remains to this day—the champion of the Strategic Defense Initiative, the so-called Star Wars defense against incoming missiles. It remains on the drawing board and in the laboratory, a high-tech and high-cost high concept that critics charge is merely provocative and is unreliable. Weinberger didn't get Star Wars, but he did order up new aircraft carriers, strategic bombers, and weapons systems, and he oversaw the development of the cruise missile. Later questioned about the impact on federal budget deficits of this gusher of military spending, Weinberger told a Harvard audience that the deficit could be controlled if Congress cut back "on a lot of unnecessary domestic spending that has big constituencies." By then it was fifty years since he'd been at Harvard, but the certainty of his views had not diminished.

Weinberger's public career ended on a dark note when he was indicted by Lawrence Walsh, the independent counsel investigating the Iran-*contra* scandal. Walsh had concluded that Weinberger had lied to Congress when he denied knowledge of the plan to sell arms to Iran and use the proceeds to arm *contra* rebels fighting the leftist Sandinista government of Nicaragua. Walsh claimed that Weinberger's own notes indicated that he did know, and that he was trying to protect President Reagan.

However, Weinberger never stood trial. In one of the closing acts of his presidency, George Bush gave the former defense secretary a full presidential pardon, describing him as a "true patriot." The country, by then exhausted by the long, complicated investigation into Iran-*contra*, barely blinked at the news of the pardon. It was already anticipating the arrival of a new, young president in Washington, Bill Clinton.

Caspar Weinberger joined *Forbes* magazine as a publisher and, on the editorial page, found a new outlet for the conservative views that had defined his lifetime.

*Lloyd Cutler (right)
with Henry Kaiser,
a client and friend*

Lloyd Cutler

LLOYD CUTLER

"We live in a multilateral world. . . . It's going to take a lot of public service."

AT THE SAME TIME Caspar Weinberger was growing up in northern California, another bright young man, who would later typify the liberal intellectual in national affairs, was growing up in New York. Lloyd Cutler became the quintessential Washington lawyer of the old school, a courtly and scholarly man who was counsel to Presidents Carter and Clinton.

He always had promise. As a child he relished trips to his father's law offices, where he would sit spellbound, listening to the tales of his father's law partner, Fiorello La Guardia, then a congressman and later one of the most colorful mayors in New York's history. It was young Lloyd's first connection to the fields that would become his life: public affairs and the law.

He was a precocious student and graduated from high school at sixteen, enrolling first at New York University and then at Yale, where he earned his law degree. Cutler was the editor of the *Yale Law Journal* at the same time another future power in Washington was president of the *Harvard Law Review*. That was Philip L. Graham, later the husband of Katharine Graham, the man who shaped the modern *Washington Post*. Cutler remembers, "We were arrogant young kids. When Justice Cardozo of the Supreme Court died, we published a joint issue of the law journals and rejected an article by a Columbia University law professor as not being up to our standards, because he was Columbia and we were Harvard and Yale."

Following graduation, Cutler went to work at the prestigious New York firm of Cravath, Swaine & Moore, but when Pearl Harbor was attacked he volunteered to take any job in Washington. He went to work for the Lend-Lease Administration, President Roosevelt's ingenious way of getting to the embattled British the war material they so desperately needed. Cutler's boss, Oscar Cox, was also the assistant solicitor general in the Justice Department, so Cutler was able to sharpen his courtroom skills as well as serve his country.

Cutler was involved in one of the more unusual episodes of the early months of the war. In the spring of 1942, eight Nazi saboteurs landed by submarine in Florida and Long Island, New York. Two of the Germans in New York decided to give themselves up, but first they wandered around for a few days before making their way to Washington, where they called the FBI. The FBI, using tips from the two defectors, quickly rounded up the other six invaders. But J. Edgar Hoover, the publicity-hungry director of the FBI, was so eager to claim credit that he announced the arrests before his agents could follow up and learn more about the network of friendly Germans the saboteurs had established in the United States.

At the time of this publicity stunt, Cutler was in a meeting with Hoover, Oscar Cox, and the secretary of war at the time, Henry Stimson. "Stimson was livid," Cutler recalls, "about as angry as I have ever seen anyone." It made no difference. Hoover continued to run the FBI just as he pleased, and he became so powerful that in subsequent years not even presidents would raise their voice to him, fearful of what files he may have had on their lives.

By 1944 Cutler was an enlisted man, in uniform and assigned to the Army's Combat Engineers. He was at a Brooklyn embarkation center, headed for England and a role in the D-Day invasion, when he checked in with some friends at the Pentagon. They decided that he would be more valuable on their team, the Special Branch. The Special Branch members were the country's intellectual elite, many of them low-ranking enlisted men in uniform, who were working on intelligence questions. Cutler was pulled out of Brooklyn and sent to the Pentagon. Later, he was told that the man who took his place was killed three days after D-Day when his jeep hit a land mine.

One of the primary missions of the Special Branch was to intercept and decode enemy messages. Cutler, who was reunited with his friend Phil Graham, was excited to be working with such a stimulating collection of former history professors, lawyers, and bankers, the best and the brightest the military could find for these critical assignments. More than a half century later, Cutler can still say, "Person for person, it was probably the most talented group I've ever worked with." They'd intercept the messages, decode them, study them, and then prepare analyses for the president or the secretary of war (as that cabinet post was called in those days), giving the Allies a critical edge. Cutler says, "Sometimes we'd intercept, say, a Japanese response to the original message from Japanese commanders. It would say, 'Please repeat, don't understand.' We were tempted to say, 'We do. Here's what you're supposed to do.' But of course we didn't."

In fact, when President Harry Truman made the decision to drop the atomic bomb on Japan, Cutler remembers, "We knew from the Japanese messages that they had authorized their ambassador in Moscow—remember, Russia was an American ally at the time—to open negotiations for a peace. The Russians never told us, but we knew. And when the time came to make the decision about the bomb . . . John McCloy, a senior man in the Special Branch, and Averell Harriman and others argued against it since Japan was ready to surrender anyway. They didn't prevail."

Having reflected on the decision all of these years, Cutler is now persuaded that it was probably the right decision to bomb Hiroshima, although he can't support the idea of the second bomb at Nagasaki. He now believes that the first bomb—and the attendant terrible damage and death toll—"kept anyone else from using it. It became a deterrent. Otherwise, we might have used one on Hanoi, or Cuba—or against the Russians. And it would have done much more harm, setting off a nuclear exchange with the Russians."

When the war was over, Cutler and some of his friends from the Lend-Lease Administration formed a Washington law firm, which eventually grew into the powerhouse Wilmer, Cutler & Pickering. During the sixties he was one of the founders of the Lawyers' Committee for Civil Rights, a response to Attorney General Robert

Kennedy's call for lawyers to help with the problems exploding across the American South and in the inner cities.

Cutler remains particularly proud of that work, believing that the committee he helped form kept the rule of law during a time when others were pressing for military occupation of embattled areas. "Now," he says, "we're up to the hard part, which is how do you undo two hundred years of slavery . . . and how do you change the pattern of life in the inner city? That's much more difficult." Cutler doesn't have a ready answer, but even though he's now in his early eighties, he isn't giving up.

He worries especially about attracting good people into the government, pointing out that anyone who volunteers for public service these days is considered to be "a fool or a knave." Now that the end of the Cold War has diminished the public's interest in foreign affairs, Cutler is concerned that "what we have left are . . . environmental threats, the terrorism threats, and the growth of third-world rogue states, which are much more complicated to deal with, and they don't arouse much immediate concern."

As a Roosevelt liberal, he's also distressed that too many people think we got to where we are today without the help of the government. "We don't simply take care of ourselves," he says. "The country needs to be led. Think about all of the great multinational institutions that were created in the euphoria right after World War II: the World Bank, the International Monetary Fund, the U.N., the European Union. Hardly anything has been created since then.

"We live in a multilateral world . . . but we have nothing to harmonize antitrust laws, tax laws, privacy laws . . . no international system to govern the information world. Those are very difficult things to do. It's going to take a lot of public service, and it's an open question whether we're ready for it."

GEORGE
SHULTZ

"My sergeant handed me a rifle and said, 'Treat it like your friend. Never point it at anyone unless you're prepared to pull the trigger.' That's a very fundamental lesson."

ARTHUR
SCHLESINGER

"I am a short-term pessimist but a long-term optimist. I think some future crisis will rally the country and bring out new leaders. These are the cycles of history."

T WO MEMBERS of the World War II generation who continue to be closely identified with their respective political parties appear to have little in common: George Shultz, a prominent and pragmatic cabinet officer in two Republican administrations, and Arthur Schlesinger, the keeper of the flame of the political philosophies of FDR and JFK, and one of America's most honored historians.

Shultz and Schlesinger are rooted in similar traditions. They both grew up in comfortable circumstances in the Northeast. Schlesinger's father was a prominent history professor. Shultz's father had a PhD in history but made his career on Wall Street. As young men, Schlesinger and Shultz attended elite prep schools, and both went on to earn doctorates in their own disciplines and become professors at Ivy League schools. After, that, however, their lives and their interests diverged.

George Shultz was a varsity letterman in two sports at Princeton, basketball and football, while Arthur Schlesinger was an exceptional history student at Harvard, already beginning the studies

George P. Shultz, Palau Islands, South Pacific, 1944

of Andrew Jackson that would bring him the Pulitzer Prize before he was thirty years old.

When the war came, Schlesinger went to work first for the Office of War Information, a writers' group determined to provide the public with an inside, truthful account of the war effort, and then for the OSS.

Shultz, an economics major, was so eager to get involved that he first tried to join the Royal Air Force. His eyesight didn't meet the exacting standards of the British, so he decided to join the Marines in the summer of 1942. One of the first lessons he learned as a lowly trainee stays with him to this day: "My sergeant handed me a rifle and said, 'Treat it like your friend. Never point it at anyone unless you're prepared to pull the trigger.' That's a very fundamental lesson." Many years later, this lesson stayed with him when, as secretary of state, he was involved in U.S. policy decisions that involved much more than one rifle.

For his part, Arthur Schlesinger was also learning lessons that would stay with him forever, and would sharpen his thinking on the social issues that occupy him to this day. As a writer for the Office of War Information, he was sent to the South, where he was shocked by the depth of racial hatred he observed.

Schlesinger was on assignment to find out the truth about reports of excessive drinking around the southern military camps. He quickly learned that the rumors of out-of-control consumption by the soldiers were exaggerated, fueled in part by leftover Prohibitionists and the southern religious establishment. He was much more likely to be told that the real problem was "Negro," although that was generally not the name used to describe the black Americans who were still being held in a form of bondage in the Deep South.

The wife of an Episcopal minister told him, "The Negroes were better off under slavery . . . they're being stirred up by northern agitators." She was absolutely sure of the existence of "Eleanor Clubs," secret cells of black women inspired by Mrs. Roosevelt and determined to escape their lives as domestic workers. The minister's wife said to Schlesinger, "Everyone in the South hates Mrs. Roosevelt."

Schlesinger finished the war in uniform, attached to the OSS, with the enviable assignment of Paris. He found a room in Montmartre, the artists' area, and began a lifelong love affair with the city.

Shultz, who met his future wife, an Army nurse, on a stopover in Hawaii, returned to the United States after the war and enrolled at the Massachusetts Institute of Technology on the GI Bill. He married Helena "Obie" O'Brien in February 1946.

Schlesinger and Shultz, each in his own way, set off on postwar careers that reflected the patterns of the best of their generation. They had distinguished academic careers while maintaining close ties to the great public-policy questions of the day.

Shultz served on the Council of Economic Advisers during President Eisenhower's administration. He left his post as dean of the University of Chicago School of Business to become President Nixon's secretary of labor, then director of the Office of Management and Budget, and ultimately secretary of the treasury. Shultz's reputation for toughness and fairness was reinforced when IRS computers kicked out President Nixon's tax return for an audit. Shultz authorized the audit to proceed. The president was livid, but his treasury secretary didn't back down.

He left the Nixon cabinet before the president was forced to resign, and became president of the Bechtel Corporation, the global construction powerhouse based in San Francisco. He returned to government as President Reagan's second secretary of state (after Alexander Haig) and stayed in that post through the end of the Reagan era. Shultz was widely credited with siding with Nancy Reagan in urging the president to establish meaningful negotiations with the Soviet Union once Mikhail Gorbachev began the historic changes in the Communist empire.

Henry Kissinger once said of this former World War II Marine, "If I had to entrust the United States to one man, George Shultz would be my choice."

Schlesinger became a Harvard professor after the war and resumed his prolific writing and teaching career. He was on Adlai Stevenson's campaign staff in 1952 and 1956 and came to know a promising young Harvard graduate who had big ambitions in Massachusetts and national politics, John F. Kennedy. When Kennedy was elected president, Professor Schlesinger went to the White House as a special assistant.

Later, he won his second Pulitzer Prize for his account of the Kennedy years, *A Thousand Days: John F. Kennedy in the White*

George P. Shultz, as photographed for the jacket of his 1993 book,
Turmoil and Triumph: My Years as Secretary of State

Arthur Schlesinger, wartime portrait

House. Schlesinger also wrote *Robert Kennedy and His Times* following the death of his friend. It won the National Book Award.

THESE TWO MEN, both now in their eighties, continue to pursue their intellectual passions, and they maintain an avid interest in the world of politics they have moved in and out of with such grace and influence over the last half century.

They both remain long-term optimists. How could they not? They've been personal witnesses to and students of the Great Depression, World War II, the Cold War, the collapse of communism, and the rise of a global economy. They've worked closely with Presidents Eisenhower, Kennedy, Johnson, Nixon, and Reagan, all of whom had triumphs and failures.

Schlesinger, ever the historian, points out that the United States healed itself after the terrible wounds of the Civil War. Theodore Roosevelt, he says, energized the country at the turn of the twentieth century when there was no great international crisis to mobilize public opinion, just as Andrew Jackson had done in the early years of the nineteenth century. Schlesinger shares the belief of many veterans that the sacrifices of his generation, the defeat of communism, and the extraordinary rise of prosperity make it possible for the younger generations to turn away from domestic politics and international affairs. "I am a short-term pessimist but a long-term optimist," he says. "I think some future crisis will rally the country and bring out new leaders. These are the cycles of history."

Ed Guthman as a young officer

ED GUTHMAN

"I was so glad to be home. God!"

MORE THAN fifty years later, Ed Guthman can still remember the palpable sense of relief he felt when he returned to Seattle after four years in the infantry, a lieutenant in the 85th Division, having fought his way through North Africa and Italy.

Ed had been wounded in Italy, and after a lengthy hospital stay he was reassigned to *Stars and Stripes,* the Army newspaper, an ideal transfer for the young Washington man who had worked summers at *The Seattle Star* before he was drafted.

So when he came home to Seattle he was able to reclaim his old job, starting out as a courthouse reporter. When the *Star* folded, he was picked up by *The Seattle Times* and went to work investigating the case of a University of Washington professor who had been accused by the Washington State Legislature Un-American Activities Committee of being a Communist sympathizer, a charge the professor vehemently denied.

The committee had promised to publicly resolve the conflicting claims but it failed to issue a report, and Guthman was assigned to the story. His editor, Russell McGrath, was an exacting boss, and when Guthman almost immediately turned up evidence to support the professor's claim of innocence, McGrath told him to check some more before they published. Guthman had already learned that the professor was in Washington State the summer the committee claimed he was at a Communist training camp in New York.

McGrath wanted more: check his whereabouts the summer before and the summer after, he instructed Guthman.

It never occurred to Guthman to question his editor's measured approach. He says now, "I think it was my military training; he was my commander and I followed his orders."

So Guthman dug some more and built a foolproof case: the professor was right, the committee was wrong. In fact, with just a little of editor McGrath's passion for the facts, the committee investigators could have come quickly to the same conclusion.

Finally, McGrath was ready to publish Guthman's story. It was complete, meticulous, and unassailable. The professor had his life back. The pernicious ways of the Un-American Activities Committee were exposed. And Guthman won a Pulitzer Prize.

To this day he credits his military training for the disciplined approach—after all, he had learned firsthand the advantages of two full years of training before his first combat. His war experience had also instilled in him a deep personal revulsion for tyranny in any form.

When he went on to become press secretary to Attorney General Robert F. Kennedy in the JFK administration, he was surrounded by many with the common experience of World War II and combat. On reflection, Guthman believes that shared experience helped everyone work as a team during crises, such as when the civil rights Freedom Riders' bus was attacked in Alabama. He says, "We knew how to quickly mobilize the resources of the government to take care of those people; every one had a role and executed it."

After his friend, now senator, Bobby Kennedy was assassinated, Guthman became national editor of the *Los Angeles Times* and, later, editorial-page editor of *The Philadelphia Inquirer*. He's now a professor of journalism at the University of Southern California. In any accounting of the good guys of American journalism, Ed Guthman is on the front page. That's how he'll be remembered: as a thoughtful, compassionate, and resourceful journalist. Most of us who have known him all these years were completely unaware of his Army experience and his Purple Heart, but they are not incidental to him or his life's work.

When his military service does come up, Ed prefers a story about his dean at the University of Washington. When Ed left the

Ed Guthman

university to answer the draft in 1941, he had not completed his ROTC requirements so he was not awarded his degree. Two years later he was a lieutenant, leading an infantry platoon on a hilltop in Italy. A large package arrived from Dean Lauer at the university with a note of explanation: "Dear Ed, We think you've fulfilled your military obligation. Here's your degree."

THE TWILIGHT
OF THEIR LIVES

"You can't pay in money for what they have done."

As an impressionable adolescent in the postwar years, I spent hours going through Bill Mauldin's book *Up Front*, his brilliant collection of drawings and thoughts on World War II's enlisted men, officers, the people they liberated, and the enemy they fought. He was just twenty-two years old when "Willie and Joe," his representations of American fighting men, first appeared. In his work, Mauldin shared with those on the front lines as well as those at home the hard truths and dark humor of life at war. As is so often the case with cartoons, Mauldin gave us the quick laugh and the lingering insight.

Recently, I read *Up Front* again. Initially I was pleased that I could recite from memory many of the cartoon captions; Mauldin's work leaves a lasting impression. When I began to reread the text, I had an even deeper appreciation of Mauldin's youthful genius. He'd put the book together near the end of the war, when he was just twenty-three. By then he was a sergeant, having entered the Army from the Arizona National Guard when he was eighteen. I can't imagine that anyone knew the minds, the frustrations, the fears, and the dreams of the average combat infantryman better than Mauldin did.

As his cartoons reflected the truth of what it was like to be up front, his writing gave us a vision of the future. Here is what Mauldin wrote of the American soldier before the war ended:

They are very different now. Don't let anybody tell you they aren't. . . . You can't pay in money for what they have done. They need people telling about them so they will be taken back into their civilian lives and given a chance to be themselves again.

There will be some good ones and some bad ones. But the vast majority of combat men are going to be no problem at all. They are so damned sick and tired of having their noses rubbed in the stinking war that their only ambition will be to forget it. They don't need pity because you don't pity brave men—men who are brave because they fight while they are scared to death.

Mauldin wrote those words more than half a century ago, even before the men headed home from the front lines, and it is as true today as it was then. They didn't want pity and they did want to forget. Of course, they could not forget, especially those who'd seen combat. When they couldn't erase the war from memory they simply confined it there, refusing to talk about it unless questioned, and then only reluctantly. That is why I think it's so important for us to hear these stories now, to know what an exceptional time that was for so many and how much they sacrificed to give us the world we have today.

Those stories come to us in so many ways. The heroes, the authors, and the politicians are part of a fixed library of memoirs and accounts, but in the course of working on this book I have realized how many stories still remain unknown to the larger world, confined as they are to the memories of the veterans and their families, or to the recollections of the people at home who made their own unique contributions.

NOT ALL of the stories are heroic or tragic. Many are memorable for the small moments they recall, for a funny line.

When his father died, Steve Friedman, a longtime friend and colleague in television, called to reminisce about what a great guy and inspiration his dad, Sol Friedman, a World War II Army veteran, had been.

Sol Friedman came back from the war and opened a grocery business in Chicago. He worked hard and raised a quintessential Chicago family: they were all active in Mayor Daley's political machine, devoted fans of the Chicago Cubs and the Bears, and life-long residents of the same neighborhood. Sol Friedman sent his children to college, and Steve rose through the ranks of network television to become the executive producer of *Today* and *NBC Nightly News* before going to work for CBS.

Steve says, "My old man and his buddies were the best, when you think of all they got done. They were in the Combat Engineers in the Italian campaign, all the way through. Later, when I asked him if he was ever scared, Sol said, 'I wasn't thinking about the bullet with my name on it. It was the one marked "To Whom It May Concern" that worried me!' " Steve and I both laughed hard, recognizing Sol's story as a perfect piece of Chicago street humor, carried to the war and back.

M Y FRIEND Jack Hemingway, the firstborn of Ernest Hemingway, was raised in the tradition of his adventurous father, so it was only natural that when the war came along he'd be involved with the OSS. Jack also thought it was natural, when he parachuted into France behind enemy lines, to carry in his pack a tool of his favorite sport, a fly rod. When questioned about it before takeoff, he told a superior officer it was a radio antenna.

In his splendid book *The Misadventures of a Fly-Fisherman: My Life With and Without Papa,* Jack describes the few opportunities he had to use the fly rod in some lovely French streams before he was taken prisoner by the Germans. When I tell this story to other fishermen, they always seem to be more interested in the quality of the fishing than in Jack's fate as a prisoner. He seems to understand.

G ENE GLICK was a combat infantryman with the Army's 45th Division and personifies to this day the "dogface" Bill Mauldin so loved: tough, smart, and capable of finding an enduring truth in the worst possible situation. Glick, an Indiana native, was fighting in Alsace-Lorraine during the big push toward Germany, late in the fall of 1944. He says, "I'll never forget November eleventh, 1944, at eleven A.M. I dove into a slit trench. You dig a slit trench when you don't have time to dig a foxhole. It's about the size of your body—

about two feet deep. There was a thin layer of ice. The shells were exploding all around. The ground shakes. You think that at any moment you're going to be killed or maimed for life. I remember thinking, Wouldn't it be wonderful if World War II ended the way World War I did—on November eleventh?"

It did not, of course. Gene Glick spent almost an hour facedown in the freezing water, with shells exploding all around him. He made a vow: "If I get out of this alive, anytime in the future, if it gets tough, I am going to remember November eleventh, 1944."

Glick survived the shelling and returned from the war to start what turned out to be one of the most successful residential construction companies in the United States, the Gene B. Glick Company. He's still on the job at the age of seventy-seven, although he's always willing to take a moment to tell you about his four daughters and his grandchildren. He took them to France in 1995 and had his grandchildren pose next to the headstones at a World War II cemetery so that, in his words, they would be reminded of "the tragedy of men not learning to live together in peace."

And what about that moment, November eleventh, eleven A.M., 1944? Gene Glick says that to this day, "It's like a guiding star. When things don't go right, when people disappoint me and projects don't work out, I think, Hey, Glick, November eleventh, 1944. No problem!"

BILL MAULDIN didn't know Mary Garber. She wasn't a dogface. She wasn't even in uniform. But in her own way, Mary Garber was changed by the war and by what came after. Moreover, what she did changed the world for so many of her gender.

She had a lifelong dream to be a newspaper sports reporter, but in the late thirties and early forties it was unheard of for a woman to cover sports—it was extremely difficult for a woman to be hired for anything except the society pages. That's how she began at the *Winston-Salem Journal* in North Carolina. When the paper offered her the job as society editor, she says, "I didn't want the job, but you had to get your foot in the door." When nearly every man on the paper's staff went off to the war, Mary finally had her chance to cover sports, but when the war ended, so did her dream-come-true. She was sent back to the society pages.

But Mary didn't give up. She volunteered to cover the contests the men in the sports department were ignoring. In those postwar years in North Carolina, the black schools received virtually no attention, so Mary became their champion on the sports pages, covering their games. She reasoned, "The parents of black athletes are just as interested as white parents."

The payoff came when a black policeman stopped her one day and said, "I don't know if you know how much the middle-aged black men in our town admire and love you."

As she quietly made her way as a woman in an all-male environment, she kept a particular eye on Jackie Robinson, who was then integrating Major League baseball. "I watched what he did," she says. "He did his job, kept his mouth shut. That's what I did." Well, not always. When Duke University barred her from the press box during a football game because she was a woman, Mary went directly to her managing editor. In turn, he fired off a letter to all of the local colleges, warning that if the practice continued, there would be no coverage of their games.

Mary went on to integrate postgame interviews, another all-male club, and to set a national standard for women in sportswriting. She was so prolific and so highly regarded in sports-crazy North Carolina that she was inducted into the state's athletic hall of fame, which also includes the legendary basketball coach Dean Smith and golfer Arnold Palmer.

Although officially retired for more than ten years, she still writes for the *Winston-Salem Journal*. To mark her forty years in sportswriting, a longer sports journalism career than any other woman in the nation, the paper published a front-page article on Mary and had it framed to hang on a wall next to the *Journal*'s Pulitzer Prize. On the back of the frame there is a note: "This is to hang here as long as the paper exists."

Mary Garber's career contributions are among the innumerable unexpected consequences of World War II, when the men went away and the women stepped in. For her part, Mary prefers that her legacy be measured by the comments of two young boys at a soap-box derby she was covering. Pointing to her, one of the boys said, "Who's that?" The other answered, "That's Mary Garber. If you do something, doesn't matter who you are, she'll write about you."

WARTIME AMERICA was forced by necessity to confront its hypocrisy concerning equality under the law. The war started the country on the road to long-overdue changes that finally came in the sixties for women and blacks. Discrimination by gender and race remains an unresolved challenge in this society, but the World War II experience accelerated the solution in ways large and small.

Dr. Helen Strauss, who was named New Jersey's psychologist of the year in 1997 for her longtime work with children and low-income families, was a WAVE during the war. She recalls Eleanor Roosevelt visiting her unit and observing, "I don't see any Negro faces here."

Shortly thereafter, two black women were assigned to Strauss's department, and as she escorted one of them, making introductions, another white WAVE, with deep family roots in Virginia, deliberately picked up her compact and began powdering her nose, utterly ignoring the new arrival.

Dr. Strauss remained friends with the black woman, Frances Willis Thorpe, until Thorpe's death in early 1998. As for the Virginia woman, so proud of her Confederate ancestors, she, too, was changed by the experience. Dr. Strauss says that years later the woman called to apologize for her behavior, expressing her deep embarrassment.

OTHER MEMBERS of the greatest generation found their life's calling in uniform, continuing to serve in the military after the war and helping it adapt to the changing times. One of these is retired Army colonel Robert Nett, who enlisted in the National Guard in his hometown of New Haven, Connecticut, as a private with no thought of staying beyond the time required.

By the time he retired in 1973, he had been in uniform for thirty-three years; had fought in World War II, Korea, and Vietnam; had been awarded the Medal of Honor for conspicuous gallantry in spearheading an attack against a heavily fortified Japanese position in the Philippines; and had a street named after him at Fort Benning, Georgia, where he continued to teach Army leadership courses after his retirement. And not incidentally, he's been married for fifty-four years to an Army nurse, Frances, whom he met while recovering from wounds. Their son, Robert Nett Jr., is a physician who retired as a major in the U.S. Army.

Colonel Nett could have lived on his Army pension and the glories of his distinguished military career when he retired, but instead he became an industrial-arts teacher in the Muscogee County, Georgia, school system for fifteen years. He liked the two fronts of his life, and moved easily between his junior- and senior-high students and his officer candidates at nearby Fort Benning. Nett felt that he could extend the lessons of his military experience by teaching young people "that they should walk proud in the light of what their fathers, grandfathers, and great-grandfathers have accomplished. In addition to education," Colonel Nett says, "students must learn to appreciate the views of others." He was so popular that he was named the county's Teacher of the Year in 1985, and one of his students successfully nominated him to help carry the Olympic torch when the Olympic Games were coming to Atlanta in 1996.

At Fort Benning, Nett is such a legendary figure that former Army students who have moved up in the ranks still call on him to help train or motivate their troops. In 1997 he visited eight training sites in Bosnia to boost the morale of forces assigned there to peacekeeping roles.

The colonel's message is built on four points:

1. Every U.S. citizen is grateful for the job the soldiers are doing.
2. The soldiers' job is important because they're preventing war.
3. As Colonel Nett often speaks at religious programs of all denominations, he *knows* that the soldiers are in the prayers of all the faithful.
4. Yes, the soldiers' job can be lonely and frustrating, but it's a lot better than fighting and, after all, they are helping people to establish a democratic way of life.

Nett is deeply impressed by the quality of today's all-volunteer military. As he says, "They're here because they want to be. When we had the Selective Service—the draft—I sometimes had to adapt my leadership to people who were angry and disgruntled. Now the officer candidates are college-educated, and by the time they get to training school they're considered the best."

Nett does, however, have some concerns about the expanding population of women in the armed services. "Even though the policy is not to have women fight," he says, "women have to be ready to fight in emergency situations. We can't have this policy of filling our military vacancies with females, but only males can fight."

Nevertheless, Nett is still gung ho on the quality of the military and the role it plays in American life. Almost sixty years after he first enlisted, he still hears the call to service. After all he's been through and all he's done for the military, you might think he would expect something in return. The colonel has another point of view. As he says, "I will go anywhere in the world to support the troops; after all, I feel so indebted to the Army for what it has done for me."

There it is again, the selfless response so characteristic of members of this generation, now coming into their twilight years. To be sure, they have gotten used to the better life, including the so-called entitlements such as Medicare, Social Security cost-of-living increases, and senior-citizen discounts—but they retain at the core of their being a strong sense of self-reliance and gratitude.

There is a common theme of pride in all that they've accomplished for themselves, their families, and their country, and so little clamor for attention, given all they've done. The women and members of ethnic groups who were the objects of acute discrimination even as they served their country remember the hurt, but they have not allowed it to cripple them, nor have they invoked it as a claim for special treatment now. They're much more likely to talk about the gains that have been achieved rather than the pain they suffered.

They have given the succeeding generations the opportunity to accumulate great economic wealth, political muscle, and the freedom from foreign oppression to make whatever choices they like. For those generations, the challenges are much different, but equally important.

There is no world war to fight today nor any prospect of one anytime soon, but racial discrimination remains an American cancer. There is no Great Depression, but economic opportunity is an unending challenge, especially in a high-tech world where education is more important than ever. Most of all, there is the need to reinstate the concept of common welfare in America, so that the nation doesn't squander the legacy of this remarkable generation by becoming a collection of well-defined, narrowly cast special-interest fiefdoms, each concerned only with its own place in the mosaic. World War II and what came after was the result of a nation united, not a nation divided.

As for me, I will always keep in my mind's eye a cool, cloudy Memorial Day on the northern plains of South Dakota. I was visiting my father's surviving brother, John, who after serving in the Navy during World War II returned to the small town of Bristol, the family seat. He stayed a bachelor all those years, working at the bank and in the municipal liquor store. He lived with two of his sisters, neither of whom, like John, ever married.

He was a small, quiet man, and on that Memorial Day he asked me to accompany him to the Bristol cemetery south of town, overlooking the broad reach of prairie. He explained that just the year before he had given up the job of placing small flags on the graves of veterans. He was worried that his successor, a veteran of the Korean War, might not know the location of all the graves that deserved to be honored.

So as I stood on a small rise, watching, these two veterans, each clutching a fistful of small American flags, made their way through the cemetery. It came to me then that this was, in many ways, the essence of the American experience. These two men had gone off to war in distant places and then returned to the familiar surroundings of their youth, the small town and farmland where life—as a result of droughts, blizzards, tornadoes, and wages that reflected the uncertainty of agriculture markets—was often difficult.

They came home to resume lives enriched by the values they had defended.

I have been witness to historic events at the U.S. Capitol and on the south lawn of the White House, at Arlington National Cemetery and the Statue of Liberty. None moved me more than the sight of my uncle and his friend, a local farmer, walking among the headstones, framed by the wide steel-gray sky and the great curve of a prairie horizon, decorating the graves of the hometown veterans on that Memorial Day.

I thought of the farmers, the merchants, the railroad men, and all their families who had gone through so much to tame the prairie and start communities, build schools and churches, and look after one another. They had gone off to war, or sent their husbands, sons, and boyfriends, and they now lay side by side beneath the sod, mute testimony to sacrifice and service. Those whose graves were decorated with the small flags were carrying the colors for all the others.

It was a ceremony of honor, remembrance, and renewal played out in countless other cemeteries across the land by members of a generation that gave so much and asked so little in return.

After talking to so many of them and reflecting on what they have meant in my own life, I now know that it is in those small ceremonies and quiet moments that this generation is appropriately honored. No fanfare is required. They've had their parades. They've heard the speeches. They know what they have accomplished, and they are proud. They will have their World War II memorial and their place in the ledgers of history, but no block of marble or elaborate edifice can equal their lives of sacrifice and achievement, duty and honor, as monuments to their time.

INDEX

"Written with a keen eye, sensitivity, and an open heart. Read it!"
　　　　　　　　　　　　　　　　　　　　—LAUREN BACALL

"Insightful . . . [a] delightful collection of personal stories . . . *The Greatest Generation* is a gift. It reminds us that we need to seek out the remaining members of this generation, to listen to them with open hearts and learn. Perhaps we may find some answers to some of the questions that plague the country today. *The Greatest Generation* reveals the private lives of people, both known and unknown, who survived these difficult times and were bound by common values of honor, patriotism, loyalty and love of family."
　　　　　　　　　　　　　　　　　—*State* (Columbia, S.C.)

"Compelling . . . [a] heartfelt tribute . . . There are stories from people you've never heard of and people you have. There are celebrated heroes and silent ones, but each one's story is essentially the same—they all had a duty in wartime that they performed without question."
　　　　　　　　　　　　　　　　　　　—*The Denver Post*

"A generation of remarkable Americans—our better angels."
　　　　　　　　　　　　　　　　　　　　—KEN BURNS

THE GREATEST GENERATION SPEAKS

I Remember

I Remember

•

_____ WHAT I REMEMBER _____
MOST ABOUT THE WAR YEARS
_____

_____

_____

_____

_____

_____

_____

_____

_____ MILITARY UNIT, JOB _____

_____

_____

_____ THE BEST MOMENT _____

_____

_____

_____

_____

_____

_____

_____

I Remember

MY LONGEST DAY

_____

_____

_____

_____

_____

_____

_____

_____

_____

_____

_____

_____

BEST FRIENDS

_____

_____

_____

_____

_____

_____

_____

_____

_____

_____

_____

_____

I Remember

•

WHEN THE WAR WAS OVER

WHAT I MISS ABOUT THAT TIME

I Remember

MY PHOTOGRAPHS

_____

_____

_____

_____

_____

_____

_____

_____

_____

_____

_____

_____

_____

_____

_____

_____

_____

_____

_____

_____

_____

_____

TOM BROKAW

·

THE GREATEST GENERATION SPEAKS

·

*Letters
and Reflections*

RANDOM HOUSE TRADE PAPERBACKS
NEW YORK

*To the men and women
of the greatest generation
with gratitude and admiration*

PREFACE

When I wrote *The Greatest Generation,* about the lives of American men and women who came of age in the Great Depression and then answered the call to arms and sacrifice in World War II, I thought of it as a letter of thanks and admiration to that generation. What I did not anticipate is that so many would write back, to express their thanks and to share their stories of a time that was at once so difficult and so triumphant. I also didn't expect to hear from so many of their children, the Baby Boomers, who seem to have found new bonds to their parents through my book.

I felt as if I had been invited to share a place at the table of the American family, to be a witness to stories parents were sharing with their offspring for the first time and to hear from the children questions that had not previously occurred to them. In many ways, I remain at that table, hearing new stories every week or meeting members of that generation and their children. I never tire of the recollections or the common pride of a worthy, even noble life at an early age and the lessons that life conveys to those who follow.

Some of the stories are here, in *The Greatest Generation Speaks,* first-person accounts of loss, courage, love, relief, struggle, achievement, sadness, and joy. All of the emotions of life during war, at home, and on the front lines.

These are the chronicles of a generation now in the last

stages of its long and magnificent life, the pure voices of men and women who gave so much, asked for so little, and remain so humbled by what they endured. These are the voices of greatness, defining in their modest fashion a legacy for the ages.

CONTENTS

INTRODUCTION

I am a child of the American men and women who grew up in the Great Depression, who came of age in World War II and then devoted their adult years to the building of modern America—the remarkable people I wrote about in *The Greatest Generation.* As I walked the beaches of Normandy on the fortieth and fiftieth anniversaries of D-Day, I first began to fully realize how they had shaped my life. They were my parents and the parents of my friends, teachers, ministers, physicians, and hometown merchants, the men and women who showed me the way through their own exacting standards of hard work, sacrifice, and personal responsibility. I began to understand how much I owed them.

As a son of working-class parents who were deeply rooted in the harsh economic realities of the Depression and the common challenges of the war, I reflected on the good fortune of my generation and the world we inherited. So many of us were the first in our families to attend college and to find that good jobs were plentiful. My generation and those that followed took their place in a world of broader horizons and expanded rights for women and ethnic minorities.

It wasn't a perfect world, of course.

Far too many of my contemporaries died in Vietnam, but others gave birth to long-overdue political and social change. The excesses of youthful rebellion in the sixties and seventies were painful, even destructive in some aspects, but the foundation of the country and its complex culture withstood the onslaught and remained secure. Moreover, my generation and those that followed were not judged by their excesses alone; indeed, we were given more opportunities in more arenas than our parents had dared to dream.

A few years ago, when I thought about my own good fortune in life and career, somehow it seemed inadequate to thank just my parents, even though their help was irreplaceable and enduring. There were so many people in the fabric of my life as I grew up who influenced me—teachers and ministers, coaches and merchants, the mothers and fathers of my friends—all men and women who had experienced great hardship during the Depression and the war years.

When I set out to write *The Greatest Generation,* I was inspired by these people and by the realization that my world of endless possibilities, despite all its imperfections, was the work of these men and women. By writing their stories, I had finally found a way to say thank you. I wanted that book to be my gift to them, an expression of admiration and gratitude for all they had achieved, and for the legacy they passed on to future generations.

Of course, I hoped that the book would be well received by the people about whom I was writing. As for younger generations, I wasn't sure what to expect. So many of the people I talked with from the World War II generation told me their kids weren't much interested in hearing about the Depression, the war, the sacrifices of the fifties. As for their grandchildren—a generation coming of age in a time of personal computers, digital video, and unprecedented prosperity—to them, stories about the Great Depression and World War II were like grainy black-and-white images in dusty schoolbooks or on late-night television. Wouldn't stories about people's lives during the 1930s, 1940s, and 1950s seem like ancient history to a thirtysomething or to a teenager shaping a life for America and the world in the twenty-first century?

And so the enthusiastic response to *The Greatest Generation* has been not only a pleasant surprise, but also deeply gratifying in ways I could never have predicted. From what people say to me on the street and write in letters, some of which appear in this book, *The Greatest Generation* seems to have inspired within many families, communities, schools, and even corners of the political arena a reevaluation of the past, and a dialogue about the core values of that time and of the present.

Children and grandchildren of the Greatest Generation are telling me they now understand the values reflected in the lives of the people they know from the World War II era, values that to many may have seemed a little tiresome in these more permissive times—the older generation's strict code of conduct and discipline; their frugality; and their expectation that once the teenage years were over, the serious grown-up years would begin.

My favorite reaction to *The Greatest Generation*, however, is expressed to me in unexpected moments—on a ski slope, in an airport, on a street in New York, in the Pentagon. Men about my age—cops, business executives, military men, construction workers—grab my hand, look me in the eye, and say, "I read your book. Thank you for helping me understand my father." Then they turn and walk away.

Any journalist would be flattered to have his or her work become a catalyst for reflection and examination, but I have no illusion about my personal role in all this. I was merely the reporter, the vehicle for people's stories and the lessons they contained. So many of the veterans said of their service during the war, "It was an honor," and I feel in turn it was an honor to have written about the people in that book.

I was totally unprepared for the avalanche of letters that appeared as soon as *The Greatest Generation* was published. Members of that generation, and their children, sent moving stories about the heroism, values, friendships, and pain of those times, and of the effect the book and its memories of the Depression and World War II had on their lives today. I wrote a book about America, and a lot of America is writing back.

The letters, many of them written in firm Palmer penman-
ship on flowered stationery, made me reflect further on the
meaning of those difficult times. I also thought the letters
contained wisdom, and valuable lessons about life, and were
of value as history too. Members of the Greatest Generation
still believe in the old-fashioned virtues of letter writing and
personal testimony. Some of them could also draw on letters
they had sent or received back then, letters written during the
war, from the front lines to people back home, or from families to their loved ones in harm's way in distant places.

In these pages, you'll hear directly from the Greatest Generation and their children; you'll hear voices and more stories, as the Greatest Generation and their families speak out,
some for the first time. Many of them say they felt they had
no audience until now. You'll also hear how the dialogue
sparked by the book caused younger generations to reexam-
ine their own lives and values, with a fresh perspective.

Most of the letters you'll find here arrived unsolicited.
Some I requested, hoping to fill in some gaps and oversights.
Even so, I know there are many more voices, experiences,
stories; we've included some pages here for you to write your
own.

If we are to heed the past to prepare for the future, we
should listen to these voices of a generation that speaks to us
of duty and honor, sacrifice and accomplishment. I hope
more of their stories will be preserved and cherished as reminders of all that we owe them and all that we can learn
from them.

I

———•———

WAR
STORIES

Frames of motion-picture war coverage taken by Raymond Daum,
somewhere on the Roer River, Germany, 1944–45.

Recently I read again Erich Maria Remarque's classic war novel *All Quiet on the Western Front*. It is a German soldier's reflection on the terror, cruelty, and absurdity of combat during World War I, yet the themes perfectly matched what American veterans wrote in their personal accounts of life at the front during World War II.

Those memoirs, many of them self-published or simply bound manuscripts, add to the rich body of literature from World War II. The best of that literature—the works of James Jones, Norman Mailer, Kurt Vonnegut, William Manchester, Joseph Heller, and Paul Fussell, for example—is well known. The homespun books will likely never be read outside the authors' immediate families. Still, the memoirs of infantrymen, fliers, sailors, and chaplains get at the essential truths of war in their own memorable and deeply personal fashion. They also remind us that for these men, in their late teens and early twenties, the lessons of death, fate, futility, and pure, unalloyed high-risk adventure were never to be matched in their other experiences.

Whenever an American flier was downed during the NATO bombing raids on Serbia, he was quickly located and picked up by elite search-and-rescue units utilizing the latest high-technology communications systems, which made it possible for the operation to be monitored thousands of miles away, in the Pentagon. In contrast, consider the Americans who were trapped by the Japanese on Corregidor in the Philippines at the outset of World War II. One of them was Clarence M. Graham, now eighty years old and living on a small landholding in Oregon. He was taken prisoner at the beginning of May 1942, and shipped off to Japan to work in a coal mine across the bay from a city called Nagasaki. For the next three and a half years he worked in the mine and then, one day in the summer of 1945, he was witness to a historic event.

This is what he wrote to me.

I am just one of many who were engaged in that war (WWII). I was stationed in the Philippines when it started and in an anti-aircraft battery. We were on the Bataan Peninsula. We were engaged in jungle fighting to the bitter end of that battle. Our battery escaped on the last night and made it back to the island of Corregidor. There we continued the defense until, on May 9th, 1942, Corregidor was captured. Nearly all of us who had survived to that point were undernourished and wounded in one way or another and most were wounded more than once.

We were taken prisoners by the Japanese and were used as slaves, tortured in various ways and maintained on starvation rations. Many were murdered. Many died of diseases and starvation. During the last year of three and a half years as a POW I worked in a condemned lateral of the Fukuoka coal mine near the city of Omuta, Japan. While there I was an eyewitness to the explosion of the atomic bomb that was dropped on the city of Nagasaki, just west and across the bay from us.

In a telephone interview, Graham took us back to the 1940s and his life in the coal mine.

It was very hot work, and very deep. The air was quite bad in there. The dust was terrible because it was a soft bituminous coal, and it filled the air and there were no currents and we had to breathe it. You had to keep your wits about you to stay alive because one false move, and your life was nothing in that country. They'd kill you in an instant if you disobeyed. . . .

In the mines, we had a shift that contained three types of work. There would be three or four men shoveling, three or four picking the coal off of the coal face, and the others would be picking up layers of slate and building pyramids of rock that hold up the ceiling. . . .

We took just one day at a time. I know that I kept saying, "I've got to keep my mind clear, and look for something good." Like . . . for one thing, I had a battery light that didn't leak on me and get acid on my skin. . . . Little things you'd keep yourself tantalized with, like . . . "Maybe soon you'll get a chance to get a break or something." . . .

I had a little belt on my waist, and all we wore was a loincloth. Sometimes I got to coughing so bad that I would take off my whole wardrobe and wrap it around my face so I could breathe. You could see only eyeballs and teeth when you looked at someone because they were covered with black coal. . . . We carried a cigar box with rice in it and that would be our ration for a twelve-hour shift. Sometimes the coal was so heavy we couldn't find our boxes. . . .

When you're a prisoner in those conditions, you don't care who it is, what his name is, who's next to you. You don't need a name. You have so little that you have to say, that you don't carry on a conversation. You're like oxen. . . . We always wondered [how the Allies were doing]. . . . Fellows made up rumors, but . . . we knew nothing. I kept thinking, well, if the Good Lord wanted me to get through this, I would make it. If he didn't, I wouldn't. I kept my faith pretty high, because so many just gave up. And you couldn't. You had to have inner drive, or you'd just die. . . .

We had just come in off of a long hard shift, and they were getting very brutal because . . . of the bombing on Hiroshima. And they were stirred up like hornets and taking it out on the Americans in the worst way. They said after Hiroshima they wouldn't give us any food, and that we would have to work until the Emperor decided that we didn't have to work anymore. We came out [of the mine] and it was daylight, and they didn't give us any breakfast. They told us to be quiet or we'd be killed. And then we had to go into our barracks—no talking. That's when . . . there was this air raid siren and we were ordered out to the trenches built in the camp between the barracks. They weren't trying to protect us [from the bombing]. . . . They needed our slave labor to get the coal to their war machines. No Japanese would go into the coal mines. . . .

We went in [to the trenches] and heard some planes but never saw them. . . . Then they blew the all clear. But just as we were coming out, I heard another plane and I looked up and saw an opening in the clouds, and I saw a B-29. I thought at the time, "Why don't they bomb, what are they joyriding for?" And then . . . we saw a brilliant flash—there's no way to describe the brightness. You couldn't tell where the flash came from—just brilliant brightness. Then seconds later there was a small tremor on the ground . . . you could feel the ground shaking. Then there was a strong wind that came from the west, which is the direction of Nagasaki, across the bay. And following that wind, there was a hot, hot wind. Terribly hot. Hotter than direct sun on your face. Then there was a lull, and a terrific wind, almost a typhoon wind from the west, which was the air rushing back to the bomb center after the heat had gone up. The wind was so strong it toppled over some of our weak prisoners, just flattened them.

That's when we saw this huge orange dome to the west, and we were wondering what in the world it was. And then out of it, there was an opening about it and all the clouds disappeared and you could see the bright blue sky. And then this column of white smoke came up just like a tornado—a column. And we're standing there watching and the Japanese are all quiet. And then all of a sudden it starts to mushroom towards the top. . . . The funny thing about it all was that I never heard it. It must have been so loud that my ears were not able to pick it up. . . .

We were in a state of shock, not knowing anything about the atomic bomb. I remember someone saying, "Wow, what a blast." Then someone else said, "They must have hit a big ammunition dump." Then after that we were ordered back to the barracks. They [the guards] were mean, but not as mean as after Hiroshima. Here, they were just in a state of shock. . . .

Six days later the war was over, and one of Graham's prison guards had an instant change of heart, saying to one of Graham's fellow prisoners, "You and I are now friends."

Graham didn't wait for a liberation force after all those years of misery, torture, and animal-like survival. He slipped through the fence, stole a bicycle, and made his way to the nearby city of Omuta to hook up with Allied forces.

He was flown out of Japan on a C-47, and as it gained altitude, he looked down to see a rainbow—a perfect circle against the deep blue waters of the China Sea. As he watched, a second rainbow formed around the first one. Graham, a lump in his throat, said to the pilot, "Do you see that?" The pilot responded, "Yes, it must be for you." Graham closed his eyes and offered a silent prayer to God. He was headed home.

ONE OF THE MOST HARROWING war stories involved American civilians who had the misfortune to sign on as the crew for a luxury cruise to the Far East just as the war broke out. June Behren's late husband, Hank, was a college student in Santa Barbara when he became a merchant seaman on the SS *President Harrison*, looking for a little adventure and college money for the following term.

This introduction to a Navy history of the *Harrison* affair by David and Gretchen Grover is a summary of what happened to the ship and crew.

In the fall of 1941 a voyage began routinely for the SS *President Harrison,* an American passenger liner departing San Francisco for the Far East. Passengers and crew were aware that their destination, although nominally still at peace, was a tense and unsettled part of the world. Nevertheless, they had no way of knowing that as they steamed toward the Orient, they were soon to be part of the opening act of a strange drama of war and captivity then beginning in the Pacific, or the Pacific theater, as, ironically, it was soon to be called. The *President Harrison* was never to know again the traditional completion of a ship's voyage: the ringing up of "Finished with Engines" on the engine order telegraph, and the beginning of a new set of pages in the logbook for the next voyage. Instead, after her heroic rescue of a Marine regiment from Shanghai she was destined to be captured by the Japanese while trying to rescue another detachment of U.S. Marines in North China from the threat of capture, then pressed into service as a Japanese troop ship, and subsequently sunk by an American submarine while transporting a load of Allied prisoners from Southeast Asia back to Japan.

Her crew was to spend three years and nine months—the entire period of American involvement in World War II—as prisoners of the Japanese, the first and largest group of merchant seamen to be so captured and the group that would spend as long in captivity as any other Americans during the war. Sixteen of her crew would not come back at all—some victims of the *Harrison*'s attempt to avoid capture, and others victims of the hardships of captivity.

Only fleeting references to the saga of the *President Harrison* and her crew appear in naval histories of World

War II and in the virtually nonexistent maritime histories of that war. Her capture a few hours after Pearl Harbor received only passing notice in the press. Even after the war, most of the limited recognition she received posthumously was as a Japanese ship and as a suspect in the disappearance of an anthropological treasure.

Mrs. Behrens updates the story with her account of what happened to her husband.

My husband skipped out on his fall semester at Santa Barbara State College. He had worked summers on the *Lurline,* a cruise ship sailing between Los Angeles and Honolulu. The run to the Orient in 1941 would provide money for the school year.

An incredible story followed over the next four years. The true account reads like an adventure thriller. After the war and his return home in 1945, Hank's wartime experiences did not entitle him to GI benefits. He worked his way through college, and did not qualify for a GI housing loan.

In 1981 we returned to China and found the location of the old prison camp. Hank and a fellow POW, Dr. J. R. Bloomfield, had tears in their eyes as they walked through the iron gates.

In 1989, while touring Santa Barbara's sister city, a senior Japanese gentleman served as our docent guide. I asked him where he was in WWII. He told me he was captain of a gunboat on the Whangpoo River. Hank couldn't believe what he heard. From his window in the POW camp he watched the patrol boat go up and down the river. The two had much to talk about. In the course of their conversation, the old captain learned that Hank had enjoyed listening to old Japanese folk songs his guards in the POW camp played on their gramophone. When we returned home, the captain had sent a cassette of the songs to Hank. A correspondence ensued until Hank's death.

Hank Behrens and all merchant seamen had a unique history in the saga of World War II. They were forty-five years in gaining veteran status. Two years before he passed away, the government presented Hank with a military discharge and a POW medal.

ROBERT WEIL AND JIM LEVY, two sons of Alabama, were best friends when the Normandy invasion was launched. Weil wrote to describe his reaction and a later visit to those beaches. He also included his friend's account of what he had gone through.

> I have never had such a feeling of guilt as I had on the morning of June 6, 1944, when I awoke to learn that the invasion was on. I was a 2nd Lieutenant, still stationed stateside, but with my conscience "over there." It was some months later that I learned that my best friend landed on Omaha Beach that morning at H-Hour. He is Jim Levy, then Captain in the 81st Chemical Mortar Battalion of the 116th Infantry Regiment of the 29th Division.
>
> Like many others, Jim never spoke to me of the invasion, and it was not until the 50th anniversary of the invasion that I read an account of it which was published on the op-ed page of the *Montgomery Advertiser*.
>
> During the '90s, my wife and I visited Omaha Beach, the cemetery, and one end of the beach to the other. As we drove down the beach, we saw a monument on the side of the hill and drove up to see what it was. I think it was a monument dedicated to the 29th Division. There was also an American couple with two children visiting the monument.
>
> As I stood there gazing at the profile of that long, steep hill plunging down to that beach, which appeared so narrow now, I could not imagine how our troops could land there with all the obstacles and gunfire. I

said to this American chap that I didn't see how our fellows ever survived on that beach, that the Germans must have been looking right down their throats.

And the chap said, "Yes, they sure were!"

I replied, "You said that just like you were here."

"I *was* here."

"What was your division?"

"I wasn't really with a division. I was with a chemical warfare mortar battalion."

"My best friend was with a chemical mortar battalion which was supposed to land several miles up the beach, but the tide brought them down to a different point."

"The same thing happened to us. . . . Who was this friend of yours?"

"His name is Jimmy Levy."

"You don't mean Captain H. F. [Jim] Levy!"

It turned out that Jimmy was his company commander, and he was one of his platoon leaders.

This is a partial first-person account of what Jim Levy went through that day, June 6, 1944.

As we began our run for the beach, features of the terrain became gradually more distinct and flashes from our bombardment and their counter-fire grew in intensity and visibility along with the tumult of sound. The early waves of engineers had been unable to clear sufficient lanes through the obstacles (much more effective than had been intimated in training) and we were forced to move down beach, parallel to the shoreline, searching for a cleared lane to the beach.

At about this time, our LCVP [Landing Craft, Vehicle, Personnel] barely nudged a land mine, which exploded, wounding a couple of men in the bow and causing the craft to take on water alarmingly. We got another of our company's LCVPs alongside, transferred all men and weapons, but shed our packs. Another of our LCVPs was hit by artillery and a transfer of men and weapons again effected some 1,000 yards offshore with still another of B Company's LCVPs. Eventually, we located a cleared path to shore, and the craft moved as far in as possible before grounding on a sandbar. All of this time my reactions were as if I were a spectator rather than an active participant, apart from what was occurring, yet mechanically responding. It was as if the mind was overloaded with the enormity of all the external events—completely beyond our control, yet somehow functioning by rote.

The water became shoulder high on the beach side of the bar, and many men—overloaded with equipment—drowned.

We had been scheduled as the fourth wave—behind the engineers and first two waves of infantry (close-in support units) to touch shore at H Hour plus 10 minutes. Time seemed interminable and really at a standstill. Gradually, the number of men at the waterline (living, wounded, dead) increased.

Believing that it was better to be killed inland than at the water's edge, trickles of men moved up the steep face of the dune line—the leaders replaced by the next in line after being killed or disabled by antipersonnel devices. Heroism was commonplace, but there was no alternative. It is easy to be selfless when there seems to be no self. We too moved across what then seemed an expanse of beach, and up the narrow tape-marked path off the beach—at times through uncleared mine fields. We established a firing position on a shelf-like path some 20 feet below the rim of the dunes—and within 100 yards of the front line infantry. It later turned out that I was the only one of the four company commanders of the 81st who survived "D" Day.

Our position above the beach and below the top of the dune line was like a grandstand seat at a spectacle we would have preferred not to watch. We were reasonably sheltered from direct weapon fire, except the few still occupied fortifications.

By way of a personal postscript. I returned to Normandy and Omaha Beach in late September 1987 for my first and only visit. It was a tremendously emotional experience and rekindled memories and feelings long dormant. I could determine within 100 yards just where we had come ashore and set up. Faces, thoughts, sounds, and happenings came flooding back—many I did not want resurrected.

We visited the American Cemetery high on the Norman hills overlooking Omaha Beach and a more serene, appropriate, immaculate, and peaceful setting I cannot imagine. A memorial stands at the north end where you enter the cemetery. A semi-circular colonnade in an arch—above which was inscribed: "These Endured All and Gave All That Justice Among Nations Might Prevail and That Mankind Might Enjoy Freedom and Inherit Peace." In the middle distance, dividing the long avenue of lawn, stands a small circular chapel; above this was inscribed: "This Embattled Shore, Portal of Freedom, Is Forever Hallowed by the Ideals, Valor, Sacrifices of Our Fellow Countrymen." How well are these lessons learned and remembered? Standing there in appreciation, sadness, and long postponed grief, I could only wonder—"Why not me?"

AN ESTABLISHED FIGURE in American life is John Whitehead, a former senior partner at the Wall Street firm of Goldman Sachs and a deputy secretary of state in the administration of George Bush, who was the last of the World War II veterans to become president. Upon returning to New York following his State Department service, Whitehead became chairman of the International Rescue Committee, a private organization working tirelessly on the problems of refugees from strife around the world.

I asked him to reflect on his war years.

I've read your book with great interest. I'm not sure that those of us who served our country in World War II deserve to call ourselves the "greatest" generation. Like any group of Americans, we were a mixed bag. But I agree that we do seem to share some common differences from other generations and I know that I would not choose to switch to another generation, even if I could.

What accounts for these differences? World War II was universally accepted by all of us who participated as a "just war." There was never a question of whether or not we were on the right side.

It was a long war, too. We were in it, most of us, for a bigger part of our lives than we had expected. While we often bitched to each other about how it was interfering with whatever it was we planned to do, we never questioned that we were in it to the end. It was a war that had to be won and we would willingly stay the course.

Just as everyone remembers where they were when President Kennedy was shot, so, too, people in my generation remember where they were when the Japanese bombed Pearl Harbor. It was Sunday, December 7, 1941, at 2:00 P.M., and I was manning the checkout desk at the Haverford College library, working off the hours of one of my various work scholarships. The attack was big news and I knew my life would never be the same.

Two of my classmates, Paul Cope and Chris Cadbury, proposed that we drive down to Washington that night and hear the President declare war. It was a little silly because, of course, we had no way to get into the Capitol where the speech was to take place. Nevertheless, off we went in Chris's ancient jalopy, and stood the next day on the Capitol steps and listened to the famous "date which will live in infamy" speech. We felt very much part of it, and so we were. It was to be a war that involved everyone.

There were a few Haverford students, it being a Quaker college, who were conscientious objectors and refused to register. Others, who registered but then declared themselves conscientious objectors, were, if they could prove a lifetime belief in pacifism, assigned to "alternative service," which meant work on a farm or driving an ambulance or some similar nonmilitary work. The boards did a pretty good job in separating the suddenly opportunistic pacifists from those with lifetime, deeply held religious beliefs. I had half a dozen Quaker classmates who fell into this category.

The rest of us were subject to be drafted at any time and most of us looked around for an alternative military program that would permit us to graduate before being called up. My friend and classmate Bob MacCrate and I discovered just such a program. It was a Navy Supply Corps program which, if we qualified, would allow us to graduate, then commission us as ensigns in the Navy, then send us for 90 days to Harvard Business School, which had been taken over for the duration by the Navy, to learn Navy accounting, and then send us off to sea.

I was called to active duty in June of 1943, assigned temporarily to the Brooklyn Navy Yard, and immediately assigned as Commanding Officer(!) of the 20th Street pier in South Brooklyn while awaiting the next class at HBS [Harvard Business School]. Here I was exposed, maybe for the first time, to being way over my head. Come to think of it, life for me has been a series of over-my-head experiences from which I had to struggle my way out.

Whitehead was assigned to the USS *Thomas Jefferson*, where he lived comfortably and relished his position as the ship's supply officer. That often involved borrowing one of the new landing craft so he could motor over to other ships and trade for the supplies he needed. He quickly became a deft helmsman, and someone was watching.

His commanding officer called him to a private meeting in the captain's quarters. Whitehead's account of the meeting follows.

"I want to assign you to some extra duty," he said.

"Yes, sir."

"Ensign R. L. Jones, one of my boat officers, has become ill and is going to be leaving the ship, and if you're willing and able, I'd like you to replace him temporarily for the next several weeks."

"Yes, sir."

"I've been watching you going back and forth to the dock. You've become pretty good at handling an LCVP."

"Yes, sir."

Now, my normal duties on the ship had to do with paying the crew, paying other bills, and helping procure whatever supplies the ship needed to operate. My so-called battle station was up on the signal bridge, the very top of the ship, where with others I was to identify incoming airplanes as friend or foe. While these duties had their risks—enemy bombings, kamikaze planes, torpedoes, etc.—they were not exactly hand-to-hand combat.

What the Captain was asking me to do was to be a boat officer in the upcoming invasion, which meant being in charge of a group of four or five LCVPs, each carrying 20 Army or Marine infantrymen from our mother ship to an enemy beach, usually at the beginning of an invasion. This was another kettle of fish!

But what could I do? I couldn't say no. And so I said yes. The Captain stood up, shook my hand, wished me luck, and that was that. I kind of floated back to my cabin, both proud and scared. Ed Carmody was there and I told him what had just happened. I think he looked at me with new respect. I don't think he thought too much of supply officers.

As soon as we reached Portsmouth, [England,] the ship was put under tight security. In Navy lingo, the ship was "sealed." No arrivals or departures. No liberty. No mail. Lots of briefings and, for me, lots to learn. Lots of poring over maps and looking at photographs of the shoreline. Lots of clambering up into an LCVP on its davits on the deck to be sure I knew every inch of it. We were to land 2,000 soldiers from the 29th Division on Dog Red Beach in the Omaha Sector of the beaches of Normandy.

Finally, on June 4, the word came to go, in spite of the weather. It was a false alarm. The weather was too bad, and partway across the channel we were ordered to turn around and come back to Portsmouth. It was a bit of a letdown.

Twenty-four hours later, however, late in the afternoon of June 5, we left again, and this was the real thing. The slower ships went first and the fastest ships last so that we would all arrive on the beach at the same time. There were hundreds of ships. It was still stormy, raining really hard, and the sea was choppy. The crossing was uneventful. No submarines.

When we were loaded, my five LCVPs found each other, formed a circle like a cat chasing its tail, and waited for other boats to form up. It was pitch dark, drizzling, and cold and the air was dark with diesel fumes. The sea was quite choppy and within a few minutes everyone was seasick. Picture 20 men, all standing packed into a 24-foot flat-bottomed boat for four hours, heavily laden with rifles and packs, all seasick. It was pretty miserable.

It was very noisy. The sound of the engines of all the boats made it impossible to shout back and forth from boat to boat and we used walkie-talkies to communicate. Somehow our five boats kept together. By about four o'clock, the first faint light of dawn began to appear and it was easier to identify the other boats. Lost boats began to find their mates. Before long, we began to hear the deep-throated explosions of 16-inch shells fired at the beach from battleships farther out at sea. And then the drone of [planes] overhead carrying paratroopers from the 82nd and 101st Airborne Divisions to land behind the beach. It was very comforting to see that some things seemed to be working as they were supposed to.

At about 800 yards, we were released to make the final run into the beach on our own. Our five little boats were still together and seemed ready to go. It was light enough now for them to see hand signs and for me to see my watch. It was five minutes of six and I waved them on in. When we got within about 100 yards of the beach, we saw there was ahead of us a solid phalanx of steel obstacles designed to keep LCVPs from landing. We had been prepared for these obstacles, which were called Element C, but not for such a solid alignment in front of us. I signaled our boats to come to a dead stop. If we had continued on to Dog Red Beach straight ahead, we all would have been hung up on those obstacles in water too deep to debark the troops. I signaled our five boats to turn sharp left parallel to the beach. After about 100 yards we found an opening and headed for the beach again. Our boats were now a little mixed up with the boats designated to land where we were now heading, but the beach was wide enough for all of us.

It was about this time that the first German mortar shell exploded, right at the waterline of the beach that we had been heading for. But we were now about to hit the beach next door and had no time to worry about mortars. The impact of the boats hitting the ground was supposed to be enough to jar loose the boat ramps, which [would fall] forward in the water, letting the soldiers debark. It worked for everyone else but our boat. Our ramp stayed closed. I left my post in back of the coxswain and went forward to help the bowman loosen the ramp. After a few blows from the hammer, our ramp came down too, and our soldiers debarked. I glanced at the other boats in our wave and saw that they were ready to withdraw.

Our job now was to get off the beach as quickly as possible to get out of the way of the second wave, which was to land directly behind us. We raised our ramps and retreated without any serious problems.

We also realized that our job with the soldiers we had landed was completed, but that theirs was only beginning, and that they had days and weeks and months ahead before their job was over. In the meantime, we were returning to the *Jefferson* for a good hot shower and a hot brunch served for the officers in the wardroom. Rather incongruous for a group of men who had just landed on the first wave at Normandy. The soldiers were the real heroes.

There was one moment of D-Day which, rather strangely, remains more vivid in my mind than anything else. It was a quiet moment, a moment of peace and introspection after a very long day of noise and fear, of chaos and seasickness, of little acts of courage, and of death.

It was about 3:00 and we had made our second landing of the day and would soon be starting again the two-hour trip back to the *T.J.* The beach was now secure. My five little boats had all made it in without serious problems and we were actually a little ahead of schedule. The ship's crew had only had two casualties from the landing. The Army lieutenant from my boat was now busy trying to get ashore a large machine gun and, for the first time since 2:00 A.M., I had a free moment.

I clambered off the boat—we were stuck on a little shoal in about two feet of water—and walked a few yards up the beach. I took a few deep breaths and looked around me. The dead and wounded had been moved up to the first dune and were being cared for. Equipment—guns and food and ammunition—was being unloaded, along with more troops. As far as I could see, in both directions, LCVPs were landing, unloading, and withdrawing and I realized that what I could see was less than 5% of the landing beaches. It wasn't orderly, but it wasn't chaos either. I got the sense that it was going to work, that what had looked like such a disaster only a few hours earlier was beginning to look like it had a chance.

I felt thankful, of course, that I seemed to have survived the worst part. I took a few deep breaths and felt suddenly elated, proud to be having even a tiny part in what was maybe the biggest battle of all history. At that moment, soaked to the skin, seasick, dead tired, cold, still scared, I would not have wanted to be anywhere else.

A NUMBER OF VETERANS wrote poignant accounts of their fear during combat. One of them, Frank Hancock of Madison, Alabama, told a touching story of a comrade who made a difficult decision as the 399th Infantry, 100th Division, crossing northern Europe, battled German forces in the Vosges Mountains. He begins with an episode from his memoir, "An Improbable Machine Gunner."

This day is a little quieter. We listen for the distant cough of the mortars and move back in the dugout to escape shrapnel when the rounds hit the trees overhead. We know the sounds: our 105-mm artillery and 60- or 81-mm mortars; their 88-mm cannon and 50- or 80-mm mortars. The ratio seems to hold; about 15 to 20 rounds go out for each one coming in. Firing continues all day. Some of our rounds fall short; a 105-mm shell hits the edge of our dugout; I am sitting inside when it bursts, not more than 2 feet from my head. My ears ring from the concussion, but the frozen dirt and logs stopped all of the fragments.

We hang a blanket to separate the dugout from the opening by the gun. Now there are three of us; one hour on and two off. Not bad! But the two sleepers are so crowded that they must turn over at the same time!

I am roused from sleep by the man I am to relieve; he lights a candle while I bundle up and put on my pistol belt. I crawl over to the hanging blanket and whisper: "Put the candle out!" He shields it with his hand and I slip under the blanket. A light blinks over my shoulder.

Furious because I think the light came from the candle, I move quickly behind the gun, and my foot strikes something in the bottom of the hole. I pick it up; it feels like a metal goose egg with a raised seam around it. I hold it inside the blanket. "What the hell is this? *It's a Kraut grenade! Git it out of here!*" I turn and throw the grenade, blind, in the dark, remembering where there is a gap in the trees. Nothing happens.

"Where is he?" The woods are silent. Nothing stirs while I strain my eyes and ears. All night I ponder: "How could he have gotten so close? What would have happened if it had not been a dud? Why did my buddy take time to insert 'the hell' in the middle of his warning?" The half-second might have been fatal if the grenade fuse had been alive.

The next evening near dusk I venture out again, and peer out from behind the tree above the dugout. With the binoculars I see a column of Germans lined up at what looks to be a horse-drawn mess cart. I pick out a tree which marks their location and then scramble down behind the gun and sight it on the tree.

A twig snaps behind me and I whirl with drawn pistol; it is our old Company Commander, now acting as Battalion Commander. I give him the binoculars and show him where the Germans are still busy dishing chow. I tell him about where the gun is sighted. He looks, then hands me the binoculars and says, "Well, what are you waiting for?"

I crouch behind the gun and fire about half a belt, maybe a hundred rounds, while traversing the gun around the tree landmark. Then I look back to where the Captain had been standing, and the forest is quite empty. I duck back into the dugout as mortar shells burst in the tree above us.

The other gunner asks: "What was that all about?" And when I tell him, he thinks it is pretty funny that the Captain vanished so quickly. It is the first, but not the last time that I see Captain Derryberry at the front.

That night I return from the chow jeep to find a new neighbor. During my absence of a half-hour or less, a rifleman has killed a German soldier, not 20 yards away from our gun. In the commotion of men going to eat, the gunner did not see the German approaching our hole, but a rifleman did. I wonder if [the dead German] is the same man who dropped the grenade in our hole the night before.

Trees move in the wind and their moonlight shadows shift across the figure lying still in the snow, so that he appears to move. I know that he is quite dead, for the medic checked him. We will not jeopardize a recovery team to bring a fallen foe from this exposed position. He will keep well enough in the bitter cold.

A few days in reserve are like heaven, walking in the streets of Siersthal, [France,] getting showers and clean clothes, three hot meals, and sleeping indoors, warm and dry. After a night or two of sleeping inside, my hips and shoulders get sore from sleeping on the floor. In the dugouts we smooth little depressions in the ground and we are padded with winter clothing.

Late afternoon, we pack to return to the front that night after dark. I show the squad how to put a new barrel in the machine gun. The old barrel looks pretty good, but someone has decided to replace it; maybe because it sat out in the woods for weeks without being oiled every day. Then too, it was not cleaned after Lt. Witt and I had fired a total of several hundred rounds through it. And I have no idea how much this gun has been used in the last two months!

The new gun barrel is full of Cosmoline, a black preservative. More like asphalt than grease; it is hard when cold. I warm the barrel next to the stove and finally get a ramrod to carry a cleaning patch through to the chamber.

Smitty the ammo bearer watches me install the barrel, and moves close to my side. At 27 he is the oldest man in the squad, maybe the oldest in the platoon. A recent draftee, he is good-humored, and well liked. Quietly, he says: "Frank, I'm not going back with you." Amazed, I put down the gun barrel. "What?" This is unheard of—what will they do to him?

"I'm not going back. I've got two little girls at home, and I want to live to see them again. I want to get back to them with enough of me left to be able to take care of them." He shows me their picture. Little charmers!

I like how lucky I am still to be single; the thought of leaving a family; or worse, coming home crippled, to be a burden—but I say: "I can't do anything about it, you'd better talk to the Lieutenant."

I install the packing around the gun barrel and fill the jacket with antifreeze: "GI" Prestone, in OD-painted cans. My mind follows the ammo bearer; men have been shot for less! We miss him later that night when we move out to relieve another battalion on the front.

I need not have worried; our understanding Company Commander assigns him to permanent KP for the rest of the war. Our kitchen is seldom out of artillery range, but it is almost never hit and has few—or no—casualties. He also serves . . . and what he did that day was an act of courage and love.

In the middle of the night, carrying our guns and

bedrolls to the front, we are almost to our new positions when we pass a dead white horse and shell-splintered trees.

I think of the options: of going home proud of my service; in shame as a deserter; or more likely, disabled or not at all.

The kitchen seems a good place to be.

GEORGE WELLS holds the record, with his friend and fellow pilot Fred Dyer, for the greatest number of bombing missions flown by a U.S. soldier during World War II. By the time he was twenty-six, his life had taken some dramatic turns.

I was born in 1919 and raised out in the country in southern New Jersey. Our family was doing all right finally, for country folks prior to the Depression. I graduated from Haddon Heights High School as president of the senior class in 1937. My parents couldn't afford to send me to college, but I was able to get a job as an apprentice in a print shop for $8.00 a week. Through the small local bank, I arranged to buy a secondhand car for $100.00. The bank let me pay $2.00 a week and no money down. I paid my parents $4.00 a week for room and board which left $2.00 a week for gas and other expenses, but not enough to take a date to a movie.

After I'd been working for two years at the print shop, in 1939, union organizers came in and told me my salary would be $16.00 a week if the print shop employees voted to join the union. Of course, we voted for it, but the print shop in order to be able to pay the increased wages laid off the last two persons hired, one of which was me.

My brother, Oliver, ten years older, had gone to college and had friends in the National Guard. He told me he was sure our country was going to be in a war and I should join the National Guard immediately and apply to take a course called the "Ten Series." When completed, it would qualify me to become a 2nd Lieutenant in the National Guard. This course usually took a working person about two years to complete. Being out of work, I completed the course in six months and passed it.

Right after Pearl Harbor, the Army Air Corps needed many more pilot officers due to their great expansion and solicited young ground force officers to transfer to the Army Air Corps for pilot training. I thought it was a great challenge and applied for it. I was promoted to 1st Lieutenant in the Field Artillery. Then I was transferred to the Army Air Corps for pilot training in 1942. I completed all the training and became the "First Pilot" on a B-25 crew in the famous Mitchell Bomber.

In 1943, my crew and I were sent overseas and joined the famous 340th B-25 Bomb Group, one of three bomb groups in the 47th Bomb Wing.

The 340th became known as the "Bridge Busters" for our many pinpoint attacks destroying bridges. Many bombing records were made by our unit. One of the most notable was when Major Fred Dyer and I established the record for the highest number of bomber missions flown by any U.S. pilot in World War II in one continuous overseas tour. We each flew 102 missions without returning home to the U.S. for rest. After a lot of effort, we were allowed to fly our 100th mission together in the same plane, which was also flying its 100th mission. We flipped a coin to see who would fly as first pilot on the mission. I won the toss and flew as first pilot and Dyer was co-pilot and formation commander for the mission. This was covered by the media.

We had thought this 100th mission was the record for World War II; but the media, who were there for the event, advised us someone had flown 50 missions in one tour in the Pacific theater and 51 missions in the European theater, during two separate overseas tours. So, Dyer and I got permission to fly two more missions and jointly share the record for the most missions in one continuous tour for any U.S. pilot in World War II.

One specific fact that I believe is God related is that I never felt very much apprehension in all of my combat experiences. I do not really understand it. I had confidence that I could meet challenges and this was a great blessing because many had great fear. It was also an advantage to be the pilot because to some degree I had more control than the others, like the gunners, bombardiers, etc.

My original bombardier, "Red" Reichard, was totally frightened of combat. Whenever he was assigned for the next day, he couldn't sleep; he perspired, rolled, and tossed all night, as he was convinced he would not survive the war. However, it did not affect his talent at all, and in spite of great anxiety he became one of the lead bombardiers for the group. In our particular group, we did not maintain crew integrity, and he and I only flew together a few times in combat.

It is amazing that our two philosophies came to play within seconds of each other. On a bombing mission over Anzio beachhead, Red Reichard was the lead bombardier in the first flight over the target. I was the lead pilot of the second flight over the target; separation between the two planes was about 50 yards.

His plane was hit with an 88-millimeter anti-aircraft shell. The plane exploded and all were killed. Within two or three seconds, an 88-millimeter shell went right through one side of my plane's tail section and out the other side. It did not explode! Each of those shells contained a time fuse, as well as a contact fuse on the nose section, which is supposed to explode on contact. His plane exploded. My plane had nothing more than two holes about six inches across in the tail section. There was no other damage to the plane and it was completely flyable.

Another bombardier of note in our squadron was Joe Heller, who later became famous when he wrote *Catch-22*. Many years later, when I read the book, I saw myself as Capt. Wren, who flew all the time. Heller wrote Captain Wren "enjoyed flying combat missions and begged nothing more of life and Colonel Cathcart than the opportunity to continue flying them. They had flown hundreds of combat missions and wanted to fly hundreds more." . . .

I received the Silver Star, two Distinguished Flying Crosses, the Air Medal with 12 oak-leaf clusters, Joint Service Commendation Medal, European African–Middle Eastern Campaign Medal with 7 battle stars, World War II Victory Medal, A.F. Longevity Service Award with one silver oak-leaf cluster, and the National Defense Service Medal with one bronze star.

I contacted Joseph Heller and asked if he remembered Captain Wells.

I remember him very well . . . but [Captain Wren] is not him. It's based on someone who had his position, which was the operations officer. I think that the one similarity to him in the book is this: George Wells just flew missions endlessly and without fear, and I just put that into *Catch-22* . . . it struck me as kind of heroic and . . . unreal.

He (Wells) doesn't know me or remember me because I was a replacement for one of fifty or seventy. I doubt we had any conversations. He was one of those people I looked up to—I was only nineteen or twenty years old, and joining a combat group! They had been around the world in combat, and I joined up only in Corsica. I was a kid and these were people I looked up to.

IN *The Greatest Generation* I wrote about the men of the 8th Air Force, which conducted the long, dangerous bombing runs from England over Europe. I had no complaints from the pilots and crews assigned to the 15th Air Force, in southern Europe, but I did get a terrifying account of a first mission from Robert Dyas of the 15th Air Force, who went on to fly fifty-two missions in the cockpits of B-24s. He sent along passages from his yet-to-be-published book, "The Liberators."

It sounded as if we were flying through a heavy hail storm. Some of the spent flak was penetrating our ship's thin aluminum skin. Bomb-bay doors were again opened, the lead ship in our "box" dropped by "Pathfinder," and [each of] the remaining ships in our box then "toggled off his drop." Our bombardier yelled "Bombs away!" over the intercom, and what was left of the original formation went into a steep, left-turning dive toward the ground. We were still in the air and still flyable. Flak had penetrated most of the ship, hydraulic fluid was spewed all over the deck as several hydraulic lines had been punctured, spent 50mm shells were piled high at all the gunners' positions, and one of the crew members could be seen, still shooting continuously out of his waist-gun position. Another crew member, with his hands clamped over his earphones as if to shut out the noise, was quivering as if he had the jungle plague, but still kept on firing. No blood yet, and no one physically hurt, thanks be to whoever is up there looking out for us.

Suddenly, directly out of the sun and coming straight at us was a single ME-109 with all guns blazing. Our nose gunner was blasting away with his trigger on "continuous fire" but our top turret gun was silent, and he should have been shooting at that crazy Hun as he was probably directly in his crosshairs. The warning light for fire in the number two engine was flashing rapidly and our engine instruments told us number two was "cooked" (inoperable and with fire). The Captain ordered that I "feather" number two and push the fire extinguisher button for that engine, which I did immediately. While we continued to try and get back into our formation, we found that this was impossible due to the decrease in power caused by the dead engine. As our airspeed and altitude slowly diminished, we found ourselves a sitting duck for the Nazi fighters still attacking us from all directions.

Our gunners were firing continuously from all gun positions, except for the top turret, as we were being raked by machine-gun fire from the Hun.

The Hun fighters, which had been dogging us all the way and which had been kept at bay by the accuracy of our gunners, abruptly disappeared. Far in the distance we could see the American fighters coming out of the south. They caught up with the slowly retreating Nazi aircraft just as we were approaching the lofty peaks of the Alps. Suddenly, an American P-38 "Lightning" peeled off his chase after a ME-109 that he was about to shoot down, when he noticed our crippled B-24. Without a second thought for his very possible air victory, he pulled alongside us and pointed to his radio headset trying to have us obtain radio contact. Captain Jawatte shook his head, indicating that we could not respond. Jawatte pointed ahead, trying to explain what he was going to try to attempt. The pilot of the P-38 threw up both of his hands to gesture that he understood and, shoving his throttle ahead, flew around us. He then took up a position directly in front of us, matched our airspeed, and guided us through the treacherous mountain range. The P-38 had more sophisticated radar and sonar equipment aboard than a B-24 and he was better able to judge how far away those jagged and deadly peaks were. If it were not for the P-38's courageous pilot leading us through the small openings in the Alps, I am sure we would have crashed into the side of the mountains.

Truly, a brave, brave man! Sacrificing a certain kill in downing a German plane, he risked his life to guide us through the Alps.

Finally, after what seemed like an eternity, we broke free of the pinnacles and saw green grass and valleys below. The P-38 dropped back, and with a wave of his hand and a flip of his wings, turned back to rejoin the action.

The pilot [Captain Jawatte] suggested that I go aft to check out the extent of the damage and try to find out what happened to our top turret gunner. I could not believe the damage suffered by the B-24. How it stayed in the air was a major miracle. The bomb-bay doors were closed but were riddled with so many flak and machine-gun bullet holes, they looked like Swiss cheese. There were so many large holes and openings, I had no trouble seeing the ground below. How any of our gunners survived was a phenomenon. No one could possibly have survived in the twisted metal and plastic covering the entire rear end of our Liberator. There was hydraulic fluid, smelly and covering the entire deck. The waist guns were still hot to the touch and the smell of cordite was overpowering. Spent 50mm shell casings covered the entire floor and you had to be damn careful as you picked your way through. The tail gunner and the ball turret gunner were just emerging from their coops and they looked like something out of a Frankenstein movie. Faces blackened, eyes popping out of their sockets, hands quivering, not saying a single word.

Also emerging from the farthest reaches of the ship's rear end was our presumably lost original top turret gunner. What a spectacle he was! Still wearing his full flying regalia, including his oxygen mask and a carry-along oxygen bottle, he had three hard-to-come-by flak vests strapped around his entire body. He was shaking so badly I was afraid that he would fall. No one said a word to him and he did not speak.

On the ground below, we noted several ambulances and fire trucks assembled in our landing area. As we all held our collective breaths, I think everyone aboard gave a silent prayer.

Our fears were ungrounded as Jawatte greased that big wounded bird in as if it had eyes of its own.

With mission number one under my belt, I felt I was invincible.

ONE OF THE MOST ASTONISHING war stories I received actually begins in Poland. It came to me from Dr. Zdzislaw Wesolowski, a college professor in Miami. It's his description of the life of his father, Stefan P. Wesolowski.

My father's military service in the Polish armed forces started in 1918 when as a boy of nine he volunteered to serve in the liberation of Lwów. His heroic action resulted in his being awarded the highest Polish decoration for valor, the Order of the Virtuti Militari, which is equal in stature to our American Medal of Honor. By 1921 he was a seasoned war veteran and at the age of twelve participated in the Third Silesian Uprising, during which time he was wounded, decorated with the Cross of Valor, and promoted to the rank of corporal, becoming the youngest noncommissioned officer in the history of the Polish armed forces.

After his war services in the liberation of Poland, my father joined the newly forming Polish merchant marine as a cabin boy on one of the first ships of that fleet, the *Gazolina*. . . . On the instruction of the captain he sewed a Polish flag. In a short ceremony he raised the flag as an act of commissioning the ship into the Polish merchant marine, which had been absent from the Baltic Sea for 350 years. And so he became Poland's first sailor of the fleet.

In 1922, Poland was reorganizing the Polish armed

forces and a call was made by Marshal Jozef Piludski, the commander in chief, to all veterans to join the armed forces. My father answered that call, presenting his military papers and decorations to the Polish Navy. At the age of 13 he was enrolled in the Polish Navy with the rank of petty officer and placed in charge of a ten-man naval observation post in Gdynia. This unprecedented event did not deter him from carrying out his duties even though his subordinates were twice his age.

Because of his twenty years of federal service, Father was thinking of retiring in 1938 and with my mother was looking for a retirement location. Little did they know that Adolf Hitler had other plans for the Polish people. By the end of August of 1938, Father received orders to report for active duty aboard the Polish destroyer the ORP *Blyskawica,* as a signalist. Father never returned to Poland and took part in the Battles of Narvik and the Atlantic. Being wounded several times and declared unfit for military duty in 1941, he now joined the Polish merchant marine as an officer. His bravery and professional reputation became well known and in 1943 while his ship was in the Brooklyn Naval Shipyard, Father was invited to meet with the commander of the U.S. Army Transportation Corps. The commander offered him the position of 2nd officer aboard an auxiliary aircraft carrier, the USAT *Ganandoc,* which was being refitted for convoy duty. At that time Father was still a citizen of Poland.

Father accepted the position at once, because he believed that by serving with the American forces he could do more to help Poland. After several convoys, the captain became ill and Father took over the command of the *Ganandoc.* The *Ganandoc* took part in the invasion of Normandy and was damaged to such an extent that Father was instructed to scuttle the ship. Instead he and his crew worked fearlessly and returned the ship to

Southampton for repairs. Needless to say, the whole ship and Father were decorated. While the *Ganandoc* was being repaired, Father was given command of a large seagoing tug, the USALT 533, which took part in convoy duty and salvage operations. On one occasion, the ship sailed into a minefield. Father took immediate action and warned the convoy commander to reroute the convoy. By doing so, Father saved the whole invasion fleet from considerable loss of life and equipment. For his heroics, he was later decorated with the Bronze Star for Valor. After the war, he joined the U.S. merchant marine and sailed worldwide until his final retirement in Miami Beach.

While Father was with the Polish and American fleet, my mother, my brother, and I were in German-occupied Poland, living in constant fear, deprivation, and danger. When the war started, I remember Mother carrying my younger brother Jeremii with me running after her across battlefields for safety while being shot at by both sides. During the years 1939–1946 my mother took care of us as well as she could by begging for food and working as slave labor in German barracks and hospitals. We moved constantly across Poland, out of harm's way. One day the Gestapo surrounded our hut and arrested Mother. They held her for interrogation for days because she had received a letter from Father via Switzerland, which was rerouted by a friend from London. It was a miracle that she was later released.

When the war ended in 1945, Father left no stone unturned looking for us, and with the help of the U.S. Embassy in Warsaw was able to locate us, being informed that we survived the war. In March of 1946 Father landed at Warsaw airport in the uniform of an American naval officer with secret orders signed by General Eisenhower. We were informed several weeks in advance of his possible arrival and left Gdynia for Warsaw. I still remember that fantastic day when I saw my father return. I was playing in the ruins of Warsaw. The joy was overwhelming. His return to Poland to get us out of Communist Soviet-occupied Poland was another one of his acts of bravery. He could have been arrested and shot because he was still a Polish citizen and because he served with the Americans. Father arranged for our departure from Poland and on July 20th, 1946, our ship, the SS *Washington,* a troop carrier, passed by the Statue of Liberty.

To try my father's life at sea, I joined the U.S. merchant marine for a few years during the Korean War, but later decided to enlist in the U.S. Air Force, retiring with the rank of captain in the reserves. Now I serve in the reserves as a colonel in the South Carolina State Guard. After receiving my higher education, I became a college administrator and currently serve as a professor at Florida Memorial College in Miami. My brother, Jeremii, also obtained a doctoral degree and held high-ranking executive positions in the pharmaceutical industry, retiring in Yorba Linda, California.

This short letter does not do justice to our parents, who dedicated their lives to two nations, their family, and the community. My parents gave us support and care and examples to live by. They sacrificed their own well-being to help my brother and me to complete our education. My father passed to me a thousand-year Polish tradition of military virtue . . . he believed that service in the military was the highest possible contribution one can make to the nation he truly loves. He loved democracy and freedom as exemplified by his contributions to Poland and the United States. He never neglected his responsibility as a father and husband. His love and commitment to his wife and sons was total and complete, as is my love to my wife, Emilia, and our children, Juliana, Stefan, and Wanda. My brother, Jeremii, shares my views in his commitment to his wife, Alicia, and their children, Ashley, Andrea, Alexa, and Jeremii, Jr.

Our mother, Antonina, was a unique person with all the virtues of a loving and caring Polish mother even at the risk of her own life. While Father was at sea, earning a living, she cared for us and helped in our education and provided a home environment in which we found happiness. Her cooking was out of this world. When I look back to those war years I thank God and my mother for our survival. Fifteen million Poles never lived to see V-E Day.

Not all war stories are about combat, heroism, life and death. Raymond Daum described his final, never-to-be-forgotten days as a combat photographer, and the rescue of priceless artifacts from the personal collection of Ludwig van Beethoven:

I was 19 in 1942, when I enlisted in the U.S. Army Signal Corps. I served in the Army as a motion picture combat cameraman following a semester's study at the University of Southern California's Department of Cinema. I was armed with a .45 revolver, and it was my job to "shoot the shooters" with a government-issue 12-pound 35mm Eyemo movie camera. We were assigned to fighting units in the European Theater of Operations, mainly the ground forces of infantry divisions. In one armored attack at about the time of the Battle of the Bulge, I was wounded as 300 German prisoners of war were rounded up at the end of a long tank battle. I got in the way of German artillery as I walked alongside our Sherman tanks and was whacked by an 88 shell that pierced my helmet as I knelt to reload my camera.

I returned to combat two days later, along with scores of GIs also hit in that German barrage. There is nothing like a close call on a battlefield to make the morning more beautiful, to make the green fields more fragrant, and to make life seem like a worthwhile journey.

There are so many experiences that your book has awakened in me—so many memories good, and some not so good. The time a Graves Registration Unit GI called me over as he processed identification of dead German soldiers lying in the fields after a firefight. He handed me a small photograph from the wallet of one young soldier. It was a picture of Ginger Rogers! (Who was my favorite movie star, too.)

As the Allied armies had penetrated deeper into Germany, and the German High Command could see that the end of the war was near, Field Marshal Hermann Göring, Commander of the German Luftwaffe, who was infamous for his looting of Europe's artistic treasures, dispatched orders to all [German] museums to disperse their collections so that they would not be looted and pillaged by the invading armies. One of these historical sites was the Beethoven-Haus in Bonn. This was the birthplace—the home—of the composer and had been converted into a museum. It was known that the museum collection included three pianos owned by Beethoven, several musical instruments, and oil portraits important to him in his life—including Joseph Haydn, Mozart, Schubert, and others. Just months before, German transport trucks had appeared at the museum, where the treasures were quickly loaded and the convoy, headed by Dr. Wildemann [the museum's curator], travelled to various rural sites in the Rhineland Province.

We took back roads. It would be a long journey to avoid the major highways that were littered with destroyed tanks and abandoned equipment left by the Germans. And what we dreaded most were the land mines put in place by the retreating enemy. I thought to myself that if this journey had taken place only a few days earlier we might have taken enemy fire. As we drove through small villages, it was obvious that some Germans were afraid to come out of their houses. They were not sure the war had ended, but some villages had white cloths of surrender hanging from windows or on poles. The children were the bravest, coming out of their homes into the street pointing handmade toy guns at us, for most of the populace in these rural regions refused to believe their country had actually capitulated. I caught the scenes in my camera's viewfinder as we approached each site on Wildemann's list [of hiding places for the museum's treasures]. I would jump out of the truck's cab as doors were hesitantly opened and I could see faces of fear—the occupants not sure what fate awaited them until Wildemann smiled reassuringly, speaking quickly, as my camera whirred harmlessly. Then out they would come—the crates, the trunks, and, from Homburg Castle, the three pianos that had been hidden in the castle's dungeon. Finally, we were led to the Siegen salt mines, where the precious art works and boxes of musical manuscripts had been stored, because the salt deposits absorbed the moisture from the air, leaving temperatures and humidity virtually constant.

Now, at the end of our quest, Dr. Wildemann asked me to hand-carry a huge bundle of autographed music manuscripts—the originals and so priceless! The manuscripts for the piano sonatas were present—including the "Moonlight Sonata," and scores of the Pastoral and Ninth Symphonies!

We finally reached Bonn, which was like a ghost town with blocks and blocks of incendiary ruins. Dr. Wildemann signaled for us to turn down a street with a sign which read, "Beethoven-Haus Gasse" (Beethoven House Street). We came to a stop before a large boarded-up portal. The first thing I noticed were German words, EINTRITT VERBOTEN—MUSEUM! ("Entry Forbidden—Museum"). In filming inside and outside the museum, I was shown, by the caretaker, the room upstairs where Beethoven was born in 1770. One question we all asked ourselves which had to be answered: How was it possible that this little two-hundred-year-old tinderbox building had survived the severe and prolonged incendiary bombings? The German caretaker's story was one of the most amazing to come out of the war. Each night, he told us—translated by Dr. Wildemann— that as the incendiary bombs began to fall, he would crawl up to the roof of the house with a garden hose turned on with as much pressure as it would afford, and he would spray—douse the walls and roof all night long until the bombing ceased, to keep the wood and plaster as wet as possible, for the structure to survive another night.

What a day it had been! A unique and gratifying experience for us all, and in a way I felt I had contributed somehow to the making of peace in Europe. I guess it has to be my best remembered story, and one not about the fighting, but about the mutual respect for one of mankind's most admirable accomplishments—great music.

As I look back to that day in Bonn—it had provided a moment of sanity in the hectic demise of the Third Reich. The experience proved that the only glory of war is in the hope of cooperation between the enemies afterward. At Beethoven-Haus, conquerors and the conquered had joined hands to preserve mankind's priceless heritage and culture.

VERONICA MACKEY HULICK, of Fort Pierce, Florida, became a Navy WAVE during World War II and before long found herself assigned to a secret project. At first she didn't know what she was working on but later she discovered it was a critical part of the Allied success.

I was 20 years old when I joined the Navy WAVES [Women Accepted for Volunteer Emergency Service] in

Jan. 1943. After boot camp I was sent, with a contingent, to Dayton, Ohio. We were assigned to a building across from the National Cash Register Co. We sat at a long table with a soldering iron, long threads of solder and inch-long wires of red, yellow, green, and blue. We were given a small wheel and a graph to follow. We soldered the little wires inside the wheel according to the graph. The wheel was then covered with graphite. Plastics had not been invented as yet.

I decided that I must not have passed the aptitude tests. This had to be the dumbest job in the Navy. However, I was surrounded by many bright young women, many of whom, like me, were former telephone operators.

One day my mother called to say a Navy officer was going all around my hometown, Wilmington, Delaware, asking questions about me. He went to my teachers, friends, employers, and neighbors. I didn't know what was going on, but I began to feel important.

We worked the swing shift and had one day off a week. The third week, we got 2 days off. It took 3 months to get a Sat. and Sun. off. We were constantly monitored by WAVE officers and had many sessions on security about our work.

This went on from April till October. I went on duty one day and saw something huge on a flatcar near our building. It was covered with a gray shroud. I said to myself, "I wonder what that is?" I know now it was the housing for the computer that was being built. NCR built the housing, the switches, and the wiring, and we women wired the rotor wheels.

That day we were told we were being transferred to Washington, D.C. We were assigned to barracks across the street from the Naval Communications Annex at Nebraska and Massachusetts Avenues.

When we went on duty, we had to show our picture and number I.D. to 2 armed Marines at the gates and a

Navy man at our building. The first day on duty, we were
taken into a chapel and a Navy officer stood in the pul-
pit and told us if we talked about what we were working
on at this station, we would be shot! About 500 women
ran these 120 computers on a shift. It was constant for
the next 2½ years. We never breached security, we'd gotten the message loud and clear.

The computer was nicknamed "the Bombe" because
of the noise it made while running. The word "computer" was not in the vocabulary at that time. Also missing in those times was air-conditioning. The oppressive
heat of the D.C. summers was unbelievable, but we
were young and full of patriotism. We lived in two-story
barracks, 50 girls on each floor. We had a bunk, a locker,
and community showers. We all got along, worked hard,
and had fun on our days off.

When we got a print-out from the computer we
couldn't read it. We tore it off quickly, ran to a door at
the end of the room, knocked, and a hand came out and
took it, I presume, to a decoding room. We had 120 computers, and when we revved them up, we got a trillion
combinations. Hitler once sent a message to a general.
We intercepted and broke it before it reached the general's hands.

It still boggles my mind, in retrospect, that first we
helped to build this computer and then ran it.

We were paid $50.00 a month for a long time because
the Navy did not know what to call us. We weren't ra-
diomen or yeomen. Finally, after a year and a half we
were given a new rating, a "Q," and raised to $60.00 a
month.

When the war was over, and we were being discharged, we were taken individually into an office and
told to put one hand on the Bible and take an oath
that we would never talk about our work. We had a
form for future employers stating they were not to ask
us about our activities during World War II. Five hun-

dred women went home, got on with their lives, and never said a word.

In 1977, President Carter declassified a lot of WWII material, and a couple of books were written about "the Bombe." The Navy never informed any of these women that the oath was lifted. My parents died never knowing what I did in the service.

In 1994 a reunion was held in Dayton, Ohio. About 80 women showed up. A Navy historian spoke to us and told us we were responsible for the sinking of between 750 and 800 German U-boats, that we shortened the war by one and possibly two years, and had saved countless lives. It was a wonderful moment. It was great to be able to tell my children and grandchildren of my work during WWII, but I wept for those who had passed away and never revealed their contribution to the war effort.

You are right, it was a different time in our history. We were patriotic, disciplined, caring, and just so thrilled to know we were doing something special to help end the war. We never sought recognition. I always thought of us as the unsung heroines of WWII.

WEIKA KOENRAAD, of Dahlonega, Georgia, was a little girl in Holland during the war, and has vivid memories of the American soldiers who liberated her town in 1945. She's now an American citizen.

I was just a little girl during the Second World War, born in Haarlem, Holland, in 1937. My husband [was born] in Amsterdam [in] 1933.

The Netherlands was occupied by the Germans in 1940, and in the western part (Holland) where I lived, the liberation came only in 1945.

The scariest thought in my mind were soldiers, with black shiny boots and a gun; nobody ever smiled, there was nothing to smile about. The games we played as children were war games. We had built a play hospital and I was the nurse. My friends were wounded and brought to the hospital. There were no toys.

The most severe winter in decades was the winter in 1944. The southern part of the Netherlands was already free, but the western part which is above the river Rhine was still occupied. Because of the weather, there was nothing more to eat. Everybody was hungry and our daily meal consisted of sugar beets, which we now feed to the hogs, and tulip bulbs. I still remember the taste of tulip bulbs. It was a nice sweet taste.

Suddenly there was spring, the bad weather was gone, and it was May 1945. Big tanks rolled through the streets and for the very first time I saw people who smiled and waved to us. They were soldiers! It was like a miracle—they were supposed to be scary, and now they were friendly and smiled. They threw Hershey's chocolate bars and chewing gum into the crowd. Something we had never seen or tasted before. I was lucky enough to catch a piece of gum. This was called by us the everlasting candy; you could chew it and it never ended. This piece of gum was, of course, shared with your friends. They all wanted to try it, but it ended up in your own mouth again.

My husband and I and our two children emigrated to the U.S.A. 22 years ago and became Americans after 5 years.

Every time I meet somebody who has served in the Second World War I give him a hug and say, "Thanks to you we are alive."

THE FATHER OF Wilfred Chatigny of Amesbury, Massachusetts, served as a staff sergeant on the front lines in Germany, where he was seriously injured. He later defied the predictions of doctors who told him that he would never walk again. Following a long recuperation after the war, Wilfred

Chatigny, Sr., went to work for a silversmith. According to his son, he is intensely patriotic and humble about his contributions to the war effort.

Dad entered France through Omaha Beach as a Staff Sergeant in the 89th Division in March of 1945, and spent one week at Camp Lucky Strike. Then his company was moved up to the front lines. The fiercest battle they incurred was at Koblenz, Germany, where they crossed the Rhine and had to hold the bridge. Shortly thereafter, they passed a concentration camp that had been liberated by another company. Dad won't talk about it. The only comment he made was that it was apparent the Germans had run over all the prisoners with their half-tracks.

Less than two months after entering the war, Dad was shot. His company was clearing the town of Darmstadt. They started early one morning and Dad said they didn't get 100 feet into town when he got hit. The bullet entered his thigh and exited below his stomach. He had substantial internal injuries that have bothered him all his life. The doctors told him he would never walk again, but he did, and still does. He credits the fact that he was always in great shape, first as an athlete in school, and then in the service after graduation in 1941. The one story Dad has told a number of times, and always gets a laugh with, is that when he woke up in the hospital two days later he couldn't understand a word anyone was saying. He asked the nurse what all the gibberish was and why he couldn't understand. Well, he was in the German ward. When he was shot, he was carrying a German Luger and a German flag. Souvenirs! They thought he was a German infiltrator, which apparently had been a problem in the field. After some discussion and a few World Series questions, Dad was moved to the American ward. He never got his souvenirs back.

VAN PARKER of Carmichael, California, was a veteran B-29 pilot when the war ended. He shared with us a letter he wrote to his parents about his final mission. It is part of his memoir called "Dear Folks."

Dear Folks,

Yesterday I experienced a privilege which will long live in my memory. It was my honor to lead a B-29 squadron over the Tokyo area while Japan's final surrender was in progress.

The purpose of our visit to the Japanese empire was to take part in the greatest display of aerial force ever assembled—this for the benefit of the Japanese people. What a sight! There were seemingly thousands of our airplanes in the air. Everywhere you looked you could see large formations of aircraft. The display must have struck awe and terror into the hearts of all Japanese who witnessed the spectacle.

We gave them a never-to-be-forgotten show of the aerial might which brought them to their knees.

As we flew low over Tokyo Bay and our big battlewagon *Missouri,* where the Japanese were signing the historic peace documents which officially ended this world's bloodiest conflict, I couldn't help but feel proud that I had played a small part in our victory.

Stretched before our eyes, and crowding Tokyo Bay to its very shores, were hundreds of ships. Never before had I seen such an accumulation of naval strength—and all ours. The Army and Navy were everywhere.

Following bomber formation break-up, prior to departure for home base, our crew seized the opportunity to do some personal reconnoitering over the Japanese homeland; [we were] especially curious about Tokyo and its environs.

It was the first time I had flown over Tokyo without being shot up. Because we were flying very low and because there were no guns firing upon us, I was able to view without distraction the terrible devastation wrought upon Tokyo by our B-29s.

Never in your wildest dreams could you visualize such destruction. There are no houses left standing. Tokyo is a mass of strewn rubble and ashes. Few people walk the deserted streets. The city has an eerie appearance of being a huge ghost town. Actually, Tokyo is no more.

Words of description fail me. You would have to view the nightmarish scene yourself to believe that such devastation could be, not only in Tokyo, but in all the cities where our B-29s paid a visit.

In sharp contrast to the ruins of the great cities is the green countryside, with its rolling, terraced hills, its valleys, rice paddies, and quaint houses with their upturned corners.

Always before in my letters to you I had described the Japanese homeland as being drab, foreboding and colorless. Maybe this description was forthcoming because I was such an unwelcome visitor there. One is not apt to get the proper perspective while looking down the barrels of unfriendly guns which are shooting flak at you. At such times you are definitely not interested in the color and beauty of the terrain below. In reality, the Japanese country is a thing of rare beauty when viewed from the air. Only the eyesores of her burned-out cities mar [her].

Thank God this terrible conflict has been terminated, and now that the war is officially over it shouldn't be long till I return to the U.S.—Happy Day.

Yesterday's "show of power" mission has been generously credited as combat on the records of all who participated. So now I'm credited with 32 combat missions over the Japanese homeland, and I have accrued well in excess of 100 points toward rotation. This record should insure an early return.

Love,
Van

II

---•---

BONDS

Lloyd Kilmer (left) and Tom Gibbon reunite on "Lloyd Kilmer and Tom Gibbon Day," May 14, 1999.

There was never a time in American life when so many people were involved in so many ways in a shared cause. It was impossible not to be affected in some fashion by the war effort, however far you may have been from the front lines.

In that common experience, old ties were strengthened and new ones were formed to last a lifetime. Whatever else may have happened later, World War II was a shared passage of trial and terror, triumph and loss, laughter and reflection. The relationships formed then have been a continuing and reaffirming link to that unique time.

The father of my friend and colleague Tim Russert of *Meet the Press* is a World War II veteran, a B-24 crewman in the 8th Army Air Force. Tim Russert, Sr.—Big Russ, as we call him—has two families: his son and three daughters—and his buddies at the South Buffalo, New York, American Legion Post 721, working-class men who are joined forever by their adventures in what so many of that generation call simply "the war."

In *The Greatest Generation* I wrote about the Dumbos, the dinner and bridge meeting of my parents-in-law and their friends from World War II. It began when the wives formed a mutual support group (although they would never have called it that) to fill the long days while their men were in harm's way in distant places. After the war, when the men came home, the group became a long-running gathering of close friends. It turns out there were an untold number of other gatherings across the land, structured in much the same way. Herb Karner of Broken Arrow, Oklahoma, wrote to my wife's aunt and uncle, Lois and Don Gatchell, in Tulsa, to describe his hometown bridge club, which reminds him of the Dumbos.

Instead of four couples, our group consisted of six couples; we have no specific name, [but are] generally known as the "bridge club." Our origin was the same: all married couples with men in service overseas, women at home raising family and keeping things rolling. When the men returned, we began a rotational meeting at each home for a home-cooked meal, with the hostess furnishing the meat and others bringing vegetables, salads, and desserts, each contributing their favorite dish. Before the meal, we had a round of drinks. Just one. Remember, liquor was expensive in those days when cash was short. To this day, my wife Ruth's favorite drink is a whiskey sour.

Following the meal we played bridge. We had a custom that when someone went down, the players who lost would put a penny in a pot. The accumulated pot went to the player who drew a 10-high hand. It seems improbable, but at one time the pot got as high as $17. Overzealous bidding, perhaps.

Who are we? I am the oldest by a few months—I will be 84 in June. The youngest is 77. Two were in the Air Corps, one was a B-17 pilot, and I was an aviation ordnance officer. Two were Navy, both serving aboard ships, two were Army, one enlisted, one officer. Sorry, no Marines. But I do have a close tie to the Marines, which is another story. Two of us, of which I am one, also saw combat in Korea, which also is another story.

Today? The group is still together. However, about three years ago we stopped playing bridge, because one of the group died. Heart attack. But those of us who can still get around get together once a month. No longer do the ladies cook. We meet at a local restaurant selected by the host. We still have *one* drink; we visit about children, grandchildren, and great-grandkids, politics, and sports, and we share the latest jokes.

When we returned from service, we all resumed our lives. My wife and I bought a house, as she had been living with her parents. Several of us completed our education and resumed careers in manufacturing, engineering, insurance, retail. I went into the newspaper business after doing other things.

During all this time there have been *no* divorces among the lot of us. Sadly, this is not true of our offspring. As a group we have 13 children; three of us have three, including my wife and me; one has two kids, and two have one each.

Our collective offspring have done well—several divorces, but professionally they include doctors and a variety of other professions and businesses. They have kept out of trouble, and so far our grandchildren are the kind you brag about. We have 10 grandchildren and three great-grands.

Most of us at one time or other have attended a reunion of our old outfit. For the most part, it's fun, but also depressing. Several years ago Ruth and I attended a reunion of the survivors of the Iwo Jima landing (my tie to the Marines) and when we walked into the hotel lobby she exclaimed, "My goodness, there's nobody here but a bunch of old, gray-haired men!"

Today I am in relatively good health, about 10 pounds over my fighting weight, active in the community and the Broken Arrow Historical Society. I belong to the Downtown Tulsa Kiwanis Club (member for 38 years) and enjoy woodworking, gardening, and photography. On a lesser scale than previously.

But I am proudest that on January 1st my wife and I have been married 61 years!

Please pardon this intrusion into your life. But I was so moved, many times to tears, when reading Brokaw's book that I felt you would understand my impulse to share our experience as a similar "Dumbo" group.

At least I feel better for having written.

I also wrote about the ROMEO Club, a band of veterans who had grown up in the poor Irish-American neighborhoods of Cambridge, Massachusetts, just around the corner from Harvard Yard. "ROMEO" stands for Retired Old Men Eating Out. The eternal leprechauns of the Cambridge ROMEO Club heard from other informal chapters and even had inquiries about whether there was an application process to start a local ROMEO Club.

ONE OF THE JOYS of the reach of *The Greatest Generation* is the rekindling of memories and relationships that had faded. I have become particularly fond of John "Lefty" Caulfield, one of the ROMEO Club members, who returned to Harvard and his baseball scholarship after Navy service during the war. Lefty had this evocative letter from a former teammate, Bill Hickey of Midland, Texas.

Dear John,

I enjoyed the article in the *Harvard Gazette* about you and your contributions to *The Greatest Generation*. I second everything Mr. Brokaw says about you, and say thank you for doing all you have done. I can remember how helpful you were to me when I was the third-base coach and you were the captain batting .438 (was your average really that high?). You were just as helpful forty years later when I visited my son Patrick at the business school. You haven't changed in forty-eight years and I love that picture of you in the *Gazette*.

What has happened to all those guys I waved around third base (some of whom were thrown out)—Cliff Crosby, John White, Benny Akilian, Sarto Walsh, Ralph Robinson, Tim Wise, John Canepa, Barry Turner—I could go on forever. I can remember my only game appearance was when Stuffy sent me in as a pinch runner against Boston College at their field in the ninth inning with two outs. I was promptly picked off and we lost by one run.

Your career in education is something to be proud of, and raising eight kids is no simple task. Keep on keeping on, John, and if you ever get close to Midland, Texas, Andree and I would love to see you.

EVERY GENERATION has a collective memory, a shared experience, but the men and women who went through the Great Depression and World War II were unique in that the events of their lifetime were so inclusive. Children of the sixties may identify with Woodstock or the Chicago 7, with sex, drugs, and rock and roll. But what about the others, who went to Vietnam or voted for Richard Nixon? For that generation the memory screen is divided, but for the Greatest Generation it is a family portrait.

Those bonds take many forms, some of them haunting, painful. Gregory Kirchner, of Bethel Park, Pennsylvania, wrote to share a story he's carried with him since the war, and to ask for help. Kirchner served as a medic with the 76th Infantry Division and has tried for more than fifty years to locate the wife of a soldier he treated on the battlefield. After the war, Kirchner worked for the postal service for thirty-six years and raised ten children, nine of whom are college graduates.

> I consider myself very fortunate to have survived. When an infantry company went into combat there were three medics such as me assigned to it. I outlived the first two men assigned with me to Company I, 417th Infantry Regiment, 76th Infantry Division. I also outlived eight replacement medics. When I was promoted, another man took my place. He was killed the following morning.
>
> I have tried without success for over 50 years to locate the family of a man I treated on the battlefield.

This man, one of five who lost all or part of a leg in a minefield, lost a leg at the hips. As I treated him, he said to me, "My God, what will my wife say?" There he was, almost blown in half, and he was thinking of her, not himself. This all happened at night during a rainfall. I have always wanted to let his wife know that he was thinking of her. This desire has been renewed when I see the scope of the research you had to do. His name was Glenn Jones. All I know is he lived in one of the Southern States. Three days before, Glenn had received a letter from his wife stating that she was about to enter the hospital for their first child. He said, "I hope she will be okay." He died in an ambulance on his way to a field hospital.

With the invaluable help of the Veterans Administration we found Sgt. Jones's widow, Virginia, living in a rural area of western North Carolina. She moved there from Winston-Salem to be with her parents and have her child after Glenn Jones was killed. She never remarried.

Virginia was surprised to hear of Gregory Kirchner's letter, since she'd never met anyone who'd served with her husband. She agreed to speak with him on the telephone but asked that he not include any gory details, explaining that even after fifty-four years, "The hurt is still there."

I arranged for Kirchner to call on an autumn Sunday afternoon, and he and Virginia talked for an hour. He said he was "thrilled to have lived so long to finally have found her." Kirchner told Virginia he was not only her husband's medic but also his friend, and he recalled their being on the move and receiving mail from home: "We were reading our letters and Glenn said, 'Well, by now my wife should be entering the hospital for our first baby.'" He also told her how Glenn repeatedly worried about her welfare as he was being treated for his fatal wounds.

As for Virginia, she said their conversation was "almost like getting a message from Glenn." She was particularly pleased that her grandson, who is a history buff, will now be able to read something of a grandfather he never knew.

Virginia said that when her husband was killed, they'd been married ten months and ten days; Glenn, Jr., arrived two months later. She said that her husband would have been proud to know that he had a son carrying his name, adding that although at first she found it difficult to call her son Glenn, after a while she was glad she had named him for his father.

Glenn, Jr., fifty-four, is an engineer with the International Paper company in Wilmington, North Carolina. He was raised by his mother, his grandparents, and his uncles. A few years ago, Virginia gave him a shadow box that contained his father's medals from the war.

Gregory Kirchner told Virginia Jones that another friend of Glenn's, Andrew Patrick of Ohio, was also wounded at the same time and returned home alive but with part of his leg missing. He said he would put them in touch as well.

Fifty-four years after a terrible night in the dark and rain of the Battle of the Bulge, when Sgt. Glenn Jones was mortally wounded, his wife now knows that his final thoughts were of her.

ONE OF THE MOST poignant stories in *The Greatest Generation* involved Jeanette Gagne Norton, who lost her husband, Camille, during the war. Camille, a paratrooper with the 82nd Airborne, was awarded the Silver Star posthumously for his heroism during the battle of Nijmegen, a critical crossing point between Holland and Germany. He died without ever seeing his son, Bob. After Jeanette's story appeared, she unexpectedly heard from one of Camille's closest friends from the service. She recounted:

> This man, Clarence Ollum, went to Fort Benning, Georgia, jump school the same time my husband did.

They went over to North Africa together, and then to Sicily. He made all the same jumps my husband did—all four of them. The last jump, of course, was where my husband didn't make it. But Clarence, who's called Bud, came back with another of my husband's buddies, Vic, and they made it a mission to find me and my boy because my husband, Camille, was always talking about me and showing them pictures of me. So they said when they got back they'd see if they could find Gagne's wife and boy. But in the course of time I remarried, and my name changed, you see. So in the course of fifty years they'd been looking for me and my boy. And of course they never found us. Vic died a few years ago.

But Bud had been telling this friend of his, Steve, "I looked for Jeanette and her boy for years and was never able to find them." He even showed him pictures of Camille. But then Steve got a copy of Mr. Brokaw's book, and he called Bud and said, "I think there's a story in here that sounds like it might be your buddy." Bud saw Camille's picture and said, "Oh my God, that's Gagne!" He was just so taken aback. And so Steve brought him over here and I met him, and it . . . oh my goodness. It was wonderful. All the things I'd always wondered about, like the different places where my husband was—his letters were censored, naturally—this Bud has been able to fill me in on, on things I never knew about. Like what it was like to jump out of the plane, and what my husband was like, and whether he was nervous. "Well, of course he was," Bud said, "just like the rest of us. We always wondered if each jump would be our last."

So I can ask him anything and he tells me. He didn't see my husband when he got killed, but he heard about it. He said to me, "I almost feel guilty because I came back and your husband didn't." And I said, "Oh, don't feel bad, Bud, it could have just as well been you." Can you imagine. . . . He showed me the same identical picture of my husband as the one in the book. On October fifteenth, I'm going to Atlanta to a Company E reunion, where I'll be meeting whoever is left of my husband's company. If it hadn't been for the book, I never would have met this gentleman. And you can't imagine how happy that's made him—and how happy it's made me!

W. E. BILDERBACK, JR., of Fort Worth, Texas, a business-man who deals in construction supplies and equipment, wrote about a letter taken from a dead Japanese soldier at Iwo Jima. Reading a translation of the letter fifty years later helped change his views about the Japanese.

> During World War II, I was a first lieutenant in anti-aircraft artillery. I made the invasion of Iwo Jima with the Marine Corps.
>
> One night at Iwo Jima, a lot of Japanese soldiers were killed. The next morning, one of my sergeants told me he had taken a letter from one of the dead soldiers and asked if I would like to have it. I said yes, I would.
>
> Fifty years later, on a trip to Maui, I had the letter translated by a young woman at the Kapalua Bay Hotel. When my wife read me the letter, I cried. It could have been written to me by my own wife. I detested the Japanese at the time the letter was written, because I had been taken from my new bride and a promising ca-reer. But this letter made me realize that the dead sol-dier didn't want to be in Iwo Jima either.
>
> The young woman who translated the letter was so emotional she cried. She asked if I would mind if she kept the letter and tried to locate the Japanese wife. A year later, the widow was found and presented with the letter.

This is the letter to Mr. Bilderback from the Japanese sol-dier's wife, Yoshi Sakuma:

I would like to express my sincere appreciation for all your and Ms. Egi's [the translator's] recent efforts on my behalf. I received the letter of memento written to my late husband, in the presence of the mayor of Fune-hiki Town and officials from the Fukushima prefectural government and Funehiki Town. Though Mr. William Bilderback does not understand Japanese, he kept the letter which was entrusted to him during the Second World War over 50 years ago. I truly feel that this letter reminds us that all the people living on the Earth can be united as one, despite the conflicts we have endured through history. I read the letter again and again and I felt that my late husband had finally come back to us after 51 years. I was flooded with a thousand emotions and tears.

As soon as I received the letter, I visited his grave to tell him of this matter. Before the war, I lived with my late husband and two daughters happily in the vicinity of the Joban coal mine. However, he was called into the army and fell in battle in Iwo Jima island. I was at my wits' end and I came back to my parents' home with my daughters. However, my youngest daughter passed away due to illness shortly thereafter. I started work as a laborer, but we earned a precarious living.

I remarried and lived with my second husband and my daughter's family and my two granddaughters for a while, and now my two granddaughters have married and I am blessed with four great-grandchildren. I am 80 years old now and I enjoy practicing gateball every day for the gateball competitions held three times annually. We live happily on a small old-age pension provided by the National Pension System of Japan.

I believe that your and Ms. Yuriko Egi's thoughtfulness, which transcends national boundaries, will contribute to building stronger ties of friendship and this will be passed down for posterity from generation to generation.

Please take care of yourselves and I wish you a peaceful life.

Bilderback also sent a copy of the letter written by Mrs. Sakuma to her husband when he was a soldier on Iwo Jima:

It's been a long time; hope you are fine as usual. When you left home it was a cold day with white clouds, but now spring has come and it's already in the month of May, with fresh green leaves. How fast the time flies!

I am fine, too, protecting family back here. Nariko is fine and growing up without catching any cold or flu.

Every morning when I say a prayer for you, Nariko also imitates me to pray with her little hands together. I think of you often and pray a lot for you. When I ask Nariko where her father is, she answers "Banzai" with both her arms up in the air. Even though she is little she does not forget.

Good-bye from your wife.

LORRAINE DAVIS of Spanish Fork, Utah, was born in 1926, so her earliest memories are of the Great Depression. As she says, "I did not know life wasn't supposed to be poor. Older siblings remember better times." By the time Lorraine was in high school, the war was on and her life took another turn. She begins by describing a bus trip she took to Salt Lake City shortly after graduating.

I sat with a former classmate who had been home on leave and was going back to Salt Lake to be sent overseas with the Marines. We talked about many things, but not his future. . . . Suddenly, an eighteen-year-old girl matured several years.

Now I want to tell you about the "girls who were left behind." Some girls married and were left alone. The rest of us were left alone, too, since all the young men were in the service. We began meeting every week or two for companionship and support. We talked about husbands, boyfriends and the war. Every day was much the same. We were all expected to get a job to help the war effort. Many worked in munitions plants or other war-related industries. Some were even "Rosie the Riveter." I started to work for the USDA a few days after graduation. Every day was about the same as we came home from work to listen to the evening news or to see it on the newsreels at the movies. Many letters were written to places all over the world. I corresponded with many young men in every part of the world since I did not have anyone special. I saved the letters for a few years and finally discarded them. Now, I wish I had not.

This same group of girls are still meeting after 55 years. After the war, boyfriends and husbands came home; the rest of us married, and we all started having those "Baby Boomers." Soon they were going to school, enjoying high school activities, getting married, and having families of their own and even grandchildren. All of this time, "the girls" were still meeting every month, supporting each other, caring for each other, and becoming even closer. At first we called ourselves the Club of '44. We later changed the name to Amity because we were such good friends. Some have passed away, but we still have close to 25 members. The only prerequisite for membership is to have been a member of the class of 1944. Amity is a consequence of World War II.

WORLD WAR II was a great equalizer. Poor kids and sons of privilege were side by side in the foxhole or bomber cockpit; Texas cowboys and street-smart toughs from Brooklyn depended on each other to stay alive; Harvard graduates learned from high school dropouts. George Chiungos of Weston, Massachusetts, shared a story about the bond between his father and a surgeon he knew during the Normandy invasion.

I recently purchased your book, *The Greatest Generation*, and was absolutely amazed as I began to read it. My father died at the age of 44 in 1963, but I can still remember the stories that he told regarding his wartime experiences in North Africa, Sicily, Italy and, of course, D-Day. He was a medic who landed sometime on that first day, and I can only imagine the horror and carnage that he witnessed. As I reflect upon his stories, he never spoke of the horrors of the war. Instead, he talked incessantly about the lasting friendships he developed, and many of the photographs in my possession today reveal wartime camaraderie, time spent with the children and other residents of any particular town or village in which his Company happened to be at any given time, and the like. In fact, I am in possession of a photo taken by a Utah Beach café owner and his wife that later became part of a Normandy postcard depicting my father and a friend relaxing on Utah Beach shortly after the Invasion. The café owner . . . billed them as the first two Americans to land on Utah Beach on D-Day. Clearly, this was somewhat of an exaggeration, but not by much! I had the opportunity to visit this family in 1972 and sat in their café while the owner and his wife tried to communicate their feelings about what my father and the American soldiers in general meant to them. I look very much like my father, and I can still remember so vividly the café owner, Felix, pointing to the original photo of my father and his friend that was hanging on the wall of the café and then pointing to me with tears streaming down his face. . . .

I will close with a story that will stay with me forever and reinforces much of what you present in your book about this incredible generation. My father learned in early 1961 that one Dr. Ballantine was senior neurologist at Massachusetts General Hospital. He had always marveled at Dr. Ballantine's incredible battlefield neurosurgical skills, as he had served in Dr. Ballantine's unit and witnessed field surgical miracles too numerous to recount. My father owned and operated a dairy products processing business. One day, he took it upon himself to drive into Boston to deliver several tubs of specialty Greek cheeses to Dr. Ballantine and renew his acquaintance. My father was taken aback by Dr. Ballantine's surprise and shock that someone would actually do that, as he simply wanted to express his admiration for what he had seen Dr. Ballantine do under some incredible conditions in Normandy. Two years later, my father was stricken with a triple brain aneurysm and requested that Dr. Ballantine perform the operation. The operation was a success, but his heart gave out and he died shortly thereafter. Dr. Ballantine's team of eight medical specialists operated for ten hours. When the uninsured portion of the bill arrived at our house (some $25,000 in 1963!), it was marked "paid-in-full" with a warm, personal note to the family from Dr. Ballantine remarking, among other things, on the impact on him of the surprise visit by my father two years earlier.

DURING THE WAR and immediately after, Hollywood movies often included this scene: a tough, battle-scarred G.I. befriending a waif, a young European victim of the long years of upheaval. It was not just the screenwriters' imagination. Many veterans recounted their memories of children and families they met in the war zones.

Yves Masson, who now lives in San Rafael, California, was a child in Paris when the Allies arrived.

I was an eight-year-old little boy when the courageous men you wrote about came to liberate me and the French capital. Of course, like all those who were there, I have very dear memories of the time: the evening when all the church bells of Paris tolled at the same time after having been silent all the years of the German occupation; the parades, the joy and the relief from fear.

In spite of all the hardships, dangers, triumphs and despairs that they had been through, so far from their land, these soldiers were so gentle. One took me on his tank and talked in a language I did not know, but his smile and his laugh made me happy; some gave me candy (the first candy I ever remember). They took me by the hand and walked with me. I was then too young to comprehend the scale of the accomplishment of the American armies, but I loved these men. I have read many books since then and know of all the battles and the great victories. The memories of those moments in late August 1944 remained vivid, yet, until I read your book, they had a dream-like quality.

It is because of this encounter with the men of the greatest generation that at the age of 29, when I had the chance, I came to America. Now a citizen, I have the privilege to live in this wonderful land.

What your book has done for me is to bridge the gap between the nameless heroes who so profoundly changed my life and the people whom I live with every day. Now these heroes are no longer part of a dream-like remembrance, they have names. Some, of course, I know because of their accomplishments in the past decades but I did not know they were there. Others, less famous, now have a name, a place where they live, and family. I may have met some of them. The word "closure" is overused in these days of stress and complexity. But in this case your book did close out that episode of my life by bringing it beyond the blind admiration and the treasured recollection to the reality of today's life in America with people I meet every day.

THE BONDS OF World War II reach across the years and even across generations. L'Myra Hoogland of Owatonna, Minnesota, knew little of her father's final days—until she found his best friend.

I, too, am a child of that generation, but I am also an orphan of one of its soldiers. My father, Myron (Mike) B. Anderson was one of the multitude of casualties of the Battle of the Bulge on December 16, 1944. He was killed two months before I was born on February 9, 1945.

My dad was one of the "older" G.I.s. The age limit had been lifted or raised. He was a 30-year-old from a small Scandinavian farming community called Gunder, in N.E. Iowa. He drove a truck, dreaming of having a larger trucking business. But it was not to be.

He has always been part of my life, especially in my deepest thoughts: "Would he be proud of me? Would he approve of my choices? What would he do?" And oh, I wish he knew my husband and had been able to love his grandchildren. . . .

My mother survived all this trauma. . . . She taught elementary school for 41 years while raising me—no welfare or help in those years. She shared her work ethic with me—just as your parents did you and all of us. She's quite a lady.

We both have been blessed, and perhaps me most of all in the last six years or so. I have met my dad's best friend, Duncan Truman from Warwick, New York, and through him others of my dad's Army buddies of the 424th AT division of the 106th Army. He and others have added information more precious than gold. Though I knew, for so long, as much as my family, he and the others have willingly shared memories of horror and honor. Until I wrote him five years ago he thought my dad was alive. It is through him that I have written to and talked to the officer my dad drove a jeep for. This is all 53 years after his death. God has blessed me through these men and their memories. Aren't we blessed?

CAUGHT IN THE MIDDLE were the civilians, especially those in countries directly in the path of Hitler's ambitions. The Belgians had not a moment of peace for five years, and Belgian families were often as brave as the most heroic soldier. Christine Winchester lives in La Grange Park, Illinois, but because of what happened to her grandfather she has another family in Belgium.

> My grandfather was a bomber pilot who had been shot down. His crew, with the exception of his navigator and himself, bailed out and were picked up by the Allies. When Grandpa went down, trying for his alternate target, several young children helped him get away from the German search party. To make a long story short, he was an escapee/evader for 9 months. A man named Emile VanVeerMeyes and [his] family hid him from the Germans at risk of their own lives for 6 of those months, while he recovered from injuries. When Grandpa snuck out just before a raid, he was picked up and spent another 9 months in a POW prison in Ghent. During this time Emile kept up with how he was doing.
>
> Even now, 50+ years away from this event, Emile and his wife and Grandma and Grandpa see each other almost every year, and are in constant correspondence. Louise and Emile are godparents to some of us, and have come to everybody's weddings, christenings, etc., for as long as I can remember. They are truly a part of our family, for without them, none of us would exist.

MARYANNE CERRA of Davie, Florida, has another version of the familiar story of an American G.I. and a young victim of the war.

> My dad, Major Riccardi, is the child of immigrant parents from Italy. During WWII, my grandparents had five sons on active duty. My dad was stationed in Italy as a bombardier, and his daily bombing missions were over the land of his parents.
>
> One of the many poignant stories my dad has shared

was one of a little Italian boy named Mario, who, during the war, would hang out at the barracks helping the G.I.'s in hopes of earning a nickel or piece of food to share with his family. My dad took Mario and his family under his wing. Before his daily missions my dad would teach Mario several English words and then review them when he returned. After several months, my dad was transferred and eventually lost touch with Mario.

On the 40th anniversary of the end of WWII, my dad organized the first reunion of the 454th Bomb Squadron and amazingly was able to locate over 500 men. (The reunion continues yearly.) Incredibly, one of the men had Mario's address. On a subsequent trip to Italy my parents were able to meet with a delighted Mario and his family, but it was not until I traveled to Italy that I realized the impact of those long-ago English lessons. Mario is now the manager of two hotels, and in fluent English he told me that had it not been for my father's influence and lessons, he would have been "a bum" (his words) and his life was forever changed.

LLOYD KILMER, a poor Minnesota farm boy who went on to fly B-24s during the war, was shot down and captured. One of his most vivid memories was of the day an American tank broke through the prison walls to free him. Fifty-four years later he made a new friend.

A couple of weeks ago a fellow called and said he was reading "the BOOK" about the 14th Armored Division of Patton's Third Army liberating Stalag 7A on April 29, 1945. He said that he was the commander on the tank that came through the barbed wire that day—and I was on his tank!!! He was my liberator.

After several conversations with Tom Gibbon of Palm Springs, California, we decided to drive over and meet Tom and his wife, Chris. We drove over last Thursday, and he had arranged for a motel for us. Upon arrival, we called Tom and they met us in the lobby of the motel. When they arrived—newspaper photographers and reporters were on hand. What a joyous meeting—big story on the front page of the paper, with a color picture. He took a group of us for a very special dinner.

They picked us up after breakfast to go to the Air Force museum for an 11:00 A.M. TV press conference. Several POWs showed up after reading the piece in the morning paper. It was a time of telling old war stories and presenting of gifts to each other. I was presented with a PROCLAMATION OF THE CITY OF PALM SPRINGS declaring May 14, 1999, to be Lloyd Kilmer and Tom Gibbon Day. Next, a "Certificate of Special Congressional Recognition" signed by Mary Bono, member of Congress (Sonny Bono's widow), and then a beautiful walnut plaque from the Narconnon International Board of Governors, their first "WE'RE NOT DONE YET!" award.

After lunch, we all took a couple of hours to rest before a reception for us with 25 or 30 people attending. Again, a time for fun and telling old war stories. After supper, we were ready to go to our motel room.

Tom and Chris came to the motel after breakfast to wish us a safe trip home. It was, and we are really looking forward to them visiting us. What a fantastic couple of days!

EVEN WHEN THE WAR WAS OVER in the Pacific, not all of the American troops were able to return home. They became part of the occupation army that moved into Japan under the command of General MacArthur. George Zimmermann, a Marine, sent me a story he wrote for a recent edition of *Leatherneck*, the Marine magazine.

It was Aug. 6, 1945, the day the first atomic bomb exploded on Hiroshima, Japan. Three days later, the city of Nagasaki on the southernmost island of Kyushu was destroyed by [an atomic bomb almost twice as powerful as] the Hiroshima bomb. Japan surrendered, and victory was declared on Aug. 15 by the Allies. The war was over, and we Marines of the Eighth Marine Regiment rejoiced at the thought of going home.

But our joy was short-lived.

Many of us found out that we would not be going home. Instead we learned that we had been assigned as part of the occupation force in Japan.

We learned Japanese phrases and customs and studied maps and photographs to help us find our way through Nagasaki to our billet near the town of Kumamoto.

When we landed, we were awed by the destruction. The city looked nothing like the pictures we had studied.

Eventually, word of an orphanage in the city began making its way around the base. Forty girls, mostly under the age of 6, were cared for by two French nuns, an elderly but spry Mother Superior Marguerite and a younger assistant, Sister Saint Paul. These women were helped by six Japanese nuns who had been raised at the orphanage.

Marines began spending their leave time at the orphanage helping the nuns and entertaining the children. Dressed in beautiful kimonos, the girls sang Japanese songs for us, and we taught them English songs such as "Oh! Suzannah," "Silent Night" and "Jingle Bells." We played games like jump rope and Blind Man's Buff with them in the orphanage courtyard.

The 8th Marines adopted the orphans for Christmas in 1945. The cook and his crew whipped up a complete turkey dinner while other leathernecks found a fir tree, which everyone decorated with hundreds of painted paper ornaments.

On one visit I asked Mother about a 16-year-old girl, named Miako, who sat by herself and never participated in anything, not even communion. The other children had said Miako had a mental problem, but Mother told me that the girl simply could not speak or hear. She lived in a silent world all her own.

As a teenager, I learned the universal sign language, which uses hand gestures for words and finger combinations for letters. I spent an hour each visit teaching Miako how to sign, and her vocabulary and knowledge of the alphabet increased steadily.

Since she knew no language at all, we were working with a blank slate. I would point to an object such as a flag and then show her one sign for the word flag as well as the signs for the letters of the word. She learned her name and the names of the nuns and some of her friends. Soon I was able to ask her what she did or ate or wanted and whether she was feeling happy, sad, angry or sick.

One small girl always took Miako's hand to help her participate in games and daily activities, and since this child already knew the alphabet and many English words, she was taught sign language as well.

Miako's silent world soon began to explode with conversation as even the nuns began to pick up some signs and communicate with her.

I was discharged in July, and while I was home for Christmas in 1946 and happy to be back with my family, I would never forget how my fellow Marines conquered boredom and homesickness by the love we shared with the nuns and the children.

To this day, I wonder what became of that little deaf girl. Did she get an education? Did she get married? Did she accomplish great things? I guess I'll never know.

JIM DIBBLE of Port Jefferson, New York, grew up knowing that an uncle had been a fighter pilot and was killed during a mission over Italy. Then he had a life-changing experience when he visited an Ohio museum.

My uncle, . . . 1st Lt. James P. Dibble, was a fighter pilot with the 94th Fighter Squadron, 1st Fighter Group during World War II. On September 9, 1943, while strafing a German convoy moving up to attack the Americans landing at Salerno, Jim was shot down by ground fire and killed.

At the time it was reported to his wife that he was last seen in his parachute and declared missing in action. One year later, with no further information, he was presumed dead. In October 1946 the Army wrote saying Jim's remains had been identified and buried in Naples, Italy. He was subsequently returned to the United States and was buried in Middleville, Michigan, in December 1948.

This was all anyone knew. For many years, questions about Jim and his last mission lingered. Everyone doubted that we would ever really know how Jim met his fate. There was even doubt that, in fact, it was Jim who had returned to Michigan.

During 1986 I was visiting the U.S. Air Force Museum in Dayton, Ohio. On the wall hung a picture of a group of men from the 1st Fighter Group in North Africa being addressed by Eddie Rickenbacker, World War I's top American ace, then a member of the 94th Aero Squadron. Was it possible that my uncle was in the picture, or was at least present? I decided the time had come to try to learn everything I could.

Over the next 13 years I went from knowing very little to knowing the details of every mission flown and everything about Jim's last flight; and, yes, he had met Eddie Rickenbacker the day of the photograph.

On September 9, 1943, both my uncle and his wingman were shot down. The wingman, Stan Wojick, was reported to have crashed with his plane. What really happened was that Stan had bailed out and Jim had crash-landed. Stan was captured and sent to a POW camp and subsequently liberated by the Russians in 1945. Jim was shot by the Germans following his crash landing and was buried next to his plane by two brothers, Vito and Paolo Cimino, who were working in the field at the time of the crash. Jim became an unknown soldier because all personal items had been removed by the Germans. It wasn't until after the war, when Stan had been accounted for and the crashed plane identified as Jim's, that an identification was possible.

When I started out to learn about my uncle, I wanted to learn what had happened on that mission. Along the way I found his crew chief, who had taken a picture of Jim standing in front of his plane on September 5, 1943. The Air Force sent me a slew of medals, none of which we knew he had been awarded. I discovered he had been nominated for the Distinguished Flying Cross, and after we fulfilled all the requirements outlined by the Secretary of the Air Force, in 1990 a formal ceremony was held at the Wright Patterson Air Force Base, with my father accepting the medal for the family. I met the pilots he flew with, sat in a P-38 fighter, and now, after searching the crash site, I have pieces of the P-38 that Jim sat in. It has been an incredible journey.

However, more important, I learned something I had not expected to. I learned about the character of the man. Character was what your book was all about, and that's why it meant so much to me. It really helped me to put into focus not only the value of the years it took to learn about Jim, but [also] the value of what he and his fellow pilots have done for those of us living in this world today.

On August 31st Jim wrote to his wife, "Yesterday I achieved the top spot in flying combat, I led the First Fighter Group into combat. I was a little nervous when confronted with the responsibility, but I just did my best and I guess it was good enough." The mission will long be remembered for the group's skill, daring and sacrifice in successfully defending a flight of B-26 bombers to and from their target area without a single bomber being lost to an overwhelming German fighter attack of over 100 planes.

On September 9, 1943, Jim flew his 49th and final mission. While strafing a German convoy he made the supreme sacrifice. His fate is no longer a mystery. We are comforted by the thought that Jim died doing what he enjoyed most, leading fighter pilots into combat. Jim didn't try to be a hero. He didn't have to. Good officers are good officers, whatever the reward.

I have learned a lot about the 94th Fighter Squadron in North Africa during the early stages of the war. I have learned a lot about my uncle, his training, his life in North Africa, and his combat missions. But the most important thing I have learned was about the character it took for these very young men to assume the responsibilities that they did and accomplish what they did. It is truly remarkable.

LURA M. WADE of Shawnee Mission, Kansas, wrote about her husband, who was taken prisoner under circumstances similar to those of Jim Dowling, whom I introduced in *The Greatest Generation.*

I . . . was amazed when I was reading about James Dowling and saw on page 48 how he was shot down, taken by train to Stalag Luft I near Barth, Germany, and eventually liberated by Russian troops in May 1945.

This is *so* like what happened to my husband, Rollin Wade, and is the first time I've ever seen anything about a fellow POW in Stalag Luft I. We were unable to take the trip there in the 1980s.

We were married after the war, on 18 August 1946, and he never talked about his war experiences until about 10 years ago, when I, working on the family genealogy, persuaded him to write his memoirs. Also, I heard about the POW medals and wanted to get one for him, so I wrote our senator Bob Dole, who arranged for him to get one. It was a surprise to Rollin when it came in the mail, but I think he was pleased to have it. He always said he shouldn't be rewarded for getting captured. He was a liaison pilot for the field artillery when he was shot down and when his plane came down he was surrounded by German troops with machine guns, so had no chance to get away. He was at Stalag Luft I for 11 months, and said the Russians who liberated them were drinking vodka and loud.

In camp he kept a notebook where he wrote down many things, from books he read in camp to cooking utensils they made from whatever was available (he made drawings of these things), names of fellow prisoners, etc. My family treasures this little book, which I found after he died suddenly on 7 July 1992, three days after his 77th birthday on the 4th of July.

We have 4 children, 9 grandchildren aged from 8 to 28, and 2 precious great-grandsons. I so wish he was still here to enjoy these little boys.

My generation (I am 77) did what we needed to do and had values and morals that seem not as important nowadays, at least to some people. I am thankful for all my memories of the experiences of my lifetime, and that my two brothers and Rollin survived the war.

In *The Greatest Generation* I wrote about Martha Putney, an African American woman who left her small Pennsylvania town and joined the Army in search of opportunity. She recently received this letter from a former high school classmate.

September 3, 1999

Dear Martha,

It is with great pleasure that I congratulate you for your accomplishments and success in life, in spite of the barricades that were in your way. While looking at the table of contents in *The Greatest Generation,* I saw the name Martha Settle Putney. It went through my mind that there can only be one person named Martha Settle. I turned to the chapter and I was right, it was you.

I was Peg Fenimore, class of '35, N.H.S. I remember you well, we were in several classes together. That was another time, I was not fully aware of the struggles that your race had to face. I have come a long way since then.

I have had a good life, mostly handed to me. There have been up and downs. The blessings are a good father, mother, and siblings and a healthy, devoted son and daughter. Some of the downs are a divorce at age 33 and widowed at age 50.

For many years I taught, first elementary school, then learning-disabled and socially & emotionally disturbed. Which were all very gratifying.

Now I am retired but work part-time at Montpelier, the home of James Madison. I volunteer at the Orange Visitors Bureau and tutor special-ed. children.

I live with my daughter, Cindy, in Orange. I enjoy good health for which I am most grateful.

I hope you are enjoying your retirement and are in good health. If you get down this way, do give me a call.

Congratulations and best wishes to you.

Fondly,
Peg Fenimore Aspden O'Connor
Orange, VA

III

·

LOSS

Ralph Stewart's grave.

TO OUR DEAR LIBERATORS

MEMORIAL DAY 1946

*The crew of Lieutenant Roland Matthew Cocker's PBM plane,
April 7, 1945 (Cocker is in the back row, third from the left).*

———————•———————

Now, more than a half-century after the end of World War II, those years have a kind of rosy glow for many. The stylish wardrobes; the handsome young men in uniform; swing music, conspicuous patriotism, and a just cause. The snappy patter of Bob Hope and the soothing baritone of Bing Crosby, the boogie-woogie of the Andrews Sisters, the jazz of Duke Ellington, Glenn Miller's distinctive melodies—all are on the sound track of the memories running across the mind's eye.

However, the stark reality is that 292,131 Americans were killed in action in World War II. They lie in lovingly tended cemeteries in France and Belgium, in the Philippines and Hawaii, in their hometown family plots and in unmarked graves where they fell in distant battle. To walk among those headstones, reading the names, ages, military units, and home states of the dead, is a humbling and simultaneously affirming experience. Most who died were very young and very far from home. Now, think of those who were left behind—the parents, wives, girlfriends, and children. Their loss is not a fleeting experience; it endures well beyond emotional visits to a cemetery.

So many young men left home at a tender age—late teens or early twenties—and were never seen again. Now the only reminder is a yellowing black-and-white photograph of a sailor in a new uniform, or a Marine on a sandy beach, or an airman with a crushed cap set at a jaunty angle, or a soldier looking at once proud and not old enough to be a warrior.

Someone's son, brother, husband, boyfriend, died in a way that even now is too painful to recount easily.

Most of those who survived know it was simply fate that saved them. Their buddies a few feet to the left and to the right were fatally wounded. The survivors carry that with them to this day; they are still asking, "Why did I survive?" Every day and every opportunity is a dividend their fallen comrades never realized. One man wrote to me about his father, a World War II combat veteran who had lost many young friends in battle. Recalling those who didn't live beyond their twenties, the dying man said to his son, "Don't sing any sad songs for me, boy. I've had my life. I've seen my grandchildren. Don't sing any sad songs for me."

I'VE TOLD YOU about Jeanette Gagne Norton, whose first husband, Camille Gagne, survived D-Day but died later in the battle for Nijmegen. He never saw their son. When the war was over, Jeanette said, "Everybody was honking their horns and yelling . . . but I couldn't really join in. . . . My heart wasn't in it."

Anne Black, now a corporate executive in Washington, D.C., was born after her father was killed in the closing months of the war. She writes eloquently of the effect on her mother, her own childhood, and their later years together.

My parents, Ceal and Ed Moloney, had been childhood friends in Englewood, New Jersey. They fell in love in their 20s but, because of the Depression, postponed their wedding till their early 30s, the coming war propelling them into action. During the four years of their marriage, my parents lived with my maternal grandmother in Englewood; my father enlisted early on in the war and was an MP on the docks in New York.

In January 1945, with the end of the war in sight and my mother four months pregnant, my father, at the "ancient" age of 34, was called overseas as part of the mop-up effort as the Allies moved across Europe. He was a sergeant in the 273rd Infantry Regiment, 69th Infantry Division. On April 14, he was killed in action near Aachen, Germany.

One of his buddies wrote, "We were attacking an A.A. [antiaircraft] position and 88s opened up on us. We were pretty far out from the town and we got orders to withdraw. Ed was at least 300 to 500 yards out front. On my way back, I noticed a medic working on one of our boys but with the 88s still coming, I didn't stop to look. When the medics got back, they told us it was Ed who had got it. They said, 'He never knew what hit him.'"

Six weeks later, while the world was rejoicing at the end of the war in Europe, I was born in New York. About to leave the hospital, my mother wrote the following to her brother: "I have neglected to write you lately but I've lost whatever pep I ever had. . . . The baby arrived on May 26 and I hope this kid has been born under a luckier star than Ed and I were. She weighed 9 lbs. and 8 ozs., so I did pretty good for an old dame. Mother is so nervous lately that she can't keep her hands still. Guess I haven't helped much with all the weeping, but I can't help it. I miss Ed so much, I can't imagine what I'll ever do, and can't find much reason for breathing. Everybody tells me that now I have the baby I'll feel better, but they don't know what they're talking about."

My mother had lost everything she was waiting for. She lost her dreams. There were an awful lot of perfect linen tablecloths in our house that never got used. So many things being saved for a future that was never to be.

And then there was me, born in the wake of my father's death, yet ready for life. I grew up living with my mother, grandmother and an ongoing parade of cats and dogs. I had a loving, stable childhood. I was close to my aunts and uncle on my mother's side and I had fun with my many cousins. I was also very close to my father's family—his brother, aunts, uncles, and my one cousin.

And then there were my father's many friends and war buddies who kept in touch with my mother over the years as best they could, sometimes just dropping into her office to chat, to see how things were going.

Growing up, it seemed to me that everyone else came from nice, perfect families made up of a mother, father and children. But, for my mother and me, our family was just the two of us. I always felt a strong need to protect her from unhappiness. On the subject of my father's death, there was for the most part silence. For me, this silence led to feelings of great shame. Shame that I did not have a father, shame that he had been killed when everyone else came home, shame that we'd been left behind, shame that we were "different."

I was a freshman in college when President Kennedy was assassinated. His death was a turning point in my life because it initiated a mourning for my own father—something I had never done. Three years later I went to Europe for the first time and found my way to my father's grave at the Netherlands American Cemetery at Margraten, Holland. After all these years, we were finally in the same place at the same time. He really had existed. It was good to know where he was at long last.

One morning in 1992, while sitting in my kitchen drinking a cup of coffee, I read in the *Washington Post* about a group of WWII "orphans" laying a wreath in Arlington Cemetery in honor of their fathers' sacrifices. I had only known one other person who had lost her father in the war and it was startling for me to read the interviews. People talking about how, as children, they had imagined that someday their dads would come home, having been held captive in some foreign country all these years. People recalling how no one ever talked about their father's death. And a woman named Ann Mix saying that for years she and her brother had always thought that when they said their prayers, "Our Father who art in Heaven" meant *their* father. I sat and cried my eyes out.

The next day, with the help of the *Post,* I was able to contact Ann Mix and her wonderful organization, the American World War II Orphans Network (AWON). My life then changed forever—and for the good. I found others who were like me. Over the years, I have made good friends, friends with whom WWII is now just part of the conversation. And the shame has mostly gone away, because now, at last, we've finally talked about it—and some days even laughed about it.

I am proud of my dad, and proud of what he did. My dearest wish is that I could have held my dad's hand, looked into his eyes and heard his voice—just once. But that was not to be.

My father left a legacy of love, good humor, courage and standing up for what you believe in. Mom carried on without him, leading a productive life, working until she was 87 and retiring (finally!) to live near me in Washington. At 90, she is with it, reads two papers daily, does some volunteer work and is eager to visit all the sights the city has to offer. From time to time, she dreams of my father vividly. She misses him always.

Sᴏᴍᴇ ᴏғ ᴛʜᴇ World War II orphans have spent years trying to determine the circumstances of their father's death and to understand the meaning of the loss in their own lives. Patricia Gaffney-Ansel of New Haven, Connecticut, was born three months after her father went down with his plane in New Guinea.

I am one of more than 183,000 war orphans who belong to the portrait of Americans heralded in *The Greatest Generation.* Most of us have lived with unanswered questions and unresolved grief; many of us have buried the pain deep within our hearts; some of us have sought a way to free the tears in order to heal. I've been given an extraordinary gift . . . a Journey of the Heart.

On March 11, 1944, my twenty-three-year-old father, Second Lieutenant George P. Gaffney, Jr., flew with the 41st Fighter Squadron on a bombing mission to Wewak, New Guinea. Instead of returning to his base, he landed at Saidor to refuel, where he filed a flash report saying he'd shot down an enemy plane and requested to have his P-47 Thunderbolt checked for damage. At 2:50 P.M. he left the airdrome heading for Gusap, a thirty-minute flight over the Finisterre mountains, and disappeared forever.

Three months later, on the day FDR signed the G.I. Bill into law, I was born a fatherless child. Fate had intervened so I would know my father only as a sepia-toned portrait of a young man in uniform, confined within a picture frame. His silence has been deafening. Although my mother spoke of him and my grandparents searched for him in my face, I could never hear that man in the picture. . . .

Several times during my childhood, the suitcase containing my father's belongings was opened. Mother would talk about him as we held his precious letters and the few personal effects that had been returned from New Guinea after he disappeared. It seems I've always known about the Finisterre mountains, the Ramu river, Saidor and Gusap, as well as the men who'd shared his tent and would later share his fate. . . .

I saw Grandpa Gaffney for the last time in 1970. As I turned to leave him, he asked if I had ever heard from my father. It broke my heart to tell him no. It was a desperate question from a dying man and remains as the saddest moment of my life.

On a morning in September 1993, in my 50th year of life and his death, one of those rare moments occurred when you know things have changed forever. I heard that the wreck of a WWII plane had been recovered in New Guinea. I thought, "Is that the crackle of static penetrating the long, dark silence? Is it meant for me?"

In May 1995 . . . I went to Papua New Guinea, as it had been known since gaining independence twenty years earlier. I passed through a time warp as our plane broke out of the clouds over the lush green grave of the man in the picture. On Mother's Day in America, pilot Richard Leahy and I flew to Gusap, where I buried a box filled with symbols of love in the kunai grass next to the airstrip to which my father had not returned. I listened for the sound of the breeze blowing through the kunai as he had described it in his last letter. I imagined his tent near the Ramu river. I was in a dream. . . .

In November 1996, a letter came from Bruce Hoy, an Australian WWII wreck researcher, saying he had information that could lead to my father's wreck site. Soon after, my quest came to the attention of Alfred Hagen, a Philadelphia businessman who'd been to PNG [Papua New Guinea] searching for the wreckage of his great-uncle, who was lost in 1943. I asked him to look for my father and sent him the Missing Air Crew Report [MACR] which includes the numbers stamped on the engine and [the] eight .50-caliber guns in the wings— *just in case.* . . .

Hagen returned to New Guinea in June 1998. He finally located the wreckage of his great-uncle's plane and then flew back to the Finisterres to continue searching for my father's wreck site. [Local] villagers led him to [a] second site. He identified the wreck as a P-47 but was unable to determine if it was my father's. He did find fragmentary evidence of remains in the cockpit area. It was, as Leahy was to fax later that day, "at the right address." We had reason to hope. The wreck was found at an altitude of 8,000' due south of Saidor, near where I had flown. The required reports were made to the CIL [the Army's Central Identification Laboratory] and soon

I called to ask when they might be going to investigate the site. Fortunately, they were preparing for the recovery of another P-47, piloted by Lieutenant Wilfrid Desilets, that Hagen had located two years earlier. Their departure would be delayed due to a tsunami, resulting in a curtailed schedule. I was devastated when they advised me there might not be time to look at "my" P-47. I pleaded with strength that came from my soul.

The weather in the Finisterres made flying difficult, but after several attempts, the CIL team got into the site on October 6. I waited for the phone to ring until Friday, October 16, when I received word from Hagen that the team had identified two of the .50-caliber guns listed on the MACR. My first call was to the CIL for official confirmation. I asked if it meant I could tell my mother. "Yes," came the response. . . .

I flew to Hawaii on June 1 [1999] to escort my father home. I was told I'm the first family member ever to have escorted the repatriated remains of an Army serviceman. As the plane left Honolulu, a lifetime of tears burst forth. This was it, my father was no longer lost and alone in those mountains. He was with me, and I was taking him home. I had daydreamed about him teaching me to fly or taking me on a Sunday drive in the clouds. Now we were on a plane together—not as I would have wanted, but it was much more than I'd ever expected to have.

Mother was waiting at the airport in Madison, Wisconsin. As we embraced she said, "You did it, Patty, you brought him home." When we went to the cargo area to wait for the hearse, the handler said, "I'm an old Army man." We stood in silence as he saluted my father's casket. On June 5 a Funeral Mass was held at St. Raphael Cathedral, where my father had been baptized and served as an altar boy. The pallbearers were his childhood friends. Twelve boys had gone to war; only one had not come home.

FOR GENEVA SHELTON of Hawthorne, California, the trauma of losing her brother in the war has not faded. He was in Belgium, advancing on Germany, in mid-December 1944.

So many of your words in the book reminded me of my brother, especially "D-Day" and the "Battle of the Bulge," as he was a part of both.

My brother, Ralph Stewart, was so very much like so many of your heroes—in his twenties and engaged to be married when war became the master of his life. He was a gentle, sensitive soul, with unbounded love for his mother and for our sister's little girl, who died after a brief illness at the tender age of five. I could never imagine him manning a machine gun. . . .

So many thoughts of my brother were aroused as I read your book, including some rather remarkable ones. First, to this day his Army Serial Number is imprinted on my mind—18035832—always ready for immediate recall. Then there was the time when I had an incredibly vivid dream: My sister and I were at a County Fair, where there was a closely-packed crowd of people. Some distance away in that crowd we saw our brother Ralph—the perfect likeness of him in his Army uniform, as in a photograph which I have. My sister and I were anxiously discussing how we were going to be able to tell our mother that we had found Ralph, who after all had not been a casualty of war! We were eagerly working our way through the mass of people so that he would not disappear among them before we could reach him. But, as seems to be the way with dreams, just as we were getting close enough to reach out to him, I awoke from the dream. Then there was a later time, about forty years after Ralph's death, when I was the principal of an elementary school. Each morning I prepared an information bulletin to post in the staff room. On two occasions that I remember, the date which I typed was

December 18, 1944—the date on which my brother was killed in battle. I was not consciously thinking of him at the time; but that date, like that Army Serial Number, was indelibly printed on my mind. . . .

When my brother's remains arrived for reburial in his hometown of Morton, Texas, attached to the end of his casket were his "dog tags"—18035832. . . .

I still have the flag which was draped over my brother's coffin, and was placed in my mother's hands at his reburial service on November 23, 1947.

F OR THOSE WHO SURVIVED, the loss of their buddies was as traumatic as the loss of a family member. Many had to ponder why they had lived, and then write to the families of those who did not. Lou Cocker Flowers of Virginia Beach, Virginia, sent a collection of letters written by her father, a Navy pilot.

Perhaps you would be interested in my father's story. [He was] Lieut. (j.g.) Roland Matthew Cocker, U.S. Navy.

On May 10, 1945, the PBM plane he piloted went down in the Pacific; nine of the twelve men on board perished. On only a few occasions did he tell the story in detail. . . . His personal account told the story of regaining consciousness and struggling to open the cockpit hatch; being injured and disoriented, underwater in the dark; holding his breath until he thought his lungs would burst; and being surrounded by fluorescent algae creating confusion as to which surface was the ocean and which was the starlit sky. It was also clear that he had a spiritual moment that night that changed his life, but that went without much discussion as I believe it was intensely private to him.

The exchange of letters between my father and the crew's families is incredibly moving. They reveal the courtesy, civility, dignity and sacrificial spirit of the time.

My father lived to be an F.B.I. agent for 30 years, a devoted husband to my mother Annie Laurie for 53 years and a beloved father to my sister, brother and me. He died of cancer November 28, 1996.

This is Lieutenant Cocker's letter to the parents of a crew member:

It was 10 o'clock at night at ███* when the plane's right side burst into flames where there is a gas tank of several hundred gallons. (Investigations determined a leaking gas line.) The fire was impossible to extinguish and the plane rapidly filled with smoke, being at a low-bombing altitude our only chance was to land in the open sea. The night was extremely dark and the glare from the flames was partially blinding, the waves had a long rolling swell which culminated in extremely hazardous landing. The plane evidently broke in two about midships. After several violent attempts to land, everyone was knocked unconscious by the impact and water filled the plane immediately as it began to sink. The co-pilot was thrown through the windshield and was seriously injured, the bow gunner escaped through the hatch nearest him, and I as pilot narrowly escaped through the window. *Your son* was at his post performing his duties to the best of his ability and you may be assured that it was through no fault of any of the crew members that this incident occurred, and it was only a miracle that three of us got out of it. The area was combed thoroughly by air and by sea for several days but no signs were ever revealed of any other survivors.

It is you loved ones [who] must bear the brunt of war, so let us all pray and work together that there may be no more of this grievance. With heads high and shoulders square, you parents and wives are the truly unsung heroes of this war.

* Censored by the military.

And here are four letters that Lieutenant Cocker received from crew members' families.

Dear Lieut. Cocker,

If you don't mind I would like to ask you a few questions. You may not be able to answer them all, but I would certainly appreciate it if you would answer all you can for me. There are so many unanswered questions running through my mind that it makes things worse. I don't know whether you are a married man or not, Lieutenant, but if you are you will understand my feelings I'm sure, and bear with me.

1. Was the Plane afire all over or just the engines?

2. Was Homer alright the last time you saw him?

3. Did you three survivors bail out or get out after the plane crashed?

4. Had the plane sunk or was it still afloat the last time you saw it?

5. Did you see Homer after the plane caught fire if so what was he doing?

6. They may not let you answer this, but was there any explosion before or after the crash?

7. Was the plane shot at, or bombed, or was the fire caused by the engine trouble?

8. Do you have any kind of proof that the other boys went down, any definite reason to believe they didn't get out too, or do you base your opinion on the fact that none of them have been found?

Answer my questions the best you can, please Lieutenant. They have been spinning around in my head unanswered so long, it's almost driven me crazy.

I can face whatever is to come, with the help of the Lord, Lieutenant Cocker, but I'm afraid I can't accept the opinion that Homer is dead, until there is some proof or time tells its own story. I have the faith you spoke of in your letter, but it's faith that somewhere, somehow, in the face of it all, God hasn't failed to answer my prayers and those of our babies.

I will appreciate anything you can tell me in regards to the answers to the questions.

Very sincerely,
Mrs. Homer Chancellor

Dear Lieutenant Cocker:

Your letter of June 10th has been received. Both Mr. Brill and I wish to express our sincere appreciation for your thoughtfulness in writing relative to our son Roland. It is gratifying to us to know that you considered him a personal friend and that his conduct and personality merited your kind words of commendation.

While we feel our loss very keenly we have the satisfaction of knowing that he was in the branch of service he liked most. We can only hope that his sacrifice and that of his comrades will hasten the coming of victory and bring lasting peace.

Very sincerely yours,
Mrs. Roland C. Brill

My Dear Lieut:

We thank you for the very sincere letter you have sent us at a time like this. The suspense was most distressing. We are thankful that Gordon was associated with a Christian pilot such as you have indicated to us that you are. We also appreciate your thoughtfulness in sending us the picture and memorial program and other details you were allowed to give us at this time.

If you wish we would appreciate corresponding with you from time to time, Mrs. Guether would like to write to the remainder of the crew also, since she can no longer write to Gordon we would like to have the present as well as the home addresses of all of you men.

I believe that this would encourage her quite much. I know she would be happy to write to all of you.

If at any time day or night you should be in Chicago or vicinity you are most cordially invited to call and stay with us.

Sincerely yours,
Mr. & Mrs. C. E. Guether

Lieut. Roland M. Cocker,
Dear Friend.

I thank you very much for letting me hear from you, and giving me as much information as you could about my boy Wiley Ross Hanson . . . that is missing in the accident at sea.

I hope that you and the other two survivors will be lucky enough that you will not have to go through with such awful experience again, and will live to get back, and when you get back don't forget to write to me and give us the full details of the accident.

You are all remembered in our Prayers.

Very truly yours. Mr. & Mrs. J. P. Hanson

SOME FAMILIES have the comfort of knowing their loved one died a hero. Shirley Colgan Goodwyne of Jacksonville, Florida, describes her brother William Winfield Colgan, a medic with the Marines. He died in one of the most ferocious battles of the war, on the island of Peleliu, where the Japanese were entrenched in deep caves on hostile terrain. William was awarded the Navy Cross, one of that service's highest decorations, for his bravery.

The whole family was affected by my brother's death and my mother got real sick and almost gave up on living. After a talk with her brother, she realized she had eight other children to raise and got on with the task. Very rarely, if ever, did we speak about William, because of the hurt it was to all of us.

During the fifty-year reunion of WWII, I met some men that did not know my brother, but who had served on Peleliu, the battle my brother was killed in. . . .

William was four months shy of his 21st birthday, but he lived a thoughtful, good clean life. . . .

It says in his yearbook, "Ambition—To be an Admiral in the U.S. Navy." He did not make admiral, but his name will always be a part of naval history, as an enlisted man who received the Navy Cross for extraordinary heroism. . . .

We now speak of William often, and every now and then, someone remembers a story that brings it back to us. His nephew Russell William Allen, who was born years after his uncle's death, has a web page dedicated to the memory of his uncle. The U.R.L. is http://www. imswebs.com/russallen~peleliu—take a look at it, he did a great job.

Shirley also enclosed a letter her brother wrote to his parents in the event something happened to him.

Dear Mom + Dad,

As you know I had 10 thousand dollars insurance and there is something I want you to do if you should have to collect. I want for you to buy a house, out near the park, you can pay it off on the F.H.A. plan, the insurance will be paid off at the rate of about 50 a month + I think the F.H.A. is on the plan of paying off a house at the rate of 30 or 40 dollars a month.

If you can, also send Edith to college when she gets old enough, don't do like you let me do get by without studying, make her. She'll probably be as smart as Dolly, it's [too] bad she couldn't have gone to college as she really deserved to go. Well there isn't much more a fellow can say, I just hope Dolly doesn't ever have to give you this letter. Love to you all.

Your Loving Son
William

P.S. Make Elwood save his money + try to get him to go to college. It really pays, get him interested in aviation or television that what is really going to pay off in the future.

THE SECRETARY OF THE NAVY
WASHINGTON

The President of the United States takes pride in presenting the NAVY CROSS posthumously to

WILLIAM WINFIELD COLGAN
PHARMACIST'S MATE SECOND CLASS
UNITED STATES NAVAL RESERVE

for service as set forth in the following

CITATION:

"For extraordinary heroism while serving with the Third Battalion, Seventh Marines, First Marine Division, Fleet Marine Force, during action against enemy Japanese Forces at Peleliu, Palau Islands, on October 4, 1944. Realizing that many wounded men were pinned down by intense enemy machine-gun, rifle and mortar fire, COLGAN unhesitatingly proceeded far in front of his own lines in order to administer first aid to the casualties. When our troops were forced to withdraw from untenable positions, he courageously exposed himself to a withering barrage from Japanese guns and directed the men to take cover until a protective smoke screen could be lowered, then skillfully supervised evacuation of the wounded until he was fatally struck down by Japanese fire. COLGAN's daring initiative and great personal valor in the face of grave peril were in keeping with the highest traditions of the United States Naval Service. He gallantly gave his life for his country."

For the President,

James Forrestal

Secretary of the Navy

CHARLES J. LEONARD, JR., was a Marine rifleman on Okinawa in 1945. He now lives in Danville, California, but he has a special connection to the American cemetery called the Punchbowl, above Pearl Harbor in Hawaii.

I enlisted in the Marines on "Armistice" Day, 1944. I trained at San Diego and Camp Pendleton. I shipped out with 5000 other 17 and 18 year old Marines the day after President (*our President*) Roosevelt died. We went to Guam for a few weeks as the advance party for the thousands of Marines who would be needed for the invasion of Japan. However, a sudden need for Marines developed in early May 1945 because of the fierce fighting on Okinawa. 2,500 of us were placed aboard an APA (the *Clinton*) and 5 days later we were off Okinawa, dodging kamikazes. . . .

We unloaded into the mud and trudged up to the front lines, which resembled WWI. The Japanese had 70 miles of tunnels and the *entire Japanese 32nd Army (116,000 Japanese soldiers) was underground.* We had to come at them out in the open and we paid the price. My Battalion (2nd Bt. 1st Regt) had landed on Okinawa with 32 officers and 869 men. When the battle ended 82 days later, 32 officers and 872 men had been *killed or wounded.* These figures don't include the hundreds of Marines who were disabled by dysentery and malaria or had their senses knocked out of them by the heaviest use of artillery and mortars by the Japanese anywhere in the Pacific. I was wounded June 12, 1945.

The war ended on Aug. 15 just as my hospital ship, the USS *Repose,* was entering San Francisco Bay.

I shall never forget the dozens of buddies who fell beside me. Every Memorial Day I become very emotional. Those of us who survived were so very lucky and we are thankful.

The following piece, also by Charles Leonard, appeared in the *Contra Costa Times*.

A Marine Buddy Cheats Death Once— but Not Twice

Eighteen-year-old private Wayne L. Lyons was my buddy. During World War II we served together in the Second Battalion, First Regiment, First Marine Division. I was a bazooka rifleman in F Company and Wayne was a rifleman in G Company.

Late in the afternoon of June 9, 1945, while Second Battalion was engaged in heavy fighting on the island of Okinawa, Wayne's platoon was caught out in the open while advancing. Eight Marines, including the commanding officer, were killed. Six were disabled by wounds and Wayne was slightly scratched in the hand by a bullet. The Japanese poured rifle fire into the bodies, so Wayne crawled underneath his dead friend, Bill Pierce. Pierce's body protected him until several of us could get to him after darkness set in. Most of the wounded were dead, but Wayne had survived.

When we got back to safety, Wayne was emotionally distraught. I held him for several minutes until he got control and then we shook hands and he went back to G Company, his uniform dark red with Pierce's blood.

Two days later, I was wounded and evacuated to the United States. Four days later, while assaulting a heavily protected ridge, a Japanese shell hit my friend, Wayne, and blew him to pieces. The shell was seen to explode where he lay, so he was listed as missing in action at the Punchbowl Cemetery above Pearl Harbor in Honolulu.

In 1985 my wife, Donna, and I returned to Okinawa and left a small memorial marker and a flag where Wayne died.

The memory of my good friend Wayne bravely returning to his company and thence to his death will live with me forever.

In *The Greatest Generation* I wrote about Mary Louise Roberts, an Army nurse who was the first woman to receive the Silver Star, for her courageous conduct while her surgical tent was being shelled on Anzio. I described how six nurses had been killed at Anzio. That caught the attention of Nancy Keister of South Yarmouth, Massachusetts, and brought back memories of one of those women.

In 1940, ten days after my son was born in Columbia Presbyterian Hospital in New York City, I was diagnosed as having scarlet fever and was taken away to Willard Parker Hospital for Contagious Diseases on the Lower East Side. I was not brave like the people in your book and felt very scared and disheartened at being separated from my husband and baby. This quarantine was to last three weeks. My husband was able to get one of the two private nurses available for this duty. Her name was Blanche Sigman. Without her loving care, I would have been a sad case.

When I returned home to my new baby and family, I kept in close contact with Blanche. She planned to go into the army and hoped to become a doctor when the war was over. Over the next few years we corresponded, and I sent packages and letters to her as she traveled through Africa and on to Italy. One day my letter was returned, marked "Deceased." As I did not know her stepmother in Ohio, I had no idea what had happened.

I learned something of Blanche when my brother, W. O. Cromwell, served in the Philippines, where he married an army nurse, Capt. Sarah Hale, sometime in the late 40's. When they came back to the U.S., I told Sarah about Blanche, saying I realized it was very iffy, but could she tell me anything about her. As it happened, she could. She said Blanche had been killed in Anzio when the Germans shelled the hospital. There was also a cargo ship, I think, named after her and I was able to spot it in the shipping news when it was in the port of New York.

And there my story of Blanche ended until today, when I got to the chapter "Women in Uniform and Out," where I read, "Ellen Ainsworth, killed by German artillery shell—one of six nurses to die at Anzio"—and my dear Blanche, also, one of them. Now, so many years later, at 81 years of age, I am able to shed tears in her dear memory.

AFTER BEING FIRED by President Harry Truman in April 1951, General Douglas MacArthur gave a speech before Congress in which he said, famously, "Old soldiers never die, they just fade away." Sadly, the veterans of World War II are now fading away at the rate of thirty thousand a month.

Mary Griffiths was married to an old soldier, a career Army officer, and they were retired in Columbia, South Carolina, when he died.

Last night my husband died as I held him in my arms, and I told him, "I love you, and go on home soldier, your mom and dad are waiting on you, give our Fay a kiss—wait for me. I will join you soon, wait for me"—with that, 2 big tears rolled down his cheeks (he hadn't opened his eyes for 2 days)—but I knew then he heard me—he took his last breath and left me.

Tomorrow I pick up his remains, and will bring him home for the last time, and take him to Beaufort, South Carolina, National Cemetery for burial. It was his wish and mine to be cremated, and be buried. He did not want any service; this is my wish too. . . .

Like so many [of those whose] personal accounts I have read in your book—he too had to be "pulled out" to talk about his experiences. He chose Army as a career—when I said goodbye to him in 1941—I did not see him for 3 years & 8 months, his war was [the] Pacific War, then he hit the Korean War again for 2 years—he wears "9 battle stripes" on his sleeve and "combat infantry badge, with a silver star"—these are the only decorations that really counted to him, that he prized. He received numerous other decorations though. . . .

The Army was our life, for 24 years. I loved every minute of it *except* the separation for wars.

I always tried to represent my husband, the Army, and the U. States honorably, wherever we were stationed.

I guess the happiest time in his life [was] when he returned to Ohio, and his 148th Regimental reunion, after 40 years or so, and he was re-united with the men that served under him [when he was] a Captain in World War II for 3 years and 8 months. . . .

Putting this down has given me much comfort to talk to you tonight.

MARTHA TILLER of Richmond, Virginia, grew up in a hurry when war broke out.

I was a sophomore in college when Pearl Harbor was attacked, so my life went from carefree—praying not to die before the next fraternity dance—to praying for all the boys I knew to come home safely. My husband and his brother were killed within six months of each other, and my favorite co-cheerleader died at Guadalcanal.

Martha was attending Sophie Newcomb College in New Orleans when she met George Tompkins, a student at Tulane. He was commissioned a second lieutenant in the Army Air Corps. They had one son, George Junior, before her husband was killed in action.

I was remarried about eight years after he was killed. I was engaged a couple of times and backed off. I was crazy about my husband. . . . It takes a long time. We had one son . . . and he is a pilot just like his father. Genes are so powerful. His father saw him just one time, and then went overseas. And then he was killed when [the child] was six months old. My son is a pilot just like he was, and he loves fast cars just like he did, and he even has the same exact signature. . . .

My father-in-law was a West Point graduate, in Eisenhower's class, and had a great deal to do in the war. They had three sons and lost two of them within six months of each other. . . . The third was a Marine, and they could have requested his return as the only surviving child of the family. But he pleaded not to be sent back home; he wanted to fight more than ever. He said that with his two brothers being killed, he wanted to fight for them. And he made it home safely, so that turned out all right.

OF ALL THOSE IN UNIFORM during World War II, only a fraction were directly exposed to enemy fire. The ratio of men in infantry divisions to those in backup positions was one to four. One of those behind the lines was Roger Newburger of White Plains, New York, who was with the Army Corps of Engineers during World War II.

I put in my time (4 years & 6 days) in World War 2. But my Corps of Engineers outfit was in battle only once and very wisely I was left behind on Oahu with six enlisted men with the company's gear that wasn't carted into the front lines.

I say "wisely" because a warrior I am not and never was. I'm sure that if I had been sent into battle I would have tried to do whatever I was told or supposed to do, but I think the guys would have been safer without me firing anywhere near them.

In fact, I also would have been safer. . . .

Saving Private Ryan is the only movie I didn't see with my wife of 48 years. I walked out of the theater, walked slowly to my car, got in and sat for about a half-hour, with one sob and a few tears rolling down my cheeks. Afterwards, I decided I was thus affected because of what the real warriors went through.

The movie's premise is that Ryan's three brothers have been killed in action and he must be pulled off the front lines before he's lost as well. In fact, many families lost more than one son. Barbara Peterson of River Vale, New Jersey, is the great-granddaughter of a woman who lost two sons. She wrote about how her family dealt with the loss of her grandfather and great-uncle, both killed in Europe.

My grandfather John W. Rockwell and his only brother, Malcolm H. Rockwell, were killed in 1944, World War II, Europe. Within two months, my great-grandmother lost her only two sons and my mother, at age three, lost her father and her uncle. To this day, my mother swears she can remember the Western Union knock on the door that changed her life forever.

My grandmother never remarried and, to my knowledge, never even dated another man after the loss of her husband. Shortly after John's death in October 1944, Malcolm wrote my grandmother to share his sorrow about the loss of his brother, her beloved husband. In his letter, Malcolm hoped that the war would soon end so as "to spare some other family the grief that is ours." That was the last time my grandmother heard from him. He was killed in the Battle of the Bulge, December 1944.

Both men are buried overseas, my grandfather at the American Military Cemetery, Normandy, France, and Uncle Mac at Henri-Chapelle Cemetery, Belgium. I had the honor of being the first family member to visit my grandfather's grave, in the fall of 1997. As you know, words cannot describe the feeling of standing on the grounds of this magnificent cemetery overlooking Omaha Beach.

ELEANOR FOSTER of Bellevue, Michigan, wrote about the pain of losing her first husband, Lawrence "Danny" Danforth, who was killed in action in Sicily in 1943.

I am 83 years old—you can say a victim of World War II. No, I was not in actual combat, but my losses are real.

It is difficult to explain the emptiness I am experiencing today. First for having lost my husband *and* to have lost the family we were to have had. It isn't because I want to lean on children; instead, it is missing the joys of seeing new families created, the sharing of family memories, the sharing of experiences and love with grandchildren, the knowledge that children are there to give guidance and support as needs arise with the aging process. All of this was sacrificed!

Danny, my husband, and I met when I was teaching in Janesville, Wisconsin. Danny was with Chevrolet Motors in Janesville, building a future with the industry. We were engaged—I had my ring—and then the draft came along. In Janesville anyone who was married was automatically exempted from the draft. Marriages occurred at an accelerated rate! With due consideration, Danny and I decided that we had an obligation to answer the need for trained men for our country and wanted to put off our wedding plans until after he had fulfilled his 2-year draft call. Drafted the summer of 1941, completed Officer Training, 2nd Lt., in 1942. I had taken a job with the University of Illinois Extension Service as Home Adviser in Belvedere, Illinois. The husband of the secretary for the Extension Service was in the regular army, Captain Cleveland. [The secretary] was concerned about our situation and, with the increased seriousness of the war, we did decide to be married in the fall of 1942. Danny was killed in action in Sicily in July 1943. I had to pull my life together and relocate in the business world. . . . Although I married many years later, a family was not in my future. Danny and I gave up being married and having a family to answer the draft . . . this we did with, as you said, a purpose and with modesty!

VINCENT DE VITTO of Lake Ronkonkoma, New York, is one of five sons of Raffaele and Luigia De Vitto, first-generation immigrants from Italy. All five of the De Vitto boys served during World War II; one of them, Liberty, was killed in France. Vincent De Vitto sent a copy of the letter that his sister Mary wrote to the brothers to break the news of Liberty's death.

Dear Boys,

I've put off writing to you for a few days now, hoping that in time I could soften the blow that I must give you. You already know that Lib was wounded in France, and perhaps you have suspected that the final results would not be pleasant.

Saturday, September 16, we received another telegram from the war department stating that Lib had died from wounds received. He was wounded on the 22nd of August and he died August 24, in France.

I know this news must be pretty horrible for you boys to take, for it hasn't been easy for us. We were so sick over it that I neglected to write to you before. I only hope that you boys can take it as well as Lib took Dad's death. Mom has been very worried about you boys not being able to take it, and it would be a consolation to her if all of you would write and assure her that you are all making the best of it. As for me, I realize how this news is going to affect you so please for Mom's sake keep well. If you'll just remember that it's God's will that these things happen. It isn't too much of a comfort, I know, but it's the only one I can give you.

You all know how Lib was well known and liked for his sincerity. Everyone feels very sad about his passing on like that.

Please be brave about this and remember to write Mom. Your letters mean as much to her as to me. I know I can depend on you.

Love, Mary

Vincent named one of his sons after Liberty and the boy grew up to be a drummer in Billy Joel's band. Vincent wrote, "On one of his world tours Billy introduced . . . Liberty, named after my brother who lost his life in action on the Brest peninsula. He told the audience that his drummer's father had helped liberate Bastogne with the 101st. Liberty received a standing ovation."

Vincent lost a brother but he said he received from the service "the deep satisfaction . . . that I joined the ranks of many before me in serving my country, and the loyalty and commitment, discipline and sacrifices that I observed and experienced will never leave my memories. I thank God for my good fortune and pray that no generation will face war again."

IV

·

FAITH

Chaplain Sam Neel. After he was released from a German POW camp, Neel carried this photograph in his wallet for more than fifty years.

Gino Merli, September 5, 1944, in Sars-la-Bruyère, Belgium, where he earned the Congressional Medal of Honor.

Were members of the Greatest Generation more spiritual or religiously faithful than their offspring or succeeding generations? Spirituality is difficult to quantify, but it's clear from the letters I received, and from anecdotal and other evidence from organized religions, that faith and religious belief were widely and openly embraced.

Certainly the combat veterans with whom I spoke were for the most part men who could testify to the truth of the saying that there are no atheists in foxholes. Philip L. Cochran of Maple City, Michigan, was not a chaplain; he was a combat Marine. But his description of what happened one night typifies what many veterans experienced.

> One night, on Guadalcanal, while leading a reconnaissance patrol, we were pinned down by sniper fire and in the ensuing melee, I was all alone, out in the middle of the jungle, not having the vaguest idea of my location. . . . I have never been so scared, but you know what, I discovered the power of prayer at that moment, a power I never had to call upon before, but a power for which I had occasion to be grateful many times during the war, a power I have relied upon throughout my life since then.

There are countless other stories of the place of faith in the lives of the men on the front lines and of their families and friends who were praying daily for their well-being. It is not surprising that after *The Greatest Generation* was published I heard from former military chaplains and their admirers, gently suggesting I should have included a tribute to their role.

They're right, of course.

Lenora F. Clark of Houston, Texas, was one of those who wrote; her husband, Lamar, was a chaplain assigned to the Pacific theater.

These persons were not conscripted, but all were volunteers. In most cases they were a little older than the average soldier because the qualifications were so high . . . all were required to have the amount of education which their denomination demanded before ordination, and ordination and recommendation were prerequisite to being accepted. Their age, however, did not prevent them going through the same hardships as the younger soldiers *unarmed*. . . . I know all of this by my personal contact with a chaplain before he entered the military and during the time he spent in actual combat with an infantry unit and recorded in letters written every day he was overseas (except when cut off behind enemy lines and unable to write). I have all these personal letters now copied and bound into five books. They tell of the dangers he faced, the men he buried, the letters he wrote to wives, or parents, or children, or sisters, or friends to try to explain what had happened to their loved one who died fighting for freedom.

Not only did these men live in foxholes, survive behind the enemy lines, starve along with all the others when there was no food, or no fresh meat or vegetables or fruit for weeks and sometimes months on end, but they gave encouragement to those who were fighting and being wounded and, in some cases, [were] wounded themselves. The particular chaplain whom I knew and from whom I received hundreds of letters, some written on a typewriter when one was available in a tent-office, but most of them in longhand, came home with a Purple Heart, a Bronze Star with several clusters, and a

Presidential Citation earned in his first combat mission on Leyte.

And [the chaplains] did not just fade away into the background at home. They became pastors, church administrators, teachers of theology, hospital chaplains and many other kinds of leaders, most of whom never earned large salaries.

Mrs. Clark elaborated on her life with her husband.

We met the first day of college in freshman English class and were attracted to each other. Very soon we were deeply in love—love that lasted the rest of our lives. We were married on April 26, 1936, and six years later, on that date, he reported to the Army in Indianapolis. When war was declared, he felt compelled to volunteer to help to pay for our freedom and all the good things that had come to us because of the sacrifice of others. I was not all that enthusiastic, because I had two small children and no home. But he felt so strongly, I could not prevail. After two years of training with a newly organized division, he asked for and got an overseas assignment and on April 26, 1944, he sailed for the South Pacific, going first to New Caledonia and then to New Guinea where he spent several months with an ordnance battalion where he built a chapel out of native materials using native labor. But that did not satisfy him. Again, he asked for combat duty. As the letters will indicate, he was assigned to a division that made the initial landing on the Philippines.

Chaplain Clark's letters home are reminders of the frontline perils of trying to serve God and combat infantrymen simultaneously.

26 October 1944

My Darling Lenora Fay,

I did not write in the mountains because the picture was such that I would not have wanted you to know what it was. I'll say this: I am sure that the papers were full of the 2nd Bn. [Battalion] 19th Regt. Things were bad, but I knew it would come out to you. I don't want to write this but it will get in the paper sooner or later through the public relations officer. I was wounded but only slightly. For polite company it was on the posterior. Yes, I got hit on the side of the "butt." . . . It was glancing and caused only a slight wound. It went through my jacket and pants and broke the skin. It only bled a little.

I am truly a veteran now. I have been through everything, but am more convinced than ever of Divine Protection. . . . Please have faith in me and our prayers to put God's love around me.

27 October 1944

Darling, I am afraid that you will feel that I have not been fair so I'll give this brief resume since I left. . . .

We had a very rough and dangerous time in the mountains with little food or anything else. Sometime I'll tell you more.

I am safe and whole and am coming back to you as I promised. I never did needlessly expose myself [to danger], and I won't.

The men are in good shape and their spirit is good. I am glad of that.

28 October 1944

My beautiful love, I love you so much. You and our darling babies are my whole life. Through you, God has taught and is teaching me what He wants me to know. I can never be grateful enough for you all. Never will I be able to pay for the blessings that are mine. It is rough here, and I'll see more, but all of that will not pay for you all. You all are worth all of this and more too. You know that all of this comes from the depth of my very being. I want you to know what you all mean to me and this knowledge will bring me back to you.

Sam neel, jr., of Bradenton, Florida, served as an Army chaplain with the 106th Infantry Division. He spent Christmas Eve 1944 as a German POW. His wife, Eleanor, sent the following letter:

> He is now 85 years old and frail. His hand is unsteady, thus I am writing for him. . . . I was not a part of Sam's life during those years. We have been married since 1971, after we both were widowed. I tell everyone that Sam's war stories do indeed show how brave he is—but the bravest thing he ever did was marry me, a widow with 6 young children.

The letter Neel dictated to his wife describes the events leading up to his capture.

> Shortly after dawn there was an artillery barrage such as I have never heard before or since. It was the beginning of the Battle of the Bulge. The Germans decided to make their break-through by hitting two regiments of our division and one regiment of the 28th Division with 12 divisions of tanks and infantry.
>
> Our regiment managed to hold its position, but the Germans broke through north of us and south of us, and they just kept on going towards Belgium and France. The last communication we received was to hold our position as long as we could. After 1½ days, a runner named Lt. Starr from headquarters finally got through to us and told us to pull out and go mount an attack on Schoenberg, which was 15 miles behind us. There was more than a foot of snow on the ground. In fact, it was a severe winter and it was almost 3 months later before we ever saw the ground again. The German meteorologist had chosen wisely and there was a low overcast for almost a week. No American planes had been able to fly supplies to us. We were out of food and ammunition. Lt. Starr told me that Schoenberg was de-

fended by a division of tanks. I decided that if we reached Schoenberg and launched an attack against the tanks with bayonets, I was going to try to find some troops near the rear to minister to.

The next 24 hours were hell. We were moving across hills and valleys, but the German tanks and artillery kept firing at us and finally we ended up on Dec. 19th on a flat-top hill completely surrounded. There were dead and wounded lying everywhere and our colonel decided to surrender. It was early afternoon and the Germans permitted me to take 25 men with picks and shovels and an armed guard. We buried American dead until dark.

At Gerolstein, the Germans herded us onto the railroad platform where we were to be loaded onto boxcars. I was walking back and forth inquiring about friends as to whether they were alive or dead. Somebody introduced me to a Dr. Sutherland from another outfit. Dr. Sutherland—Chaplain Neel. We talked rather formally for a couple of minutes and then I turned and started on. Evidently there is a characteristic way that I carry one arm because Doc took one look at the way I walked and he yelled, "Hey, are you Sam Neel?" I turned and took another look at him and said, "Yes, are you Josh Sutherland?" We had been classmates for three years in college. We were so bearded and haggard that we didn't recognize each other from the front, but he recognized my back.

The Germans gave us a little food and water and then we were piled into the old "40 and 8" boxcars of World War I vintage. The cars were supposed to carry 40 men and 8 horses. Evidently they had the horses on before us, because we were crowded in on 6 inches of horse manure. There were so many of us that no one could lie down. We all had to sit up.

They kept us in the cars like animals for 3½ days. We weren't permitted to get out and there was no food or water. I began to wonder if the Germans were systematically torturing us.

Finally, near nightfall on December 23rd, our train stopped in the railroad yard of Limberg, Germany. We were permitted out of the cars for a few minutes; then they gave us a little food and water. Each of us had a small piece of black bread which was so coarse it looked like it was made out of sawdust. They also gave us a spoonful of molasses each. Doc Buxton, who was sitting next to me, had let them use his helmet to bring our molasses in, and they had given him a spoon to dish it out. Before we ate they asked me to give a prayer of thanksgiving for the food. Just as I was finishing the prayer, the air raid siren in Limberg sounded and a host of RAF bombers came flying over. Our railroad yard was the target for the night. As we heard the first bomb swish in the air, one man yelled, "Watch out men, here come the bombs, put on your steel helmets." So, Doc Buxton threw on his helmet and molasses went all over him. It was a nerve-racking ordeal but after it was over we had a good laugh as we helped Doc lick his way out.

The next morning when we looked out there was one crater within 30 yards of our car. When that one hit, we must have had the feeling that you have just before you go off into eternity. We also saw dead Americans lying all over the railroad yard. These were the men who had broken out of their cars in trying to run away from the bombs.

As the morning moved along, the men still alive sat in their cars and the train wasn't moving. You could feel the tension mounting because each of us was thinking, "If this train doesn't move, we will still be sitting here tonight and the bombers will come again." Finally, an interpreter in our car who could speak German talked to one of the guards. He suggested that the Germans permit me, the chaplain, to go from car to car and try to quiet the men. To our surprise, the guard consented.

As I went from car to car, I reminded the men that it was Dec. 24th, Christmas Eve. I suggested that they go, in their hearts and minds, back to their homes where their families were gathered around the Christmas trees, and that they have a Christmas service of some kind in each car.

When I got back to our car, darkness had fallen. I recited to our men the Christmas story from Matthew which begins, "Now when Jesus was born in Bethlehem of Judea, in the days of Herod the King . . ." Then I gave a Christmas prayer and we began to sing Christmas carols. When we sang "Silent Night, Holy Night," which is a German carol of course, our guard knocked on the side of the car. Through our interpreter he asked us to sing the carol again. He did not recognize the English words, but he recognized the tune. As we sang I could see the men beginning to relax. Then, in conclusion, one man with a beautiful voice sang Brahms's Lullaby. We began drifting off to sleep. Then suddenly, our car gave a jolt and the train began to move. A great shout of joy went up from all of us, because we were moving out of that dreadful railroad yard. It was the best Christmas present any of us had ever had.

The prison camp itself was quite an ordeal. They didn't have room for us at permanent American camps, so we were taken to a prison camp for the Russians.

It was a very challenging experience for me. The first Sunday we had worship service. The men crowded into barracks and stood the entire time. I was up on a small platform and beside me was a can with a pussy-willow in it which someone had found to use as a worship center. As I looked out I could see the men's eyes saying, "You talked a lot about religion back in the States, but what can it do for men who are faced with being cold and hungry day after day, week after week?" I couldn't have met the challenge on my own, but I had an old battered New Testament which I had managed to keep each time we were searched by the Germans. That week I had run across a passage in Philippians. I reminded the men that

Paul wrote this letter when he was a prisoner and was being persecuted. Then I read Philippians, the 4th chapter, the 11th through the 13th verses: "I have learned, in whatsoever state I am, therewith to be content. I know both how to be abused and how to abound. Everywhere and in all things I am instructed both to be full and to be hungry, both to abound and to suffer need, I can do all things through Christ who strengtheneth me." I didn't need to preach, the Scripture preached for me. And that's how it was Sunday after Sunday.

JOHN CRAVEN of McLean, Virginia, was a military chaplain in four campaigns during World War II and three during the Korean War. His story came to us from an April 6, 1995, article in the *Religious Herald*, the Virginia Baptists' weekly. The author is Pam Parry.

Traumatized by mortar fire, the young Marine huddled outside a military hospital, his body trembling, clenched into a fetal position. "John the Baptist" took his hand and began to pray, "Our Father which art in heaven, hallowed be thy name." The trembling continued. "Thy kingdom come. Thy will be done on earth, as it is in heaven."

In a moment, the Marine composed himself enough to join the chaplain: "Give us this day our daily bread. And forgive us our debts, as we forgive our debtors."

As they finished the Lord's Prayer the soldier began to relax and the shaking subsided. The most effective antidote for shell shock is the Lord's Prayer, says Chaplain John Craven of McLean, who lived that dramatic scene numerous times during seven combat campaigns spanning more than 30 years of military service. Now retired from active duty, Craven, 79, is a chaplain at Vinson Hall Navy–Marine Corps Officers Retirement Residence in McLean.

Craven, a Southern Baptist, is thought to have seen more combat than any living chaplain. He participated in four campaigns during World War II, including the one at Iwo Jima, and three during the Korean War. On the 50th anniversary of the Iwo Jima campaign, Craven reflected on his participation in the historic battle. Craven, known affectionately as John the Baptist by the Fourth Marine Division, ministered to hundreds of wounded, dying and scared men. "I tried to visit the troops as often as I could to encourage them, talk to them," he said. For the most part the chaplain's role was helping to tend to the wounded, he added.

Often, all that Craven could do for the [Iwo Jima] wounded was to take some moistened gauze and wipe the volcanic ash from their eyes. . . .

Craven, a member of McLean Baptist Church, also baptized four men during his five weeks at Iwo Jima. Those men accepted Christ on the boat before they landed. To witness such new birth amid the death and devastation of attack was miraculous, he recalls. Five decades later, he returned to that island in the Pacific to participate in the dedication of a monument to the casualties on both sides. The Japanese and American veterans sat on opposite sides of the monument. After leading a prayer, Craven and a former Japanese captain who had become a Buddhist priest embraced, setting an example for the men. Later, Craven wrote: "Before leaving the beach and the spot where our command post had been, I photographed a small, green plant with a small, red bloom. To me, it represented the hopes and dreams for peace rising out of the blood-soaked sands of Iwo Jima. . . ."

One of Craven's many lasting memories of World War II is the time he shared a foxhole on Iwo Jima with a Catholic chaplain, Henry Druffel. As Craven recalled in a telephone conversation more than fifty years later, that experience shared by two men representing different expressions of Christian faith linked them forever. In a letter, Craven reaffirmed his impression.

We were both assigned to the 14th Marine Regiment, and we had about 3000 men. It was an impossible situation. The Army had four chaplains with each regiment. But with the Marines, the Navy provided just one Catholic and one Protestant chaplain per regiment. . . .

I tried to visit the troops, the men, as often as I could. We had five battalions, so that took quite some time. I spent quite a lot of time at the aid station, where the wounded were being brought in. . . . Iwo Jima was a difficult situation from beginning to end.

I landed at about five o'clock on D-Day, and it was two days later that we fixed our foxhole together. It was a pretty good foxhole. The volcanic ash at Iwo Jima wasn't solid ground, it was easy to give way. It was all volcanic ash, so it wasn't easy to walk in. The two of us managed to get part of a Japanese airplane that had been shot down—part of the fuselage of the wreckage. So we put that over the top of the foxhole and put some sand on top of that. It worked fine. . . . We were in there during fire, but then we looked up at the jagged pieces of this fuselage above us that were shot up, and we thought that if we were hit, we'd get more damage from the fuselage than the enemy shell. . . . So we flipped the fuselage over and started enlarging the foxhole. But while we were digging, the Japanese opened up with firing right on us. So we'd dig a while and then duck down in the hole because they were firing over our heads. But when we were down, Chaplain Druffel looked at me and said, "This sure gives you an incentive to dig, don't it?" I'll always remember that! So we finished it, and got a piece of lumber from the beach and fixed up a pretty good foxhole. Just the two of us . . .

You always have some fear, though of course I'd been

through three campaigns before that . . . so I was pretty well ready for combat. . . . But it was my first time in the foxhole with another chaplain. We were together about 45 days . . . we coordinated and knew what the other was doing, in lining up services and where we were going to be during the day. . . . And when we got back to Maui, we saw each other every day . . . but then I'd been overseas 18 months so I came home. . . . After the war, the Marines transferred me to Norfolk to serve on amphibious ships. I was an enlisted Marine in the 1930s, so I liked to serve with Marines. . . . And after Druffel got out he went to Indiana to his order and he taught school. He didn't have a regular church—he worked in this Catholic community as a priest.

He was a really great guy . . . really wonderful. We communicated about once a year. He came to stay with us once at our home. But he's been dead at least 10 years now. He had a good sense of humor, but was a very pleasant, devoted priest . . . he was out to serve the men and help them and minister to them, in every way he could. A great individual.

Henry Druffel wrote to Chaplain Craven on June 29, 1953, right after the Korean War.

Chaplain John H. Craven, USN
Arlington, Virginia

Dear Chaplain,

Hi! John. Sure good to hear from YOU again. Wish I could attend the Reunion of the old 4th Division (I still wear its shoulder patch on my coat lapel and tell the kids it stands for the 4th Commandment) in Washington, DC, next week but on Monday I'm embarking for the other Washington on the other end of the country, namely, Washington State which is my original home.

Greetings and best regards to your wife and family whom I met out in California and have not forgotten.

I'll be thinking about you all next week while traveling westward. The thought of you will be good company on a long lonesome train ride. Have a good time and tell all our old friends you see I haven't forgotten them.

Thanks a lot for writing and if we don't have the pleasure of meeting again here in this world I shall continue to hope and pray that we meet where we both thought we might meet while we were in that "super-foxhole" together out there on Iwo Jima some eight and a half years ago now.

God bless you always.

Your old teammate on "Maui no ka oi!"

RABBI JUDAH NADICH was the first Jewish chaplain to serve in the European theater. He was summoned on the orders of General Dwight Eisenhower after a Jewish soldier was killed in a training accident and there was a dispute over whether he would be buried in a Jewish cemetery, as the local rabbi in Belfast urged, or in a military cemetery. Nadich became an important adviser to Eisenhower when the concentration camps were liberated. The camps led him to question his faith in God, but eventually he became one of New York City's most important spiritual leaders as rabbi of the Park Avenue Synagogue for thirty years.

I enlisted immediately after Pearl Harbor. At that time, I was a rabbi in Chicago, and I thought, if a rabbi should not be in the war, then who should? We had been reading in the press about what had been happening to the Jews. Of course, compared to what happened to them later, what happened in the beginning was very little. But still, it was very offensive that the windows of Jews were being smashed, and they were boycotted, and things like that. After I enlisted, I was ordered to Fort Bragg, North Carolina, where I served as the Jewish chaplain for the troops there. We had over 100,000 troops at Fort Bragg, including the 101st Airborne. . . .

I was sent from Fort Bragg to Brooklyn, New York, and after a brief wait at Fort Hamilton in Brooklyn, I was put aboard a Dutch freighter with about 14 or 15 officers. Three days out from England, we were attacked by German submarines. We lost three ships, but we were some 50 ships altogether. It wasn't very pleasant, especially when we would gather in a little room on the ship and listen to the radio. We could hear the German radio too, and we heard a woman, whoever she was, speaking in very good English, saying that the German submarines had sunk a number of American ships coming to Europe, and they would keep attacking us until every ship was sunk. She was boasting about the German successes to boost the morale of the German people.

When we arrived at Liverpool, I was ordered to Northern Ireland where we had our first troops stationed, and I served there until the troops emptied out for the invasion of North Africa. Then, I was ordered to England, where I was stationed at the American Army cemetery in Brookwood, near Surrey. They carried out funerals three days a week—on Tuesdays, Thursdays and Saturdays—but I told them there should be no Jewish burials on Saturdays. That gave me five days that I could travel throughout England and Scotland to visit bases and to meet with Jewish troops and officers and conduct services.

After the Normandy invasion in June of 1944, I became very busy at the Brookwood cemetery. With the first landings at Normandy, we were busy burying men, sometimes as many as 300 or 350 a day. I would make certain that I had a Catholic chaplain and a Protestant chaplain present, and bulldozers would dig long trenches. The bodies were carefully prepared, and carefully placed in the trench. And when all of the bodies

were placed in the trenches, each of the three of us conducted his own religion's burial service. It was difficult
emotionally, and that happened day after day. There was
no burial place as of yet in France, so that continued for
quite a while.

And then in August of '44, I was ordered to Normandy. . . . In the Army, you're supposed to help men of
all faiths who come to you for counseling. The only
distinction would be the service of a particular faith. I
had Catholic and Protestant soldiers who came to me
for counseling, if I happened to be the chaplain closest. . . . Soldiers were much more open to faith in times
of danger than people are generally, and the attendance
at services was always good. I have no doubt that having
a deeper faith helped these soldiers go on. . . . We knew
the business we were in—it wasn't child's play. We knew
that a good number of the men were going to die. We
hoped that we wouldn't be one of them—chaplains
were being killed too.

The only time I was actually close to death during the
war was in Normandy, when I was with my Catholic senior chaplain, and his deputy. . . . I was sitting in the
front seat with the driver, and the two more senior officers were in the rear. We were going through the woods
when we heard the crack of a rifle. And I suddenly felt a
cold wind go past the back of my neck. And the two officers said, "Wow, that bullet just missed you!" . . .

In the summer of 1945, I was sent to Frankfurt, Germany, by orders of General Eisenhower. When I arrived,
I was told that I had a new job. I was to travel to dis-
placed persons camps—DP camps—to meet with Jewish survivors who had been liberated by the American
army from the German concentration camps, in order
to find out what the needs of these survivors were and to
report that to General Eisenhower. . . .

I was horrified by what I saw. No one had told us that
there were concentration camps. On one of my first

trips, I went to Dachau, before it was cleaned up. I walked into a large room, and it had a lot of clothing hooks on the wall, and there was a nice polite German sign that said, "Remove your clothes, hang them on the hook, and remember where the hook is so that you can get your clothes afterwards, and then proceed to the showers." Then I went into the supposed shower room, and I see to my horror that it's what I had been told about. It was a gas chamber. I looked at the door through which I had just come—the heavy metal door—and I looked at the inside, and it was covered by scratches from top to bottom. I at once knew what they were. They were made by people. When the gas had been thrown in from the top, they were desperate in their futile attempt to get out, scratching at the door.

From there, I was sent into the next room, where there were three large furnaces, a crematorium. The bodies were carried from the gas chamber and shoveled into these furnaces. At the back of the room there were large sacks that looked like potato sacks. I looked to see what was in them, and I saw that they were still filled with what I'd seen in the bottom of the furnace: human ash. Each sack had been stamped in German on the outside, "Fertilizer." The ash was to be used to fertilize German farms. I rolled up my sleeve and plunged my arm into one of these sacks. I rubbed the ash against the palm of my hand with my fingers so that I should never forget what my eyes had seen there. As you can see, I have never forgotten. . . .

When I came back to the States, I did not know whether I could continue serving as a rabbi. In my own mind, I was wrestling with the idea that of course occurs to any person who believes in God—how could a good God permit this to happen? Fortunately, I was asked to be a fund-raiser, a speaker, by the United Jewish Appeal, which sent me on a six-month speaking tour in 40 states to speak at mass meetings of American Jews to tell them what my eyes had seen and what I had done. When those six months were over, I was asked to go to South Africa to speak to the Jewish communities there for the same purpose. By that time, I had in my own mind resolved my difficulties. I simply said to myself, "If I believe in God I have difficulty. If I don't believe in God, I have more difficulties." . . .

I have no doubt that the war experience affected me as a rabbi. It made me see life whole, with its good and its evil. It made me see how wonderful human beings can be—how heroic, and how evil.

THE ONLY Congressional Medal of Honor awarded to a chaplain went to Father Joseph O'Callahan, a professor at Holy Cross. His nephew, Jay O'Callahan, wrote this narrative about his uncle.

Just before World War II, two professors were arguing at Holy Cross College. One of them was Joseph T. O'Callahan, mathematics professor, and he was saying, "I don't know, I love teaching, but I've got to leave."

"What are you talking about, Joe?"

"I'm talking about the war. I'm talking about Hitler raging over Europe. We're just about to go to war. There are going to be a million kids involved. What am I doing safe in a classroom? If I were a chaplain, I could at least be some kind of help to those kids."

"Come on, Joe. You're thirty-six years old. You've got claustrophobia so bad you can barely stand under an umbrella. You've got high blood pressure and poor eyesight. You're a priest and a professor of mathematics. Let somebody else comfort the kids, Joe. Somebody who could lend a hand in an emergency."

Four years later, you, Lieutenant Commander O'Callahan, are on an aircraft carrier, the USS *Franklin*—Big Ben, they call her. It's seven in the morning March 19th,

1945, you're fifty miles off the coast of Japan. Every eye scans the sky nervously, afraid a Japanese plane is going to break through the air cover and drop a bomb. Just after seven in the morning, a Japanese plane does break through. It flies fifty feet above the deck of the *Franklin* and drops two 500-pound bombs.

One bomb drives through the flight deck. Then it drives through the fo'c'sle deck and finally explodes on the hangar deck. In moments, the hangar deck is one massive flame. Everyone in the hangar deck is dead. One- and two-thousand-pound bombs burned loose from the planes are rolling on the hangar deck, beginning to explode. Bombs and rockets are exploding at the rate of one a minute. Hundreds of thousands of gallons of aviation fuel are creating an inferno. There are hundreds dead already, hundreds more burned and wounded, and through the smoke somebody yells, "Padre! Padre! Flight deck forward."

You, the padre, Joe O'Callahan, make your way through the choking smoke to the forward flight deck. You turn around, and see behind you eight hundred feet of the flight deck, a mountain of fire. The black smoke churns away in a huge dark plume rising to the sky. You turn and see before you one hundred feet of the flight deck still clear of flame. Men are lying, groaning, all over that part of the deck. Even out in the air the stench of burned flesh is terrible. You run over, kneel down and take a sailor's hand.

"Padre, we're dead," he says.

The explosions are so loud it is difficult to hear, but you know what he means. The ship has lost power; it is dead in the water. . . . The *Franklin* is drifting toward Japan. There is fire, smoke, and confusion everywhere. Suddenly, you understand what's so important. Communication has broken down. There's terror everywhere. If a sailor looks for a petty officer for leadership, the petty officer is probably dead or in shock from burns. If a petty officer looks for an officer, the officer is probably trapped below decks or floundering in the water. There is no leadership because nobody recognizes anybody. Not in that smoke, not with faces smeared with it. You, the padre, realize everyone can recognize that white cross on your helmet. So you rush down to the fo'c'sle. There are forty or fifty sailors standing there. Not just in terror. They are in awe. The ship is blowing itself apart.

"Lads, lads! Want to save our happy home?"

They gather 'round you as if you are a magnet. You lead them up to the flight deck and turn those men into firefighting parties. . . .

Now, on the *Franklin*, that March 19th, at 9:52 in the morning, comes the biggest explosion of the whole day. The whole ship is rocked. It's like an angry cat that takes a rat in its jaws and shakes it. One more explosion like that, and the whole ship will go down.

You, the captain, Les Gehres, look down from the bridge, and you see two enclosed gun turrets. There are flames all around those gun turrets. If the shells in those turrets explode, the ship might go down. Down below you see the padre, Joe O'Callahan, with a fire hose, leading a group of sailors right through the flames. The padre gets right to the first gun turret and opens the door.

You, the padre, don't want to step into that gun turret. You have claustrophobia and your flesh crawls at the thought of it. It's dark in there, and you're going to be trapped, but you force your body in. The sailors follow you. You lift up a five-inch 38 shell and hand it to the sailor next to you, who passes it down the line, saying, "Padre, praise the Lord and dump the ammunition."

You, Captain Gehres, turn to your XO, Commander Joe Taylor, and say, "Get a tow on this ship!" It's impossible without power. Impossible. But you're drifting.

You're only forty miles off the coast of Japan. An air battle is going on above you. The Japanese will sink you unless you're towed out of here. So you say, "Get a tow on this ship!"

So you, the XO, run down to the fo'c'sle and manage to get eighty men. The USS *Pittsburgh* comes astern and hands over a cable. The men have got to drag that cable along the fo'c'sle. There's a huge loop on its end, and that loop has to be put around a great hook on the deck, and then the ship can be towed. But eighty men cannot move the cable. That cable is six inches of steel. It's a quarter-mile long. It weighs thirty tons. You'd need a thousand men. Eighty men cannot move it. But they must.

Now imagine you are Frank Frasure, and you're on that cable. You're a steward's mate, second class, and you're a black man. All by yourself you start to sing slowly, "We're gonna take this line, and make a tow. Heave, ho. It's time to get on home." One by one, the other black sailors join in the song, "We're gonna take this line, and make a tow. Heave ho. It's time to get on home. Heave, ho." Now the white sailors begin to sing. There are eighty sailors, young men and some older officers, all on the cable, singing that song of yours, "We're gonna take this line, and make a tow. Heave ho. It's time to get on home. Heave!" You're beginning to move that tow line. It's impossible, but you are beginning to move it.

Now you, Captain Gehres, look down on that flaming, slanting deck. The ship is at a thirteen-degree list. It might capsize. You see a five-hundred-pound bomb slithering along that slippery flaming deck toward a hole. If it goes through the hole, it will explode in the fo'c'sle where those men are moving the tow line. They will die, and the ship will continue to drift. You, Captain Gehres, see six sailors run through the smoke and stop the rolling bomb. They stand the bomb up on end and even from up there you can see the sailors shaking because the bomb is hot and about to explode. Two officers run over, kneel down, and try to defuse the bomb, but can't because they are too nervous. Then you, the captain, watch the padre, Joe O'Callahan, run over to the bomb. He stands right beside it and folds his arms. Everybody calms down. And they defuse the bomb.

April 3rd, the battered USS *Franklin* steams into Pearl Harbor. It's been out just one month. . . . The *Franklin* is in Pearl Harbor only a few days when the Navy says, "Take the *Franklin* to the Brooklyn Navy Ship Yard." And so the battered *Franklin* steams east almost 11,000 miles. . . . On May 17th, 1945, in the Brooklyn Navy Ship Yard, on the flight deck of the *Franklin,* awards are being presented. "Klimkiewiez, Morgan, Frasure . . ."

You, the padre, are standing on the flight deck having to blink a lot. The sun must be awfully bright. You're just a little disappointed for your mother, because she's just come aboard. And you know your name is not going to be called out today. You know your mother is going to say, "Well, I bet Joe did something."

What you, Joe O'Callahan, don't know is that the moment your mother came aboard, Les Gehres, the captain, went over to her and said, "I'm not a religious man. But I watched your son that day and I thought if faith can do this for a man, there must be something to it. Your son is the bravest man I have ever seen."

On January 23, 1946, at the White House, President Harry S. Truman awarded Commander Joseph T. O'Callahan the Congressional Medal of Honor.

ANOTHER RECIPIENT of the Congressional Medal of Honor, Gino Merli, kept the faith after facing death again and again through a long night during the 1st Division's advance on Germany.

The night of September 4th, in Belgium somewhere, our company was ordered to stop the troops that were moving through Belgium and Germany—they were trying to get back to their homeland, the German soldiers were. And in the afternoon about six o'clock our company commander got notice saying that they needed a section of guns to set up a roadblock and 14 men to support it. They loaded up the two jeeps and we began marching towards the objective of the roadblock. We finally reach the town of Sars-la-Bruyère, and that's where [Sergeant] Patinski said, "This is where we set up the roadblock." So everybody got to work and then dug their foxholes, and we were prepared then to hold that roadblock at all costs. As we were digging our emplacement, the neighboring village citizens were coming over to the sergeant since he had the highest rank and telling him there were many, many enemy soldiers along that cobblestone road we came down. This is about 7:30 in the evening. Sergeant Patinski then sent a patrol out in front of the guns to see where the enemy was. They returned half an hour later and reported at least a hundred German soldiers marching down the road. Patinski got the two guns ready for an all-out stand to hold that roadblock.

When we opened fire in the first volley, the enemy soldiers coming down the cobblestone road were like ants. We couldn't believe our eyes when we saw the silhouette of the enemy soldiers—they were ahead [of] us, beside us, inside of us. We were holding the roadblock— by this time there were two of us that were killed, four injured, and many of the remaining had been taken prisoner. We were fighting under the cover of darkness. They came down four times to try to knock us off [the gun emplacement]. The last time they came around four a.m. and found the two lifeless bodies. We . . . my assistant gunner and myself . . . were stationed in our foxholes, the two of us. They turned around and left and said the job was done. No sooner had they turned around did we open fire—we killed them. . . . My assistant gunner was killed at this point. And so I stayed by myself.

Merli was now the only man on the machine gun in the foxhole. He pretended he was dead.

Another group came down later . . . they said something in German, I assume it was that nobody was there. So when they moved on, I opened fire by myself . . . from my foxhole. Later . . . I realized that there was this one German soldier left, out twenty yards in front of the gun emplacement. . . . He was wounded . . . but he knew that I was there. . . . I could hear him moving, calling to his comrades that he was wounded. He was moving and I was moving. We knew the other was there. . . . So from four a.m. to six a.m. he knew I was alive and I knew he was alive. He was watching because . . . there was a bright moonlight that night and you could see an outline of a human being. So he was watching for me . . . watching for my silhouette. . . . He tried to shoot once.

Then his medic came to help him, and he tried to convince his own medic that there was someone still alive at the position. But the medic didn't believe his own soldier, and said "We don't have time to worry about one man in a foxhole." . . . I can vividly remember now every move, every second from eight that evening to nine the next morning. You had to stay alive, stay awake, if you wanted to survive. . . .

Finally, at dawn, Merli's outfit rescued him.

The morning after, they took us to the chow house and there was breakfast. And afterwards I asked Sergeant Patinski if he wouldn't mind if I went and prayed for the dead—our dead and their dead. No matter how bitter you were against the enemy, you still had the heart to pray for him. Because he was in the same boat as you and I . . . We went to the small church nearby and sat down and said some prayers. . . . The sergeant came with me, and one or two others of the squad came with me. We prayed in silence . . . I'd say for a good 15 minutes. I was thinking of my assistant gunner who was killed. . . .

I prayed for the ones that lost their lives that night. But I also prayed for that one wounded soldier who waited and waited to find my silhouette. But that never happened. And thank God it didn't. That's why I went to the church and prayed. I felt that if anybody out there was given a chance to knock me off that gun emplacement, it was that German soldier. . . . I still think about him. . . . Many, many times I've felt that this individual who lived through four o'clock to six o'clock—that he is looking for me, somewhere, somehow. . . . I've always felt that he is out there looking for me. . . .

Rita valdrini morasco of Pittsburgh was part of a personal and spiritual pilgrimage with her husband, Robert, in search of his father, who was killed in combat.

I thought you might be interested in a no less than miraculous event which brought together, after 50 years, a father and son mortally separated by WW II German gunfire. The event evolved from a trip my husband and I made in the mid-'90s to visit my extended family in northern Italy.

50 years ago at that time, on February 4, 1945, my husband's father, Robert Anthony Morasco, was gunned down on La Serra mountain by enemy mortar fire while trying to free the little town of Pianosinatico and the surrounding countryside from German occupation. Robert was a Private, First Class, of the elite infantry group, the 10th Mountain Division of the United States Army.

We had hoped to "know" Robert better by immersing ourselves in history itself. And this would be made possible for us with the assistance of my Italian cousin from Genoa, a Jesuit priest, who could serve as translator for us in our travels.

We arrived in Pianosinatico with my cousin the next day to be greeted by the community elder, who had prepared dinner in her home for us, and this special "someone" by the name of Valerio Petrucci, a quiet, sweet-looking 67-year-old man with a gentle voice. The following is his revelation to us:

Valerio was 17 when his home town of Pianosinatico was finally freed from occupation when the German forces in Italy surrendered to Allied forces on May 2, 1945. And it was late May of that year, as the snows in this mountain tower were finally melting, that Valerio made a life-changing discovery while picking mushrooms in the woods high above his parents' home.

In a small clearing, he found, separated by several hundred yards, the bodies of two individuals who he knew were American soldiers because of the color of their uniforms. The one body had apparently been exposed to the sun for some time because the body was partially decomposed. The soldier had been severely wounded in the head. His spectacles and a bullet-ridden helmet lay nearby.

Several hundred feet from the first soldier, Valerio found the body of the second. This soldier was lying about 10 feet from the edge of a cliff overlooking the town.

This second soldier was lying on his side with his head tilted back and facing upward toward the sky. His mouth was open, and Valerio recalled that the teeth he could see were straight and even. The soldier had been severely wounded in the side and the wound was packed with gauze bandages that were now stained with blood. The soldier had apparently received medical attention for a time following his wounding . . . until he died. This soldier also bore no identification.

But *we* knew his name.

Valerio said that, over the years, he has frequently returned to that clearing to light a cigarette and to ponder his sacred discoveries. He said that for 50 years he has imagined what it would be like to meet the families of those two brave, fallen American soldiers who sacrificed their lives for his people. He wept heavily as he gazed at my husband.

And we did return in September of the following year. We brought with us a bronze ground marker on which was inscribed in Italian, in addition to Robert's name and date of death, "Mortally wounded for the liberation of Pianosinatico." We would place the marker on the exact spot indicated by Valerio.

About 30 townsfolk met us at our hotel in the mountains and walked with us up the mountain. One old soldier had been completely blinded in the war, and his daughter and son-in-law assisted him in his ascent of the mount. We were profoundly touched by his presence. People brought beautiful fresh-cut flowers, the American and Italian flags were carried, and one man in his 60's made the trek with a wooden altar on his back for the celebration of mass at the top. The climb took an hour.

As we rounded the summit and stepped into a small clearing about 50 feet from the edge of the mountain, we looked into the blue heavens beyond, high above the town of Pianosinatico below. Piercing the infinity of that blue sky was a 7-foot wooden cross rising majestically from the precipice . . . a 7-foot cross erected in the previous months by Valerio, his nephew and some local artisans to mark the spot where Valerio had found Robert so many years ago. At the base of the cross was a stone monument with an Italian inscription, "As the sun rises, so it illuminates Your glory." I began to cry. My

husband wept, too, as we stood there holding each
other. It was deeply moving to think that Robert's body,
alone for so long, alone as his wife was giving birth back
home to his child, many a morning greeted the sun as it
rose over that precipice. Yes, his body, alone, greeted the
sun, but his spirit had long been with God.

We return every year to that town, to that mountain.
We all make the journey, together with Valerio, his wife
and son, the priest, soldiers, and many townspeople. Advance notice of our coming is announced in the local
newspaper so that townspeople can plan their schedules
to be with us. We meet at the base of the mountain,
walk together upwards, celebrate mass at the foot of the
cross, talk about the war and what town residents remember or have heard from others about that time in
1945, and afterward, for a day or two, visit with the many
new friends we have made and "family" my husband has
finally found for himself in Italy.

My husband still loves to hear his mom tell of her romance with Robert . . . how handsome and dashing he
was, how intensely patriotic, idealistic and good. He
was the stuff that an heroic tale is made of. But now he
is even better than that. Now, 54 years after Robert lay
dying on foreign soil, 54 years after the birth of the son
of whom he only dreamed and who would bear his full
name, 54 years after the end of that horrible war, U.S.
Army Pfc. Robert Anthony Morasco, I do believe, is
looking down with a father's love and pride on the son
who cared to share with him the final moment of life.

We thank Robert for his sacrifice . . . and we salute
him in love.

V

REUNIONS

Thomas J. Broderick, Joseph P. Wall, Linda Murphy, Margaret Ray Ringenberg, Dorothy Dowling, Peggy Assenzio, James Dowling, John Assenzio, Maureen Caulfield, John "Lefty" Caulfield—guests at the 1999 meeting of the USS Missouri Association

—————————— • ——————————

An American ritual—little known by those who do not participate—is the annual reunion of military units from World
War II. Foot soldiers and sailors, pilots and tank drivers, rear-
echelon outfits and battle-scarred companies are bound together by their common experience during W.W. Two, as they
like to call it.

The reunions are getting smaller now. Some men prefer
not to attend. The memories of war are too painful, or their
new wives don't understand the appeal, or their postwar lives
never measured up to that distinctive time when they were all
together, doing something so dangerous, so adventurous, and
so honorable.

Jack Van Ingen, a retired lieutenant colonel, wrote to tell
me about the reunion of the 457th B-17 Bomb Group in Get-
tysburg, Pennsylvania; R. L. Rimmer was in the Coast Guard,
and his Patrol Frigate Association met in Atlanta in the summer of 1999; the 194th Field Artillery Battalion met in Amana,
Iowa, on Labor Day weekend 1999 to talk over old times. The
V-12 Sailors and Marines of Colorado College, Colorado, an
officer training program, got together in the fall of 1999. Joe
Liberto invited me to a Philadelphia reunion of the 607
Graves Registration Company, the men who had the grim
task of collecting the dead on D-Day beaches and helping to
establish the first permanent American cemeteries in France.
The list goes on and on, through all the branches of the ser-
vice, from the celebrated outfits to the obscure.

I wish that I could attend them all. Instead, I have chosen

a few that are representative of the personal reunions that grew out of *The Greatest Generation*.

Lee Stratton Walter of Perkasie, Pennsylvania, wanted to tell us about her husband's war buddy.

> Trusting that you are not too overcome with stories to hear another, here is one that portrays how the human experience spills over again and again.
>
> You can imagine that the wife of a WWII flier has heard fifty years full of war, and then some. So I was not at all surprised when someone called my husband, George, announcing that he was a WWII buddy. It was August of 1981. I was in the stable saddling up one of my horses, and my husband was up a hill, across the lawn, in the driveway. I went to the door and shouted, "There's someone named Ervie Cloyd on the phone. Says he was in the war with you." My husband returned dryly, "That's not possible. Ervie Cloyd is dead. Shot down over Romania!" Nevertheless, he had dropped everything and taken off, full throttle, for a house phone.
>
> I would soon learn that Cloyd, one of my husband's tent mates in Italy, had come east from Arizona to attend a reunion of the Association of Former Prisoners of War of Romania, in Cherry Hill, New Jersey.
>
> Although my husband had not been a POW, we were invited to attend. The guest of honor was Princess Catherine Caradja of the Romanian Royal Family, who at that time was in her eighties. She had assisted Allied fliers shot down in her country, insisting they were prisoners of Romania, to keep them from being captured and sent to Germany. She had also taken food to those imprisoned in Bucharest.
>
> And the Princess went on to locate scores of former POW's, whom she referred to as "her boys."

Al Feliksa of Saint Ignace, Michigan, writes about his reunion with an RAF pilot whom he helped rescue from the Adriatic Sea in 1945.

Rather than destroying lives in battle, I had the privilege of being part of the 1st Emergency Rescue Squadron, whose task was that of rescuing air crews that were shot down and ejecting over water.

During WWII, our Search and Rescue crew was assigned to the US Army 12th Air Corps, based on a 15th Army Air Corps Field at Falconara, Italy. Our orders came from the British Command. We flew in Navy PBY-5A's (Army number OA-10A). On March 14, 1945, we were patrolling over the northern part of the Adriatic Sea. A radio message informed us that a fighter pilot was shot down off the coast of Venice and gave us the pilot's approximate location. Our on-board radar pinpointed the pilot in the water and the rescue was successful in spite of heavy shore battery cannon fire causing some damage to our aircraft.

He was a Jewish pilot in the South African Air Force and flew with the British Royal Air Force out of Italy. While flying a British Spitfire and strafing and bombing anti-aircraft installations at Madre, a city near Venice, his plane was hit by anti-aircraft fire, but he managed to climb to 5,000 feet before bailing out into the icy cold Adriatic. I often wondered what happened to the downed pilot. I never knew his name . . . but somehow he remembered mine.

THEN—after 53 years, came a voice out of the past. It was a letter from that rescued pilot, Boris Senior. . . . He located me through Jim Thompson and Jim Morrison, founders of the PBY Catalina International Association, of which I am a member.

Boris Senior described his life after his rescue.

After World War II, I went to England to study at London University, but after learning about the murder of six million Jews in the Holocaust (about one third of the entire Jewish population of the world), I felt unable to continue to study and went immediately to Palestine to prepare for the War of Independence in 1948, hoping to ensure the creation of a safe homeland for Jews from anywhere. Together with a small number of volunteers we started the Israel Air Force, flying what was available, at first even dropping bombs we carried in our laps.

In time, we managed to get fighter aircraft, strangely enough Messerschmidt 109's made in Czechoslovakia, which I flew against the Egyptian Spitfires. I went through the entire war plus more years in 1956, 1967, and 1973.

Feliksa concludes:

Boris recently retired as a leader of the present Israeli Air Force. By the sound of his life, he led a significant role in establishing and keeping Israel a solid nation. I told him that I thanked GOD that he survived the war and had an opportunity to live a full and meaningful life.

W HEN HE ATTENDS the reunion of his World War II outfit, Marty Fritz of Northfield, Massachusetts, who has been a farmer for fifty years, can look back on a long life of poverty, hard work, and pride.

I was born May 22nd, 1922, the oldest of 6 children. My dad was working 6 days a week for $17.00. Memories of the depression years are still so vivid in my mind. We lived close to the railroad tracks in the poor section of town. I went to Catholic school taught by the Sisters of Saint Joseph [and that time] has long since blessed me with many fond memories of my formative years.

When I came home from school my mother would make me change my clothes right through to the skin and put on old clothes. We had to save our good clothes for church and school. After which I would take pails and walk the railroad tracks, picking up coal that fell off all the coal cars heading North. I would pick coal until dark. When I came home with the coal, I would find my younger brothers whining, "Mama, I'm hungry." I would ask my mother, "Ma, what's for supper?" She would snap back, "Wind pudding and air sauce." I would then find her crying. I felt so bad.

When I was a freshman in high school, I became acquainted with a farmer who needed help on his farm. He told me he would pay me $15 a month. I talked my folks into letting me go there, thinking my share could go to my brothers and sisters. I had to get up at 4:00 A.M., work in the barn until 6:30, run up the house, change my clothes, have my breakfast, then walk two miles to meet the school bus. After school, the same walk back. I had to work in the barn until 9:00 P.M. Then to the woodshed to split.

On Sundays I walked 7 miles to go to church. When I got paid, I gave my mother $10. With the $5.00 I had left I bought and paid for my own clothes. I worked on that farm for five years. The last 6 months I worked for the farmer, he had no money to pay me. On the night of December 7, 1941, lying on my bed listening to music on the radio, the music stopped. They said, "We interrupt this program to bring you a special news bulletin. The Japanese have bombed Pearl Harbor." I did not even know where Pearl Harbor was. All night I listened to all the reports coming in from all across the Pacific. In view of the fact that I had not been paid in 6 months, and [the farmer] owed me $90, I thought it was time for me to change course. The next day I asked the man I was working for if he would mind if I had the day off. I walked 7 miles to enlist in the U.S. Navy. After 6 weeks at the Naval Training Station in Newport, R.I., I was assigned to the new battleship U.S.S. *Massachusetts,* where I served 4 years.

I will be forever so grateful that I had the honor and

the privilege to serve my beloved country in her hour of need. To this very day I still thank God for helping us win the war, and for the great leaders we had at that time. The admiral, the generals, and all the fine young men, and women, who laid their lives on the line to preserve our precious freedom.

After I returned home from the war I met, and later married, a wonderful lady "like your mother." I was indeed truly so blessed. We were married 50 years last April 24. We have three lovely daughters and two grandchildren. I have been farming for 50 years. With God's help, I am still farming.

I went to my ship's 53rd reunion last June. So many of my wonderful friends and old shipmates now dwell in the house of the Lord forever. As each one takes leave they seem to take a piece of me with them.

ONE REUNION that didn't happen saddens me. It would have involved my late father-in-law, Merritt Auld, a battalion surgeon who died in 1980. Molly Hunter and Krista Markway, the granddaughters of Marcellus Markway of Jefferson City, Missouri, wrote to tell me of Markway's assignment as an ambulance driver for Dr. Auld.

When we were in high school, we were required to interview a World War II veteran for our American History course. Of course, we interviewed our grandpa and it was always a difficult and emotional time for him. He just would not open up about his experiences. So we learned that the war was not a subject to approach Grandpa about. Then your book was published. He received the book as a gift and began reading it (though many of us doubted that he would). Since the day that he began reading it, our grandpa has changed. The book is now dog-eared, placed prominently on the table next to his reclining chair. There are all sorts of markers hanging out of it, including the list of the men that he served with. He even marks up the pages, underlining names and places.

Now when we go to visit him, he talks to us about his experiences. He once told us that his commanding officer or company leader (we are not sure of the title), Dr. Merritt Auld, is one of the finest men he has ever known. That in itself is a tremendous compliment coming from our grandfather, who is a loving Christian and father, a good judge of character and the most talented worker that we have ever seen. Grandpa now tells us stories about the war, shares a scrapbook filled with pictures and all sorts of mementos that have been hidden for years, and has a look of pride in his eyes that we have never seen.

Mary Beth Markway Rieke, the daughter of Mr. Markway, wanted to share a war story involving her father, which later led to a reunion.

One day he was driving his ambulance on the beautiful hillsides of rural Italy. Bombers and machine gunners appeared overhead. He ran for cover in the only place he could find—a church, under the altar stone. Waited there several hours until the bombing and machine-gunning subsided. Felt it safe to radio his captain, Merritt Auld. (He has a small photo of the church and his ambulance, both pierced with hundreds of bullet holes.)

[To Auld he said:] "Sir, I'm stranded. All tires on my ambulance shot out. Need four new tires."

A couple hours later a shining faced private, Freddy St. John, showed up with four new tires.

Recently Mother told me this story: A month ago she was at home in the house that my dad had built for them. There was a knock at the door. An older fellow, it was Mr. Fred St. John, from Georgia. He was looking for my dad, Mark.

I'm sorry, my mom says, he's not here now, he's playing cards with his friends at the bowling alley.

Mr. St. John asks directions and goes to the bowling alley. Walks in. Sees my dad. Says, "Who are you?" to my dad.

My dad, not quite recognizing him, doesn't give his real name, lightly jokes.

Mr. Fred St. John says, "You're Mark."

"What's your name?" says my dad.

"I'm Freddy St. John."

They hadn't seen each other since that day so long ago. Mr. St. John had come to see my dad because as young men 56 years ago they had met when my dad needed four new tires on the war-torn hillside of rural Italy, and a deep, deep bond of human gratitude and glory was formed.

Mary Kay Duckworth, Markway's sister, picked up the narrative in her letter about the 109th Medical Battalion of the 34th Infantry Division.

What really impressed me was his close friendship with his fellow soldiers in a medical company, made up mostly of National Guard members from Iowa. The group of farm boys soon made and have retained lifetime connections. Throughout the war years his letters were a running commentary on the incidental daily happenings, often mentioning by name his good friends. Thus, they became our acquaintances also.

Having experienced the war together, it is a blessing for these men to retain a warm and close relationship today. I experienced this on a trip through Iowa in the fall of 1998 with him and his wife. We had wonderful meals and good visits with his wartime friends in their homes, and at the local cafés. These appointments were set up the night before by telephone as we traveled the highways and byways of Iowa. Usually the men gathered together and perhaps reminisced while the ladies got reacquainted . . . these visits had continued over the years. We "toured" homesites, witnessed their various hobbies and interests, shared family news, important and not-so important news . . . good conversations. I have never met more quality-minded, personable individuals, now in their eighties.

VI

LOVE
STORIES

The last family photograph of Helen, Sandra, and John Chichilla, 1944.

George A. Yates, U.S. Navy, with his bride-to-be, Juanita Greenwell.

Mr. and Mrs. Joe DeMaggio, November 11, 1945.

In researching *The Greatest Generation*, I quickly discovered that almost every war story had a love story connected with it. That led to a chapter called "Love, Marriage, and Commitment."

The chapter, in turn, elicited more love stories from the men and women of that generation. It does seem that the common struggles, the risks, the long separations at an early age, the relief of survival did forge some uncommonly strong marriages. Those couples look back on their lives together and count the durability of their union and the family it produced as their greatest achievement.

To be sure, there were failures. Passions born of youth, war, and the prospect of early death led to whirlwind romances and quickie marriages before a man was shipped overseas. But once the war was over, it was sometimes difficult to reignite those fires. Some men returned from war hardened, troubled, abusive, unable to stay in a loving relationship or fit in to a life with softer edges. Marriage counseling and other forms of psychological help were not widely available in the immediate postwar years.

So it is all the more a wonder that many marriages did endure, did flourish, especially when so many of them were embarked upon when the couples were of tender age, with little or no experience in the grown-up world they were expected to inhabit.

After a long lifetime together their love affair has come full circle. As they were once giddy with anticipation about their common future, now they have the quiet satisfaction of a promise kept.

JUANITA YATES of Monroe City, Missouri, lived happily with her husband's other love: his time in the U.S. Navy.

> My husband, George A. Yates, Petty Officer First Class (cook), was in the Navy four and one-half years and spent three and one-half years on the destroyer USS *Badger 126*, most of it in the North Atlantic protecting supply ships headed for the Allied troops. He died September 18, 1997. I lived with the love of his life, the U.S. Navy, as my only competitor for his affections for 52 years. The 11 children, 36 grandchildren, and four great-grandchildren were raised to "swab the deck, fore and aft, bulkhead to bulkhead," and we always ate in the galley rather than the kitchen. Sound familiar? They knew his stories by heart and he was always ready for another telling.
>
> George died of congestive heart failure and was on a heart pump, but we were privileged to care for him at home the last six months of his life. A farmer and sales-man of farm machinery, he literally worked the day he died, from his bed. A man called that morning with something wrong with his machine and George told him how to fix it over the phone. So weak he could hardly talk, he handed the phone to me and said, "I knew I could still do it." A few hours later he was dead.
>
> What a privilege we had. Constantly surrounded by family, he would tell his Navy stories to yet the third generation on any occasion. At 4 a.m. the family was still there when he breathed his last. We got to say our goodbyes, listen to his advice whether we wanted to or not, and hear him say how much he loved all of us. It was easier then than in his early years when he worked so hard and the emotion was buried so deep. He was a deeply religious man, grateful to his God that his life

had been spared. Those last eight hours were full of prayer, tears and a lot of laughter. Oh, how he loved to laugh!

You, George, and they truly were the greatest generation.

SOME WIVES still marvel at the ability of their combat veteran husbands to see everything in life after the war as a dividend. One of those wives is Dorothy A. Talbott of Golden, Colorado.

My husband and I have both read your book, and found it very interesting and heart warming. It did take us back a few years!

My husband, John, is almost 76 years old, was a "Depression kid" who went to New Mexico Military Institute in the thirties (courtesy of a great-uncle), then to OCS, and on to the Tenth Mountain Division at Camp Hale, Colorado. He got there because he had worked with horses at NMMI, so was sent to Camp Hale as a "mule officer" only to discover that they'd done away with mules some time before! So, they put him in a line company, because he'd written on his info sheet that one of his hobbies was skiing, even though he'd only been once! He was transferred out (before the Tenth went overseas) as a replacement officer in the Massachusetts National Guard, and eventually to the Battle of the Bulge in Europe. He was wounded (his helmet saved his life from a hand grenade), and after recovering in England was with the occupation forces, and spent some time in Munich as a censor for a German newspaper (he'd learned German at NMMI).

I am 70 years old, was also a "Depression kid," whose banker father had lost everything in the crash. I, however, was in high school during the war, and graduated in 1946, and am appalled now at how unaware I was while the war was going on. We didn't have TV then, of course, and I suppose I was a typical teenager—not terribly interested in much beyond my own small world. . . .

The real purpose of this letter is to tell you that until I read your book (reinforced the other night by your interview), I never really understood the impact that the war must have had on my husband. I'm sure that his experiences in military school and the army molded his character like nothing else. And it explains why he has conducted himself with such courage battling a neuromuscular disease for the last forty-two years. He was diagnosed with a form of muscular dystrophy, called spinal muscular atrophy, when he was 34. It was very slow progressing, and he even skied until he was in his fifties. However, he's been quite disabled for the last ten years or so, and can do very little for himself. He was a stockbroker when diagnosed—thank goodness—because he didn't have to change occupations. He's just made his living on the telephone all these years, and is STILL working (although finally has decided to retire the end of the year). He's truly an inspiration to all who know him, because he's always cheerful, never complains, and only occasionally gets angry at something he can't do (but only I overhear that!). So, this has been truly the biggest battle of his life, and he has managed it remarkably well, with great dignity and grace. I think that his war experiences really pale in comparison, because this has gone on so long.

Joe demaggio of Albuquerque, New Mexico, described how he and his wife, Anne, were married and included a poem one of their children wrote for their fiftieth wedding anniversary.

On December 7, 1941, my girl friend and I had gone to the movies for her birthday and [were] faced with the truth when the picture was stopped, the lights went on and the theatre manager announced that all military personnel had been ordered to their commands immediately. When we came out of the theatre the newspaper boys were telling the story of the Japanese attack on Pearl Harbor. We had been dating for about a year and a half and looking forward to a married life together. However, I was expecting to be drafted and decided that I would not put my wife at the risk of becoming a widow. We [remained] engaged and two months later, February 6, 1942, I reported to the Induction Center and [was] sent to Camp Upton, Long Island, N.Y., and then on to Fort McClellan, Alabama, for basic infantry training. . .

.

When the war ended in Europe, our battalion was in the vicinity of Kassel awaiting the possibility of going home after thirty-nine months of overseas duty. Instead, our Battalion Commander informed us that our next move would be to the Pacific. I immediately wrote to my fiancee and told her not to wait for my return because I didn't expect to survive such a mission. Thanks to the A bomb our battalion was ordered to the coast of France for demobilization. I was discharged on October 11th and Anne and I were married on November 11th, Armistice Day.

We have been married for 53 years and have been blessed with two children and three grandchildren of whom we are very proud. On our 50th Anniversary, which was attended by about 75 people, including family and friends from many parts of the country, we were presented with the enclosed "Now We Are One," written by our son, Paul, and I was asked to read it aloud for everyone to hear. I was doing fine until the last paragraph when the lump in my throat was choking me.

Their Parents Came from Foreign Lands,
In Search of "the Dream."

They were to work at the early age,
But also to learn and be the best they could.
Their Papas and Mamas taught them to be as One.

They Played With Cans, Sticks, Rocks,
whatever imagination could fabricate for fun.
They met at work and enjoyed friendship, while
earning their way as their parents had done.

The War Disrupted Their Fun With Duty,
Honor and Love of Country.
One of them would fight the war on foreign soil,
put his life on the line for a future.
One would work in the factories at home
and pray for him to return there.

They Were Apart, But Now They Were One.

Fifty Years of Their Life Together
with all of its meaning,
Bring us here to celebrate how Two became One.

Learn Life's Lesson, Never Forget,
How You Came to This Time & Place;
You Are Who You Are,
Because They Are One.

WORLD WAR II may have been the last great age of the love letter. Love letters have been written since, but never on such a scale. Mail call for those in uniform and the daily postal delivery for those at home were cherished rituals of life. Those letters brought news of family, neighborhood gossip, confessions of loneliness and fear, expressions of sympathy from commanding officers for families whose young men were wounded or dead—the full spectrum of human emotion, but most of all, love.

Patricia Matthews Dorph of Staten Island, New York, shared letters exchanged by her parents during the war:

Both my parents grew up on Staten Island, just a few doors from one another. They attended the same grammar and high schools. When my father started Columbia University in 1935, my mother got a job in Manhattan. Not until senior year in Columbia did my father start his courtship with my mother. In 1939 my father started Columbia Law School. Probably one of the most magical days was August 23, 1941, when they were married. They lived near Columbia for almost a year until my father graduated from law school. Then the draft took him away to boot camp in July 1942. Officers Training School followed, where they lived together in Georgia for a few months. My father was sent overseas in July 1943—first to Iceland, then England, then, about a month after D-Day, he went to France. Some time was spent in Belgium and Germany. He was an officer assigned to Eisenhower's Communications Division.

My parents wrote almost every day. They not only wrote what was happening in their personal lives but their hopes, dreams, fears and most profoundly their love and dedication to one another. . . .

My father died at a young age in 1962. My mother raised the three of us always looking on the best side of life and instilling in us honesty, compassion and to live life to the fullest. No one could ever understand why my mother never dated or remarried. She had a lot to offer someone. It was not until I read all the hundreds of letters that they wrote to each other during the war that I realized that my father was my mother's one true love. No one could ever take his place.

Roger Matthews's nickname for his wife Sophie was Joe. This is a letter he wrote in August 1944.

Dear Joe,

I have shown your very fancy salutation to the proper people and they are impressed; must be convinced that you love me more than their gals love them. And incidentally, I know that they know that much as they might like some female, they can't even get near the way I feel about you. They should, anyway, because I mention it often enough. I suppose that my attitude may become boring to them at times but I have to tell someone about it, don't I? I have just heard a very familiar cry . . . a chorus by my friends who have just walked into the office . . . it is "Deeeearrrrrr Sophie!" That happens every time they see me at the typewriter. . . .

So you want to know what nights I go riding in the jeep? If I could count on meeting you, I would make it any night or any day. I would even *walk!* One year's being alone, when it hits you all at once, hurts a little, doesn't it. Aww, why feel sad; I'm going down and take a look at your picture. As long as I have you, nothing can be really wrong.

All my love,
Roger

At home, Sophie was volunteering to wrap bandages for the Red Cross, a vital chore that went on everywhere in America. Here is a letter she wrote Roger in August 1944.

My darling Roger. I'm very tired. It's 11:30 but I could not go to sleep without telling you how many dressings we made tonight. We broke all records. 3094 dressings for 21 workers in 3 hours—that's impossible but we did it. I'm a slave driver—you know me. . . .

Roger dear, the R.C. ladies all approve of your pictures. I'm getting such pleasure out of them dear. You sure minded all my instructions. I could just see you saying "Sophie wants me to smile and look pleasant"— You are an angel to do me such a favor. Good night my darling one. I love you so very much dear. Kiss me— your own dear,

Sophie

Here is a letter from Roger to Sophie, dated early August 1944.

Dear Sophie,

This is one letter you probably won't get for a long time—so now that you finally have it, I hope it lives up to your expectations.

At the moment I'm relaxing on a bunk with two more bunks over my head. Urg is in one, Willie in the other. Altogether there are 9 1st Lts. in this one stateroom. But we are getting along pretty well.

Maybe you've already guessed where I am. Correct— on a boat. Name, capacity, location, etc. all military secrets. I think I can say it's not moving.

But censorship doesn't affect my saying that I love you, does it? That's no military secret; in fact it's no secret at all. I keep loving you more and more, and now I'm really beginning to miss you.

Sophie to Roger, August 3, 1944:

My darling Roger—Today my joy at receiving two letters from you—my first since last Sat.—was rather dimmed by a very sad letter from Karolyn. Roger dear, Bill is missing in action since June 23rd. It was such a shock to me. He only went into action on June 17th. She said that there was a possibility of his being a prisoner because where he and his men were there was no identification of any kind at all found. I'm so sorry for her. She said though that Patsy was such a blessing now. I can well imagine. Needless to say, I wept some very wet tears. Maybe I'll get another letter soon giving me more information. Well dear, the pictures of you are enough to make even me happy. Such a lovely nice smile—the sun gleaming in your eyes. What do you mean by saying that you are funny looking. You are the handsomest feller in this whole army snooks.

Hey snooks—what are you practicing shooting for. Don't you know that I don't like such goings on? Guns are too dangerous and I don't want you to get too familiar with them. My angel, I think that you have gained some weight—don't you? You look swell to me and I wish I could just hug you to pieces.

Roger to Sophie, August 13, 1944:

I have some letters of yours but the most important item in today's delivery was the anniversary card. A very nice looking one, of course, but the big thing was that it came. I will feel ashamed when you get the one I am sending to you; we can't get very fancy ones over here but I know that you will understand. It *is* the idea that counts, isn't it? I also have yours of the 2nd and 3rd of July. That was terrible news about Bill Quinlan and Karolyn must feel just [awful] about the loss, not knowing what to do. That's the worst thing about it; there is nothing that she can do but wait and hope that some good news will come out of it. I hope that's what happens. . . .

The worst part of war and being in it is not what may happen to you individually but what the effect will be on those that mean something to you. I realize more than ever now how much I love you and how much I want you to be happy. . . .

Art is now putting the pressure on me to get done with this and hand over the typewriter to him so that he can get to work on a letter to his wife. I told him that he has to wait so now he has gone outside and stolen another machine from somewhere. See how tenacious I am when I'm writing to you? Must be love.

Love
Kisses
All kinds of stuff
Roger

Roger to Sophie, August 26, 1944:

Dear Sophie,

OK! Don't go hitting me on the head! This will have to represent the letters for the 24th and 25th too. First of all, I am not where I used to be but I'm still not sure where I'm going. But since I won't be able to mail this anyway until we land, it's OK to say that it will be some-place in France. Now don't you start chewing on your nails! Of course, I don't actually know anything.

I've seen my first proof of how well the Allies have this sector of the world under control. It's amazing to see the number of ships, plying back and forth, just like a busy highway back home. It looks as though England ought to be emptied soon if it keeps up.

Remember what I said earlier—no worrying. I hon-estly can say that. And I love you very much and miss you even more.

All my love,
Roger

Roger to Sophie, August 31, 1944:

Dear Sophie,

As you can see we have finally got our various cases open and the typewriters are available again. Art is here with me busy on a letter to his wife, with a French phrase book open before him. He wants to make her think that he is picking up the language rapidly. . . . That's the one out of which the *Stars and Stripes* picked the phrase "My wife doesn't understand me," for use of soldiers going to France, and got itself in a lot of trouble with many soldiers' wives! (You don't have to worry about that with me. The gals are around here are even less interesting than those who were in England.)

Good night, Joe
All my love,
Roger

Sophie to Roger, September 19, 1944:

Do you miss me today? I sure miss you. I've had an "experience" today. I think that I really hit bottom this morning. My nerves were all shot to pieces and I was shaking like a leaf. When Gussie called to say that there was a letter from you I was completely cured. What do you think it is snooks—love? I am getting pretty certain of the fact that I love you so much. Of course the news about Kent's death last night upset me quite a bit. I still don't realize it—even though I can say it.

Roger to Sophie, September 22, 1944:

Dear Sophie,

The letters are still arriving all out of order. The latest batch that I have to report are those of the following dates: August 26th, 29th, 30th, and 31st. And for all of them my sincerest thank-yous. Letters from you are the nicest things that I can get in France or England or any place else that you might think of. Just as soon as I get all of them gathered together from out of my various shirt pockets and field jackets I am going to line them up in order and read them all over again just to get a clear picture of what you really were doing the last few weeks of August. . . .

I had about ten minutes' worth of business out around Versailles today so Rose and I went out, took care of the business and then took in the Chateau or whatever it should be called. Gosh, Hon, how I wish you could be here to get to places like that with me!

Sophie to Roger, June 19, 1945:

Roger dear—

How's my favorite friend this fine day! I've thought it all over very carefully and just decided that I like you more than anyone else in the whole wide world and want you home soon. Gets lonesome without you! . . .

Today is the day that NYC is welcoming Eisenhower. If it had been a regular parade I'd have gone but it was only a motorcade—zip, and it's over. Give me the old fashioned kind of a parade where the bigshot sits on the steps of St. Patrick's and watches the show go by.

Georgie's Purple Heart medal reached home today. A pretty fancy looking hunk of stuff. He'll be a fancy looking fancy when he gets home don't you think. I'll bet 5 cents he did not find you. Made a sort of a rush trip through Europe—don't you think?

On Friday, darling, it will be 3 years that you are in [the] U.S. Army. That was your induction date—remember? Also 3 years out of Law School—3 years on the 29th that you were admitted to the Bar—such a world. Gussie and Jack are married 4 years on Thursday. Does it seem real to you that we will be married 4 years by the end of summer? . . .

Our little Susan is rapidly becoming a Big Susan. We are going to weigh her again tonight. She's a doll and I love her. At first they sleep about 23 hours of the day but now she's awake for a few hours at a time and just lies still—no weeping—no nothing—just kicking and eating. . . .

I'll say, so long for a while my pet. You are my most favorite darling pet and I wish you were here because I'd like very much to neck with you.

Your own dear
Joe

Roger to Sophie, June 26, 1945:

SUBJECT: Report of Mission to PARIS, FRANCE
TO: COMMANDING OFFICER, 24 Dudley Ave. Detachment, Matthews Family, APO 1, Sunnyside, S.I.
THROUGH: The same old channels.

In that letter, Roger described in great detail his trip into Paris and included a hand-drawn map (opposite).

Roger and Sophie—Joe—did find their way back into each other's arms after the war and, as their daughter says, their romance continued.

Not all of the love letters home had a happy ending. Sandra Eve MacDuffee's father, John Chichilla, was killed in 1945. His letters from the Christmas season of 1944 have a special poignancy.

> My dad was killed two days before my second birthday in 1945, so I have no memories of him, which to me is the saddest part of it all. I have a lot of pictures, thanks to my mom's diligence and she and I talked about him a lot as I got older. My dad is buried in a military cemetery in Luxembourg and when I was sixteen, my mom ordered an aerial photo of the cemetery with his cross circled in pencil. We also got a close-up snapshot of his cross that enables us to read his name and outfit. The day that picture arrived was a day of many tears for both Mom and me, and of an overwhelming sense of loss. . . .
>
> I miss him more and more as I get older, not ever having known him and wondering what my life would be like today if he had come home safe.
>
> My mom remarried, but she never stopped loving my dad and she never stopped grieving for him. Mom also had a "Lost Love Remembered" scrapbook full of newspaper clippings, cards from dad and photos of the two of them and me.

Nov. 15, 1944

Hello Darling,

Here I am sitting in a cellar safe as can be writing under a candle light. I love you, I adore you, my sweet Darling. Darling, Joe & I got split up yesterday, and to-

day the fellow from New York & I got split up. So now I have two new pals—one from Idaho & one from Ohio, they are a lot of fun. . . . I love you darling wife, I adore you my sweet. A million hugs & kisses may God bless you & Sandra, I sure do miss you both my two sweet Darlings.

I love you, I love you, your loving husband,

Johnny

Nov. 27, 1944

Hello my little Sandra,

Sandra, how are you & Mother? Are you both well & pretty as you both were when I was home? I hope you are, because when I come home I am going to kiss the daylights out of you both. So, Sandra, be a good girl to Mother & hurry up & learn to help Mother with the housework. I have a little toy dog I am going to send to you for a Christmas present. If I was home I would get a live dog for you. So you will have to wait until I come home. Sandra, give Mother a big kiss for me—also tell her that Daddy loves her with all of [his] heart. So long, my little daughter. Keep Mother happy for me. A million hugs & kisses to you and Mother & may God bless you both.

Your
Daddy

Dec. 28, 1944

Hello Darling,

. . . My Sweet Darling, I trust that you had a wonderful Christmas without me. As for me we spent Christmas eve & Christmas day in a fox hole. There [were] a lot of pine trees covered with snow surrounding us. At one thirty Christmas eve I was thinking of the last Christmas when I went to the Midnight services & came home & found you listening to the radio. You had the services from St. Patrick's Cathedral in New York. I sat down & we both listened to it. After the service was over we listened to Bing Crosby sing Christmas carols. Christmas day I got out of my fox hole & sang a carol & went from one hole to another & wished the boys a Merry Christmas. So today we are going to have our Christmas dinner. . . .

My Sweet Darling wife, please don't worry about me because I am well & safe. But I need a shave & I am very dirty. So today I am going to clean up & it will be a relief to be clean again for a while. . . .

Darling, I love you so. All I ever dream & think of is the day that I come home & live peaceful again. So until then a million hugs, & kisses to you & Sandra. May God bless you both.

Your loving husband
Johnny

VII

APPRECIATION

Martha Barnett, president of the American Bar Association, 2000–2001, and Chesterfield Smith, president of the American Bar Association, 1973–1979

Terry Supple and the Gaynor Army

When I shared some of these stories with a friend, he was moved and then, after a moment, he commented on the nature of the world in which we live: "You hear something like that and you resolve to keep it in your mind forever, but twenty minutes later you're wondering what's for lunch." It was a thoughtful and perceptive comment on the pace of modern life and the selfish agendas that preoccupy too many of us.

Nonetheless, the stories in *The Greatest Generation* did strike a chord with many readers. Their response was uncomplicated and heartfelt. Both members of that generation and those who came later seemed grateful for the opportunity to say thank you, without apology or condition. Those expressions of appreciation came in a variety of forms and across generational lines.

Harold W. Duket of Nashotah, Wisconsin, wrote about how he felt after being thanked by a Vietnam veteran at a recent Memorial Day parade.

> I am 76 years old, a veteran of the European Theatre of Operations and went in to Omaha Beach on the 14th of July, 1944 when the Germans were just six miles inland.
>
> This past week ago Monday my wife and I attended the Memorial Day services at a small town in Wisconsin. As was my custom I wore my Eisenhower jacket (which I can get on but can't button) with my T5 rating on the sleeve along with 4 gold stripes for two years

overseas and the few ribbons I picked up along the way and my overseas cap. I stood at the right times and saluted at the right times. As we got up to leave an army officer from the Vietnam conflict who had been on the band shell as one of the speakers came up to me and said: "I saw you in your uniform and I just wanted to say thank you."

It was later on that day when I realized he hadn't said "Thank you for coming to the ceremonies" or "Thank you for being here." He just said, "Thank you."

As I approach the 55th anniversary of my going ashore in France, I must say that this is the first time anyone ever said thank you for what we assumed was just our duty and obligation.

Douglas Barker of Groton, Massachusetts, wrote about his admiration for his father, William Barker, an Army lieutenant decorated for his service in Italy:

My father had a hankering to become part of the United States Army at a young age. He quickly enlisted the help of his parents in enrolling him at Valley Forge Military Academy. He graduated from the academy as a 2nd Lieutenant in the U.S. Army Infantry and left for North Africa and Italy in 1944.

My father had a knack for leading as well as staying alive. Throughout his campaigns he led his "E" Company valiantly through battles in North Africa and up into Italy. He was lucky in the respect that he had a company full of good men and a guardian above looking after him and most of his troops. . . .

During this Italian campaign he was awarded the Distinguished Service Cross for extraordinary heroism in action at the first battle of Cassino. He was later awarded the Bronze Star, the Purple Heart (with four clusters) and two invasion arrowheads. He was also awarded the Military Cross of Valour and the Bronze Medal for Valour by the Italian government.

The fifth time my father was wounded was somewhat of an end to his active military career. A barrage of incoming artillery shells turned out to be friendly fire that had missed its mark. While [he was] surveying the combat scene a shell dropped in front of him within ten yards' distance. He instinctively covered his face behind his arm as he heard the shell come in and explode. A large shell fragment ripped through his forearm and ricocheted off his helmet. Fortunately, after years and rounds of surgery he was able to recover 80% usage of his arm. . . .

I have enclosed, as well, a picture of my father as he returned from his tour of duty back in 1945. His left arm is in a cast from his shoulder to his wrist, his right leg in a steel brace due to bone and skin grafts. . . .

I am still to this day amazed and honored that the man in this picture (Captain William R. Barker, "E" Company, 2nd Battalion, 141st Infantry, 36th Texas Infantry Division), at 19 years of age, volunteered and went to war, fought for our country and returned home to build a successful business career; all in what amounted to be little more than just a fraction of his lifetime. Truly great accomplishments in my book.

AN UNANTICIPATED BENEFIT of World War II was the lasting effect of military training and discipline on millions of young people who returned home to the challenges of civilian life. Philip L. Cochran of Maple City, Michigan, was a Marine then and, like all Marines, remains one to this day.

As I initially reflect on my experiences in the Marine Corps during World War II, as I have so often during the past half century, I am still overwhelmed with a tremendous sense of gratitude . . . gratitude first of all that I returned home in 1946 sound in mind and body, returning a vastly different young man than the one who had left in the Fall of 1941, a much, much better person in so many ways . . . gratitude for the opportunity to be a

United States Marine, a pride inculcated in all Marines from day one of their service, in my case from the moment I arrived in Quantico, Virginia in the Fall of 1941 for their Officers Training Program, a pride that will never leave me . . . once a Marine, always a Marine.

I do not recall many negatives . . . certainly great sadness over the loss of many comrades and good friends . . . Frank Shafer from Hinsdale, Illinois, Reid Woodward from Leroy, New York, Bob Cassels from Clarendon Hills, Illinois, Kenneth MacLeod from California, and when my closest friend and fellow Marine officer, Harry Edwards, who was like a brother to me, was killed on Saipan, I wept openly and copiously. I was deeply saddened, also, that I couldn't be home to see my Dad before he died and to help Mom with her grief. . . .

Before the war, as the third boy in a family of three boys and three girls, puny and underweight, with two athletically talented older brothers, I had a strong inferiority complex. Indeed, one of my motivations in trying to join the Marine Corps, "the rough and tough foot soldiers," was to prove to my Dad that I was as good as my older brothers. Becoming a Marine, graduating tenth in my class at Quantico out of 320, serving the Corps honorably and retiring as a Major gave me a high sense of self-worth . . . not an ego trip, but just feeling good about myself, a feeling that has never left me. Without question, this sense of self-worth, which the Marine Corps gave me, has been a source of strength and well-being through my life. (Incidentally, Dad, indeed, became very proud of me. On one occasion, as Mom and Dad were entertaining at an open house in our home one Christmas Eve, as was their custom, Dad, having been slightly over-served with Tom and Jerry's, a popular Christmas season alcoholic beverage at the time, announced to the assembled guests that I had just been promoted to First Lieutenant and was in charge of all the Marines in the South Pacific!!)

During my service years, I had developed significant organizational skills, both as a staff officer in our battalion and, after returning from the South Pacific theater, on the staff of the Commandant of the Marine Corps in Washington, D.C. This experience had a substantial effect on my career after the war. Returning to my pre-war position as a salesman for a large insurance agency in Chicago, I missed being part of an organizational management and resigned as a salesman. Our chairman, Wade Fetzer, a great and wise man, refused to accept my resignation and instead offered me a job as director of recruiting and training. I became a member of his staff, and eventually became chairman and CEO of the firm, the largest private insurance agency in the Midwest, as well as a director of three New York Stock Exchange companies. . . .

I returned to civilian life in 1946 with a feeling of great debt for having been spared injury or disabling illness, with a resulting heavy sense of obligation to my family, my community and my country. Without question, this sense of obligation motivated me significantly in striving to repay the debt I believed I owed. As a consequence, I have had a lifetime of devotion to community service, in my home town, Hinsdale, Illinois, in Chicago, and, after I retired, in Glen Arbor and Traverse City, Michigan.

With all these positive impacts on my life since the war, not for an instant could I think that my service in World War II represented a sacrifice. To the contrary, my life gained so much from those experiences. I returned way ahead of the game, and I'm still ahead. I owe so much to my experiences during the war and to the United States Marine Corps.

WILLIAM "BUD" ANTHONY of Muldrow, Oklahoma, was a child of the Depression whose life was changed by military service.

I too, have buried my memories of my life in the 40's. First, poverty, we had a dirt floor in our one room house. A man, woman and eight children. I was the oldest, and when I turned 17 years old, I enlisted in the Army. This was the first time I had more than one pair of shoes and more than two pairs of pants. I remember telling the supply sergeant, "What am I to do with all of these clothes?" He replied, "Keep moving, soldier." That was the first time anyone had called me soldier. I still think about how I swelled up with pride.

At that early age in our lives, we trusted everyone, and anyone older was "Mr. or Mrs." Respect was coveted and demanded. Trust was a part of our lives. If we were asked if we did something, we never thought of denying it. Good moral character was the only way we knew. . . .

I didn't realize we were poor until I went into the service. . . .

I know in my heart that if we hadn't gone to war, I would not have been successful at anything. President Truman saved my life. We were scheduled to go in Tokyo Bay on the 2nd wave. I feel to this day, if he hadn't dropped the bomb . . . I would have perished. Yes, I saw Hiroshima, but at that time in my life, I didn't realize what I was looking at. It just looked like nothing had been there for a thousand years. Only cement rubble and devastation. Yes, it killed thousands, but on the other side, we killed thousands and saved a lot more Americans and Japanese than the bomb killed.

I am starting to remember things I don't want to, so I will close my letter.

JOE COPPOLA of Paramus, New Jersey, was a youngster when war broke out.

I was almost 12 when Japan attacked Pearl Harbor, and my memory of that whole era is very vivid. Three of my older cousins who lived across the street joined up, as did all the other young guys in the neighborhood. I never doubted their ability to win the war because I knew no one could defeat the American soldier.

The years right after the end of the war are also quite vivid. It was difficult to walk down our main shopping avenue because of all the baby carriages. I can still see the embarrassed look on some returning veteran as he is given a spontaneous hug by an eight-months-pregnant ex-classmate. . . .

In 1980 we helped close the Westinghouse Elevator plant in Jersey City by conducting an outplacement program for their last 220 employees. Many of the men involved were World War II veterans who were employed as machinists, electrical technicians and maintenance people. They could do anything with their hands, and several had unusual hobbies. One had played the piano at Carnegie Hall, another made artistic wall creations from sheet copper, one was an artist and another owned and raced horses. I commented at the time that if I were ever marooned on an island I would like it to be with these men because they could build a city. The greatest generation was also the most capable generation. They could and did do it all.

LINDA MATTHEWS of Doylestown, Pennsylvania, learned lessons of life and death as a result of her father's experiences as a Marine sergeant.

My father [Walter Ciesielka] was a Marine in the Pacific Campaign and through the years, prompted by his reminiscences, I have striven to learn as much as possible about the Pacific and European Campaigns. To discuss this with my peers, however, has been a disappointment for me as I have found that many in my generation have a general sense of apathy regarding this period of history and the experiences of their parents. . . .

As for my father, he passed away ten years ago. The doctors told him that he had inoperable lung cancer with six months to live. He never discussed his illness, nor did he complain about his pain. He worked at his electrical business until two months before his death, which was three years after they told him he had six months to live.

I will always remember his strength and the one thing he told me before his death. He was in the second wave at Iwo Jima; mortar shells were hitting his unit and he jumped into a trench with four other Marines. A shell hit the trench and he was the only one to walk out alive. The way he viewed it, he could not complain about his impending death as he was given forty-five years he should not have had. . . .

I am sure there are many such stories of the common soldier who did not make it into politics, take advantage of the G.I. Bill or start major lucrative businesses. My father was a product of the depression, with both parents deceased before he was fourteen and with only a ninth grade education. His major contributions in life were to marry at eighteen, participate in a war, have two children, [and] become a policeman and later an electrician. Above all, he loved and provided for his family. If there is a sequel to your book you might want to consider dealing with the common soldier or "grunt" who did not end up with wealth or fame but was just absorbed back into the population making the best of what life doled out.

AMERICA, A NATION OF IMMIGRANTS, had in its military force young men not long removed from the countries they were now expected to fight. Carole Lalli of New York City wrote about her uncle, Armand Casini, an Italian-American, and his friends.

They were architecture students at Cooper Union, and the friendship, along with many others from Cooper, was life-long. Uncle Armand served in Italy, in the Apennines, and his hand-drawn maps were used by the 10th Mountain Division. . . .

Armand always said that he and his friends, who were terrific skiers, joined the 10th Mountain Division so that they could enjoy the sport. I think they actually were dropped from planes on skis into the mountains, but Armand never talked about any heroic adventures.

The other thing that always has struck me about the war is that so many first-generation Americans were sent back to the countries from which their parents had emigrated. This too seems to have been taken in stride, which I deeply suspect would be very different for our more self-involved generation. I have a letter that Armand sent to my grandmother when he was stationed in Rome, updating her on various family members still living there; the letter has the casual tone of someone on vacation. . . .

Following the war, Armand had a marvelous career with Skidmore Owings and Merrill; he was design chief on projects around the world before he joined the San Francisco office. Years later, he was about to become a partner when everyone realized that, because he had volunteered in the middle of his final year at Cooper Union, he did not have a degree. So, at the height of his career, he spent a semester at Berkeley, which he enjoyed enormously—no whining.

HENRY KISSINGER was one of thousands of European Jews who came to this country to escape Hitler's extermination campaign. Kissinger returned to Germany during the war as a uniformed member of the U.S. Army.

Herbert Owens of New York City escaped from Vienna in

1938. Austria had been annexed by Hitler, and Herbert's father had already spent a year in a concentration camp. Owens writes about the struggle to survive that refugees faced in New York, and the euphoria he felt on returning to Austria in 1943 as an American soldier and citizen. He told me he considers this his greatest achievement.

I was born in Vienna, Austria, in June 1924. My father was the third-generation owner of a Drugstore in the center of town. My mother died when I was 8. I attended public school from age 6 to age 10, then entered high school, learning Latin and English.

In March 1938 Hitler annexed Austria, the "Anschluss." The route into town was down our street. I was then not quite 14. In May 1938 most of the Jewish Men were arrested, my father included, and sent to Dachau Concentration Camp. I lined up at Gestapo headquarters and was told that Hitler wanted all Jews to leave Austria and as soon as we found a place to go to, my father would be released.

There were few options. Very few countries opened their doors. Entry to the United States was by a quota system, so I registered for a number. A sponsor was needed. Two cousins who themselves had just emigrated to the United States based on an employment contract sent us the required "Affidavit of Support" in December 1938.

Permission to leave Austria could be obtained only by leaving all possessions behind. This meant dealing with financial matters about which I had very little knowledge. Fortunately a good friend of my father who was not Jewish helped me, and sometime around my 15th Birthday the exit papers were complete.

Providence shone on us when shortly thereafter I was notified by the American Consulate that our quota number had been reached, the "affidavit" [had been] accepted and a visa would be issued, subject only to a physical.

When I presented this to the Gestapo, they did approve my father's release, after he was imprisoned more than a year, with the proviso that we would leave within 60 days.

We almost didn't make it out of Vienna. On September 3, [1939,] World War II started, our passage was booked from Trieste, Italy, to New York for early November. We managed to hide out and finally left in time to get the boat, taking only one suitcase with clothes and no money.

We arrived in November and found a furnished room on the West Side. My father got a minimum wage job to deliver packages. It was not easy to make ends meet so when I was 16 I got working papers and continued High School at night. There were many other "refugees," as we were known, attending for the same reasons, including my wife who I was fortunate to meet there. She too, coincidentally, had recently come from Vienna.

On my 18th Birthday I registered for Selective Service and was called to active duty in February 1943. I was assigned to Fort Dix for basic training. The very first day we were taken to Federal Court in Newark and sworn in as Citizens of the U.S.

After completing the basic training, I was sent to the Signal Corps in Ft. Monmouth, N.J., to attend Radar school. In July 1943, now 19, my wife and I were married. After completing some preliminary courses we [soldiers] were trained by engineers from A.T.&T. to operate a new "Top Secret" Microwave communication system which they had just developed for the U.S. military.

A unit was formed and we were sent to Wiesbaden, Germany. The war in Europe ended. The cable and telephone systems were totally destroyed. The Chief Signal Officer happened to come to our compound looking for personnel who spoke German. Plans were made to rehabilitate German installations somewhat similar to what we had been trained on, located on mountaintops throughout the country.

Together with another few men, I was selected and assigned to General Eisenhower's headquarters, with the task to rebuild and operate stations to carry telephone and telegraph traffic.

I interviewed prisoners of war, looking for soldiers who had operated this equipment; [I] assembled a crew, established a repair shop and our team successfully reestablished communications. My travels took me to Frankfurt, Munich, Cologne and to Vienna.

The euphoria of returning as a soldier of my new country, just six years after leaving, remains a lasting memory.

My wife and I just celebrated our 75th Birthday and our 56th Wedding Anniversary. Not a day passes without us thinking about our past and how very fortunate we are to live in freedom in the greatest country in the world.

Not all of the veterans were able to pick up where they left off. Some were changed forever by their wounds. Terry M. Supple of Woodland Hills, California, and his family came to know the cost of war and the exceptional strength of two veterans.

During the war, Birmingham Hospital (later Birmingham High School) was built in Van Nuys, California, and it became the center for servicemen with spinal injuries. Hundreds of young men came to this facility for medical treatment. But more often, it was for rehabilitation and training in the use of devices such as wheelchairs that allowed them to return to civilian lives as paraplegics or quadriplegics. . . .

It was in this neighborhood and environment that my four brothers and I grew up. On our street in Encino were a couple of these paraplegic veterans. And in the neighborhood surrounding ours, there were several more. . . .

I finished your book while flying to Chicago on April 18th. I was saddened to learn that Randall E. "Uppy" Updyke died the following day at the Veterans Hospital in Seattle. In all respects, he was larger than life. As a young infantry lieutenant, he was seriously wounded by a land mine in Europe. As a result of his injuries, he became a paraplegic and was sent to Birmingham Hospital. While there, he met and fell in love with a young nurse named Lil. She was at his bedside as he died 54 years later.

Uppy was a very outgoing man who gained substantial girth confined to his wheelchair. He never lost the "colorful" infantry language that went well with his gregarious personality. Because of his handicap, Uppy and Lil could not have children, so instead they drew all the kids in the neighborhood to them like a magnet. With a group of 6 to 10 year olds, Uppy organized the "Gaynor Army," named after the street where we all lived.

He became active in the Disabled American Veterans (DAV) organization in the San Fernando Valley, and was the first commander of their chapter that is still going strong. About 40 years ago, they moved to the Hood Canal area in Washington and set up a marina. Uppy became quite well known and was often visible driving his tugboat throughout the Puget Sound. About 10 years ago, he was honored as the Veteran of the Year for the State of Washington.

They had a huge impact on our family as dear friends to my parents and us. Since they couldn't have children of their own, they "adopted" my younger brother, Casey, as their own. After they moved to Washington, he would spend the summers working with them at the marina. During the Vietnam War, Casey joined the Army (just like Uppy) and served with distinction in the 101st Airborne in Vietnam. When the war was over, he remained in the Army until he retired a few years ago from Fort Lewis, Washington. He still lives in the area, and he and his wife were with Uppy and Lil when Uppy passed away. . . .

Edward L. "Shorty" Gordon was an Air Force tail gunner, shot down over Europe. His story is similar to Uppy's in that he was sent to Birmingham Hospital, where he met and married a young nurse, Jeanie. Shorty and Jeanie lived across the street from us, and like the Updykes, always enjoyed being around the neighborhood kids.

Shorty was a handsome Texan who had a wonderful upper body physique. It must have been very difficult for him to be confined to a wheelchair. It didn't stop him, however. He enjoyed shooting hoops with the kids on the driveway, and could sink a two-hand set shot from 30 feet away. He was employed in sales at a steel supply yard and got me a job driving a truck for them during my high school years.

He and Jeanie also "adopted" one of my brothers, Rory. Even after we all moved out of the neighborhood, Rory returned often for dinner . . . or to sit around for a few drinks with Shorty and some of his buddies. Both Shorty and Jeanie have passed away. But I was always struck by the love that bound the two people together, knowing as they did that once they committed to each other, it really was "for better or worse."

As I noted earlier, the group of men and their wives were wonderful to be around. Although they experienced many physical hardships, they moved on with their lives, making them as normal as possible.

In this age of self-absorption the selflessness of many veterans strikes a chord. Jonathan Birenbaum of Scarsdale, New York, described his appreciation of his father.

Having read *The Greatest Generation,* I find myself compelled to write to you. . . . I am writing to thank you for helping me, after 45 years, to understand more fully my 85 year old father. Your observations and commentary have caused me to have a greater appreciation for a man I have loved and whose life has been devoted to my sister, my mother and me in a way that I am not sure even he has understood.

THE AMERICAN FLAG remains for many World War II veterans an almost sacred symbol of patriotism. They have been the primary promoters of a so far unsuccessful campaign to make desecration of the flag unconstitutional. Edward F. Jonat of Great Neck, New York, became a tireless promoter of the flag when he came home from the war and joined the New York City fire department. His devotion to the flag never wavered; neither did his sense of right and wrong.

Like many of the people in your book, I found the war to be a great adventure. I found myself leaving N.Y.C. for the first time, seeing many parts of our beautiful country and living with shipmates from many of our 48 States. That thrill I felt sailing out under the Golden Gate on a beautiful new submarine into the Pacific, China and Yellow seas. Every day presented a new challenge, thrill and experience. In the conning tower I learned leadership from my Captains that held me in good stead when I became an officer in F.D.N.Y. [the Fire Department of New York City]. . . .

In '66 and '67 I was a chief in the 4th Div.—Harlem— and facing a strange test. . . . The children at Columbia [University] were rioting and burning our flag and the N.Y.P.D. asked us to open our hose and deck pipes on them. Boy was I happy when I received the shortest and best directive I received in the F.D.N.Y. It stated, "FDNY fights fires not people."

At a Christmas party last year I was again reminded of the impact my love of our Flag had on my career when after 22 years in retirement I met an old friend of mine. He greeted me by saying, "Ed Jonat, every time your name comes up people remember the Flag."

THOSE WHO LIVED THROUGH the Depression and World War II learned lifelong lessons in the importance of working together. As a result, later in life they became another kind of army, a formidable force of volunteers. Roderick Berry of Mount Dora, Florida, is typical.

Although I can relate somewhat to the individuals you chronicle, I never felt I was of the greatest generation. I spent 40 months overseas, mainly in Hawaii and the El-lice Islands, and I never fired a shot. Hardly arduous duty, merely maintaining radio communication. In truth I felt I was wasting my time and the government's. But I did what I was told, caused no trouble, made sergeant and some good friends.

Your book prompted me to rethink my thoughts after my generation. I began talking about it to friends about 15–20 years younger than me. You must understand, far too many of my generation have already left me. I was surprised to learn many people agreed with you and consequently disagreed with me. There is a difference among generations. Far too vividly, I remember the De-pression, and serving in the army was better than what we left home. . . .

I erred when I decided not to attend college, but I made a living by working until [the age of] 74. I am in Florida for 23 years now. I volunteer in elementary school a few days a week teaching proper English, grammar, and how to write any type of letter, essay, story, etc. I work with 3rd graders who need extra atten-tion because they are behind. I will note that this comprises about one third of the class. My reward is having some student state, "Thank you Mr. Berry, now I get it." Although I was never a hero during the war I now give back to the people of the U.S.A. In return I get even more back.

I almost forgot. I was born in England and arrived here when I was three years old, became a citizen at 24 while in the service.

Now I am proud of my generation, thanks to you, and wish I could have contributed more.

In *The Greatest Generation* I wrote about Chesterfield Smith, a World War II veteran who later became president of the American Bar Association and took a courageous stand against Richard Nixon during Watergate. His protégée Martha W. Barnett was recently elected to the ABA office her mentor once held. She will be forever grateful to him.

Let me give you just one example of how Chesterfield mentors by transferring his personal credibility. When I was a young lawyer at my first ABA convention, Chesterfield spent a great deal of time introducing me to his friends and colleagues. One afternoon, noticing, I suspect, that I had nothing better to do, he decided that I needed to meet Warren Burger, then Chief Justice of the United States Supreme Court. He introduced me by saying, "Mr. Chief, I want you to meet *my* lawyer, Martha Barnett." For many years thereafter, that is how I was known—as Chesterfield Smith's lawyer. Believe me, being known by that title makes a difference.

Many years have passed since the first ABA meeting. Following in his footsteps, I now begin my tenure as president-elect of the American Bar Association. In this role, I have the opportunity to represent the legal profession and to perpetuate the ideals exemplified by Chesterfield Smith. I have been fortunate in the past few years to receive recognition for various accomplishments. My greatest personal accolade, however, was captured a number of years ago in an article about future presidents of the American Bar Association. In talking favorably about my prospects, a reporter attributed them to the fact that I had Chesterfield Smith at my side. . . . How right he was! As blessed as I am to have Chesterfield in my life, I am but one of thousands who benefit from this remarkable man.

JULES RIEDEL of Red Hook, New York, wrote about his father-in-law, William (Bill) Hull, who served at Iwo Jima and recognized himself in a *Greatest Generation* picture of sailors posing in a Panama photo studio.

Bill is originally from Troy, NY, a veteran of WWII, a former Golden Gloves boxer who after being discharged from the Navy started as a janitor for and retired from Niagara-Mohawk after 35 years as a Gas Line Crew Foreman. His passions were camping, fishing and trapping and he now enjoys the quiet joy of bird-watching and the Travel Channel. A far cry from what he endured as a young man. . . .

His first wife, Eileen, had tuberculosis and died of pneumonia 8/15/56. Their daughter, Barbara Ann (my wife), was raised solely by Bill for almost six years and never had a baby-sitter. She tagged along everywhere with her father—the Irish pubs, American Legion, the non-tourist Catskill bars, etc. When Bill married Doris in 1961, the family became whole again and thrived on determination, guts, pride and a terrific sense of humor. . . .

He served aboard the USS *Jupiter,* basically a supply ship for the 5th Fleet in the Pacific Theater that prior to the war was a cargo ship named the SS *Flying Cloud.* During the war, she traveled one hundred thirty-five thousand two hundred eighteen miles, carrying thousands of tons of supplies and troops to various fronts, all of which involved crossing the equator 14 times and picking up 10 battle stars along the way. [Supply ships] were often considered the first and easy pickings for the enemy. Cutting off supplies to the other warships was considered critical and they, many times, came under greater attack than other vessels. At one point, Bill was continuously at sea for 18 months and under fire.

From what I've been able to piece together, based on documents Bill still has . . . he actively participated in twelve battles, eleven of which are described below, and was awarded the Philippine Liberation Ribbon with two Bronze Stars for bravery.

Battles William L. Hull participated in and has been officially cited for:

> Guadalcanal, Solomon Islands (enemy attack)
> Tarawa, Gilbert Islands (landing operation)
> Saipan, Marianas Islands (initial landings)
> Palau Islands (initial landings and support-reserve force)
> Leyte, Philippine Islands (initial landings)
> Battle for Leyte Gulf (early phase)
> Leyte, Philippine Islands (reinforcement)
> Dutch New Guinea (enemy air attacks)
> Lingayen Gulf, Luzon, Philippine Islands (initial landings)
> Iwo Jima, Kazan Retto (initial landings and disembarkation)
> Okinawa Shima, Nansei Shoto (landing of supplies and equipment)

While spending time with [my in-laws] back in June, at the cabin he and Doris built 31 years ago in Vermont (the American flag always flies on the grounds), I had left the book on a table. . . . He was browsing through it, when suddenly he began making exclamations about a photo. It turns out he is the sailor third from the left and they had the same photo at one time.

You have no idea of how emotional it was for him and how excited and animated he became at the discovery. For us it seemed unbelievable, mostly because of the pure coincidence of him just happening to pick up the book and thumbing through it. Because of his vision problems, he just looks through books with lots of photos in them. . . .

Bill is a fixture in the Albia neighborhood of Troy, NY, having been born there and then lived in the same house for over 50 years. He is recognized by all during his summer motorized wheelchair excursions throughout the neighborhood and to the American Legion, which he visits regularly. The book accompanies him on these daily trips and to anyone who is willing to try and listen, he shows the picture and proudly points to his chest saying, "Me, me . . ."

Mr. Brokaw, as a direct descendant of "the Greatest Generation" myself, I found your book to be a great inspiration and feel it should be required reading for all high schoolers. . . . It woke up a stirring of pride in a member of our family who for 13 years has not been able to express himself about his accomplishments during the horrors of battle. To begin with, he is a humble man, used to hardship, a non-complainer and like many other veterans downplays [his] role in wartime. Your book freed up emotions in him and made family members and friends aware that this man demonstrated the greatness you describe so well in your book. We thank you for that.

ONE OF THE GREAT California success stories of the postwar years involved the San Francisco–based real estate empire of Walter H. Shorenstein. He remains a major force in real estate development, Democratic party politics, and philanthropy. He credits his Army service with getting him started.

When the draft was started in 1940, President Roosevelt personally drew the numbers to select the first one hundred groups of draftees. Out of thousands of numbers, FDR chose mine on his 25th pick, and in November 1940 I joined the first group of inductees at Camp Upton, on Long Island, New York.

Even as thousands of young men descended on the place, it was clear that Camp Upton had neither the staff nor the facilities to receive us. After an abbreviated basic training, I was pulled into the Classification Section, interviewing the incoming waves of draftees and recommending assignments. The need for qualified staff was such that I remained there for my whole year of military service, and was discharged in November 1941. Just a few weeks later, I was driving into New York when I heard that Pearl Harbor had been bombed. I turned around and drove back to Camp Upton to reenlist. . . .

With classification duties reassigned, I was selected for quartermaster officer training at Camp Lee, Virginia, late in 1942. . . . We worked around the clock to get air units prepared for Operation Torch, the invasion of North Africa.

The challenges and stress that were such a big part of every day led to a huge burnout rate. For relief, the Colonel would send us to various schools for brief periods. I attended Field Grade Officers Training, and later was selected for the Air Corps Command and General Staff School. This in-depth training, combined with the skills I was learning from my duties, gave me what I consider the equivalent of an MBA. Though I was only 26 and a first lieutenant, I had responsibilities unlike anything the civilian world could have offered. . . .

Despite the long, stressful hours, the job never really

felt like work. We knew that we were accomplishing something very important. When I consider my accomplishments subsequently, I feel very well served by the discipline and analytical skills I developed in the service. Having had my endurance and resourcefulness tested under the most critical circumstances, I came away at the end of the war with the confidence and independence to make a new start in a new city with just $1000 in my pocket and a pregnant wife.

I think for many people the drive and determination that sustained them during the war carried over into their civilian lives. In my own career I have tried to operate by the same standards of achievement that were demanded of me by the service. Even more importantly, I think the strength and shared values derived from the war have set a high standard for each subsequent generation. From civil rights to technological transformation, America's younger generations have grown up with the idea that dedicated people working together can truly change the world. To me, this is the greatest and most enduring legacy that my generation has passed on.

ONE OF World War II's larger-than-life heroes was Marine fighter pilot Joe Foss, who earned the Congressional Medal of Honor for his exploits in the skies over the Pacific. When I wrote about him in *The Greatest Generation* I described the postwar years when one of his children was struggling with cerebral palsy. The following letter from William Smith, now living in California, recounts the role Joe Foss played in the life of Smith's son, another cerebral palsy victim.

Living in Kansas City, Missouri, during the mid-forties, my wife and I learned that our three-year-old son, Billy, had cerebral palsy. We were devastated. We knew nothing about the affliction.

The United Cerebral Palsy Association invited parents to a local church to learn about the dilemma we were facing. We drove to the church one snowy Sunday evening and found only one other couple there. But soon a large man entered the room. He had flown down from South Dakota. Joe Foss. He told us about his daughter with cerebral palsy.

Although this was some fifty years ago, I still remember his words of encouragement. We left the small gathering that night with hope and feeling that we and Billy would be able to cope with the disease.

However, when he was in high school, and [during his] first year of college, we were advised by his counselors that we should not encourage Bill to go on and get a college degree. We were told the best we could expect was the possibility he could work with Good Will Industries in some manner.

Apparently some of the words of encouragement we received from Joe Foss that night in Kansas City had rubbed off on Bill. He went on to graduate and was employed by the U.S. Forest Service in their computer operation. He wrote programs that were used throughout the country and he supervised a computer office. He will complete a very successful career with the federal government in a few years.

ANOTHER VETERAN from the pages of *The Greatest Generation*, California schoolteacher Luis Armijo—Army Joe, as the kids called him—inspired a number of letters of appreciation. One came from Paul H. Limon of Fullerton, California.

Dear Mr. Armijo,

Just wanted to drop you a few lines to say hello and to tell you how very proud I am to be one of your former students.

I know you probably don't remember me. I was very quiet and shy back in those days. You were my typing teacher my final year, in 1966. I truly enjoyed taking typing and you as my instructor. I always remember you as a fair and honest man. . . .

I enjoyed reading your stories in Tom Brokaw's book. Little did I know that within a year and a half of graduation, I would be in the Army and in Vietnam. As you and I know, war is a terrible thing. But it makes you really appreciate this great country of ours.

Thanks again for all you have done, for me and all the students you have touched.

God bless you and your family.

CHRISTOPHER GILLESPIE, another Vietnam veteran, who now lives in Westport Point, Massachusetts, has often reflected on the differences between the experiences of his parents and what he endured.

In 1942, my father was a 30-year-old classics teacher, five years into his teaching career, with one small child and me on the way. He came home from class one day and announced he was joining the Navy. In his school community, there were many young [men with] families in similar circumstances, none required to go off to war. But my father, along with many of his colleagues, felt strongly that he needed to be a part of this war, so he became a 90-day wonder at Fort Schuyler, New York. Because he stammered badly, the Navy would not let him become a ship's officer, with the difficulty of issuing orders on a bridge, I suppose. Frustrated, he asked for the next most hazardous duty, and he was assigned to the Greenland Patrol. He ended up on a support base in Greenland teaching English to other servicemen. He loved that tour and loved Greenland, sending us back Eskimo crafts and a 45 record he had made, wishing his little family back home a Merry Christmas. . . .

My mother, her world turned completely upside down, went bravely along with these developments, and had already joined the American Red Cross Motor Corps. There she met her best friend in life, and the two of them were like naughty kids in the back of the classroom. Her circumstances were not unique. All three of her brothers went off to war, two of them [going] away for at least four years.

They all made it home eventually, and I remember as a young boy the feeling in our town, a sense of communal homecoming, reunion, getting joyfully back to normal life. I remember wounded veterans panhandling on the sidewalk, the packed Memorial Day parades and red paper poppies.

That clarity of purpose and sense of community makes my tour in Vietnam seem all the more solitary and confused. The differences between my father's war and mine are enormous—ironic and poignant, at least to me. I find myself oddly envying my father's experience.

My mother looks back over a long, happy life punctuated by worry, waiting and wars: waiting for her father to return from the trenches of World War I France, waiting for her brothers and husband to return from World War II and waiting for me to return from Vietnam.

CERTAIN BATTLES have become symbolic of World War II; D-Day tops the list. It was massive, daring, and successful, a critical turning point in defeating Germany. A veteran of the Pacific theater, Frank G. Nolte of Lincoln Park, Michigan, had a memorable encounter when he finally got to Normandy.

I took advantage of the GI Bill, earned a graduate degree and went on to teach at a community college for almost 40 years. I traveled from a new home purchased on the GI Bill benefits and still live in it. No member of my family ever graduated from college [before me]. I am probably the very typical man you wrote so glowingly of.

I went to Omaha in 1988, missing D-Day by about 44 years. . . .

I sat alone on the low stone wall that separates the cemetery from the beach, filled with this tremendous emotional upheaval. Our French guide interrupted my moment and the following conversation ensued.

"Were you here then?"

"No, chère. I was in Finschhafen, New Guinea, on D-Day."

"But these men, they are your peers?"

"Yes."

"I know how you feel."

"How could you, chère? You are 25, born in Paris, and a graduate of the Sorbonne. How could you know how I feel?" Rude, maybe, but given the moment . . .

"Down the road a few kilos is another cemetery [she said "Seem a Tear ee"] where my grandfather is buried. He was shot by the Gestapo on D-Day for having a radio." Not a transceiver, just a radio.

"Then you do know."

Suddenly she said, "May I sit with you for a few minutes and hold your hand?"

I probably nodded; too far into tears to speak.

After a few minutes, she stood up and said, "The tour must move on." And then she said, "May I kiss you?"

My Lord, Mr. Brokaw, what is an emotional basket case to do? I kissed her while weeping unashamedly and with considerable enthusiasm.

Do you know the lines from Emerson? When it seemed that the Civil War was nearing and when by contemporary standards the young men seemed to be fops and weaklings, Emerson wrote:

> *So nigh is grandeur to our dust,*
> *So near is God to man,*
> *When Duty whispers low, Thou must,*
> *The youth replies, I can.*

VIII

CHILDREN

Pat Zack with her father, Paul W. Tittel, Sr., 1954.

———————— • ————————

Few children relate easily to the young lives of their parents. Events that precede our own births automatically fall into the category of "history," a distant time however few years have actually passed. For the baby boomers, the army of children produced by the men and women who began their families once the war was over, the disjunction between their world and the world of their parents could hardly have been greater. One represented deprivation, sacrifice, and hard-won prosperity; the other, greatly expanded opportunity and, even during Vietnam, more personal choices.

Those differences led to some historic and well-documented rifts—indeed, to a cultural revolution that since has cooled. Now, based on many of the letters I received, as the boomers grow older they also become much more aware of what their parents had endured and the legacy of their early challenges.

In watching her father care for her mother after a debilitating stroke, Janet McKeon of O'Fallon, Illinois, realized that the strength of their relationship grew out of their war experience.

As a member of the early Baby Boom generation who lived through the Vietnam years, I thought we were the group who had been wronged, with our boyfriends/husbands fighting in a faraway place in a war that nobody wanted to be a part of, and with no appreciation by others of what we went through.

Your book certainly gave me a different perspective on that. But that's not all your book did for me. It made me wonder about my own parents' participation in and life during the war. Of course I knew my dad had served and that my older sister was born during the war, but he never talked about it and I guess I was never interested enough to ask.

Sad to say, but during the past year my dad and I have had a lot of time to talk since my mother had a stroke and required constant care. I made a three-hour trip home every week to help with her care and it was during this time that he started telling me about their life during the war.

What an eye-opener these stories were to me. It was hard to believe that in all those years since the war they had never complained about those hardships, the separations and the fear of the bombing missions (my dad was a bombardier who flew missions out of England). I had always seen my parents as good, hardworking people but the year that we cared for my mother showed me their strength, which they obviously also had during the war years. My dad cared for her 24 hours a day, never complaining, always appreciative of the help my sisters and I gave, but never demanding or expecting it. My mother endured the helplessness and, at the end, the hopelessness with quiet dignity until she died in May. . . .

My real reason for writing to you is to urge you to use your public voice to remind members of my generation who are still lucky enough to have one or both parents alive, to listen to their stories before they are lost forever.

Mike McReaken, of Manvel, Texas, wrote to describe a similar experience:

My father passed away last year after a three-year struggle with the effects of a severe stroke. He was at home because of the love and devotion of my mother, his wife of 55 years. My dad was at Pearl Harbor on one of the few ships of the line that was able to escape the sneak attack. For many years I tried to get my dad to tell me what it was like on that Sunday morning. He never would—or could—talk about it. . . .

It was difficult to read *The Greatest Generation* without tearing up or being emotionally choked up to know of the hardships, loss, and joy that my parents' generation suffered through. After watching my mother care for Dad since the day of his stroke, I always knew it was because of her unconditional love for him, and his deep-seated fear of being placed in a nursing home. But after reading about the many others in *The Greatest Generation,* I also understand and appreciate more why my parents made the choices and decisions that they did throughout their entire lives together.

I MET PAT ZACK in Louisville, Kentucky, while signing copies of *The Greatest Generation.* She wanted to tell me more about her father, Paul W. Tittel, Sr.

My father served in the 537th Quartermaster Battalion of the US Army. Among other battles and campaigns, he experienced Normandy firsthand. Apparently, his experiences there changed him forever. My father refused, or was unable, to talk about anything that happened to him, or the things that he saw, during the war. As children, we thought it would be exciting to hear about how "he alone" beat the Nazis and the Japanese. He never seemed to understand our "childish fascination" and would always grow quite serious and change the subject. [When we were] high-schoolers, looking for more insight into the history we studied, he would again become very serious, only confirming or commenting on the facts. When asked for his personal reactions, he would only say, "Just pray that you never live during a world war."

In 1984, on the 40th anniversary of D-Day, my father returned to Normandy. I was told that when he stepped onto Omaha Beach, and later, Utah Beach, he fell to the ground, shaking and sobbing like a child. Still, on his return, he would not discuss his reliving of that moment. . . .

I was born in 1950, a child during the years of rebuilding after the war, experienced adolescence throughout the turbulent 60's, established a career in the 70's, became a "boomer," and began a family of my own in the 80's, and finally, reached some level of maturity in the 90's. Throughout all those years, I never really knew or understood how my father became the great man that he was. What I did know was that he never wanted his children, or future generations, to experience what he did during the war, and did all that he could to ensure that the world, at least our world, would be a better place for us.

Throughout sixteen years of formal education and hours of independent study, none of the US history courses I took or books I read gave me the insight into the people who served in WWII as your book did. The stories told in *The Greatest Generation,* I believe, were my father's stories, the stories that he could never bring himself to tell. Their missions, their goals, their dreams, were his. Thank you for writing this book. Thank you for providing me with the opportunity to get to know my father.

THE PARENTS of the baby boomers are in their seventies and eighties; this is their twilight time. The father of Barbara Yearing of Ridgewood, New Jersey, suffers from terminal cancer.

My father was a recent graduate of the University of Illinois in 1943 when he joined the Army Air Corps. He hurriedly got married and then he and my mother traveled with gas rations from Chicago to California, where he was stationed as a meteorologist. Their experiences during that time organized their thinking and became part of our family history.

Today, my father lives a good distance away and is dying of cancer. I had been searching for some way to tell him how much I appreciated my childhood and all that he had done for me, but could not seem to find the words to tell him face-to-face. My dad, like many of the World War II era, has had a hard time with expressed feelings. He would have found it strange to be thanked for something that was for him a matter of course. That's when I stumbled upon your book and thought I might use it as a Christmas gift and also as a means to open up a discussion with him about his life and what an impact it has had on me.

The book captured for me what I have been trying to say to him for some time about the qualities exemplified by his generation, qualities that I have taken for granted all these years. Honesty, integrity, hard work, personal responsibility and perseverance were all around me and I absorbed them almost imperceptibly. Your book has also helped me to see my father as part of his generation and not so unusual in his somewhat intractable and unyielding beliefs.

So I sent my father your book with a letter that attempted to express my gratitude to him. I tried to let him know that I understood the uniqueness of his time in history and was proud of the way he had come through it all. Mostly I thanked him for being a great father. He called me on Christmas Day to thank me for the note and to say that it "tugged at his heart." He finally heard me and we were finally able to connect in a meaningful way. Thank you for writing such a wonderful tribute to my father and others like him. Thanks to you I feel I have been able to say something important to him before he dies.

THE GRANDCHILDREN of the Greatest Generation are hearing these stories of life in the thirties and forties for the first time. One of them is H. Harrison Wheeler of Village of Golf, Florida. He greatly admires his grandfather, who served in the Counterintelligence Corps.

The Greatest Generation was a recent college graduation gift from my grandparents who, it occurred to me as I progressed through the book, could have easily been among those you profiled. The day my grandparents were married, in the late 1930's, their collective savings totaled a meager twenty dollars. But they loved each other, and they knew how to work. During World War II my grandfather enlisted and, failing an entrance exam into the Army Air Corps because of poor eyesight, was placed in the relatively thin ranks of the Counterintelligence Corps . . . As I have taken an interest in him and his generation (thus the book was an appropriate present), he occasionally opens up to me about the war—a topic that unfailingly piques my curiosity. But even with me, his namesake grandson, he is often reticent and unwilling to discuss his Army days. They were, he says, some of the worst days of his life, and he has no wish to relive them.

After the war he returned home and prospered in the restaurant business in Buffalo and in the Northeast at large, eventually selling his business to Del Monte. . . . Yet despite his stupendous financial success and his achievements in the war (I know he was decorated in one capacity or another), what my grandfather is most proud of are the five sons he and my grandmother raised and the subsequent families the boys established. My grandfather is the most brilliant, compassionate, reflective person I know. But, after having read your book, it seems obvious that many other grandchildren would echo my sentiment to describe their own grandparents.

THE RENEWAL of interest in World War II has prompted many schools to assign essay themes on the topic. Bessie Luttrell lives in Shepherdsville, Kentucky. Her social studies teacher, David Bock, sent a copy of an essay Bessie wrote about her grandfather, entitled "The Bravest Man I Will Never Know."

He stands firmly in the back of my mind; I will never know this man. He is who my father speaks proudly and passionately about. He is my grandfather, Harold Wilber Luttrell, better known as Curly. He lived from March 10, 1915, to March 14, 1980.

My grandpa has been a major factor in my life, despite the fact that he died two years before I was born. Through the memories my father and my uncle have passed down to me, I feel I have a close relationship with him. This relationship was built upon my father and uncle's connection with their father, but has grown into a much deeper bond between my grandfather and me.

As I've learned more about my grandpa and his experience through World War II, it has strengthened my ability to stand up for what I believe in and never let people trample on my dreams. He taught me to have courage even under extremely harsh conditions. . . .

August 23, 1942. The Air Force sends my grandfather a telegram requesting his presence in the war. He leaves his wife and a baby daughter to proudly defend his country.

He was first stationed at the Air Force Mechanic School (bombers) in Lincoln, Nebraska. During his study at Nebraska he advanced to Ford, Michigan's Mechanic School. When he finished his training at Michigan, the Air Force placed him in Wendover, Utah's Gunner School. At each school he studied the most well-known American heavy bomber of WWII, which was known as the B-17 Flying Fortress.

The B-17 achieved fame in the daylight precision-bombing campaign over Germany in 1943, 1944, and 1945. It obtained a reputation of being capable of absorbing a large amount of battle damage and still continue to fly. B-17s dropped 640,036 tons of bombs on European targets during the war. Boeing records claim that the Fortress destroyed 23 enemy aircraft per thousand attacks. Approximately 4,750 B-17s were lost on combat missions, which is about ⅓ of all B-17s built. . . .

There were 340,000 people in the 8th Air Force, including 135,000 combat crewmen. 28,000 of them would become POW's (Prisoners of War), including Harold Luttrell, who was reported missing in the line of duty on January 11, 1944. . . .

He was taken to Dulag Luft (transit camp for airmen) in Wetzlar, Germany. The German soldiers moved him to Stalag Luft III (main camp). . . . As he walked to the camp, he saw [the] dead bodies of his fellow soldiers and [of] Jews piled along the roadside. He stayed in this prison for the remaining 17 months of the war.

After he arrived in Stalag Luft III the German soldiers took all of his clothing and threw him into a 50-ft. hole. Each hole was designed to hold one prisoner and the purpose for them was simple cruel torturing. . . . After the war was over, the German troops made the remaining prisoners march 200 miles for their freedom. . . . My grandfather made it through the march to freedom.

In August 1945 he was honorably discharged from the Air Force. He received a Silver Star for saving three of his crew members, by sharing his oxygen at 30,000 feet and keeping them alive while under heavy fire. Three

Air Medals were given to my grandfather, [one] for each German fighter he shot down singlehandedly. He also received four Oak Leaf Clusters, [one] for each assisted kill (shooting down a German fighter).

When he entered the war he weighed 240 pounds, but when he returned home he only weighed 99 pounds.

His weight was not the only thing that changed during the war. He never forgot the total destruction of the bombs they dropped on the countries. He always thought of the women and children that were killed. The image of bombing the small towns always stuck in his mind.

Two statements my father remembers his dad saying were "A man who bragged about what he did in the war, did not see nothing or was never in the war." Also "I'm proud to be an American, and I love my country." He fought boldly to defend the country he loved most.

I never got the chance to meet my grandfather. He died on March 14, 1980 (four days after his birthday). . . .

I wish I could have had a chance to meet my grandfather before he passed away. He was a true hero to many people and I'll always hold a special spot in my heart for the man I'll never know.

ALLEN A. BEAUMONT of Sun City Center, Florida, sent a copy of the inscription his grandson wrote inside *The Greatest Generation.*

I am 78 years old and served in the Army Air Corps, the U.S. Air Corps and the U.S. Air Force from 1939 through 1973 in both active and reserve duty. I entered in September 1939 as a private and retired in September 1973 as a colonel.

My grandsons (3) have always been interested in my services to the country and I feel this particular note from #3 Grandson shows that there are still some offspring from the "baby boomers" who realize the importance of World War II and the results thereof.

Pop Pop & Nini—

After going to Europe and Normandy, I think this book's title captures what we all feel about our grandparents. Thanks for giving us the world.

Love,
Richard #3

B RIAN W. HAAS of Gainesville, Florida, writes about the sacrifices of his grandfather, who died when he was two years old.

I never knew my grandfather, Clarence Kennish, a World War II veteran. I was 2 years old when he died twenty-one years ago. I often imagine the conversations that we might have had. Unfortunately, as seems to be the case often, he rarely talked about the War. Neither my mom nor her sister knows much about what he did during the War in Europe.

The only remembrance I have from my grandfather is his old duffel bag. This is a treasure to me. It contains his Army-issue clothing, toiletries bag, a few pictures, and other small items. It is the only thing I have from him but I am so thankful to have it. But because of the stories you have gathered I feel like I know something more about my grandpa. By seeing the people who he likely fought along with, I can better imagine his experiences.

I wish that more Americans today would take the time to look back and see the sacrifices these great people made for our great country. Perhaps if they did, they would appreciate more the precious freedom that we enjoy. I am so proud of my grandfather; although he's been gone for over twenty years, in a way I feel that he lives on. America, the beautiful country that he was willing to give his life for, continues to go strong today. Every time our flag is raised, our national anthem sung, and freedom is enjoyed, I believe he lives on.

LISA M. PEDERSEN of Roy, Utah, sent her impressions of her father and a poem she wrote as a tribute to his war years and later life. She plans to move back to the family farm in Iowa.

I sometimes find it incredible how an Iowa farm boy faced being sent off to parts unknown, to live in Times Square as he attended training, to see Frank Sinatra for a quarter, to sail across the Atlantic and have your ship rammed and limp into port, to liberate Moosburg and enter Dachau. . . . I intend to gather and document all these stories, experiences and feelings from my father this summer, not for any literary project but for my family history. . . .

I am sharing with you a poem I wrote for my dad this spring and which was read at the Memorial Day service at a small cemetery in Inwood [Iowa] by the American Legion in front of a small group. My father is in his 80's and recuperating from a broken leg. He was very concerned about who would put the flags on the graves or raise the flags on the Avenue of Flags. It got done. And he was able to attend, sitting in the car. I share this with you as a fellow defender of the heritage of all our veterans. Thanks and if you ever are in northwest Iowa traveling Highway 182 north of Inwood and you come across Sunny Side Farm, feel free to drop on in, the coffee is always on.

He followed his orders with strength and resolve,
No challenge too great that he couldn't solve.
But war has a way of not favoring sides,
Bombs fall where they may leaving no place to hide.

No safe arms of family to help ease his pain,
No warm hand to hold as his life slipped away.

But the comfort of buddies, one of their own,
His war finally over, 'twas time to go home.

And what of the soldier who lived to fight on?
Was it fate, was it luck, was it trust in his God?
No time for his grief or the sorrow of tears,
For his duty was battle, he must silence his fears.

He fought on through each battle, etched deep in his brain,
Memorized every town, every bridge, the terrain.
His prayer would be answered and peace reign again,
But how would he fit? For he wasn't the same.

He pledged an allegiance when battle was done,
To carry the torch, the victory won.
He lived all these years upright and true,
To be worthy of those who had paid war's due.

SOME CHILDREN of the Greatest Generation have their own memories of the war years. John E. Smith of Soldotna, Alaska, was living in California as a young child.

My first memories are of my grandfather, grandmother, aunt, and mom gathered around the radio at night listening to the news. Night after night this took place. No talking on my part was allowed as every word was listened to with a gravity I have never since felt. Sometimes the broadcasts were very hard to hear, as there was a great deal of static noise. I still remember looking around at my family and seeing faces so serious that I was afraid.

Over time, I learned that my dad was in England getting ready to fight Hitler. I didn't learn until after the war exactly what he did. I did not find out from him, either; my grandmother had to tell me. My father never spoke to me in any detail about the war. I learned that he was part of the Red Ball Express hauling mostly fuel to Patton. He went to Europe six days after D-Day as a buck sergeant and came home a battlefield-commissioned captain. After the war, the Army Air Corps became the Air Force and my father went with the Air Force.

The reason we moved to California was also for the war effort. My mother drove a wrecker for the military. My aunt and grandmother were building airplanes, and my grandfather was a tool and die maker also involved with building airplanes. One of the things that I to this day remember clearly is that I once saw a poster for Rosie the riveter and she had a blue and white hankie tied around her head. That night when my aunt came home she was wearing the same hankie around her head, and I thought the poster was of her.

I also remember shortages. My grandmother complained the most. Grandma liked to bake and the two most essential things, butter and sugar, were always in short supply. Many people also talk about gasoline being rationed, but rubber, i.e., tires, was also in short supply. My grandfather was something of a genius in repairing tires that were no good. He had built a little "vulcanizer," he called it. He would recap portions of old tires that other people said were not repairable. I remember people coming over at night with an old damaged tire asking Grandpa to please fix it, and he would.

When I was four years old I went from house to house with other kids asking people to donate any old aluminum pots or other aluminum they might have so it could be made into airplanes. . . .

I remember V-E [Day] as very confusing. My mother and aunt broke down and cried. My mother was essentially out of control and no one was able to make her stop crying. I was very scared, and everyone tried to tell me it was because she was so happy, but I could not believe this until much later when she did stop. My dad finally came home in 1946! I didn't even know him.

My father never really spoke to me (or anyone) about the war. When I asked him about his being commissioned an officer in the field, he only said that they were short of experienced men and that he was most experienced so they "appointed" him. He did not like being an officer and resigned his commission in 1946 to become a master sergeant.

My father passed away in 1972. His civilian funeral was held in Riverside, California. We then placed his flag-draped casket on a train. My mother was not in good health and could not go with him on the train. I rode with him in the baggage car to San Francisco, where he had a military burial with full honors. This is where I learned about some of what he had done in Europe. I still do not know how his fellow soldiers learned about his funeral but there were about fifteen men [there]. We spoke a little after the ceremony and they informed me of his bravery and leadership under fire. Most of these men were in tears and there was a lot of emotion displayed for a few moments. Then it was suddenly over, and they all (to a man) began to change the subject and start telling jokes. Each seemed to be embarrassed that they had spoken at all.

I will never forget that day, or those men. I have tears in my eyes now, just writing about it. Like you, I was raised by those men and women who rarely spoke of their sacrifice and heroism. Thank God they were there!

MAJOR JOHN CARY served as a field surgeon in the Army, and when he came home he was chief of staff at St. Luke's Medical Center in Milwaukee. One of his sons, John M. Cary of Mequon, Wisconsin, still senses his presence and feels connected to what he went through.

Permit me to tell you about my dad, who was in the Army for 5 years and ultimately served in the Battle of the Bulge as a field surgeon. As was the case with so many of your "heroes," Dad never talked about the war. His only comment was "Those who talk the most, did the least." . . .

He settled in Milwaukee after the War and later became chief of staff of Milwaukee's most prominent medical center. His staff meetings were brief and run without unnecessary banter, probably [as] a result of his military days. When someone would talk too long, his standard response was "Write me a letter, next question!" He saw a son return from Vietnam. . . . Another son has made a career in the Navy medical service and will retire in a year or two. He buried his oldest son [who died of] cancer following 30 years of chronic kidney disease. . . .

Since [my father's] death in 1995, I had his Bronze Star, battle ribbons, dog tags, religious medal and medical insignia framed along with his Army portrait as a 34-year-old major. They proudly hang in what was his living room and is now a room enjoyed by our family. It was an amazing feeling to read your book in that room while seeing him "look over" my shoulder.

I also enjoyed your book since I had the good fortune to meet the subject of one of your first stories, Tom Broderick. Mr. Broderick's daughter Molly married a friend, Wayne Barnett, about 10 years ago. . . . Wayne is now general manager of NBC's affiliate in New Orleans, WDSU, Channel 6.

I met Mr. and Mrs. Broderick at Wayne and Molly's wedding, and sadly a few years later at Molly's funeral, after her valiant battle with cancer. I was impressed with Mr. Broderick. I never knew the cause of his blindness. It was amazing to read about him in your book and make the connection. I read his story at midnight on a Saturday and had to wait until Monday morning to call Wayne and ask if it was in fact "that" Mr. Broderick.

Wayne proudly said that it was. I have since written a note to Mr. Broderick to thank him for his service and tell him how much I enjoyed his story. . . .

I didn't intend for this letter to be so long. I think it became therapeutic for a son who misses his dad a great deal.

JENNY THARP YOUNG of Hackensack, New Jersey, wrote to say that while sorting through her father's belongings after he was killed in an accident in January 1999, she and her siblings discovered documents indicating that he had been awarded two Purple Hearts and four Bronze Stars while serving in the 101st Airborne Division—honors he never mentioned to his family. They also learned that their mother had saved hundreds of letters he wrote to her during the war.

Although my sisters and brother at various intervals of our childhood would attempt to question Dad about the war, he had great difficulty talking about it. We grew up in a household filled with books, articles and documentaries regarding the war, but could not discuss it with Dad, except for him to say, "Whatever you read or see, it was much worse." . . .

In reading your book, a memory came flooding back, of when my younger sister, 13 at the time, ran away. When the police called our home the next morning after picking her up during the Chicago riots, my dad insisted she was in her room sleeping. Upon returning home with her, he flew into a rage, telling her what could happen to a young woman unprotected. He recalled a horror from the war, as my sister and I stood speechless. He broke down into uncontrollable tears and walked away. That was the only time we saw him break down. We knew he had much hidden pain, and yet we had no clue. . . .

In closing, it is only after reading your book and after the death of our father that we are really and truly beginning to understand him. And in understanding our father, we are beginning to know ourselves a bit more. These men returning from war had a huge impact on all of our lives. I am sure that many or all of the children of these men who read your book will feel the same.

Here are three of the letters David Tharp wrote to his then sweetheart:

Somewhere in France—July 7, 1944
My Dearest Lou,

I'd like to tell you what I got or rather what I had for my birthday, and if I live to be a hundred I'll never forget that day. I can't tell you the whole story, but my buddies and I stopped at a French home for some cider and while drinking that my partner told them (the French people) of my birthday. They made quite a fuss over it and gave me a bouquet of roses—red, white and blue— and a big red rose to put on my jacket. To top all this off, they gave me a bottle of very special wine, which was very good and quite old. It was only about an hour that we spent there, but it will not be forgotten.

Forever yours, David

P.S. Don't call me Davie anymore. If you do, I'll get even one of these days. That isn't a threat. Happy happy.

Austria June 6, 1945
My Darling,

D-365 and still kicking. One year ago to-day I was a very scared lad. First I was mad and then I was scared then both of them. That was one day I shall never forget. I pray that in my future years I shall never live such a year as this past one has been.

I'm not giving you any hopes, but rumors are that I'll be coming home around Aug. or Sept. However, don't pin your hopes on it. That's strictly talk. So, Hon, if I should, you either have a vacation then or we'll take one.

You go right ahead and buy those pajamas, Hon. I'll try and remember what they're used for. Ha. . . .

Oh yes, I've been wanting to ask you something. Do you think you'll still want a short engagement? I might consider four or five days.

Auxerre, France
August 9, 1945

Darling, I'm so glad you feel the way you do about the racial problems of to-day. At least we shouldn't be fighting over that. I want my children to be brought up to feel that they are equal and not to hate people because they are black. Oh I can't really explain it here on paper, but I'm sure you know what I mean. As you said, Hon, we wouldn't have the large racial problem we have today if the parents didn't teach their children about it.

GORDON MORRIS of Lancaster, Texas, described how *The Greatest Generation* brought him closer to his father.

Dad began college with little idea of what he wanted to do in life. When the war began he enlisted and served with the Chinese army in Burma under the command of General Stilwell. Dad never talked about the war. I don't know if it was because of the horror of what he experienced, or the belief that it was simply a job to be done and done without fanfare. He went on to a career in the Army, and although there were the obvious drawbacks of moving, we gained a respect for other cultures which helps us today in our dealings with others of diverse opinion.

The following is part of a letter Morris wrote to his father.

Thank you for your hospitality during our visit. We had a great time and were glad for the opportunity to come spend time with you and Mother. I was especially glad to see how well you were able to get around and how much your health had improved.

The enclosed book is a small gift to help us commemorate Father's Day. I wish we could be with you. Although I have not read the entire book, I have read segments and heard a great deal about it. It's Tom Brokaw's chronicle of the age of America's WWII vets, your generation. It focuses on the growing up and the silent sacrifice given by the men and women of this time. It is certainly a unique and important perspective my generation seems to have misplaced. I hope you enjoy reading it. I look forward to borrowing it from you the next time we're home. I will celebrate my first Father's Day on Sunday and will think of you and give silent thanks for the direction and abilities you have passed on to me. I am, and will continue to be, forever grateful.

THERE WERE so many branches of the main service groups that not all received the attention they deserved in *The Greatest Generation*. Thomas Uhlman of St. Petersburg, Florida, reminded me that those who served in submarines were not given much wartime credit because of censorship and their "stealth" duty in dangerous waters. In fact, 52 subs and their crews, more than 3,500 men, were lost during World War II. It was hazardous duty and heroic: American submarines were responsible for 55 percent of all Japanese vessels sunk during the war.

Many members of the Merchant Marine and their families were also disappointed that their branch of the service didn't get more attention. They reminded me that the merchant seamen who sailed into hostile waters with cargoes of vital war material were also in the service of their country and on dangerous assignments. In fact, even though more than six thousand Merchant Marine seamen lost their lives as a result of enemy action during the war, they weren't recognized as true veterans eligible for benefits until a congressional act in 1988.

By then it was too late for many of their families.

Mary C. Matranga, of San Clemente, California, wrote about her father and what he left behind after the war. As testimony to the dangers of Merchant Marine service, she also included a report on the sinking of his wartime ship, the SS *Pennmar.*

> I am writing to you about my father. His name was Capt. Sigmund Charles Krolikowski. He had served on many ships. One of them was the *Pennmar.* It was sunk in the Atlantic on September 23, 1942. He later transferred to a tanker in the Pacific. At war's end he was offered [the position of] port captain of Long Beach. They needed a captain to take a tanker to Australia. While there, gas was leaking in the hold and he went down to rescue some men. He either had a gas mask on and it was defective or he did not have one on. We never got the whole story. He died saving men's lives and was buried in Australia. My mother was left with six children in ages from six months to fifteen. She did not receive any money or benefits from the government. She was about destitute. She went back to work. My sister started working at fifteen and I at 13. If my father had some benefits, life would not have been so hard. My mother and family suffered untold misery and hardship. Now after so many years they finally recognized the worth of the merchant marine. What value is it now after so many years. We couldn't engage in any activities after school and we had to work. Going through college working two jobs, working in the college to help pay for the tuition, and being restricted in extra curricular activities because of work

and pressure. We could have had a normal life if he had benefits.

———

FROM: Harold F. Spinney
             3rd Officer, SS *Pennmar*
TO: Port Director, Reykjavik, Iceland
SUBJECT: Statement Regarding Loss of Two Men

I have been presently employed as the 3rd Officer of the SS *Pennmar,* having left the United States for the United Kingdom. On the 23rd of September at 21:51 the vessel was torpedoed. My usual post is #2 lifeboat, but this had been lost two days previous in a heavy gale. Therefore, I had taken command of one of the two remaining life rafts, two of these also having been lost in the storm.

After the torpedo hit, the Master ordered abandon ship. I made my way to my raft, which was on the port side of the afterdeck of the vessel. Arriving at my station I found that Harry Lane, AB Seaman, on my watch had released the tripping gear and the raft was overboard towing on its painter. There were two men on the raft, and as I stood there Lane jumped for the painter and slid down to the raft. As he did so his right leg was caught and crushed between the ship and the raft.

The vessel was still making way, and seas were breaking over the raft threatening to wash the men overboard. Two messmen, R. Gooden and Cecil Thompson, and an oiler, A. Mock, had assembled near me. I instructed them to jump over the side and swim to the raft as soon as I cut the painter. Going forward I cut the painter, and climbed back over deck cargo. I found A. Mock still on deck. I told him to jump, which he did immediately, and [I] followed at once.

The raft had by this time drifted to the ship's stern and I swam towards it. On getting aboard I had the men break out the oars and begin to get the raft away from the ship's stern as the wheel was turning over. A. Mock had made the raft and R. Gooden also, but the other man, Cecil Thompson, was still swimming for the raft. He had been calling out to us on the raft but suddenly he disappeared from sight never to be seen again.

While paddling around the starboard side of the vessel to get clear of her sinking, I suddenly saw a red life preserver, light burning, and upon bringing the raft alongside found it to be Harry Lane floating face down in the water. He had a deep cut across the back of his head and blood was running from this cut and from his mouth. I have not the slightest doubt that he was dead. I released his body.

Rounding the bow of the ship we floated there until the ship went down and then tied the two rafts together with the #1 lifeboat.

[signed] Harold F. Spinney
3rd Officer, SS *Pennmar*

IX

·

LESSONS

John H. Chafee, USMC, 1943,
following the battle of Guadalcanal.

Ozzie Sweet
(extreme left, holding
camera), Camp Callan,
California, 1941.

Walter Morris
preparing for his
first jump.

There may never again be a time when all the layers of our complex society are so completely absorbed in a monumental challenge as they were during World War II. Everyone had a role; everyone understood that the successful outcome of the war was critical to the continuing evolution of political and personal freedom.

The nation was infused with a sense of purpose and patriotism. Political leaders, the popular culture, advertising, newspapers, and radio cheered on the war effort once the fighting began. For many young men and women, that call to duty and the constant reminders of its importance marked their lives both during the fighting and long after.

They brought home from the war fundamental lessons in the random nature of mortality, the gratification of entering into a common effort for the greater good, and the true reward of unconditional love of family. They also returned mature beyond their years, and eager to have a life of renewal and not destruction.

John Chafee, the late U.S. senator from Rhode Island who died recently at age seventy-seven, was the teenage son of a wealthy New England family when war broke out.

I had had a wonderful freshman year at Yale, going there in September 1940, and had been on the wrestling team, which greatly attracted me. I was captain, and our team was undefeated and I was undefeated. It was a big thing in my life. And the war was declared, and I was a sophomore wrestling on varsity at the time. But as deeply attached to wrestling as I was, I had no qualms about enlisting—even though I was in the ROTC and could have stayed there until I was commissioned. I decided to join the Marines, and why the Marines I'm not quite sure. Maybe it was that they had a big poster that showed a Marine coming off the beach with a rifle over his head, saying "First to Fight—Join the Marines." I went down to the recruiting office in Providence, Rhode Island, and signed up. . . . My parents were quite enthusiastic about it. They didn't counsel against it at all.

Six months after he enlisted, Chafee was in the Pacific as a nineteen-year-old Marine private, armed with a Springfield rifle that had been designed about forty years earlier. He asked for a combat assignment and was sent to Guadalcanal as part of the invasion to secure Henderson Field, a strategically vital airstrip. Chafee was dug in when the Japanese counterattacked.

The Japanese came down with tremendous precision and sank four cruisers—three American and one Australian. They just caught us napping—they came down at full speed, at night. The Americans couldn't seem to handle things at night at that point. They switched on their lights and caught the Americans—boom boom! We were on the shore and when those big guns shoot at night, you can follow the projectiles for a while because they come out red hot. We were leaping with excitement because we thought the Americans were whipping the Japanese! And the next morning, we saw what was left of the American vessels. . . . I'll never forget the Coast Guard hauling in these Americans—the survivors—and they were just drenched with oil. You didn't have to be a Phi Beta Kappa to know that we hadn't won that battle. So it dawned on everyone that we took a beating. And particularly when we saw that our four protective vessels were gone. And the supply vessels had left because they'd be easy prey to the Japanese, and we knew that there hadn't been much time for anything to be unloaded. We're thinking, Hey—this is kind of lonely! . . .

Somebody once asked me, Did you ever think the Japanese would chase you off of Guadalcanal? It never occurred to me! I never even dreamed it, even after that! I don't know what we thought, but we weren't panicked. We just thought, Well that's today, but tomorrow's another day and the United States is not just going to leave us here.

In December, after four months at Guadalcanal, Chafee's division was sent to Australia. The following September, Chafee was selected for Officer Candidate School and returned to the United States for training at Quantico and at Fort Ritchie in Hagerstown, Maryland. On June 14, 1944, he was commissioned a second lieutenant, and then sent to Okinawa in May 1945:

> There, the fighting was fierce—but by this time we had wonderful equipment. Way better than Guadalcanal . . . Okinawa was much more in the open, whereas it was more jungle fighting at Guadalcanal. It was different. I had a small unit—my job, as part of an intelligence unit, was to assess the frontline situation and report to my superiors by radio.

On Okinawa, Chafee went through a combat experience that gave him a perspective on fate that guides him to this day.

> I remember we were going across a rice paddy, and they had these draining ditches that the farmers had made and they were very narrow, but at least it was a ditch, maybe 12 or 14 inches deep. We started across this open rice paddy and got vigorously shelled by artillery. At this time, we were a rifle platoon moving forward, so there were maybe 40 in this group. On those occasions, you want to make yourself as small as possible and everyone tried to squeeze into one of those ditches, which was tough going but it made you feel better. I was squeezed

into one of those ditches—it seemed like an eternity, but the shelling probably lasted only 10 minutes. Afterwards, the fellow who had been in the ditch in front of me didn't get up. And I suddenly realized he was dead, he was killed from the shelling. . . . It's all luck. It just happened that I could have been the guy. I wasn't any better or braver or anything . . . it's just one of those things.

When World War II ended, Chafee went back to Yale and then on to Harvard Law School. He married and returned to Rhode Island, where he joined a prominent law firm in Providence. In 1951 he was recalled to active duty as a Marine captain in Korea. He was surprised, but, he says, "I always liked military service so it didn't bother me much to be called up."

[I] found it a great experience commanding a rifle company. It's one of those things that's unique. You're responsible for some 270 men and how you disperse them and lead them is a great experience. And you have young lieutenants working for you and you want to give them good leadership, too. It's a leadership post where you're still very close to the enlisted men. I don't think there's a better job in the Marine Corps. . . .

During World War II . . . no one needed to have explained what we were doing. Everyone understood what we were involved with. And now, with Kosovo, there was a long debate about should we be there. And back and forth it goes. Whereas there was none of that in World War II. Everyone understood.

I'm not one who believes this country is going to pot . . . or that people in my generation are of some grand status above all others. The people I work with here [in Washington] are for the most part from a younger generation. I'm 76 now and the vast majority of the people I deal with are in their middle 50s . . . and these people are terrific! And they're just as good as our generation, and I truly believe that thrown into a similar situation, they'd do just as good. . . .

After serving in Korea, Chafee returned to Rhode Island and his law practice but it wasn't long before he was active in Republican party politics in that tiny state with its long tradition of Democratic party rule. Chafee served first in the state legislature and then won three terms as governor, where he became a champion of the environment, health care, and education. After three years as secretary of the Navy during the Nixon administration, he decided to run for the U.S. Senate from Rhode Island, losing to longtime incumbent Claiborne Pell. In 1976 Chafee ran again, this time successfully, and he was elected by landslide margins in three subsequent campaigns.

Throughout his life, Chafee enjoyed an enviable reputation as a man of conviction who often found common ground between ideological opposites. He took great pride in building a consensus and getting something accomplished, especially in the areas of environmental protection and expanded health care. Shortly before his death, Chafee drew on his early years as a combat Marine to put the current Washington climate and his own life in perspective.

It's the way you approach things in life. In my case, I had my 20th birthday on Guadalcanal . . . and later I was selected for officers school . . . so you got a sense of confidence in yourself. It was very helpful because later in life, you have these challenges, and you think these guys are so bright! But then you think, I've been in the fast league and made it, and so I can make it in this league too! . . . You'd have a challenge and people would say how difficult it was. At Harvard, they'd say, Look to your left and then to your right—one of you will flunk. I thought, Look, I've been through tougher times than these. I think I'll get over *this*. So people say when you run for governor, that's so hard. But someone else has done it! I guess when you've been through a series of things in your life, you think, If I lose, I lose, what the heck. It's not like I've been shot. I just don't win. . . .

FOR THOSE WHO SURVIVED, World War II was a gateway to opportunities they might never before have imagined. The writer Paul Fussell says bluntly, "World War II made America."

It certainly changed the life of Miguel Encinias, who grew up in the thirties in New Mexico, a difficult time and place for working-class families—especially for poor Hispanics, who were treated as second-class citizens or worse. Yet when war broke out, the Hispanic population responded with alacrity. Hispanics earned twelve Congressional Medals of Honor. Encinias wrote to tell his story of the war and its aftermath.

In 1939, at age 16, [when I was] a junior in high school, I joined a New Mexico N.G. Combat Engineers Company. I served for a year before we were federalized on September 16, 1940. I always wanted to be a fighter pilot, but I was too young, and I didn't have two years of college. In early 1942, the standards were dropped to 18 and an [intelligence] test. That April, I would be 18 years of age.

I became a Spitfire fighter pilot, and flew combat missions for nine months in Africa, Sicily and northern Italy out of Corsica. On February 19, 1944, I was shot down and wounded over a German airbase at Viterbo, [Italy,] about 100 miles north of the front line. I was captured immediately and became a POW and started my month's trip to Stalag Luft I on the Baltic coast—the only Hispanic among 10,000 officer aircrew members.

After the war, I became a charter member of the D.C. Air Guard, flying the P-47, while attending Georgetown University, from which I graduated in 1949. Just as the Korean War was nearing, I left the squadron to study at the Institut d'Etudes Politiques in Paris. The war was on when I finished my year of graduate study. I went straight to Bolling AFB, and volunteered for active duty and Korea where I flew the P-51 and later the F-86. I was shot down behind the lines and wounded on my 65th mission. We had helicopters then, and I was picked up and taken to a MASH hospital. After hospitalization elsewhere, and convalescence leave, I went back to fly 46 more missions.

When Vietnam came, I volunteered, and flew a good bit of combat missions as an advisor to Vietnamese fighter pilots.

In a later conversation, Encinias said that after he retired as a lieutenant colonel in 1971 he enrolled at the University of New Mexico, where he earned a Ph.D. in education and Spanish literature. He already had a master's degree in French from Middlebury College, courtesy of the Air Force.

Wanting to use his degrees, as he put it, "to give something back to the country and to the children," Colonel Encinias went from flying high-performance jets to a new job as a director of cross-cultural and language instruction for Albuquerque's public schools. He conducted teacher training seminars and developed performing arts activities to raise cultural awareness. In 1985 he returned to the University of New Mexico to design a curriculum more relevant to the large Hispanic student population.

During his military career, Encinias flew more than 5,000 hours and earned three Distinguished Flying Crosses, fourteen Air Medals, and two Purple Hearts.

WHEN *The Greatest Generation* was published, it had a striking photo on the cover—a couple standing next to a jeep, his duffel bag nearby. Their embrace appeared to be a farewell. I had several letters from couples saying it brought back memories of their own parting. Then the man who took the picture wrote. His name is Ozzie Sweet, and taking the photo launched him in a new direction: he went on to have a distinguished career as a magazine and sports photographer.

Sweet, who had worked as an extra in Hopalong Cassidy movies before enlisting, explained that he got the idea for the picture from a dog at Camp Callan in Southern California.

I took the photo when I was still in basic training, just because I thought it would be fun. It was taken with an old-time folding Kodak camera and a tripod that I borrowed. . . . The dog (which belonged to a sergeant on the base) gave me the idea. He always looked so sad, and since it was a replacement center, and G.I.s were being sent out every week, I thought it was a fitting picture.

It was the thing of shipping out—that's a sad, sad time. There wasn't the glory connected with going off to war. It was a very sad thing. And of course all the guys who did were very brave, but it wasn't a pleasant experience. So I have a special place in my heart for that photograph. . . . The soldier in the picture was a friend of mine, and the thing was finding a girl with pretty legs. I found her at a dry cleaner's place on the base. It was just putting two people together, really. I told her what I was going to do, and she was willing to do it. No model's fees then!

It was always a favorite picture, because it was my first to be published in any way. It was published in the *Range Finder,* the Camp Callan newsletter, and then in one of the newspapers in San Diego. Then it was picked up by the picture services, and that's how it got around. . . . So when it came time to be shipped out, I was transferred instead to the Signal Corps as a PR man, and that gave me lots of opportunities to take pictures. That's where my career started. It was that photograph that kept me from being shipped out, and it was that photograph that gave me all the opportunity to take pictures. If I'd been shipped out, I might not have had the career I did.

Sweet, who now lives in New Hampshire, went on to shoot magazine cover photos of Albert Einstein, Ingrid Bergman, Helen Hayes, Grace Kelly, Dwight D. Eisenhower, John Wayne, Walt Disney, and Herbert Hoover, among others. His book on Mickey Mantle is considered a sports photography classic.

Walter morris was a military pioneer as a result of World War II: he was responsible for the formation of the first unit of black paratroopers. Morris, now retired in Florida, was a sergeant at Fort Benning, Georgia, with an all-black outfit. He remembers to this day the depressing effect of the worst kind of discrimination: while black soldiers were banned from the post store, Italian and German prisoners of war who had been shipped into Fort Benning were free to use the facility.

In an interview with NBC News, Morris described how his men, who were relegated to guard duty, reacted to that egregious policy and what he decided to do about it.

> You automatically develop an inferiority complex. There must be something wrong with me . . . if I can't ride in the front of the bus, and the only thing I can think of is the color of my skin, because I've gone to school. I put my pants on in the same way everyone else does. So it must be the color of my skin that causes this. And . . . when you realize that, you're in a position where you are saying[:] . . . What in the world can I do to overcome this?
>
> . . . I saw the morale of my men at such a low ebb [that] they came off guard duty and we would go into the barracks and sleep all day. They had no initiative, and it occurred to me that as the First Sergeant of this company, I should do something about the low morale. And the idea [came to me that] to imitate the white parachute students going through their calisthenics might be one way of uplifting our men.
>
> So we started at four o'clock every afternoon. When the white students would march off the field, the black students would march on the field.

What Morris didn't know at the time is that in Washington, black leaders such as A. Philip Randolph and Roy

Wilkins were putting pressure on President Roosevelt to develop a black paratroop outfit.

At Fort Benning, the commanding officer called Morris in
and told him he would be the first member of what became a
discrete unit, the 555th Parachute Infantry Battalion. Morris
led a platoon of sixteen fellow Negroes, the term used then,
who successfully completed their parachute training. The
platoon came to be known as the Sweet Sixteen.

Morris remembers their first jump.

A lot of butterflies. A lot of anxiety. We were scared to
death. But we couldn't show it because the whole world
had their eyes on us and they were betting that we
would not jump out of any airplane in flight. And we had
to prove that we could do it.

The worst-looking jump I have ever seen was our first
jump. We were trained to jump with the proper attitude,
which was knees together, slightly bent, the feet together, arms tight, held. And when I look at the first
jump we made, I have to laugh because it was nothing
like the training we received. But it was improved; by
the time we got to our fourth jump, we were looking
pretty good. But we came out of the plane fast.

We realized now that we were soldiers. Not guard
duty soldiers, not servants, not cooks. We were actually
training for combat. We were going to be paratroopers.
And that . . . gave us all incentive to succeed.

The Sweet Sixteen were ready for combat. They received
additional training in California and they were sure they were
headed to the Pacific and the closing days of the war against
Japan. Instead, with no advance warning, they were sent to
the Pacific Northwest as smoke jumpers, to fight forest fires
started by Japanese incendiary balloons.

Morris was deeply disappointed. As he prepared to jump
into a fire in Washington State, he asked himself why he was
doing this, and then he found the answer:

It occurred to me that the reason I was doing it is because of my children and my children's children. And I knew I had in my heart that . . . , this country, as great as it is, would overcome the stigma of separation and prejudice, and of course, we've come so long a ways from [the] 1945 era. And of course we have a long ways to go. But I can see the light.

I'm seventy-eight years old now and I can see the light at the end of this tunnel.

Morris has special respect for General James Gavin, the scholarly and heroic commander of the 82nd Airborne, who led the Allied forces into Germany. When Gavin returned to Fort Benning after the war and learned that the 555th Parachute Infantry Battalion was a segregated outfit, he had it disbanded and folded into the 82nd Airborne. When Morris and his fellow pioneers from the 555th hold reunions now, they always invite General Gavin's daughter.

In 1946 Walter Morris left the Army to return home to Seattle and learn his trade from his father, a bricklayer. Morris brought those skills to New York, where he became one of the first African Americans in the bricklayers' union. He worked steadily on New York area construction projects until his retirement as superintendent of the Bedford-Stuyvesant Restoration Project in 1983.

One of his daughters is a law professor at Howard University and the other is a health department worker. He has a grandchild in the U.S. Army. How does Morris see his legacy as the first black military paratrooper?

That we succeeded where we were not expected to succeed. And we overcame the pitfalls that were put there. We overcame. And it's a warm feeling to know that, that color has nothing to do with it. It's what's in one's heart. One's spirit. And that . . . should be a lesson to all of us. We should have, and we will have, a colorless society one day. And that will be the crowning jewel in this great country's history.

THE CLOSING DAYS of the twentieth century and the renewed interest in the World War II era have prompted many veterans to revisit the early impressions of life they described in letters home. Kay Voss, a retired businessman in Michigan, wrote the following:

> Let me start by saying that I am a part of the WWII generation. I served in the Eighth Air Force as a co-pilot on a B-17, flying 31 missions.
>
> We came home to forget what hell we had gone through and we all wanted to just get married, settle down and live like "normal" people. I arrived home on Labor Day 1945, and was at work at my old job the very next day at 8:00 a.m. My father had a grocery and meat market in which I had worked from the age of 12. He and Mother had a rough time while the war was on. Help was hard to find, rationing, customers sometimes difficult to please when you didn't have what they wanted. Dad was more than happy to have me back.
>
> I can still remember how I felt those first few days. I was HOME!! All of those horrible days were behind me, and I was still alive!! Anyone would have had to experience that to really know what I mean.
>
> I married my sweetheart shortly after and raised four wonderful children, two boys and two girls. The war was all behind me and as far out of my mind as I could put it.
>
> It wasn't until my parents had both passed away, and we cleaned out their attic, that I began to think much about my Eighth Air Force days. For in a box, all bundled neatly according to date, I found every letter I had ever written to my folks clear through college and my three years or so in service . . . several hundred of them.

The last of those letters reflect the euphoric relief and joy servicemen and women everywhere must have felt in the summer of 1945:

HURRAH!! HURRAH!! I'm COMING HOME!!! I may not be able to write again for a few days, so if my letters are rather scarce from now on for a while you'll know why. I have lots to do and little time to do it. I haven't even started to pack. Everything is A-OK. All of us are so happy we can hardly keep our feet on the ground. I am going to cut this short. Hope you'll forgive. *SEE YOU REAL SOON!!*

Excerpts from my May 21st letter:

Our time is completely our own. We have been doing absolutely nothing. I'm putting on the weight I lost last winter when we were doing all the flying. My pants almost fit again!

So, I have quite a bank roll back there now, eh Dad? Well, it's not nearly as big as it will be before I'm home again for good. There ought to be a nice little nest egg waiting for me. I don't know if I'll buy a plane or not. Right now, I have all the flying I want for a while. I'm going to be content to keep my feet on the SOLID GROUND!! Right now I have too many bad memories of things that have happened up there. Of course, civilian flying will be a lot different. I'll wait to see how I feel when I get home for good! And besides, I don't want to spend all my money on a plane . . . I've got to start thinking about settling down!

Voss eventually took over his father's grocery business, and he stayed in that line of work until he retired in 1982. In his letter to me he concluded with this passage:

I remember the chapel service we attended just before our first mission. The chaplain prayed for our safe return, and the last song we sang, "Be Still, My Soul," returned to me many, many times in the uncertain days of combat. There seemed to be someone singing it to me. I liked to think it was my mother—and she still does, from her Heavenly Choir.

BE STILL, MY SOUL; THE LORD IS ON THY SIDE.
BEAR PATIENTLY THE CROSS OF GRIEF OR PAIN.
LEAVE TO THY GOD TO ORDER AND PROVIDE;
IN EVERY CHANGE, HE FAITHFUL WILL REMAIN.
BE STILL, MY SOUL; THY BEST, THY HEAVENLY FRIEND
THROUGH THORNY WAYS LEADS TO A JOYFUL END.

BE STILL, MY SOUL; THY GOD DOTH UNDERTAKE
TO GUIDE THE FUTURE, AS HE HAS THE PAST.
THY HOPE, THY CONFIDENCE, LET NOTHING SHAKE;
ALL NOW MYSTERIOUS SHALL BE BRIGHT AT LAST.
BE STILL, MY SOUL; THE WAVES AND WINDS STILL KNOW
HIS VOICE WHO RULED THEM WHILE HE DWELT BELOW.

BE STILL, MY SOUL; THE HOUR IS HASTENING ON
WHEN WE SHALL BE FOREVER WITH THE LORD,
WHEN DISAPPOINTMENT, GRIEF, AND FEAR ARE GONE,
SORROW FORGOT, LOVE'S PUREST JOYS RESTORED.
BE STILL, MY SOUL; WHEN CHANGE AND TEARS ARE PAST,
ALL SAFE AND BLESSED WE SHALL MEET AT LAST.

CONCLUSION

This has been a deeply satisfying personal journey for me. Reading the letters, hearing the stories, and sharing the emotional themes was a familial experience, intimate and nurturing. In this age of electronic communication overload, there is something reassuring and eloquent about a single voice speaking in direct, honest, and sometimes painful fashion about a passage when time was measured day by difficult day.

In a time of conspicuous self-indulgence, it is comforting to be absorbed in the lives of others who are selfless and grateful for whatever they have. Even those who were unhappy with oversights in *The Greatest Generation* made their points quietly and respectfully.

As a final note I have chosen two different stories. One came to me while I was signing books in Big Timber, Montana, a favorite small town hard by the Yellowstone River. Betty Van Mullem gave me the letters her grandparents wrote to her uncles—their sons—Raymond and James Todd on the day the Japanese surrendered. Harry Todd and his wife, Millie, in their western hamlet spoke for America.

The first letter is from Harry, who was treasurer of Golden County, Montana.

Dear Boys,

My emotions are so mixed, mingled with gladness and sadness, that I hardly know what to say to you tonight. All afternoon we gathered about the radio in the sheriff's office about every quarter hour. Finally about 3:30 P.M. National Broadcasting Co. picked up Max Jordan at Berne, Switzerland, who said the text of Japan's reply was on the way to Washington and we should have it in two hours. Talk about sweating it out—I smoked more cigarettes in the past 24 hours than I usually do in three days.

Mom and I are so happy tonight it's no use trying to tell you why and a lot of stuff like that but to be able to look forward to the time you are home again and to be sure you are coming home, well it just almost overwhelms me. I just feel like getting out the Remington and burning up all the skeet shells you brought home, Jim. This little town has very few methods of making noise but the fire bell and the Methodist church bell have rung out and the sheriff went about town sounding his siren. The Governor has proclaimed tomorrow and Thursday as holidays and the President has designated Wednesday and Thursday for all government people as holidays. Stan called us up at about 5:30 A.M. this morning to tell us the war was over. However, it was announced from the White House at 5:00 P.M. (Mountain Time) today. . . .

From now on I am going to check off the days and weeks till you get home.

Love,
Dad

Their mother, Millie, was equally relieved and joyful:

O Darling—you will never know how happy your Dad and Mother are tonight. The past four days have been such a tense—nervewracking time. We have been having [the] radio on constantly day and night and it seemed the news would never come. Papa and I are so thankful tonight that Our Heavenly Father has spared our loved ones . . . and hope and pray they may be coming home to us soon. We do have so much to be thankful for—Raymond—that our family circle has not been broken, and how we pray you may be under the home roof soon. And while we are rejoicing—we cannot forget those who have loved ones *who will not be coming home*. There are many sorrowing broken hearts tonight—while we are rejoicing. There are so many broken homes, may God comfort these broken hearts. There are many who have made the supreme sacrifice so that we have these happy homes of ours. To them we owe much of our freedom.

Love from Mother

The final letter—and the final word—is from Ruth Chamberlain, the grandmother of Jeremy Brunaccioni of Greenfield, Massachusetts. He sent the letter she wrote to her children on July 4, 1991. It is typical of the experiences of young couples across the nation and the tone is also characteristic of the generation. It is quietly matter-of-fact and, at the end, devoid of self-pity.

She describes her romance with Roland, her husband, from the moment they met on an ice skating rink as teenagers. He had dropped out of school at the age of sixteen to work in a shoe factory to help support his family. They went to a movie on December 7, 1941, in Manchester, New Hampshire.

Sunday was movie night and we were sitting in the State Theater on Elm Street, when the news of Pearl Harbor was flashed on the screen. I don't think there was a sound in the theater as all the uniformed men in there quietly arose and left to report to their posts. The inevitable had arrived—we were at war. . . .

We were married the next spring—1942—and Dad managed to be home till Feb. 22, 1943. By then I was pregnant 6 mos. and heartbroken when we saw him off at the train station. . . .

It was about 6 wks before I heard from him and learned he was at Camp Bliss in Texas near Austin for basic training. He was in the 365th Field Artillery Battalion attached to the 97th Infantry Div. To this day, his Serial #, 31266957, rolls readily from my lips. I wrote every day for 3 yrs except when having Nancy or the few times I saw him. . . .

In January of '44 he was stationed at Ft. Leonard Wood in Missouri and I could visit him there. . . .

When Dad thought he'd be stationed there, I returned home for Nancy. We went back out in April on an old train with wooden seats. Lots of standing room only, but a crazy young girl with an 11 mo. old baby got preferred treatment. It took several days, sitting there with a baby to bottle feed and change. And remember, no Pampers. I'll never figure out how I did it. Dumb and dumb luck! . . .

Had to wash all our clothes by hand. What diapers! Somehow managed all that alone—got all the laundry on the line and the clothesline broke dropping everything into the red clay dirt of Missouri!

Dad made Staff Sgt. and I was so proud. He was slated to go to OCS—Officer Candidate School—but by that time the war was getting worse with Japan and in June we had to come home because the outfit was going to California. . . .

They were shipped to Camp San Luis Obispo, California, and outfitted with hot weather gear. By then, the Battle of the Bulge in Belgium was waging and they were needed in Europe instead. It's a wonder we won the war!

So back they came to the East Coast in Jan. '45 and headed for a brief stop in England and then to Le Havre, France. . . .

By 1945, the Germans were really on the run, and Gen. Patton was chasing them right on to Berlin. The 97th was attached to his outfit, so Dad followed in his wake. . . .

Then came unconditional surrender in May 1945 and

Alice and I celebrated on Elm St. with thousands of others. What joy!

We still had Japan to contend with, so he ended up in Bremmerton, Washington, and boarded a ship for Japan. The day they sailed, Japan also surrendered, but of course the ship sailed on. . . .

In February of 1946, exactly 3 years after being called, he returned home for good. There was a time of getting reacquainted and readjusted to a normal way of life.

A whole chunk of three years out of [our] lives and apart!

So ends the saga—any questions?

Mom

ACKNOWLEDGMENTS

This is a book crafted by many memories, youthful insights, and the wisdom that come with seasons of despair and triumph. It is, most of all, another tribute to the men and women who rode the treacherous currents and sailed with the fair winds of most of the twentieth century.

It would not have been possible to have produced this book without the tireless and enthusiastic assistance of a remarkable group of young women who are making their own mark of greatness at an early age:

Elizabeth Bowyer, who was indispensable in assisting me with *The Greatest Generation*, reenlisted for this book, working late nights and odd hours while she held down a summer job at a prestigious New York law firm and studied at Columbia Law School. I am in awe of her ability to do so many tasks so well simultaneously. I am also grateful for her personal passion about this subject.

Catherine Balsam-Schwaber and Tara Pepper of NBC News were invaluable in their roles as readers, researchers, and organizers. No matter how large the stack of new mail or how difficult the research project, they went about their assignments with quiet efficiency and good cheer.

My friend Frank Gannon read the manuscript (as he did the manuscript of *The Greatest Generation*) and made several helpful suggestions for which I am very grateful.

As she did with *The Greatest Generation*, Erin O'Connor managed to keep my NBC News responsibilities, author's role, and personal life in balance and mostly on schedule. She knows when to say yes and how to say no without offending anyone, including me (although she is wisely trying to get me to say no more often). I am forever in your debt, Erin.

At Random House, my peerless editor and great friend, Kate Medina, cheered me on while gently and thoughtfully steering the book from start to finish. She is a brave and brilliant inspiration.

Her assistant, Meaghan Rady, has an editor's eye and the cool of an air-traffic controller. She kept *The Greatest Generation Speaks* from crash-landing on any number of occasions. She also makes me laugh with her impish sense of humor.

The other members of the Random House team who performed so gracefully under the enormous pressure of looming deadlines are Benjamin Dreyer, Carole Lowenstein, Jolanta Benal, Evan Stone, Maria Massey, Andy Carpenter, and Richard Elman. Thank you all.

The real authors of this book deserve the greatest accolades: the men and women, young and old, who shared their stories, their tears, their gentle criticisms, and their quiet pride in lives lived well. There is no single American voice, but the chorus is thrilling.

The stories that you will read here have been edited and they are reprinted with the permission of the authors. We have attempted to verify all of the factual information, but in some cases these are memories and impressions more than a half-century old.

The selection process was difficult because there were so many letters and memoirs. I am deeply grateful to all who wrote, and I treasure each of the stories. They widen and enrich the family portrait I wanted to present in *The Greatest Generation*.

To be sure, there are stories that I missed, and for that I accept full responsibility. I hope they will find audiences in family gatherings, schools, community celebrations, barrooms, and churches. They are too important, too instructive, and too entertaining to be cloistered forever.

TOM BROKAW, is the author of six bestsellers: *The Greatest Generation, The Greatest Generation Speaks, An Album of Memories, A Long Way From Home, Boom!,* and *The Time of Our Lives.* A native of South Dakota, he graduated from the University of South Dakota with a degree in political science. He joined NBC News in 1966, serving as the White House correspondent during Watergate, and anchoring *Today* on NBC from 1976 to 1981. He was the sole anchor and managing editor of *NBC Nightly News with Tom Brokaw* from 1983 to 2005. He continues to report for NBC News, producing award-winning long-form documentaries and providing expertise during breaking news events. Brokaw has won every major award in broadcast journalism, including two DuPonts, a Peabody Award, and several Emmys. He is a regular contributor to the op-ed pages of the *New York Times,* the *Washington Post,* and the *Wall Street Journal,* and to *Time, Newsweek,* and *Men's Journal.* He lives in New York and Montana.

ABOUT THE TYPE

This book was set in Fairfield, the first typeface from the hand of the distinguished American artist and engraver Rudolph Ruzicka (1883–1978). Ruzicka was born in Bohemia and came to America in 1894. He set up his own shop, devoted to wood engraving and printing, in New York in 1913 after a varied career working as a wood engraver, in photoengraving and banknote printing plants, and as an art director and freelance artist. He designed and illustrated many books, and was the creator of a considerable list of individual prints—wood engravings, line engravings on copper, and aquatints.

ALSO BY TOM BROKAW

The Time of Our Lives
Boom!
A Long Way From Home
An Album of Memories
The Greatest Generation Speaks
The Greatest Generation